First World War
and Army of Occupation
War Diary
France, Belgium and Germany

2 DIVISION
19 Infantry Brigade
Headquarters
22 August 1914 - 31 July 1915

WO95/1364

The Naval & Military Press Ltd
www.nmarchive.com
Published in association with The National Archives

Published by

The Naval & Military Press Ltd

Unit 10 Ridgewood Industrial Park,

Uckfield, East Sussex,

TN22 5QE England

Tel: +44 (0) 1825 749494

www.naval-military-press.com

www.nmarchive.com

This diary has been reprinted in facsimile from the original. Any imperfections are inevitably reproduced and the quality may fall short of modern type and cartographic standards.

© **Crown Copyright**
Images reproduced by permission of The National Archives, London, England, 2015.

Contents

Document type	Place/Title	Date From	Date To
Heading	2 Div 19 Bde H.Q. 1914 Aug to 1914 Dec		
Heading	2 Division 19 Infantry Brigade 1915 Aug-1915 Nov		
Heading	War Diary Headquarters, 19th Infantry Brigade (2nd Division) August And September 1915		
War Diary	Laventie	01/08/1915	16/08/1915
War Diary	Le Verrier	17/08/1915	24/08/1915
War Diary	Cuinchy Sector	25/08/1915	03/09/1915
War Diary	Bethune	04/09/1915	12/09/1915
War Diary	Givenchy	13/09/1915	16/09/1915
War Diary	Gun St.-RI	17/09/1915	24/09/1915
War Diary	Cambrin Sector Between La Bassee Road And Vermelles-Auchy road.	25/09/1915	25/09/1915
War Diary	Cambrin Sector	25/09/1915	27/09/1915
War Diary	Cambrin	28/09/1915	30/09/1915
Heading	Brigade Operation Orders and Instructions.		
Operation(al) Order(s)	19th Infantry Brigade Operation Order No. 44	14/08/1915	14/08/1915
Miscellaneous	19th Infantry Brigade March Table.	14/08/1915	14/08/1915
Miscellaneous	Officer Commanding, 19th Field Ambulance.	15/08/1915	15/08/1915
Miscellaneous	19th Inf. Bde.	16/08/1915	16/08/1915
Miscellaneous	March Order No. 45 19th Infantry Brigade	18/08/1915	18/08/1915
Miscellaneous	March Table-19th Infantry Brigade	18/08/1915	18/08/1915
Miscellaneous	B.M.4.18th Officer Commanding 5 Battns	18/08/1915	18/08/1915
Operation(al) Order(s)	19th Infantry Brigade Operation Order No. 46	23/08/1915	23/08/1915
Miscellaneous	March Table 19th Infantry Brigade Table "A"	25/08/1915	25/08/1915
Operation(al) Order(s)	19th Infantry Brigade Relief Order No. 47	31/08/1915	31/08/1915
Miscellaneous	Officer Commanding	01/09/1915	01/09/1915
Operation(al) Order(s)	19th Infantry Brigade Operation Order No. 48	03/09/1915	03/09/1915
Miscellaneous	Relief And March Table.	03/09/1915	03/09/1915
Operation(al) Order(s)	19th Infantry Brigade Operations Order No. 49	12/09/1915	12/09/1915
Miscellaneous	Relief And March Table	12/09/1915	12/09/1915
Operation(al) Order(s)	19th Infantry Brigade Operation Order No. 50	16/09/1915	16/09/1915
Miscellaneous	Section "B" Givenchy.	16/09/1915	16/09/1915
Miscellaneous	19th Infantry Brigade Instructions	22/09/1915	22/09/1915
Miscellaneous	Reference 19th Infantry Brigade	22/09/1915	22/09/1915
Miscellaneous	Reference 19th Infantry Brigade	23/09/1915	23/09/1915
Operation(al) Order(s)	19th Infantry Brigade Operation Order No. 52	24/09/1915	24/09/1915
Miscellaneous	Appendix "A" to 19th Inf. Bde. Operation Order No. 52	23/09/1915	23/09/1915
Miscellaneous	Memorandum	23/09/1915	23/09/1915
Miscellaneous	19th Infantry Brigade Orders For The Assembly Of The Brigade For Operation Order No. 52	24/09/1915	24/09/1915
Heading	Messages		
Miscellaneous	To Adjutant 1st Middle	24/09/1915	24/09/1915
Miscellaneous	C Form (Duplicate) Messages And Signals		
Miscellaneous	A Form Messages And Signals.		
Miscellaneous	Messages And Signals.		
Miscellaneous	A Form Messages And Signals.		
Miscellaneous	Daily Tactical Progress Report		
Miscellaneous	Daily Report Up To 12 Noon 1st August 19th Infantry Brigade	01/08/1915	01/08/1915

Miscellaneous	Daily Report Up To 12 Noon 2nd August 19th Infantry Brigade	02/08/1915	02/08/1915
Miscellaneous	Daily Report Up To 12 Noon 3rd August 1915 19th Infantry Brigade	03/08/1915	03/08/1915
Miscellaneous	Daily Report Up To 12 Noon 4th August 1915 19th Infantry Brigade	04/08/1915	04/08/1915
Miscellaneous	Daily Report Up To 12 Noon 5th August 1915 19th Infantry Brigade	05/08/1915	05/08/1915
Miscellaneous	Daily Report Up To 12 Noon 6th August 1915 19th Infantry Brigade	06/08/1915	06/08/1915
Miscellaneous	Daily Report Up To 12 Noon 7th August 1915 19th Infantry Brigade	07/08/1915	07/08/1915
Miscellaneous	Daily Report Up To 12 Noon 8th August 1915 19th Infantry Brigade	08/08/1915	08/08/1915
Miscellaneous	Daily Report Up To 12 Noon 9th August 1915 19th Infantry Brigade	09/08/1915	09/08/1915
Miscellaneous	Daily Report Up To 12 Noon 10th August 1915 19th Infantry Brigade	10/08/1915	10/08/1915
Miscellaneous	Daily Report Up To 12 Noon 11th August 1915 19th Infantry Brigade	11/08/1915	11/08/1915
Miscellaneous	Daily Report Up To 12 Noon 12th August 1915 19th Infantry Brigade	12/08/1915	12/08/1915
Miscellaneous	Daily Report Up To 12 Noon 13th August 1915 19th Infantry Brigade	13/08/1915	13/08/1915
Miscellaneous	19th Infantry Brigade Daily Report	14/08/1915	14/08/1915
Miscellaneous	Daily Report 19th Infantry Brigade.	15/08/1915	15/08/1915
Miscellaneous	Daily Report 19th Infantry Brigade.		
Miscellaneous	Daily Report Up To 12 Noon 25th August 1915 19th Infantry Brigade	25/08/1915	25/08/1915
Miscellaneous	Trench Mortars In Action	25/08/1915	25/08/1915
Miscellaneous	Daily Report To 12 Noon 26th August 1915 19th Infantry Brigade	26/08/1915	26/08/1915
Miscellaneous	Daily Report To 12 Noon 27th August 1915 19th Infantry Brigade	27/08/1915	27/08/1915
Miscellaneous	Daily Report To 12 Noon 28th August 1915 19th Infantry Brigade	28/08/1915	28/08/1915
Miscellaneous	Daily Report Up Till 12 Noon 29th August 1915 19th Infantry Brigade	29/08/1915	29/08/1915
Miscellaneous	Daily Report Up Till 12 Noon 30th August 1915 19th Infantry Brigade	30/08/1915	30/08/1915
Miscellaneous	Daily Report Up Till 12 Noon 31st August 1915 19th Infantry Brigade	31/08/1915	31/08/1915
Miscellaneous	Daily Report Up Till 12 Noon 1st September 19th Infantry Brigade	01/09/1915	01/09/1915
Miscellaneous	Daily Report Up Till 12 Noon 2nd September 19th Infantry Brigade	02/09/1915	02/09/1915
Miscellaneous	Daily Report Up Till 12 Noon 3rd September 1915 19th Infantry Brigade	03/09/1915	03/09/1915
Miscellaneous	Trench Mortars In Action	03/09/1915	03/09/1915
Miscellaneous	Brigade Major 19th Inf. Brigade		
Miscellaneous	Daily Report Up Till 12 Noon 4th September 1915 19th Infantry Brigade	04/09/1915	04/09/1915
Miscellaneous	Trench Mortars In Action	04/09/1915	04/09/1915
Miscellaneous	To Brigade Major		
Miscellaneous	Summary Of Daily Operation Work And Intelligence Reports	04/09/1915	04/09/1915

Miscellaneous	Daily Tactical Progress Report		
Miscellaneous	Weekly Report Shewing Areas Shelled By The Enemy	16/09/1915	16/09/1915
Miscellaneous	Daily Report Up To 12 Noon 14th September 1915 19th Infantry Brigade	14/09/1915	14/09/1915
Miscellaneous	Trench Mortars In Action	14/09/1915	14/09/1915
Diagram etc	Diagram		
Miscellaneous	The Adjutant 5th S.R.		
Miscellaneous	Daily Report Up To 12 Noon 15th September 1915 19th Infantry Brigade	15/09/1915	15/09/1915
Miscellaneous	Trench Mortars In Action	15/09/1915	15/09/1915
Miscellaneous	Daily Report Up To 12 Noon 16th September 1915 19th Infantry Brigade	16/09/1915	16/09/1915
Miscellaneous	Trench Mortars In Action	16/09/1915	16/09/1915
Miscellaneous	19th Infantry Brigade. Summary Of Operations Work And Intelligence	17/09/1915	17/09/1915
Miscellaneous	19th Infantry Brigade Daily Progress Report	17/09/1915	17/09/1915
Miscellaneous	Trench Mortars In Action	17/09/1915	17/09/1915
Miscellaneous	Daily Progress Report Up Till 12 Noon 18th September 1915 19th Infantry Brigade	18/09/1915	18/09/1915
Miscellaneous	Daily Progress Report Up Till 12 Noon 19th September 1915 19th Infantry Brigade	19/09/1915	19/09/1915
Miscellaneous	Trench Mortars In Action	19/09/1915	19/09/1915
Miscellaneous	19th Infantry Brigade Daily Report Up To 12 Noon 20th September 1915	20/09/1915	20/09/1915
Miscellaneous	Trench Mortars In Action	20/09/1915	20/09/1915
Miscellaneous	19th Infantry Brigade Daily Report Up To 12 Noon 21st September 1915	21/09/1915	21/09/1915
Miscellaneous	Trench Mortars In Action	21/09/1915	21/09/1915
Miscellaneous	Daily Report Up To 12 Noon 22nd September 1915 19th Infantry Brigade	22/09/1915	22/09/1915
Miscellaneous	Trench Mortars In Action	22/09/1915	22/09/1915
Miscellaneous	Report On Patrol Night		
Miscellaneous	Report on enemy's wire and intervening ground		
Miscellaneous	Daily Report Up To 12 Noon 23rd September 1915 19th Infantry Brigade	23/09/1915	23/09/1915
Miscellaneous	Trench Mortars In Action	23/09/1915	23/09/1915
Miscellaneous	Daily Report Up To 12 Noon 24th September 1915 19th Infantry Brigade	24/09/1915	24/09/1915
Miscellaneous	Reconnaissance Of Wire In Front Of The German Support Lines	24/09/1915	24/09/1915
Miscellaneous	Left Battalion Report		
Miscellaneous	Summary Of Operations	25/09/1915	25/09/1915
Miscellaneous	Daily Report Up Till 12 Noon 30th September 1915 19th Infantry Brigade	30/09/1915	30/09/1915
Heading	Plans And Sketches.		
Map	Map		
Diagram etc	Diagram		
Heading	War Diary Headquarters 19th Infantry Brigade (2nd Division) October 1915		
War Diary	Sailly Labourse	01/10/1915	02/10/1915
War Diary	Bethune	03/10/1915	15/10/1915
War Diary	Cambrin	16/10/1915	29/10/1915
War Diary	Gonnehem	30/10/1915	05/11/1915
Miscellaneous	Brigade Operation Orders Nos. 53 54 55 56 57 58 59		
Operation(al) Order(s)	19th Brigade Operation Order No. 53	01/10/1915	01/10/1915
Operation(al) Order(s)	19th Brigade Operation Order No. 54	03/10/1915	03/10/1915

Miscellaneous	March Table	03/10/1915	03/10/1915
Operation(al) Order(s)	19th Brigade March Order No. 55	10/10/1915	10/10/1915
Operation(al) Order(s)	19th Infantry Brigade Operation Order No. 56	15/10/1915	15/10/1915
Miscellaneous	Relief Table	15/10/1915	15/10/1915
Operation(al) Order(s)	19th Infantry Brigade Relief Order No. 57	20/10/1915	20/10/1915
Operation(al) Order(s)	19th Infantry Brigade Relief Order No. 58	24/10/1915	24/10/1915
Operation(al) Order(s)	19th Infantry Brigade Operations Orders No. 59	26/10/1915	26/10/1915
Miscellaneous	19th Infantry Brigade Relief And March Table	26/10/1915	26/10/1915
Miscellaneous	Daily Reports.		
Miscellaneous	Daily Report Up To 12 Noon 17th October 1915 19th Infantry Brigade	17/10/1915	17/10/1915
Miscellaneous	Daily Report Up To 12 Noon 18th October 1915 19th Infantry Brigade	18/10/1915	18/10/1915
Miscellaneous	Daily Report Up To 12 Noon 19th October 1915 19th Infantry Brigade	19/10/1915	19/10/1915
Miscellaneous	Daily Report Up To 12 Noon 20th October 1915 19th Infantry Brigade	20/10/1915	20/10/1915
Miscellaneous	Daily Report Up To 12 Noon 21st October 1915 19th Infantry Brigade	21/10/1915	21/10/1915
Miscellaneous	Daily Report Up To 12 Noon 22nd October 1915 19th Infantry Brigade	22/10/1915	22/10/1915
Miscellaneous	19th Infantry Brigade Daily Report Up To 12 Noon 23rd October 1915	23/10/1915	23/10/1915
Miscellaneous	19th Infantry Brigade Daily Report Up To 12 Noon 24th October 1915	24/10/1915	24/10/1915
Miscellaneous	19th Infantry Brigade Daily Report Up To 12 Noon 25th October 1915	25/10/1915	25/10/1915
Miscellaneous	19th Infantry Brigade Daily Report Up To 12 Noon 26th October 1915	26/10/1915	26/10/1915
Miscellaneous	19th Infantry Brigade Daily Report Up To 12 Noon 27th October 1915	27/10/1915	27/10/1915
Miscellaneous	19th Infantry Brigade Daily Report Up To 12 Noon 28th October 1915	28/10/1915	28/10/1915
Miscellaneous	Daily Report Up To 12 Noon 29th October 1915 19th Infantry Brigade	29/10/1915	29/10/1915
Heading	War Diary Headquarters, 19th Infantry Brigade (2nd Division) November 1915		
Miscellaneous	Headquarters, 19th Infantry Brigade November 1915		
War Diary	Cambrin	06/11/1915	27/11/1915
War Diary	Gonnehem	28/11/1915	30/11/1915
Heading	Brigade Operation Orders Nos. 60 61 62 63 64 65 66 67 68 69		
Operation(al) Order(s)	19th Infantry Brigade Operation Order No. 60	03/11/1915	03/11/1915
Miscellaneous	Relief And March Table Issued With 19th Brigade Operation Order No. 60		
Operation(al) Order(s)	19th Infantry Brigade Relief Order No. 61	11/11/1915	11/11/1915
Miscellaneous	Relief Table	09/11/1915	09/11/1915
Operation(al) Order(s)	19th Infantry Brigade Relief Order No. 62	11/11/1915	11/11/1915
Miscellaneous	Relief Table	12/11/1915	12/11/1915
Operation(al) Order(s)	19th Infantry Brigade Relief Order No. 63	17/11/1915	17/11/1915
Operation(al) Order(s)	19th Infantry Brigade Relief Order No. 64	19/11/1915	19/11/1915
Miscellaneous	Relief Table	19/11/1915	19/11/1915
Operation(al) Order(s)	19th Infantry Brigade Relief Order No. 65	21/11/1915	21/11/1915
Miscellaneous	Relief And March Table	21/11/1915	21/11/1915
Operation(al) Order(s)	19th Infantry Brigade Relief Order No. 66	22/11/1915	22/11/1915
Operation(al) Order(s)	19th Infantry Brigade Operation Order No. 67	26/11/1915	26/11/1915

Type	Description	Date From	Date To
Operation(al) Order(s)	19th Infantry Brigade Operation Order No. 68	28/11/1915	28/11/1915
Miscellaneous	Preliminary Instructions For Relief	28/11/1915	28/11/1915
Operation(al) Order(s)	19th Infantry Brigade Operation Order No. 69	29/11/1915	29/11/1915
Miscellaneous	Relief Table	29/11/1915	29/11/1915
Miscellaneous	19th Infantry Brigade	29/11/1915	29/11/1915
Heading	Daily Reports		
Miscellaneous	Daily Reports Up To 12 Noon 7th November 1915 19th Infantry Brigade	07/11/1915	07/11/1915
Miscellaneous	Daily Reports Up To 12 Noon 8th November 1915 19th Infantry Brigade	08/11/1915	08/11/1915
Miscellaneous	Daily Reports Up To 12 Noon 9th November 1915 19th Infantry Brigade	09/11/1915	09/11/1915
Miscellaneous	Daily Reports Up To 12 Noon 10th November 1915 19th Infantry Brigade	10/11/1915	10/11/1915
Miscellaneous	Daily Reports Up To 12 Noon 11th November 1915 19th Infantry Brigade	11/11/1915	11/11/1915
Miscellaneous	Daily Reports Up To 12 Noon 12th November 1915 19th Infantry Brigade	12/11/1915	12/11/1915
Miscellaneous	Daily Reports Up To 12 Noon 13th November 1915 19th Infantry Brigade	13/11/1915	13/11/1915
Miscellaneous	Daily Reports Up To 12 Noon 14th November 1915 19th Infantry Brigade	14/11/1915	14/11/1915
Miscellaneous	Daily Reports Up To 12 Noon 15th November 1915 19th Infantry Brigade	15/11/1915	15/11/1915
Miscellaneous	Daily Reports Up To 12 Noon 16th November 1915 19th Infantry Brigade	16/11/1915	16/11/1915
Miscellaneous	Daily Reports Up To 12 Noon 17th November 1915 19th Infantry Brigade	17/11/1915	17/11/1915
Miscellaneous	Daily Reports Up To 12 Noon 18th November 1915 19th Infantry Brigade	18/11/1915	18/11/1915
Miscellaneous	Daily Reports Up To 12 Noon 19th November 1915 19th Infantry Brigade	19/11/1915	19/11/1915
Miscellaneous	Daily Reports Up To 12 Noon 20th November 1915 19th Infantry Brigade	20/11/1915	20/11/1915
Miscellaneous	Daily Reports Up To 12 Noon 21st November 1915 19th Infantry Brigade	21/11/1915	21/11/1915
Miscellaneous	Daily Reports Up To 12 Noon 22nd November 1915 19th Infantry Brigade	22/11/1915	22/11/1915
Heading	2 Division 19 Infantry Brigade H.Q 1914 Aug-1915 Nov		
Miscellaneous	B.H.Q. 19th Infantry Brigade August 1914		
War Diary	Valenciennes	22/08/1914	23/08/1914
War Diary	Quivrechain	24/08/1914	24/08/1914
War Diary	Jenlain	25/08/1914	25/08/1914
War Diary	Le Cateau	26/08/1914	27/08/1914
War Diary	Olezy	28/08/1914	28/08/1914
War Diary	Pointoise	29/08/1914	30/08/1914
War Diary	Culoisi	31/08/1914	31/08/1914
Miscellaneous	Narrative of Events of 19th Infantry Brigade		
Heading	B.H.Q. 19th Infantry Brigade September 1914		
War Diary	Sentines	01/09/1914	01/09/1914
War Diary	Fresnoy	02/09/1914	02/09/1914
War Diary	Longperrier	03/09/1914	03/09/1914
War Diary	Chanteloup	04/09/1914	05/09/1914
War Diary	Grisy	06/09/1914	06/09/1914
War Diary	Villneuve St Denis	07/09/1914	07/09/1914

War Diary	La Haute Maison	08/09/1914	08/09/1914
War Diary	Signet-Signy	09/09/1914	09/09/1914
War Diary	Jouarre	10/09/1914	10/09/1914
War Diary	Certigny	11/09/1914	11/09/1914
War Diary	Marizy St Genevieve	12/09/1914	12/09/1914
War Diary	Busancy	13/09/1914	13/09/1914
War Diary	Carreire Leveque	14/09/1914	14/09/1914
War Diary	Venizel	15/09/1914	20/09/1914
War Diary	Septmonts	21/09/1914	30/09/1914
Heading	B.H.Q 19th Infantry Brigade October 1914		
War Diary	Septmonts	01/10/1914	05/10/1914
War Diary	St Remy	06/10/1914	06/10/1914
War Diary	Vez	07/10/1914	07/10/1914
War Diary	Bethisy	08/10/1914	08/10/1914
War Diary	Pont St Maxence	09/10/1914	09/10/1914
War Diary	St Omer	10/10/1914	11/10/1914
War Diary	Renescure	12/10/1914	12/10/1914
War Diary	Borre	13/10/1914	13/10/1914
War Diary	Rouge Croix	14/10/1914	14/10/1914
War Diary	Mont De Lille	15/10/1914	15/10/1914
War Diary	Steenwerck	16/10/1914	16/10/1914
War Diary	Vlamertinghie	17/10/1914	19/10/1914
War Diary	Laventie	20/10/1914	20/10/1914
War Diary	Fromelles	21/10/1914	21/10/1914
War Diary	La Boutillerie	22/10/1914	31/10/1914
Heading	B.H.Q. 19th Infantry Brigade November 1914		
War Diary	La Boutillerie	01/11/1914	14/11/1914
War Diary	Bac St Maur	15/11/1914	17/11/1914
War Diary	Houplines	18/11/1914	30/11/1914
Heading	B.H.Q. 19th Infantry Brigade December 1914		
War Diary	Houplines	01/12/1914	26/12/1914
War Diary	Armentieres	27/12/1914	31/12/1914
Heading	Attached 6 Division 19 Infantry Brigade 1915 Jan-1915 May To 27 Division		
Heading	War Diary Headquarters, 19th Infantry Brigade (6th Division) January 1915		
Heading	D.A.A.G The Base War Diary For January 1915 herewith		
War Diary	Armentieres	01/01/1915	02/01/1915
War Diary	Bois Grenier	03/01/1915	31/01/1915
Heading	War Diary Headquarters, 19th Infantry Brigade (6th Division) February 1915		
War Diary	Bois Grenier	01/02/1915	28/02/1915
Heading	War Diary Headquarters, 19th Infantry Brigade (6th Division) March 1915		
War Diary	Bois Grenier	01/03/1915	31/03/1915
Heading	War Diary Headquarters, 19th Infantry Brigade (6th Division) April 1915		
War Diary	Bois Grenier	01/04/1915	30/04/1915
Heading	War Diary Headquarters, 19th Infantry Brigade (6th Division) May 1915		
War Diary	Bois Grenier	01/05/1915	31/05/1915
Heading	27th Division 19th Infy Bde Bde Headquarters Jun-Jly 1915		
Heading	War Diary Headquarters, 19th Infantry Brigade (27th Division) June 1915		

War Diary	Bois Grenier	01/06/1915	30/06/1915
Heading	Operation Order No. 41		
Operation(al) Order(s)	19th Infantry Brigade Operation Order No. 41	26/06/1915	26/06/1915
Miscellaneous	19th Infantry Brigade-Relief Table	22/06/1915	22/06/1915
Heading	Intelligence Reports.		
Miscellaneous	19th Infantry Brigade Intelligence Summary	12/06/1915	12/06/1915
Miscellaneous	Daily Intelligence Report 19th Infantry Brigade.	13/06/1915	13/06/1915
Miscellaneous	Intelligence Report Night	14/06/1915	14/06/1915
Miscellaneous	Intelligence Report Night	15/06/1915	15/06/1915
Miscellaneous	Intelligence Report Night	16/06/1915	16/06/1915
Miscellaneous	Intelligence Report Night	17/06/1915	17/06/1915
Miscellaneous	Intelligence Report Evening and Night	18/06/1915	18/06/1915
Miscellaneous	Report On Patrol	16/06/1915	16/06/1915
Miscellaneous	Headquarters 19th Infantry Brigade	17/06/1915	17/06/1915
Miscellaneous	Intelligence Report Evening and Night	19/06/1915	19/06/1915
Miscellaneous	Intelligence Report Evening and Night	20/06/1915	20/06/1915
Miscellaneous	Intelligence Report Evening and Night	21/06/1915	21/06/1915
Miscellaneous	Intelligence Report Evening and Night	22/06/1915	22/06/1915
Miscellaneous	Intelligence Report	23/06/1915	23/06/1915
Miscellaneous	19th Brigade	22/06/1915	22/06/1915
Miscellaneous	Intelligence Report	24/06/1915	24/06/1915
Miscellaneous	Intelligence Report	25/06/1915	25/06/1915
Miscellaneous	Intelligence Report	26/06/1915	26/06/1915
Miscellaneous	Intelligence Report	27/06/1915	27/06/1915
Miscellaneous	Intelligence Report 5-pm-5am	28/06/1915	28/06/1915
Miscellaneous	19th Infantry Brigade Intelligence Report.		
Miscellaneous	19th Infantry Brigade Intelligence Report.	30/06/1915	30/06/1915
Heading	War Diary Headquarters, 19th Infantry Brigade (27th Division) July 1915 (19th-31st)		
War Diary	Bois Grenier	19/07/1915	31/07/1915
Heading	Operation Orders		
Operation(al) Order(s)	19th Infantry Brigade Operation Order No. 42	18/07/1915	18/07/1915
Miscellaneous	B.M./D.3	18/07/1915	18/07/1915
Miscellaneous	Issued with Operation Order No. 42 March Table	18/07/1915	18/07/1915
Miscellaneous	Warning Order	21/07/1915	21/07/1915
Operation(al) Order(s)	19th Infantry Brigade Operation Order No. 43	22/07/1915	22/07/1915
Map	Map		
Miscellaneous	19th Infantry Brigade After Order To Be Attached To Operation Order No. 43	22/07/1915	22/07/1915
Miscellaneous	March Table Battalions 19th Infantry Brigade	22/07/1915	22/07/1915
Miscellaneous	Relief Orders	30/07/1915	30/07/1915
Miscellaneous	Relief Orders Of 19th Infantry Brigade.	31/07/1915	31/07/1915
Heading	Intelligence Reports		
Miscellaneous	19th Infantry Brigade		
Miscellaneous	Intelligence Report	02/07/1915	02/07/1915
Miscellaneous	Intelligence Report	03/07/1915	03/07/1915
Miscellaneous	Intelligence Report	04/07/1915	04/07/1915
Miscellaneous	Intelligence Report	05/07/1915	05/07/1915
Miscellaneous	Intelligence Report	06/07/1915	06/07/1915
Miscellaneous	Intelligence Report	07/07/1915	07/07/1915
Miscellaneous	Intelligence Report	08/07/1915	08/07/1915
Miscellaneous	Intelligence Report	09/07/1915	09/07/1915
Miscellaneous	Intelligence Report	10/07/1915	10/07/1915
Miscellaneous	Intelligence Report	11/07/1915	11/07/1915
Miscellaneous	Intelligence Report	12/07/1915	12/07/1915
Miscellaneous	Intelligence Report	13/07/1915	13/07/1915

Miscellaneous	Intelligence Report	14/07/1915	14/07/1915
Miscellaneous	Intelligence Report	15/07/1915	15/07/1915
Miscellaneous	Intelligence Report	16/07/1915	16/07/1915
Miscellaneous	Intelligence Report	17/07/1915	17/07/1915
Miscellaneous	Intelligence Report	18/07/1915	18/07/1915
Miscellaneous	A Form Messages And Signals.		
Miscellaneous	Daily Report	25/07/1915	25/07/1915
Miscellaneous	Daily Report	26/07/1915	26/07/1915
Miscellaneous	Daily Report	27/07/1915	27/07/1915
Miscellaneous	Daily Report	28/07/1915	28/07/1915
Miscellaneous	Daily Report	29/07/1915	29/07/1915
Miscellaneous	Weekly Report On Exploits.	30/07/1915	30/07/1915
Miscellaneous	Daily Report	30/07/1915	30/07/1915
Miscellaneous	Daily Report	31/07/1915	31/07/1915
Heading	WO95/Stray/BBB		

BEF

2 DIV
19 BDE H.Q

1914 AUG TO 1914 DEC.

ATTACHED 6 DIV 1915 JAN — MAY
27" 1915 JUNE & JULY

2. DIVISION

19 INFANTRY BRIGADE

1915 AUG — 1915 NOV

(TO 33 DIV DEC 1915)

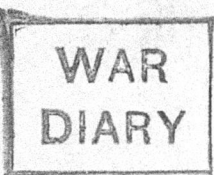

Headquarters,

19th INFANTRY BRIGADE.

(2nd Division)

AUGUST AND SEPTEMBER

1915

Attached:

    Bde. O.Os. & Instructions.
    Messages.
    Daily Tactical Progress
    Reports.
    Plans & Sketches.

Army Form C. 2118.

WAR DIARY
or
INTELLIGENCE SUMMARY.

(Erase heading not required.)

Instructions regarding War Diaries and Intelligence Summaries are contained in F. S. Regs., Part II. and the Staff Manual respectively. Title pages will be prepared in manuscript.

Hour, Date, Place	Summary of Events and Information	Remarks and references to Appendices
LAVENTIE		Casualties
Anatal 1st.	The 19th Infantry Bde on taking over the	August Orantr
" 2nd "	trenches N of FAUQUISSART found that they	1. Killed — 7
" 3rd "	were in a deplorable condition. Parapets	" Wounded — 1
" 4th "	were not bullet proof, no parados covered in	2. Killed — 3
" 5th "	and communication trenches were very	" Wounded — 1
" 6th "	bad. The wire in front was also very	3. Wounded — 1
" 7th "	poor.	4. " — 1
" 8th "	The Brigade set to work and during	5. " — 1
" 9th "	the 15 days decidedly improved the	6. " — 1
" 10th "	trenches in every way.	7. Killed — 1
" 11th "	The upper hand was got over the enemy	" Wounded — 5
" 12th "	who appeared to do what he liked before	See Daily reports attached
" 13th "	Great improvements were carried out	8. Wounded — 1
		9. " — 3
		10. " — 2
		11. " — 5
		12. Wounded — 1 " — 2
		13. Nil

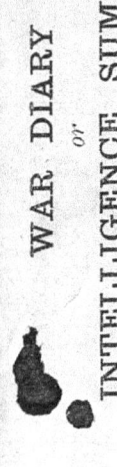

Army Form C. 2118.

WAR DIARY
or
INTELLIGENCE SUMMARY.
(Erase heading not required.)

Instructions regarding War Diaries and Intelligence Summaries are contained in F.S. Regs., Part II. and the Staff Manual respectively. Title pages will be prepared in manuscript.

Hour, Date, Place	Summary of Events and Information	Remarks and references to Appendices
LAVANTIE		Corporals Glles
August 14.	Operation Order No 44 attached. ✓	6 GR
" 15.	See Daily report.	14 {wounded 7}
LAVANTIE. 16.	19th Brigade moved to L.E. VERRIER	15 {wounded 1} {wounded 1}
LE VERRIER August 17th		16 {d 1} {wounded 1}
" 18th	Operation Order No 45. In Billets. ✓	17 {d 1}
August 19th	19th Inf Bde march past LORD KITCHENER.	18 {d 1}
" 20th		19 {d 1}
" 21st	BETHUNE. 19th Inf Bde joins the 2nd Div } In Billets.	20 {d}
" 22nd	replacing 4th Guards Brigade. Operation Order No. 46.	21 {d}
" 23rd		22 {23rd Ind}
" 24th		{24th Ind}
CUINCHY Sector.		25 {Killed 1} {Wounded 1}
August 25.	See Daily Tactical progress reports.	26 {Killed 2} {Wounded 10}
" 26.	Enemy quiet. Nothing to report.	27 {Killed 1} {Wounded 3}
" 27.		

Army Form C. 2118.

WAR DIARY
or
INTELLIGENCE SUMMARY.
(Erase heading not required.)

Instructions regarding War Diaries and Intelligence Summaries are contained in F. S. Regs., Part II. and the Staff Manual respectively. Title pages will be prepared in manuscript.

Hour, Date, Place	Summary of Events and Information	Remarks and references to Appendices
August 28	CUINCHY.	Casualties O/R B.P.
" 29	See Daily reports. (Tactical)	28 { Killed — 1
" 30	Operation Order No 47. attached ✓	Wounded — 2
" 31		29 { Wounded — 2
September 1		30 { Killed — 1
" 2	Operation Order No 48 attached. ✓	Wounded — 3
September 3rd		31 { Killed — 2
September 4 — 12		Wounded — 5
4		1. —
5		2. —
6	in Billets.	Wounded — 1
7		3. — 5
8		4. —
9		5. —
10	Operation Order No 49 attached. ✓	6. nil
11		7. —
12		8. —

WAR DIARY
or
INTELLIGENCE SUMMARY.

Army Form C. 2118.

Hour, Date, Place	Summary of Events and Information	Remarks and references to Appendices
GIVENCHY.		Casualties
September 13th	Daily reports attached.	13. Wounded Off. O.R. 3
September 14th	2 R.W.F. very heavily shelled.	14. Killed 5 Wounded 1 22
September 15th		15. Killed 1 Wounded 1
September 16th		16. Killed 1 Wounded 2
September 17th	Operation Order No. 80 attached.	17. Killed 2 Wounded 2
September 18th	19th Inf Bde relieved one battalion of the 28th Inf Bde and one battalion of the 6th Bde.	18. Wounded 1
September 19th	See Daily reports.	19. Wounded 1 2
September 20th		20. Wounded 5
		21. Killed 3 Wounded 1 2
		22. Killed 2 Wounded 10
		23. [Killed] 1 5

Army Form C. 2118.

WAR DIARY
or
INTELLIGENCE SUMMARY
(Erase heading not required.)

Instructions regarding War Diaries and Intelligence Summaries are contained in F. S. Regs., Part II. and the Staff Manual respectively. Title pages will be prepared in manuscript.

Hour, Date, Place	Summary of Events and Information	Remarks and References to Appendices
September 21st	1st Day of bombardment commenced at 6.0 a.m.	Casualties Nil
September 22nd	2nd " " " " " "	Nil
September 23rd	3rd " " " " " "	See daily reports attached
September 24th	4th " " " " " "	
	Two reliefs were carried out during the bombardment, 1 Mich'lesex & 2. A & S Highlanders were relieved by 2 R.W.F. and Cameronians and vice versa. Evening of 24th September position was as follows :- In trenches on the right 1 Middlesex in support 2. R.W.F. On left 2nd A & S Highlanders in support Cameronians. 5th S.R. W. MASON Rouge deposits. Operation Order No 32 attached	

WAR DIARY or INTELLIGENCE SUMMARY.

Army Form C. 2118.

Instructions regarding War Diaries and Intelligence Summaries are contained in F.S. Regs., Part II. and the Staff Manual respectively. Title pages will be prepared in manuscript.

(Erase heading not required.)

Hour, Date, Place	Summary of Events and Information	Remarks and references to Appendices
CAMBRIN – sector between LABASSEE road and VERMELLES – AUCHY road.		

September 25th 3.30 a.m.	All units were in position of assembly in the trenches south of the LA BASSEE road from GUN STREET – R.1 (Z2) by 3.30 a.m. Middlesex Regiment on the right holding from R1 – D crater. 2nd A & S Highlanders from D – GUN ST. 2nd RWF supporting Middlesex, Cameronians supporting 2nd A & S Highlanders and 5th S.R. in BRADDEL TRENCH and MAISON ROUGE.	Casualties
		      Offrs O.R.
		      20 240.
		 Killed
		 Wounded 17 585
		 Missing 2 80
		 Gassed 1 41.
		 Total Casualties
		 40 Offrs.
		 946 O. Ranks.

3.45 a.m.	Gas & smoke attack "Zero" is 5.50 a.m.	
5.50 a.m.	Gas attack commenced. Wind very slight and changed travelling in S.E. direction. Gas went slowly and in some parts blew back into our lines. Germans are putting on smoke helmets and lighting fires all along their line at intervals of 25–30 yards. Snipers were also seen to be used. Middlesex and 2nd A & S Highlanders advanced and are met with a very heavy rifle and machine gun fire. Gas had not affected the Germans, who are now firing very accurately. 2nd A & S Highlanders	Operation Order No 52. attached.

WAR DIARY or INTELLIGENCE SUMMARY

Army Form C. 2118.

Hour, Date, Place	Summary of Events and Information	Remarks and references to Appendices
September 25. CAMBRIN sector.	leading companies hung up on the wire. Misalliance unable to get on owing to the heavy fire, lies closer. Germans seen leaving their front parapet very thickly. Apparently the enemy were firing from their front and second lines. Both battalions hope very heavily. Reserve company of the Misalliance then goes over but losses very heavily. Position at 7.20 a.m. 1/Misalliance about 100 × in front of our front line trench, 2nd A&S Highlanders lying under cover of the German parapet by this time. 2nd A&S Highlanders withdraw to their original trenches leaving many men behind including two complete platoons who reached the German front trenches. 1/Misalliance trying to get on still 100 × in front. Artillery shells the German front line very heavily. A bombardment under 7?Divisional orders was arranged to start at 9.0 a.m. after which Infantry was to advance. 2nd R.I.S? were push out 2 companies to support the Misalliance but they are met with fierce opposition and lose heavily.	

Army Form C. 2118.

WAR DIARY
or
INTELLIGENCE SUMMARY.

(Erase heading not required.)

Instructions regarding War Diaries and Intelligence Summaries are contained in F.S. Regs., Part II. and the Staff Manual respectively. Title pages will be prepared in manuscript.

Hour, Date, Place	Summary of Events and Information	Remarks and references to Appendices
26th September CAMBRIN Sector	Bombers of 1/Middlesex reach the craters at R, but are heavily fired on by our own artillery	
9.45am	Orders received from II Divn to say that Notpower progressing favourably on our right and that no further attack was to be made by the 6th or 19th Infy Bdes. Orders were received to reorganize and	
12.45pm	consolidate. In order to help the troops on our right as much as possible we were to adopt an active attitude. Position of the Batt at 2.0 p.m. 2nd R.W.F. in place of 1/Middlesex. Communications on flank of 2nd A&S Highlanders 5th S.R. moved up to support 2 R.W.F. and 2nd A&SH supports. Communications with Maison Rouge dug outs.	Casualties:
11.42pm	Mdx have withdrawn to MAISON ROUGE dug outs. Germans fire gas shells into our left & certain amount of confusion caused.	Killed Off: 1 OR: 4
5.30 am	All quiet. Germans delivering attack towards Hulluch being given were affected by the asphyxiating shells. Day spent in reorganizing and consolidating. Very bad weather	Wounded: — 18
		Missing: — 1
		Gassed: 1 14
		Total: 2 37.

WAR DIARY or INTELLIGENCE SUMMARY.

(Erase heading not required.)

Army Form C. 2118.

Hour, Date, Place	Summary of Events and Information	Remarks and references to Appendices
September 27th 5.0 am	Quiet night. Little enemy gun at our stretcher bearers. Enemy and then some shells which passed over of the 6th S.R.	Casualties.
CAMBRIN Sector 2.25 p.m.	Position on FOSSE 8 reported to be overrun by the 28th Bdze and we were asked to "Stand to arms".	Officers. O.R. Killed. 2. 9 Wounded. — 17 Missing. 1 5 Gassed. 1 10 Total. 2 41
3.0 pm	Confirmation of the reoccupation of FOSSE 8 by the enemy. 19th Inf Bde ordered to cooperate by a pre attack in order to help the counter attack which was being delivered against FOSSE 8.	
4.45 pm	Division orders Hour "Zero" is at 5.0 pm. Gas was to be let off and after 26 minutes patrols were to be pushed forward to ascertain position of the enemy. Objective was ALLEY from MINE POINT - FRANKS KEEP. Wind was from NNW at 5 miles per hour	
5.0 pm	Gas attack commenced. Generous light fire but however smoke helmets. Generous than the parapets. Enemy shell fire ? At 5.26 pm gas was turned off and Cannons and pushed forward patrols. All officers are shot. Enemy hostiling	

WAR DIARY
or
INTELLIGENCE SUMMARY.
(Erase heading not required.)

Army Form C. 2118.

Hour, Date, Place	Summary of Events and Information	Remarks and references to Appendices
CAMBRIN Sector September 27th	his front line very strongly. Our M.G.s and artillery cause casualties to the enemy, who maintain keep up and reply to our attack.	
6.0 pm	All quiet, enemy doing a little shelling.	
September 28th		2' Casualties Officers O.R. Killed — 1 Wounded — 4 Missing — 1 Sick — 4 Grand — 3 Total — 13
11.50 am	Orders received from II Div to their HQrs cylinders of wind in	
CAMBRIN.	favourable. A quiet day and night. Occasional bursts of rifle and machine gun fire from the enemy whom collecting parties. Night spent in organising and collecting dead.	29th Killed — 1 Wounded — 2 Grand — 1 Total — 4 O.R.
September 29th	A quiet day. Cannonians were relieved by the A&S High. Enemy resorted to shelling our support lines on the left.	
September 30th	He is very heavy at rights and keeps up a good deal of sniping and machine gun fire.	30th Officers O.R. Wounded — 5 O.R Missing — 1 O.R Grand — 10 O.R Total — 16 O.R
CAMBRIN.	During the afternoon we were told to take over part of the line held by the 5th Bde. (2nd Div). The Middlesex took over from N1 - P3 (exclusive) on the right and	

Army Form C. 2118.

WAR DIARY
or
INTELLIGENCE SUMMARY.
(Erase heading not required.)

Hour, Date, Place	Summary of Events and Information	Remarks and references to Appendices
	The 5th S.R. took over from P3 inclusive to R1 exclusive. The line was now 3000 yds in length and the Brigade was allotted as follows. From Right to left - 1/Middlesex - 5th S.R. - 1st R.W.F. - 2nd A & S Highlanders. A very cold night which hampered the relief.	

CR. Nurai Capt
for Brigadier General
Commanding, 19th Infantry Brigade

BRIGADE OPERATION ORDERS AND INSTRUCTIONS.

SECRET

Copy No: 1.

19th Infantry Brigade Operation Order No: 44

Ref. 1/40,000 maps,
Sheets 36, 36 A.

14th August, 1915.

1. The Brigade will be relieved by the 59th Infantry Brigade (20th Division) on the nights 15th - 16th and 16th - 17th August as per March Tables attached.
The Brigade will be billeted in area VIEUX BERQUIN - NEUF BERQUIN - DOULIEU (F.7 and 30 and L.8) till 19th August when it will march to 1st Corps area to replace the 4th (Guards') Brigade in the 2nd Division.

2. The Train, Supply Column, Ammunition Column and Field Ambulance will remain in their present billets till 19th August.

3. The Officers Commanding 2nd Royal Welsh Fusiliers and 1st Middlesex Regiment will arrange details of relief with the Officers Commanding 11th Rifle Brigade and 11th K.R.R.C. respectively at Brigade Headquarters at 11.am to-morrow 15th August. Officers Commanding remaining units will meet at same place and time on Monday 16th August.

4. Billeting parties and regimental transports will move under Battalion arrangements. Time of starting to be reported, for approval, to Brigade Headquarters. They can move by daylight - route SAILLY Bridge.

5. Lists showing S.A.A., Hand Grenades and Trench Stores, etc. to be handed over have been issued to units concerned.

6. Sapping platoons will march with and be billeted with, Brigade Headquarters. Parties at the Brigade Grenade School will report to their units at 10.am to-morrow.

7. After reliefs are completed on night of 16th - 17th August, Brigade Headquarters will be at BLEU, F.19.b

Major,

Issued at 10.pm

Brigade Major 19th Infantry Brigade.

Copy No: 1 File
      2 Staff Captain,
      3 2nd R.W.Fusiliers,
      4 1st Cameronians
      5 1st Middlesex Regt.
      6 2nd A. & S.Hrs.
      7 5th Scottish Rifles
      8 Brigade Transport Officer
      9 19th Bde. Train
    10 19th Bde. Supply Column
    11 19th Bde. Amm.Column
    12 19th Field Ambulance
    13 H.Q. 8th Division
    14 H.Q. 20th Division.
    15 H.Q. 59th Inf.Bde.

No. 1.

To be attached to
19th Inf.Bde.
O.O.No: 44.

19th INFANTRY BRIGADE MARCH TABLE.

SUNDAY, 15th AUGUST.

UNIT.	Relieved by.	Starting Point.	Time of Starting	ROUTE	BILLETS.	REMARKS.
2nd Royal Welsh Fusiliers. (LAVENTIE)	11th Rifle Brigade	Cross Roads G.34.d 8.8	8.15.pm	Cross roads G.28.d - SAILLY Bridge - DOULIEU	L.5, F.26	11th Bn.R.B. arrive at LAVENTIE about 8.45.pm. 2 Advanced platoons will take over Post ESQUIN before arrival of battalion.
1st Middlesex Regiment (Trenches)	11th K.R.R.C.	Road junction M.5.b 9.2	On completion of relief.	Cross Roads G.29.d - SAILLY Bridge - DOULIEU	L.1,2,3, and 8.	Head of 11 Bn. K.R.R.C. will reach road junction M.5.d 1.1 at 9.7pm where guides from 1st Middlesex Regt. will meet them.

14/8/15.

H E Ryan
Major,

Brigade Major 19th Infantry Brigade.

No. 2.

19th INFANTRY BRIGADE MARCH TABLE.
MONDAY, 16th AUGUST.

UNIT.	Relieved by	Starting point.	Time of starting.	ROUTE.	BILLETS	REMARKS.
5th Cameronians (in trenches)	11th R.B.	Cross roads, G.29.d	One completion of relief.	SAILLY BRIDGE.- DOULIEU	F.21 & 22	Leading platoon of 10th K.R.R. will reach road junction H.3.d 4.4 at 8.30.pm. 2 platoons will relieve 2 platoons 2nd A. & S.Hrs in PICANTIE Post.
Half Battn. 5th Sco.Rifles (in trenches)	Half 10th K.R.R.C.	Road junction H.10.d	On completion of relief.	Cross roads G.34.d - cross roads G.29.d - SAILLY Bridge.	F.10, 15 & 15.	10th K.R.R.C. reach road junction H.10.d about 9.pm where guides of 5th Sco.Rifles will meet them
Half Battn. 2nd A. & S.Hrs. (La-Bacquerot).	Half 10th K.R.R.C.	Red House H.3.d 2.1	On completion of relief.	Cross roads G.29.d - SAILLY Bridge.-DOULIEU	F.14 & 15.	10th K.R.R.C.reach road junction H.10.d about 9.pm where guides from 2nd A. & S.Hrs. will meet them They will take over billets in RUE BICQUEROT and Posts HOUGEMONT and DEAD END.1 platoon in each. PICANTIE Post will be relieved by 11th R.B. (see above)
Half Battn. 5th Sco.Rifles (LAVENTIE)	Half 10th R.B.	Cross roads G.34.d 9.8	8.pm	Cross roads G.29.d - SAILLY Bridge.- DOULIEU	F.18, 15	10th R.B. reach LAVENTIE about 8.45.pm
Battn. 2nd A. & S.Hrs. (LAVENTIE)	Half 10th R.B.	Cross roads G.34.d 9.8	8.15.pm	Cross roads G.29.d - SAILLY Bridge.- DOULIEU	F.14 & 15	Ditto.

14/8/15.

Brigade Major 19th Infantry Brigade.

O.37

Officer Commanding,

    19th Field Ambulance.
----

1. Reference March Tables attached to Brigade Operation Order No. 44 of yesterday, the following horse ambulances will be provided by you:-

Today, 15th August.

2 (a) One horse ambulance, to accompany 2nd Royal Welch Fus., to be at Cross Roads, O.34.d.8.8. at 7-45 pm.

(b) One horse ambulance, to accompany 1st Middlesex Regt., to be at Road Junction M.6.b.3.6. at 9-30 pm.

Tomorrow, 16th August.

3.(a) One horse ambulance, to accompany 1st Bn. The Cameronians, to be at Cross Roads, O.29.d., at 9-45 pm.

(b) One horse ambulance, to accompany half battalion 2nd Argyll and Sutherland Highlanders, to be at Cross Roads, O.34.d.9.8., at 7-45 pm.
    This ambulance will also be used by half battalion 5th Scottish Rifles, who will be marching on same road ahead of 2nd A. & S. Highrs.

(c) One horse transport to accompany half battalion 5th Scottish Rifles, to be at Cross Roads, O.34.d.9.8., at 10 pm.
    This ambulance will also be used by half battalion 2nd A. & S. Highrs. who will be marching on same road ahead of 5th Scottish Rifles.

4. On each of the above dates, the ambulances can remain for the night at the transport lines of the units they accompany, returning to 19th Field Ambulance next morning.

5. Please acknowledge.

                                               Major,

15/8/15.   Brigade Major, 19th Inf. Bde..

                3.

Officer Commanding,

    For information.

15/8/15.
                                                Major,

                        Brigade Major, 19th Infantry Bde..

G.3884

19th Inf.Bde.
_____

Copy of wire from 3rd Corps 15/8/15.

Begins. warning order aaa 19th Inf.Bde. 19th Bde Signal Section 19th Field Amb and 19th Inf.Bde. train will march on 19th inst to join 1st Corps to destinations as follows aaa Bde.H.Q. Signal Section three battalions and Brigade Train to BETHUNE aaa One battalion and Field Ambulance to VENDIN LEZ BETHUNE aaa one battalion BEUVRY aaa Staff Officer 2nd Div. will meet Brigade aaa Orders for march will be communicated later to the 19th Bde. ends.

H.T. Walker

16th August, 1915.

Major.
General Staff, 8th Division.

MARCH ORDER No: 45   Copy No: 5

19th INFANTRY BRIGADE.

Ref. 1/40,000 squared map (3rd edition)
and 1/100,000 HAZEBROUCK Sheet 5 A.

18th August, 1915.

1. The Brigade will march into billets in and near BETHUNE
to-morrow 19th August as per attached March Table.
A halt for dinners will be made at the farm 300 yards N. of
AIRE - LA BASSEE Canal (Q.34.c and d).
On receipt of further orders to continue the march, battalions
will move forward in the following order:-

    2nd Battn. Argyll and Sutherland Highlanders,
    1st Battn. The Middlesex Regiment.
    1st Battn. The Cameronians.
    2nd Battn. Royal Welsh Fusiliers,
    5th Scottish Rifles.

During the second half of the march, the Brigade will march past
Lord Kitchener at the Windmill ½ mile South of HINGES Cross roads.

2. 1st line transport will accompany units. All other transport
will march with the Brigade Train. They will be ready loaded at
regimental centres not later than 7.30.am.

3. The Sapping Platoons will be at road junction W.N.W. of N
of NEUF BERQUIN (L.13.a. 10.8.) at 7.10.am and join their
respective units there. They will be billeted and rationed by
their own units until further orders.

4. O.C. 19th Field Ambulance will send 5 horse ambulances to be
at Brigade starting point at 7.45.am. They will follow in rear
of the Brigade.
In addition 2 motor ambulances will be at farm 600 yards N. of
AIRE - LA BASSEE Canal (Q.34.c. 6.2) at 10.am

5. The Brigade Train and 19th Field Ambulance will move
independently to BETHUNE under their own arrangements.
Route: LA GORGUE - LESTREM - LOCON.

6. Separate orders have been issued to the Brigade Supply Column
and Brigade Ammunition Column. They will leave the Brigade
to-morrow.

7. Brigade Headquarters during the march will be at the head of
the column; afterwards in Rue GAMBETTA, BETHUNE.

Issued at 6.pm

                                        Major,
                          Brigade Major 19th Infantry Brigade

Copy No: 1 Office
          2 Staff Captain,
          3 2nd R.W.Fusiliers,
          4 The Cameronians
          5 1st Middlesex Regt.
          6 2nd A. & S.Hrs.
          7 5th Sco.Rifles.
          8 Bde. Transport Officer
          9 Bde Supply Column.
         10 Bde. Ammunition Column
         11 Brigade Train.
         12.Lieut.Stanway (O.C.Sapping Platoons)
         13 H.Q. 2nd Division.
         14 8th Division.

To be attached to March Order No: 45.

MARCH TABLE – 19th INFANTRY BRIGADE

19th AUGUST, 1915.

UNIT.	Starting Point	Time of passing starting point	Distance from starting point to BETHUNE.	Approximate distance from billets to starting point	ROUTE	BILLETS	REMARKS.
1st Middlesex Regiment.	Cross road junc. HAZEBROUCK - ST.V. - BLK UIR road 1/40,000 map L.13.b.	7.30.am	10½ miles	1½ miles	MERVILLE - PACAUT -	BETHUNE	1st Middlesex Regiment 2nd R.W.Frs. and 1st Cameronians will reach starting point via Rue PRUVOST (L.8.)
2nd R.Welsh Fusiliers.		7.37.am		2½ miles	Cross Roads, South of N of Le CORNET MALO -	BETHUNE	
The Cameronians		7.44.am		4 miles	HINGES - Cross Roads	BETHUNE	2nd A. & S.Hrs and 5th Sco.Rifles via LA COULONNE. (E.30.a)
2nd A. & S. Highlanders		7.51.am		4 miles	South of G of OBLINGHEM.	BETHUNE	
5th Scottish Rifles		7.58.am	9½ miles (to VENDIN)	4¼ miles		VENDIN - LEZ BETHUNE (W.27.c)	

NOTE: Midday halt for dinners at 300 yards North of AIRE - LA BASSEE Canal (N.34.c.) 6½ miles from starting point.

Halts. The column will halt for 10 minutes on head reaching:-

    1. N. end of MERVILLE

    2. PACAUT.

18/8/15.

[signature]

Major,
Brigade Major 19th Infantry Brigade.

B.M.4. 18th

Officer Commanding
       5 Battns

B.M. 3 of today is cancelled.

Owing to the Brigade having to march past Lord Kitchener
at an earlier hour, leading battalion of the brigade will
pass starting point at 7.30.am. Breakfasts will be
eaten before starting and dinners will be given at
half way halt at 11.am.
Order of march:-

    1st Middlesex Regiment
    2nd Royal Welsh Fusiliers.
    The Cameronians
    2nd A. & S. Highlanders
    5th Scottish Rifles.

Orders are now being issued.

18/8/15.   Major,

                            Brigade Major 19th Infantry Brigade.

SECRET.   Copy No:

           19th Infantry Brigade Operation Order No: 46.

                                                23rd August, 1915.

Ref. trench map, and
1/40,000 BETHUNE Sheet.

        1. The Brigade will relieve the 6th Infantry Brigade in
    Section A (CUINCHY) to-morrow 24th August, as per attached
    Table "A".

        2. The sapping platoons will rejoin Brigade Headquarters
    and be billetted at ANNEQUIN F.25.d.

        3. The Brigade Machine Guns will take over machine gun
    positions to-morrow morning under separate instructions
    issued through the Brigade Machine Gun Officer.

        4. Supporting batteries of 34th brigade R.F.A. are as
    follows:-

        For A.1: 70th battery, R.F.A.)
        For A.2: 50th battery, R.F.A.) all 18 pdrs.
        For A.3: 16th battery, R.F.A.)
            56th howitzer battery is also in communication with all
    battalion Headquarters in front line and can be called upon
    direct by battalions for assistance or retaliation.
            Further assistance from Heavy Artillery can be given
    if application is made, through the affiliated field battery,
    to 34th brigade R.F.A., repeating to Brigade Headquarters.

        5. Transport, except such 1st line and officers' kits as
    accompanies units, will be billeted in BEUVRY.

        6. Brigade Headquarters will close at Rue GAMBETTA, BETHUNE,
    at 5.pm and open at same time at CAMBRIN A.19.d.7.3.

                                            H. Braine
   Issued at 3.pm   Major,

                               Brigade Major 19th Infantry Brigade.

      Copy No: 1. Office,
               2. Staff Captain,
               3. 2nd Bn. Royal Welsh Fusiliers,
               4. 1st Cameronians,
               5. 1st Bn. Middlesex Regt.,
               6. 2nd Bn. A. & S. Highlanders,
               7. 5th Bn. Scottish Rifles (T)
               8. Captain Stanway and Bde. Sapping Platoons,
               9. H.Q. 6th Infantry Brigade.
              10. H.Q. 2nd Division,
              11. Brigade Transport Officer.

Table "A".

To be attached to Operation Order No: 46.

MARCH TABLE, 19th INFANTRY BRIGADE.

Battn. to be relieved.	Battn. to be attached to	Section of front & posts, or billets.	Rendezvous	Time of arrival of loading platoons.	Approximate number of miles from billets to rendezvous.	Route.	REMARKS.
1st. N.F. Fusiliers							
2nd Battn. R.W.Fusiliers Regt.	1st Bn. Royal Berks Regt.	A.2 and The KEEP - The HOLLOW - LOVERS REDOUBT	A.19.d.6.2	3.pm	5¼	BEUVRY - ANNEQUIN.	
2nd Battn. A.& S.Hrs.	1st Bn. King's Regt.	A.3 and ORCHARD REDOUBT	North end of POPE FIVE POINT A.14.d.10.3	3.pm	5¾	Road junction E.11.b.5.8.- to QUESNOY road junction F.14.b.6.9 - to PRIEZ bridge F.10.c.8.0 - Vauxhall bridge A.13.b.4.4.	Vauxhall bridge not shown on map. Battn. crosses to North bank of canal by 1t. March by Companies at 400 yards distance to road junction F.14.B.6.9 thence by platoons at 100 yards distance.
1st Battn. Cameronians.	1st K.R.R.C	A.1 and PARK LANE REDOUBT, STAFFORD REDOUBT, CAMBRIN Post.	A.19.d.6.2	4.pm	5⅝	BEUVRY - ANNEQUIN.	
1st Battn. Middlesex Regiment.	2nd S.Staff. Regiment.	Billet in ANNEQUIN (2¾ companies) and BRADDELL Post - CARTERS Redoubt - TOURBIERES Redoubt - CUINCHY Post (1¼ companies).	F.29.b.4.6	4.30.pm	4½	BEUVRY - ANNEQUIN.	
6th Battn. Sco.Rifles.	1st Herts. Regiment.	Billets in BEUVRY.	F.14.c.0.4	4.45.pm	5½	BETHUNE - BEUVRY.	
Sapping platoons. (O.C.Captain Stanway.)	6th Brigade Grenadier Company.	ANNEQUIN.	F.29.a.4.9	5.15.pm	4½	BEUVRY	Platoons will assemble at Bde.H.Q.,Rue GAMBETTA at 5.pm.

Note. Battalions will march by companies at 400 yards distance to BEUVRY, thence by platoons at 100 yards distance. If shelling takes place platoons will open out by sections.

Guides for each platoon and each redoubt or post will meet platoons and post garrisons at the rendezvous.

23/8/15.

M. E. Browne
Major,
Brigade Major 19th Infantry Brigade.

Copy No: 1.

19th Infantry Brigade Relief Order No: 47.

Ref.1/40,000 BETHUNE map,
and Trench map.
                                               31st August, 1915.

1. The Brigade (with 11th Field Company, R.E.) will take over subsection Z.2 from 3rd Infantry Brigade to-morrow 1st September.
Subsection Z.2 extends from BETHUNE - LA BASSEE road (exclusive) to VERMELLES - LA BASSEE road (inclusive).

2. The following reliefs will be carried out to-morrow 1st September:-
(a) 5th Scottish Rifles (less 1 company) will relieve The Cameronians in subsection A.1 and posts held by them. Relief will commence at 10.am from A.19.d.7.3, where guides for each platoon and post garrison will be met.
On completion of relief The Cameronians (less 1 company) will take over the billets vacated by the 5th Scottish Rifles in F.20.b. and 21.a.

(b) 2nd A. & S.Highlanders with 1 company 5th Scottish Rifles, will relieve 1st South Wales Borderers and 2 platoons 4th Royal Welsh Fusiliers in Z.2.
The company 5th Scottish Rifles, will be under the command of O.C. 2nd A. & S.Highlanders, but will be rationed by its own battalion.
O.C.company 5th Scottish Rifles will report to O.C. 2nd A. & S. Highlanders at 10.am to-morrow 1st September for orders.
Relief of Z.2 will commence at 3.45.pm from Headquarters 3rd Infantry Brigade (A.19.d.5.2) where guides will be met.

(c) One company The Cameronians, will relieve Headquarters and 2 companies 4th Royal Welsh Fusiliers in the dugouts at MAISON ROUGE (A.20.d.4.2)
Relief will commence at 4.30.pm from road junction A.20.c.5.5, where guides will be met.
The Company will be under the direct orders of Brigade Headquarters and will be rationed by its own unit.

3. The redistribution of machine guns will be carried out during the morning of 1st September under separate instructions issued through the Brigade Machine Gun Officer.
Guns, on completion of relief, will be in position as follows:-

    Subsection Z.2:   8 guns
                           (including 1 in   (4 of 2nd A. & S.Hrs.
                           STAFFORD Redoubt) (4 of 1st Cameronians.
    (Guides for 7 guns will be at A.19.d.5.2 at 11.30.am)
    Subsection A.1:   6 guns   (4 of 5th Sco.Rifles.
                                                         (2 of 1st Middx.Regt.

    Subsection A.2:   6 guns   (4 of 2nd R.W.Frs.
                                                        (2 of 1st Middx.Regt.

Officers Commanding Sub Sections will arrange to ration the detachments in their respective Sub sections.

(4)

4. Officer Commanding 10th Trench Mortar Battery will arrange to send 2 mortars into subsection Z.2 to-morrow morning. This section will be under the orders of O.C. 2nd A. & S. Highlanders.

5. The allotment of batteries of A group, R.F.A. will be notified later.

6. A list of trench stores in Z.2 to be taken over will be issued later.

7. On completion of relief the new section will be under the command of the G.O.C. 19th Infantry Brigade and will be known as Section A.
    Subsection Z.2 will become A.1
    Subsection A.1 will become A.2
    Subsection A.2 will become A.3.

Issued at 5.30.pm.
                         Major,
              Brigade Major 19th Infantry Brigade.

Copy No: 1 Office,
        2 Staff Captain,
        3 2nd R.W.Fusiliers,
        4 The Cameronians,
        5 1st Middlesex Regiment,
        6 2nd A. & S.Hrs.,
        7 5th Scottish Rifles
        8 Brigade Transport Officer,
        9 O.C. 11th Field Coy., R.E.,
       10 O.C. 10th T.M.Battery,
       11 O.C. A group, R.F.A.,
       12 3rd Infantry Brigade H.Q.,
       13 2nd Division, H.Q.

SECRET   O.69.

Officer Commanding
_____

1. Reference para.5 of Relief Order No: 47 of yesterday, supporting batteries are allotted as follows:-

    Subsection A.1 (105th battery, R.F.A.
    (South of LA   (
    BASSEE Road) (C.50. battery, R.F.A.

    Subsection A.2   70th battery, R.F.A.

    Subsection A.3   50th battery, R.F.A.

    All above are 18 pounders.

2. In subsection A.1 the 105 battery can fire in enfilade along the whole of the German front trenches.

C.50 battery can fire on German front trenches opposite the right of the subsection and on all German trenches in rear of the front line.

3. For howitzer support or for assistance or retaliation from heavy artillery, application will be made by Officers Commanding subsections to Headquarters "A" Group R.F.A. through their affiliated field batteries.

4. Officers Commanding subsections will report at 7.pm today whether they are in communication with their supporting batteries.

1/9/15.

                                            Major,
                    Brigade Major 19th Infantry Brigade.

Copy No: 1

19th Infantry Brigade Operation Order No: 48

Ref.1/40,000 map BETHUNE
and Trench Map.

3rd September, 1915.

1. The Brigade will be relieved by the 6th Infantry Brigade to-morrow, and will be billetted in BETHUNE as Divisional Reserve.
No: 10 Trench Mortar Battery will remain in Section "A" (CUINCHY) and will be attached to the 6th Infantry Brigade until relieved by No: 6 Trench Mortar Battery at 10.am on 5th September.
The 11th Field Company, R.E. will also remain in Section "A" and will be affiliated for work to 6th Infantry Brigade.

2. Reliefs will be carried out as per attached TABLE. Guides will be provided by units for each platoon and post garrison.

3. The machine guns of the Brigade will be relieved under instructions issued through the Brigade Machine Gun Officer. Guides for each gun will be at Brigade Headquarters at 11.am to-morrow.

4. The 2nd Royal Welsh Fusiliers will take over Guards and Control Posts, in and near BETHUNE, from The Cameronians at 4.pm to-morrow.

5. Transport will march to BETHUNE under regimental arrangements.

6. Trench stores will be handed over as per instructions already issued.

7. The Brigade Sapping Platoons will rejoin their respective units on arrival in BETHUNE.

8. Brigade Headquarters will close at CAMBRIN at 5.pm and reopen at same hour in RUE GAMBETTA, BETHUNE.

Issued at 8.30.pm

Major,
Brigade Major 19th Infantry Brigade.

Copy No: 1 Office,
2 Staff Captain,
3 2nd R.W.Fusiliers,
4 The Cameronians,
5 1st Middlesex Regt.,
6 2nd A. & S.Hrs.,
7 5th Scottish Rifles,
8 Brigade Transport Officer,
9 ~~Captain Pelton~~, O.C.Bde.Sapping Platoons,
10 O.C. 11th Field Coy., R.E.,
11 O.C. "A" Company The Cameronians (MAISON ROUGE)
12 O.C. No: 10 T.M.Battery,
13 H.Q. "A" Group, R.F.A.,
14 H.Q. 2nd Division,
15 H.Q. 6th Infantry Brigade.

To be attached to
Operation Order No: 48.   RELIEF AND MARCH TABLE: 19th INFANTRY BRIGADE:

UNIT	Relieved by.	Rendezvous for guides.	Time of arrival of leading platoon.	Subsection & Posts to be relieved.	Billets in BETHUNE	REMARKS
5th Sco.Rifles (less 1 Coy.)	1st King's Regt. (less 1 Coy.)	Hedgegrow Lane near Bde.H.Q. A.19.d.6.3	12.50.pm	A.2 & Park Lane Redoubt(1 platoon) Stafford Redoubt (1 platoon) CAMBRIN Post (½ platoon)	Feuillarde Barracks.	
1 Company, ½ platoon 2nd R.W.Frs.	1 Company, ½ platoon, R.Berks.Regt.	Ditto.	1.15.pm	CUINCHY supporting Point (1 Company) BRADDELL Post (½ platoon)	Rue d'Aire	Party of R.Berks.Regt will follow in rear of 1st King's Regt.
1st Middx. Regt.	2nd S.Staffs Regt.	Ditto.	1.30.pm	A.3 and The Keep (1 platoon) Lover's Redoubt (½ platoon)	Ecole Sevigne Ecole Paul Bert Ecole Libre.	
2nd A.& S. Hrs. and one Coy. 5th Sco. Rifles.	1st K.R.R.C. and 1 Coy. 1st King's Regt.	Ditto.	2.15.pm 3.pm	A.1 and Russell's Keep, Arthurs Keep (1 platoon each)	Montmorency Barracks.	
"A" Company The Cameronians	1 Coy. R.Berks.Regt.(?)	Ditto.	3.pm	MAISON ROUGE Dugouts.	Cemetery Area.	
2nd R.W.Frs. (less above)	R.Berks.Regt. (less above)	Cross Roads F.29.b.4.6	3.pm	ANNEQUIN billets & Carter's Redoubt TOURBIERES Redoubt (1 section each)	Rue d'Aire.	
The Cameronians (less 1 Coy)	1st Herts or 5th King's Regt.	Cross Roads F.14.c.4.4	3.pm	BEUVRY Billets.	Cemetery Area.	
Brigade Sapping Platoons.	6th Brigade Grenadier Company.	Cross Roads F.29.b.4.6	3.pm	ANNEQUIN Billets.	With their respective Bns.as above	6th Bde.Grenadier Coy. will be in rear of R.Berks.Regt.

3rd September, 1915.

H. E. Erskine Major,
Brigade Major 19th Infantry Brigade.

19th Infantry Brigade

Copy No....1....

OPERATIONS ORDER No. 49.

Reference trench map and 1/40,000, BETHUNE SHEET.

12th September, 1915.

1. The Brigade will relieve the 5th Infantry Brigade in Section "B" (GIVENCHY) tomorrow, 13th September, 1915.

2. The relief will be carried out as per March Table attached.

3. The Brigade Machine Guns will take over positions from 5th Infantry Brigade tomorrow morning under separate instructions issued through the Brigade Machine Gun Officer.

4. The 95 millometre trench mortar battery will leave Brigade Headquarters at 10 am and be at 5th Infantry Brigade Headquarters (F.10.b.8.0.) at 11-30 am. whence it will be guided to its position in the trenches.

5. Battalion Grenadier Officers of units in front line will take over grenade stores, &c. in their respective subsections tomorrow morning, reporting to 5th Infantry Brigade Headquarters (F.10.b.8.0.) at 11 am.

6. The Brigade Sapping Platoons will march with their own units until they reach the neighbourhood of LE QUESNOY and LE PREOL respectively, when they will march independently to their billets at LE PREOL in F.16.a.3.2.

7. Orders concerning transport and billeting parties have been issued sepabately.

8. Brigade Headquarters will close at RUE GAMBETTA at 3 pm tomorrow and open at F.10.b.8.0. at same hour.

H. E. Braine

Major,
Brigade Major, 19th Inf.Brigade.

Issued at 4-30 pm.

Copy No.		Copy No.	
1.	Office.	7.	5th Scottish Rifles
2.	Staff Captain.	8.	Bde. Transport Officer
3.	2nd R.Welch Fus.	9.	Bde. Trench Mortar Office
4.	1st Cameronians.	10.	O.C. Sapping Platoons. (Captain Stanway)
5.	1st Middlesex R.		
6.	2nd A.& S. Highrs.	11.	O.C. "B" Group, R.F.A.
		12.	5th Inf. Bde.
		13.	2nd Division.

To be attached to Operation Order No. 4.

Relief and March Table, 19th Infantry Brigade.

UNIT.	Relieving.	Sub section and posts or billets.	Route.	Rendezvous for Guides.	Time leading Platoon to reach rendezvous	REMARKS.
1st Cameronians.	2nd H.L.I.	B.2. The Keep (1 platoon) Hilders redoubt (2 sections) Mairie redoubt (1 platoon)	Canal towpath North of canal as far as PONT LEVIS (H.3.c.) thence by tow path S. of the canal.	WATERLOO Bridge (F.10.d.3.8.)	2-30 pm.	Intervals between platoons from PONT LEVIS. Distribution in trenches. 2 Companies front line. 1 Company support (less 2½ platoons in posts) in GUNNER Siding. 1 Company reserve at WINDY CORNER.
5th Scottish Rifles.	Glasgow Yeom.	B.1. Orchard Redoubt (1 platoon).	BETHUNE cross roads F.14.b.6. 9. - LE PREOL bridge, (F.16.a.8. 10.); thence by road S. of railway to VAUXHALL Bridge.	VAUXHALL BRIDGE. (A.13.b.5.5)	3-0 pm	Intervals between platoons from LE PREOL Bridge. Distribution in trenches. 2 Companies front line. 1 Company support (less platoon in Orchard Redoubt.) in STRATHCONA Walk and BAYSWATER. 1Company in reserve at SPOIL BANK.
2nd R.Welch Fus.	2nd Oxford & Bucks. L.I.	B.3. Poppy redoubt (2 sections)	Road S. of canal and railway to PONT LEVIS (F.3.c) thence by tow path S. of canal.	WATERLOO Bridge (F.10.d.8.8)	3-30 pm.	Intervals between platoons from PONT LEVIS. Distribution in trenches; 2 Companies front line 1 Company (less POPPY redoubt garrison) in PARK Lane and SCOTTISH trench 1 Coy. reserve at WINDY Corner.

Relief and March Table (Continued)

UNIT.	Relieving.	Sub section and posts or billets.	Route.	Rendezvous for guides.	Time leading Platoon to reach rendezvous.	REMARKS.
2nd A.& S. Hrs.	2nd Worcestershire Regt.	LE PREOL.	Road S. of canal and rail way to LE QUESNOY F.8.b.8.7. - Cross Roads F.14.b.6.9.		Billetting parties to be sent on ahead.	Head of Battalion to reach LE QUESNOY at 4 pm.
1st Middlesex Regt.	1st Queen's.	LE QUESNOY.	Road S. of canal and rail way to LE QUESNOY F.8.b.8.7.		Billetting parties to be sent on ahead.	Head of battalion to reach LE QUESNOY at 4-30 pm.

12th September, 1915.

A.S.M'Carr / Major,

Brigade Major, 19th Infantry Brigade.

19th Infantry Brigade.   Copy No...........

Operation Order No. 50.

Reference tracing of trench map   16th September, 1915.
and 1/40,000, BETHUNE MAP.

1. The Brigade will be relieved by the 5th Infantry Brigade in "B" Section (GIVENCHY) tomorrow, and will, on the same day, take over from 6th Infantry Brigade and 28th Infantry Brigade, (9th Division) that portion of the trench line lying between GUN STREET (A.21.b.4.0.) and a point known as R.1. (A.27.b.8.0)
   This new sub-section will be known as Z.2.

2. The Northern boundary of the Brigade area will be from GUN Street to junction of TOWER Reserve trench and THE LANE, thence Westward along the Southern edge of the LA BASSEE Road.
   The 6th Infantry Brigade is responsible for the defence of the road.
   The Southern boundary will be R.1. - SIM'S KEEP - LEWIS ALLEY - LEWIS KEEP (All inclusive to 9th Division) thence to road junction in F.30.b.2.8.

3. The respective reliefs will be carried out as per attached Relief Table.

4. The Brigade Machine Guns will be relieved in B. Section tomorrow morning and will move to new positions in Z.2. sub-section and billets under instructions issued through the Brigade Machine Gun Officer.

5. Lists of trench stores handed and taken over, respectively, will be sent in by units to Brigade Headquarters, as soon as possible after relief.

6. Brigade Sapping Platoons will take over billets of one Company 6th K.O.S.B. and one Company 10th H.L.I. near CAMBRIN Church and will arrive there at 1-30 pm.

7. The O.C., 95 mm trench mortar battery will bring out three 95 mm trench mortars on relief, and put them into that part of Sub-Section Z.2. to be held by 2nd A. & S. Highrs.

8. East Anglia Field Company, R.E. is attached to the Brigade from tomorrow.

9. Distribution of supporting batteries will be notified later

10. Brigade Headquarters will be established at the Chemist's shop at A.19.d.5.2. at 4 pm tomorrow, but a report centre will remain at present H.Q. until relief of "B" Section is completed

H. E. Browne
Major,
Brigade Major, 19th Infantry Brigade.

Issued at 8-30 pm.

Copy No. 1 Office.
  "   2 Staff Captain.
  "   3 2nd R.Welch Fus.
  "   4.1st Cameronians.
  "   5 1st Middlesex R.
  "   6 2nd A. & S. Highrs.
  "   7 5th Scottish Rifles.
  "   8 Brigade Transport Officer.

Copy No.9 (O.C. Sapping
          (Platoons.
  "   10 (O.C.95 mm trench
          (mortar battery.
  "   11 O.C."A" group, R.F.A.
  "   12 2nd Division.
  "   13 6th Brigade.
  "   14 5th Brigade.
  "   15 28th Brigade.

Operation Order No. 80.

Section "B", GIVENCHY.

UNIT.	Sub-Section.	Relieving or relieved by	Rendezvous for Guides for Platoons, & posts.	Time.	Billets.	Remarks.
5th Scottish Rifles	B.1.	Glasgow Highlanders.	VAUXHALL BRIDGE.	3-30 pm.	LE PREOL.	Transport lines at LE PREOL.
1st Cameronians.	B.2.	1st Queens.	VAUXHALL BRIDGE.	4-30 pm.	Cemetery area, BETHUNE.	Transport lines in BETHUNE. 1 platoon (1 officer 50 other ranks) in billet at Chicory Factory.
2nd R.Welch Fus.	B.3.	2/Worcesters.	WINDY CORNER.	5-50 pm.	ECOLE PAUL BERT, BETHUNE.	Transport lines in BETHUNE.
			Z.2. Subsection.			
2/A. & S.Highrs. (less 1 Company)	Left half of Z.2. & RUSSELL'S KERR.	1/K.R.R.C.	CARRIE supporting Point.	2 pm.	Transport lines at LE PREOL.	Trench from GUN STREET Southward to 50 yards N. of Point "D"(A.21.d.3.2.)
1 Company, 2nd A. & S. Highrs.	MAISON ROUGE Dug-outs.	1 Company, 1st Kings.	--ditto--	2-30 pm.	-	Battalion Reserve.
1st Middlesex R. (less 1 Company).	Right half of Z.2.	10th H.L.I.	CARRIE Church. (A.26.a.3.30.)	3 pm.	Transport lines at LE PREOL.	Trench from VERMELLES - LA BASSEE Road Southward to point known as R.1. (A.27.b.8.0.)
1 Company, 1/Middlesex R.	Right half at Z.2. & ARTHUR's KP.	1 Company, 1/K.R.R.C.	CARRIE Supporting Point.	2-45 pm.	-	Trench from VERMELLES - LA BASSEE Road Northwards to 50 yards N. of point D. (A.21.d.5.2.

Brigade Major, 19th Infantry Brigade.

S. O. S.
=====================

Brigade major

19th Infantry Brigade instructions.
----

1. The 19th and 6th Brigades of the 2nd Division will take part in the main attack in conjunction with the 9th Division, on the enemy's lines South of the Canal. Other troops will again be on the right of the 9th Division. The 6th Brigade will be on the left of the 19th Brigade
   The 5th Brigade will make a subsidiary attack North of the canal from GIVENCHY.
   The date and time of the assault will be notified later.

2. The Brigade will attack as follows:-
FRONTAGE. R.1 (about A.27.b.8.0.) - GUN STREET (inclusive).

OBJECTIVE. Canal Alley from B.25.b.7.7. inclusive, to A.24.b.4.2. exclusive.

DIRECTION OF RIGHT *FLANK*
    LES BRIQUES FARM - Road Junction A.29.a.3.9. - Cross Roads A.30.b.4.7. - HAISNES (marked 74 on 1/10,000 map)- Road and Railway junction B.25.b.7.7. (all inclusive).

DIRECTION OF LEFT *FLANK*
    CHATEAU ALLEY - CROSS ROADS A.22.b.1.2. - cross roads A.23.a.5.2. - road junction A.23.b.8.1. - road junction A.24.d.1.9. (All inclusive).

The 19th Brigade is responsible for maintaining touch with the 28th Brigade. The 6th Brigade for maintaining touch with 19th Infantry Brigade.

3. (a) The attack will be made in a series of bounds corresponding to the following intermediate objectives :-

1st Objective.	2nd Objective.	3rd or MAIN objective.
LES BRIQUES FARM & VERMELLES RAILWAY line as far N. as road crossing A.22.b.1.2. (inclusive.)	AUCHY - LEZ - LA BASSEE and TRIANGLE ALLEY from A.29.b.4.8. to A.23.a.6.2. *(Both inclusive)*	Railway line from B.25 b.7.7.(inclusive) to A.24.b.4.2. (exclusive)

(b) The ground gained will be made good by consolidating at first certain intermediate points, including :-
(i) RYANS KEEP: existing oblong work A.21.d.9.3.

(ii) LES BRIQUES FARM: road crossing A.22.b.1.2.

(iii) Posts in TRIANGLE ALLEY at suitable points.

(c) Communication trenches from our present line to the German present front line will at once be dug through as follows:-

    (1) T6 MINE POINT.
    (2) From ETNA.
    (3) From SHORT CUT.

4. The Brigade will attack with two battalions in front and two in support. The 5th Scottish Rifles being in Brigade reserve.
    No. 1 (right) battalion/front will be R.1 - to point D inclusive.
    No. 2 (left) battalion front will be from point D (exclusive) to GUN STREET.
    The dividing line during the advance between the two battalions will be :-
    (1) Point 85, where DOOK ALLEY crosses the railway.
    (2) Point A.23.d.2.6. (North East of AUCHY Church)

(During the advance here, the left battalion will keep its right flank on the North side of DOOK ALLEY)

(2)

(3) Siding B.19.c.4.5. (inclusive to left battalion).

No. 3 battalion will be in rear of No. 1 battalion in sidings between BURBURE and MAISON ROUGE ALLEYS.

No. 4 battalion will be in rear of No. 2 battalion in sidings between BURBURE ALLEY and WILSONS WAY.

5th Scottish Rifles will be in trenches near MAISON ROUGE

5. The exact position of the four regular battalions, i.e. which assault and which follow in support, depends on the date finally fixed for the attack. The 1st Middlesex Regt. and 2nd R. Welch Fus. will co-operate on the right, the 2nd A. & S. Hrs. and 1st Cameronians on the left.

S.A.A.   6. Every man, except as below, will carry 200 rounds of S.A.A.
Grenadiers will carry 50 rounds each.
Men of Sapping Platoons will carry 120 rounds each.
Signallers 50 rounds each.

Reserve ammunition will be distributed as follows:-
Trench reserve - All spare ammunition in the trenches to be collected in each of the front battalions areas and placed in depots near the points where forward communication trenches are to be dug.
The battalion mobile reserve (1 G.S. limbered wagon, 4 S.A.A. Carts and 9 pack animals per battalion) and the Brigade Mobile reserve (3 G.S. limbered wagons and 5 S.A.A. Carts), will be parked at LE PREOL.

SANDBAGS.   7. Every man will carry two sandbags.
Men of Sapping Platoons and Sappers of East Anglian Field Company R.E. will carry 6 sandbags.

GRENADIERS.   8. Each grenadier will carry 6 "ball" bombs in special canvas
GRENADES.   carriers.
600 special bombs (Lachrymator) will also be issued to units in the front line to be used during the bombardment, immediately prior to the assault.

In addition to the above, each battalion, except 5th Scottish Rifles, will receive 200 "ball" bombs with 100 canvas carriers, each carrier holding 2 "ball" bombs and also 200 No. 1 Grenades per battalion to be carried on the belt.
These will be distributed among platoons and will be carried forward as a battalion reserve for redistribution to grenadiers. The distribution of bombs will be as follows :-

On the man.		Ball grenades.	Canvas Carriers.
Battalion grenadiers	600 X 5. =	3,000	500
Selected men in each) of 4 regular Bns.)	400 X 4. =	1,600	(1) 400.
Battn reserve) in bomb depots)	500 to each Bn (2)	2,000.	in boxes.
Brigade reserve at) Brigade reserve depot)		2,000	in boxes.
		8,600	
Special Lachrymator bombs.		600	
		9,800.	

(5)

The Lachrymator bombs will be distributed for special purposes. They are reported to have a very good effect on the enemy. They should not be used indiscriminately, but should be used in places where the hostile defence is particularly obstinate and where the ordinary bomb has not sufficient effect. They should not be used against any points through which our troops will have to pass.

(1.) 800 will be No. 1. Grenades which clip on to the belt.
(2.) These 2,000 bombs will be in four depots in the trench. Depots will be numbered one to four and each will contain 500 "Ball" Grenades.

ENTRENCHING TOOLS AND R.E.STORES.
9. (a) Besides the light entrenching tools each Battalion will carry 160 G.S. shovels and 50 picks. These will be issued equally to platoons and will be carried on slings specially provided for the purpose.

(b) Wire cutters will, if possible, be made up to 64 per battalion. These will be distributed by Officers Commanding Battalions as required, with due regard to the fact that the wire which will probably require most cutting will be that which is behind the hostile front line.

(c) Stores of R.E. Material will be situated in the trenches as follows :-

Right attack   -   near Vermelles
                          VERMELLES Road.

Left attack.   -   In rear of ETNA.

Brigade reserve.   -   MAISON ROUGE.

Advanced Depot.   -   CAMBRIN SUPPORTING POINT.

(d) In addition to the above, the following stores will be provided for battalions in the front line.

Right battalion.   -   60 bridges, 300 ladders.

Left battalion.   -   30 bridges,   80 ladders.

Both battalions will also receive a certain number of light bridges to carry forward for crossing the hostile trenches.

RATIONS & WATER.
10. (1) In addition to the haversack ration and iron ration, one extra cheese ration will be carried on the man.

(2) Dumps of reserve rations will be established in the trenches one in each section, near

(i) VERMELLES ROAD (Right attack),
(ii) Rear of ETNA. (Left attack).

Each dump will consist of 3,500 complete iron rations.

Two reserve stores of water will be established near the two above positions - each consisting of 180, two gallon tins.

MEDICAL.
11. (a) The Advanced dressing station will be at No.1 HARLEY STREET.
(b) Collecting station for walking cases - BEUVRY; F.14.c.
(c) First aid posts will be established at
1. In MAISON ROUGE dugouts near Western end of BURBURE ALLEY.
2. In BURBURE ALLEY 200 yards from its Western end on North side of ALLEY.

(d) An Advanced collecting post of No. 3 Mobile Veterinary Section for sick and wounded horses, will be at F.8.d.6.5. The injured horses will be taken over there by the M.V.S. and the conducting parties will return immediately to their units.

A Veterinary officer will be on duty there, and his assistance can be obtained by units having no Veterinary Officer of their own.

CONTROL POSTS.

12. Blocking posts will be established on the line MAISON ROUGE - CAMBRIN SUPPORTING POINT.

These will be found by the Brigade police, assisted by a proportion of Regimental Police.

The duties of these posts will be

(1) To prevent any man proceeding West of the line of posts, unless on duty or provided with a pass.

(2) To prevent civilians getting East of the line.

(3) To collect stragglers and send them to a central collecting station, where they will be reorganised and returned to units under police arrangements.

PRISONERS OF WAR.

13. (1) A Divisional collecting post for prisoners will be established near the road junction West of the BEUVRY Canal branch (F.15.b.3.2.)

(2) All prisoners taken by the Brigade will be sent under escort to the above depot, where they will be taken over. Escorts will then return to the front.

(3) Prisoners should be despatched from the front in convenient batches, as escorts can be provided. Escorts should vary in strength from 15 to 20 percent of number of prisoners.

(4) Batches should rarely exceed 100. An officer will be sent in command of a party of 100 or more.

(5) Prisoners physically unfit to march must be handed over to the nearest dressing station.

(6) Officers and N.C.Os. commanding escorts will
   (a) Count prisoners before starting
   (b) Escort should be divided in front and rear, flanks being lightly guarded.
   (c) Slowest movers to be placed in front.
   (d) Allow no conversation between the prisoners and any other person (civil or military).
   (e) When on the road, keep prisoners concentrated.
   (f) When halted, civilians and soldiers to be kept at a distance.
   (g) Any prisoner attempting to escape to be shot.
   (h) After handing over the prisoners to the collecting post and obtaining a receipt for them, return with escort at once to unit.

(7) A Brigade prisoners collecting post will be formed at MAISON ROUGE, just South of Exit of BURBURE ALLEY - where escorts from units will hand over prisoners.

From here special escorts will take them on to the Divisional collecting post.

DOCUMENTS.

14. Officers are not to carry on their person any documents, copies of orders, instructions, air photographs, maps, plans of our trenches, etc. which might be of use to the enemy in the event of the documents falling into his hands.

(5)

FIELD COMPANIES.
R.E.
MINING PARTIES,
R.E.

15 (a) 1st East Anglian Field Company, R.E. (less 2 Sectio will be attached to the Brigade.

(b) With a view to discovering and dealing with hostile mine galleries, a certain number of officers, N.C.Os. and men of the Tunneling Company with the necessary equipment will be attached to the Brigade.

95 mm. TRENCH MORTARS.

16. The Brigade 95 mm Trench mortar battery will be issued with a certain number of smoke bombs.
These smoke bombs can be thrown as far as the German trenches in front of the Division — the mortars will be registered early with the ordinary bomb and then not used, in order to avoid drawing fire on our front trenches.

Half the battery will advance with right supporting battalion, half with left supporting battalion.

MACHINE GUNS.

17. A Brigade reserve of Machine Guns will be formed as follows :—

    2 guns   2nd R.Welch Fusiliers.
    2 guns   1st Cameronians.
    4 guns   5th Scottish Rifles.

This includes "B" teams for each of the above guns.

The remaining guns will operate with their respective battalions.

At the moment of the assualt each gun will have 14 belt boxes of ammunition, i.e., 3,500 per gun.

Flags will be issued to Machine Gun Sections as follows:-

2nd R.Welch Fusiliers.   Blue.
1st Cameronians.   Green.
1st Middlesex Regt.   White.
2nd A. & S. Highrs.   Red.
5th Scottish Rifles.   YELLOW

These flags will be used as sign posts to ensure the ammunition supply being brought to the proper guns when they move forward.

COMMUNICATIONS.

18. (1) There will be a central signal station on FOSSE No. 9 , ANNEQUIN, F.29.d.

Detailed instructions regarding communications have already been issued.

(2) Distinctive screens (yellow on one side, khaki on the other) have been issued to units of the 2nd Division at a scale of 1 per platoon.

The 9th Division will use red and yellow diagonal screens. The 7th Division Red and Blue diagonal screens.

These screens will be erected to designate any ground of which troops are in fairly secure possession, and which they are consolidating. The screens should be placed, if possible, out of sight of the enemy, and leave the khaki side towards the enemy. Troops whose advance is too rapid, or whose position is too insecure, to allow of the erection of the identity screens, will make their presence known to the Artillery by raising their caps on the points of their bayonets.

(6)

These methods of identification do not however, relieve units of the responsibility of sending back information regarding their progress.

(3) Smoke candles firing yellow smoke and men raising caps on bayonets will also be used as signals to denote positions gained by our Infantry.

(4) Smoke candles will be carried by the Infantry during the advance and used to notify their position to our own artillery.

When a body of troops finds its advance is impeded by the fire of our own artillery it will burn a smoke candle. Every man carrying candles will also be provided with a box of fuzees.

(5) Electric torches are of great value for night signalling. Officers and N.C.Os. in possession of electric torches will assist battalion signallers by the loan of these whenever possible.

(6) There will be a telephone instrument and operators at the following places

(7) Three linen arrows about 15 feet long and one and half feet wide with arrow head at one end will be carried by battalion Headquarters.

These will be used, when Infantry is held up by hostile fire from trenches, houses, etc., to ask for artillery support; the arrows being laid out on the ground pointing in the direction of the named object

This will enable aeroplanes to distinguish the particular target more accurately.

Artillery will continue to fire on targets until arrow is removed.

(8) There will be an Artillery F.O.O. with each of the battalions carrying out the assault and with the two in immediate support.

ASSAULT. 19. Every precaution must be taken to ensure that, when troops are forming up for the assault, bayonets are not allowed to show over the parapet.

H.E.Braine
Major,
22/9/15. Brigade Major, 19th Infantry Brigade.

SECRET.

Reference 19th Infantry Brigade Secret Instructions of 22/9/15, paragraph 18 (6) "COMMUNICATIONS", the following are places where telephones will be operating:-

RIGHT BATTALION.

1. Support trench between Boyaux 7 and 8.
2. Boyau 10.
3. Boyau 11.
4. Support trench between Boyau 14 and 15.
5. Battalion Headquarters West end of Boyau 9.

LEFT BATTALION.

6. Junction of Boyaux 16 and 15a.
7. West end of Boyau 19.
8. West end of Boyau 21.
9. Battalion Headquarters West end of Boyau 18.

LEFT SUPPORT BATTALION.

10. WILSONS WAY between sidings 4 and 5.

RIGHT SUPPORT BATTALION.

11. MAISON ROUGE ALLEY between sidings 1 and 2.

ADVANCED BRIGADE HEADQUARTERS.

12. 100 yards North of MAISON ROUGE and 100 yards South of West end of BURBURE ALLEY.

22/9/15.

H. E. Braine
Major,
Brigade Major, 19th Infantry Brigade.

S E C R E T.   O.107.

Reference 19th Infantry Brigade Secret instructions of 23/9/15 para. 18 "COMMUNICATIONS" sub para. (7).

1. Sub para. (7) is cancelled and the following will be substituted :-

" White linen arrows about 15 feet long and 3 feet wide, with arrow head at one end, also five other strips six feet by one foot six inches, will be carried by battalion headquarters.

When Infantry are held up by hostile fire from trenches or houses, or other features at close range, and requires support from heavy howitzers, and arrow will be laid out on the ground near the obstacle as it can be brought, pointing towards it, with one 6 feet strip laid cross ways wise for every 200 yards that the obstacle is estimated to be distant from the arrow.

The result will be that as soon as the aeroplane notices the signal, it will, if it can distinguish the target call up a heavy howitzer and range it on the target, keeping the fire up until the signal is removed.

Example: A signal points at a house estimated to be 400 yards from the signal:-

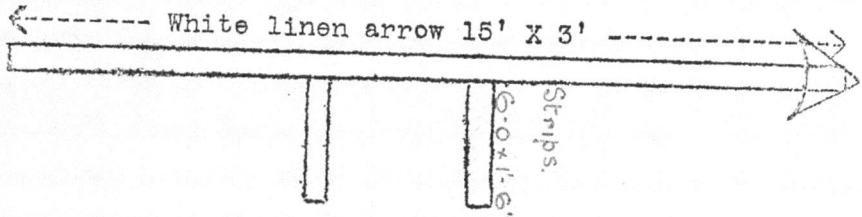

The aeroplane on calling up a battery for this work will use a pre-arranged prefix, and the battery will only fire when "G" is sent by aeroplane.

Immediately the signal is removed, the aeroplane ceases sending "G" and the firing ceases.

Arrows must be picked up as soon as fire is required to cease.

23/9/15.

                                                           Major,

                        Brigade Major, 19th Infantry Brigade..

S E C R E T.   O.105.

1. Reference 19th Infantry Brigade Secret instructions, of 22nde September, para. 18 "COMMUNICATIONS" sub-paras (3) and (4), the following instructions have been issued by the 2nd Division to avoid any possibility of doubt or misunderstanding.

"The burning of a smoke candle by the infantry is a signal <u>only</u> to show the position of that body of infantry. It is <u>not</u> a request to the artillery to lift their fire".

"If infantry are being fired on by our own artillery, they will burn a candle so that the artillery Observation Officers will be able to locate their position, and regulate the fire of the guns accordingly".

In other words both the above mean the same thing, i.e. the position of our infantry.
If the artillery F.O.Os. find that their guns are firing on this line of smoke candles, they will know they are firing on our troops, and consequently lift.

2. Paras.(3)and (4) will be cancelled except that men raising caps on bayonets will still also be used as signals to denote positions gained by our infantry, and that every man carrying candles will also be provided with a box of fuzees.

3. 100 single and 125 triple candles will be issued to the Brigade, which will be similar to those used during the period previous to the assault.

These candles will be distributed as follows:-

	Single.	Triple.
To each of 4 Regular Battns.	20	28.
5th Scottish Rifles.	20	13.
	================	
	100	125.
	================	

23/9/15.

Major,

Brigade Major, 19th Infantry Brigade.

Copy No. 1.

19th Infantry Brigade Operation Order No. 52.

Reference 1/10,000 Trench Map. 36 c N.W. Sheet 1
and tracing of Brigade Trenches.

24th September, 1915.

1. The 1st and 4th Corps of the 1st Army will assume the offensive, South of the LA BASSEE Canal, on 25th September with the object of securing the line LOOS - HULLUCH northwards to the LA BASSEE Canal.

The 2nd Division (with 19th Brigade on the right and ... Brigade on the left) will take part in this attack, advancing with its right in touch with 9th Division, and its left along the LA BASSEE Canal, to CANAL ALLEY (Railway line HAISNES So LA BASSEE Canal)

The assault will take place at 6.40 o'clock. The hour of zero (9.00 o'clock) will be notified later.

North of the LA BASSEE Canal the enemy is to be engaged vigourously in order to prevent him withdrawing troops for a counter-attack, and a subsidiary attack will be made by the 5th Infantry Brigade from GIVENCHY.

Wherever the enemy gives ground he must be followed up with the greatest energy and the utmost rapidity in order to take advantage of the first surprise and to prevent his reserves occupying his rearward defensive lines.

2. The Brigade will attack the following intermediate objectives, in a series of bounds :-

1st Objective.	2nd Objective.	3rd or main Objective.
LES BRIQUES FARM. and VERMELLES Railway line as far N. as road crossing A.22.b.1.2. (inclusive).	AUCHY - LEZ - LA BASSEE and TRIANGLE ALLEY from A.29.b.4.8. to A.23.a.6.2. (both inclusive)	Railway line from B.25.b.7.7. (inclusive) to A.24.b.4.2. (exclusive).

and will advance towards the main objective with 1st Middlesex Regiment leading on the right and 2nd A. & S. Highrs. on the left.
    The 2nd R.Welch Fusiliers will support the 1st Middlesex Regiment - The 1st Cameronians will support 2nd A. & S. Highrs.

    5th Scottish Rifles, with their grenadier platoon, will be in Brigade Reserve.

3. The outer flanks during the advance of the Right and left battalions will be :-

Right attack.   LES BRIQUES Farm - Road junction A.29.a.5.5.
(1st Middlesex -Cross Roads A.30.b.4.7. (marked 74 on
R. & 2nd R.   1/10,000 map) - Road and railway junction
Welch Fus).   B.25.b.7.7. (all inclusive).

Left attack.   CHATEAU ALLEY - cross roads A.22.b.1.2. -
(2nd A. & S. Hrs. Cross roads A.23.a.5.2. - Road junction
& 1st Bn. The
Cameronians).   A.23.b.8.1. - road junction A.24.d.1.9.

(2).

The dividing line during the advance between the right and left attack will be :-

(1) Point 85, where DOOK ALLEY crosses the railway.

(2) Point A.23.d.2.6., N.E. of AUCHY Church (DOOK ALLEY inclusive to right attack).

(3) Siding B.19.c. (inclusive to left attack).

The right battalion is responsible for keeping touch with the 28th Infantry Brigade (9th Division) on its right; the 6th Brigade is responsible for keeping touch with the left battalion.

4. The assualt will be carried out as follows :-

(a) 1st Middlesex Regiment, against Railway trench from A.27.b.9.5. to VERMELLES - LA BASSEE Road.

A special bombing party, with escort, both detailed by this battalion, will attack enemy's trenches opposite Point "D".

(b) 2nd A. & S. Highrs. against MINE TRENCH from A.21.d.6.4. to A.21.d.7.7.

Two special bombing parties with escorts, will be detailed by this battalion; one to co-operate with 1st Middlesex Regt. bombers from Point "D", and one to attack hostile trenches and craters opposite ETNA and VESUVIUS, between points A.21.d.7.7. and 7.9.

5. As soon as assualting battalions have vacated their trenches, 2nd R.Welch Fusiliers will occupy trenches vacated by 1st Middlesex Regt. and 1st Cameronians those vacated by 2nd A. & S. Highrs.

5th Scottish Rifles will move forward to assembly trenches CHURCHILL'S CUT and Sidings 4,5, and 6.

6. The ground gained will be made good by consolidating, at first, certain intermediate points, as follows:-

(a) <u>Right Battalion.</u>   RYAN'S KEEP.

    <u>Left Battalion.</u>   Oblong work A.21.d.9.6. - C.1.9.

(b) <u>Right battalion.</u>   LES BRIQUES FARM.

    <u>Left Battalion.</u>   Road crossing A.22.b.1.2.

(c) Posts in TRIANGLE ALLEY at suitable points (both battalions).

Points in (a) will be consolidated by Sapping Platoons of 1st Middlesex Regt. and 2nd A. & S. Highrs respectively.

7. Communication trenches, as soon as the first assault is successful, will be dug forward as follows:-

(a) To MINE POINT by Sapping Platoons, 2nd R.Welch Fus. & detachment of 1st East Anglian Field Company, R.E.

(c) From ETNA by Sapping platoons 1st Cameronians and detachment of 1st East Anglian Field Company, R.E.

(c) From Southern end of QUARRY Trench to point 51 by Sapping Platoon of 5th Scottish Rifles and detachment of 1st East Anglian Field Company R.E.

O.C. (a) will keep in touch with O.C. 1st Middlesex Regt.

Os. C. (b) and (c) will keep in touch with O.C. 2nd A.& S.Hrs.

As soon as a communication trench is marked out and started, the R.E. detachment of the 1st East Anglian Co. R.E. will move forward and assist the remaining two sapping platoons in consolidating RYAN'S KEEP and the Oblong work in A,21.d.9.6. - d.1.8.

8. The four machine guns of 1st Middlesex Regiment and 2nd A. & S. Highrs. will accompany their respective units in the assualt.

The 2nd R.Welch Fusiliers and 1st Cameronians will each take forward with them 2 machine guns.

Their remaining machine guns and those of 5th Scottish Rifles will be in position in the trenches to cover the assualt and afterwards form a Brigade Reserve under the Brigade Machine Gun Officer.

9. The Brigade 95 mm trench mortar battery of 8 mortars, will be attached, half to 2nd R.Welch Fusiliers and half to 1st Cameronians and will move forward with the Headquarters of those battalions respectively.

10. The section No. 6 Trench Mortar Battery (1½ inch mortars) will take up positions so as to fire on hostile trenches at MINE POINT and those opposite ETNA and VESUVIUS. When the assualt is launched, the section will be in Brigade reserve.

O.C.Section will get into communication with Brigade Headquarters, through the trench headquarters of the left battalion (near junction of HIGH STREET and Boyau 18).

11. A party of 173rd Tunnelling Company, R.E. will be attached to the Brigade for special duties.

It will be divided into 3 detachments, as follows:-

No. 1. at West end of Boyau 15.
Nos.2.& 3 In HIGH STREET between Boyau 21 and GUN STREET.

These detachments will move forward as soon as the hostile front line has been made good.

12. Artillery Barrages are shewn in Appendix "A" attached.

13. Attention is drawn to 19th Infantry Brigade Secret instructions of 22nd September,1915,

14. Depots of S.A.A., grenades, R.E.material, rations, and water have been established in two areas.

(1) In area of ARTHUR'S KEEP.

(2) In area of RUSSELL'S KEEP.

15. The Brigade transport will be parked as follows :- S.A.A CARTS, cookers, water and tool carts at F.10.c.; East of BEUVRY Canal, remainder of transport at LE PREOL, West of canal. Branch

16. For communication through the trenches BURBURE ALLEY will be "DOWN STRETCHERS"; WILSONS WAY & MAISON ROUGE will be "UP".

(4).

17. Advanced Brigade Headquarters will be in Dugouts near MAISON ROUGE (A.20.d.3.2.)

H. E. Browne

Major,

Brigade Major, 19th Infantry Brigade.

Issued at 11 am.

Copy No. 1 & 2 Office.
"   3   Brigade Machine Gun Officer.
"   4   2nd R.Welch Fusiliers.
"   5   1st Cameronians.
"   6.   1st Middlesex Regt.
"   7.   2nd A. & S. Highrs.
"   8   5th Scottish Rifles.
"   9.   Section No. 6 Trench Mortar Battery.
"   10.   Brigade 95 mm "   "   "
"   11.   East Anglian Fd. Coy. R.E.
"   12.   173rd Tunnelling Coy. R.E.
"   13.   O.C. Brigade Sapping Platoons.
"   14.   Z.2. Group, R.F.A.
"   15.   Brigade Transport Officer.
"   16.   H.Q. 2nd Division.
"   17.   6th Infantry Brigade.
"   18.   28th Infantry Brigade.
"   19.)
"   20.)   Spare.

APPENDIX "A" to 19th Inf. Bde. Operation Order
No. 52 of 23/9/15.

ARTILLERY BARRAGES.

(A) SHRAPNEL (18 pr. guns).

(1) 5 minutes before
    0.00 hours to
    0.10 (15 minutes)
                  From A.27.b.9.3. to the canal.

(2) 0.10 - 0.30
    (20 minutes).
                  The barrage moves East to a line
along W. face of AUCHY and then
moves West again till at 0.30 it
is on the German front line as in
(1).

(3) 0.40 - 0.50
    (10 minutes).
                  The assualt.
Barrage lifts to:- from junction
of TRAIN ALLEY and LES BRIQUES
trench along the railway through
A.22 central, to the canal at
A.16.d. 3.7.

(4) 0.50 - 1.0
    (10 minutes)
                  Barrage lifts to the following line.
From road at A.23.c.2.0. - along
West face of AUCHY - Cross Roads
at A.22.b.9.10. - to the canal
A.16.d.10.8.

5. 1.0 - 1.20.
    (20 minutes)
                  Barrage lifts again to :-
From A.23.c.10.0. - along East
face of AUCHY - houses at A.23.a.7.5.
- to canal at A.17.c.9.7.

(B) HOWITZERS AND HEAVY GUNS BARRAGE.
9.2", or 8", 6" Howitzers, 4.5" howitzer; 6" and 4.7" guns.

1. 0.0. - 0.10.
    (10 minutes)
                  HAISNES Trench, AUCHY & HAISNES,
PEKIN Trench.

No. 5 Group H.A.R. (15" & 9.2" Howitzers).

2. 0.10 - 0.50.
    (40 minutes)
                  AUCHY.

    0.10 - 1.15.
    (65 minutes)
                  HAISNES Trench. PEKIN Trench.

4.5" Howitzers.

3. 0.50 - 1.30
    (40 minutes)
                  Trench along and N.W. of railway
from A. 24.a.10.4. to A.24.a.

N O T E S.

1. All Vermorel Sprayers with battalions, together with any brought up by the Special Company, will be distributed in front trenches amongst the emplacements.

These sprayers, with spare petrol tins must be taken forward with the attack in order to clear hostile trenches, where required for consolidation and occupation by us.

2. During the attack all ranks will wear their smoke helmets with vizor up. Caps will be carried. After the belt of ground affected by the cylinders has been passed, helmets can be removed, but must be carefully preserved and carried, and not thrown away.

3. It is possible that exits underneath the parapet may cause a back draught, which may bring the gas back into our trenches. All such exits will be blocked with sandbags while the gas is being used.

The sandbags are only to prevent back draught and ought to be easily removeable if required.

23/9/15.

H. E. Browne
Major,
Brigade Major, 19th Infantry Brigade.

SECRET.   O.108.

MEMORANDUM.

(Not to be taken forward in the assault)

1. Previous to the assault a GAS attack will take place from 0.00 hours to 0.40 hours.

The assault will be launched at 0.40. hours.

2. There are 39 Gas emplacements along the Brigade front, with 12 cylinders, 8 smoke candles, and 2 Triple candles in each.
The cylinders will be worked by the Special Company R.E., who will be distinguished by Green, White and Blue brassards.
The candles will be worked by men detailed by the two battalions in the front line.
These men will also assist the Special Company R.E. and will be at the disposal of the battalion to which they belong as soon as their candle work is finished; i.e. at 0.40 hours.

3. The candle men will be found as follows:-

Unit.	Emplacements.	Candlemen.
1st Middlesex R.	22.	44.
2nd A. & S. Highrs.	17.	34.

Four of the 1st Middlesex Regtiment's emplacements are N. of the VERMELLES – LA BASSEE Road and lettered "A" to "D", the remainder S. of the road.

23/9/15.

Major,

Brigade Major, 19th Infantry Brigade.

19th Infantry Brigade.

O.109.

U R G E N T.

Orders for the assembly of the Brigade
for Operation Order No. 52.

INFANTRY.
1. (a) The leading platoon of 2nd R.Welch Fusiliers will pass Brigade Headquarters (A.19.d.6.2. at 12 midnight to take up their position in BOOTS Trench and Sidings .1,2,&3.

    ROUTE - CAMBRIN Church - MAISON ROUGE ALLEY.

(b) The leading platoon of 1st Cameronians will pass Brigade Headquarters at 1 am to take up their position in CHURCHILLS ALLEY and Sidings 4,5, & 6.

    ROUTE - CAMBRIN Supporting Point and WILSONS WAY.

(c) The leading platoon of the 5th Scottish Rifles will pass Brigade Headquarters at 2 am to take up their position in MAISON ROUGE ABBEY trenches.

    ROUTES.- CAMBRIN CHURCH and MAISON ROUGE ALLEY (Headquarters and 3 Companies).

    CAMBRIN Supporting Point and entrance of WILSONS WAY (1 Company)

SAPPING PLATOONS
and R.E.
2.(a) The Sapping Platoons of 1st Middlesex Regt. and 2nd A. & S. Highrs. will report at their battalion Headquarters at 6 pm.

    ROUTES - 1st Middlesex Regt.   MAISON ROUGE ALLEY.

    2nd A. & S. Highrs.   WILSONS WAY.

(b) The sapping platoon of 2nd R.Welch Fusiliers with detachment of 1st East Anglian Field Company R.E. will be in position in KINGSWAY (S. of WILSONS WAY) by 12 midnight.

    ROUTE - WILSONS WAY.

(c) The sapping platoon of 1st Cameronians and 5th Scottish Rifles each with detachment of 1st East Anglian Field Coy. R.E. will be in position in TOWER Reserve trench (Between BACK STREET AND BRAINES ALLEY) by midnight.

    ROUTE - WILSONS WAY.

DETACHMENT
of 1st East
Anglian Coy.
R.E.
3. The detachments of 1st East Anglian Field Coy. R.E. will join the Brigade Sapping Platoons at CAMBRIN Church at 8 pm.
    O.C. East Anglian Coy. R.E. will arrange at that hour that his three detachments join up with their three sapping platoons respectively.

The senior Officer of each combined detachment (Sapping platoons and R.E.) will be in command of the detachment.

4. The detachment of 173rd Tunnelling Company, will be at Brigade Headquarters at 7 pm and move forward from there to their positions in the trenches.

    ROUTE - CAMBRIN Supporting Point - WILSONS WAY.

5. The 95 mm Trench Mortar Battery will remain in its present position in the trenches.

Os.C. each half section will report to the O.C. Unit they are attached to.

6. Officers Commanding all units directly they are in position will report to Advanced Brigade Headquarters at MAISON ROUGE Dugout (200 yards S. of exit of BURBURE ALLEY).

24/9/15.

H. E. Barrie

Major,
Brigade Major, 19th Inf.Brigade.

MESSAGES.

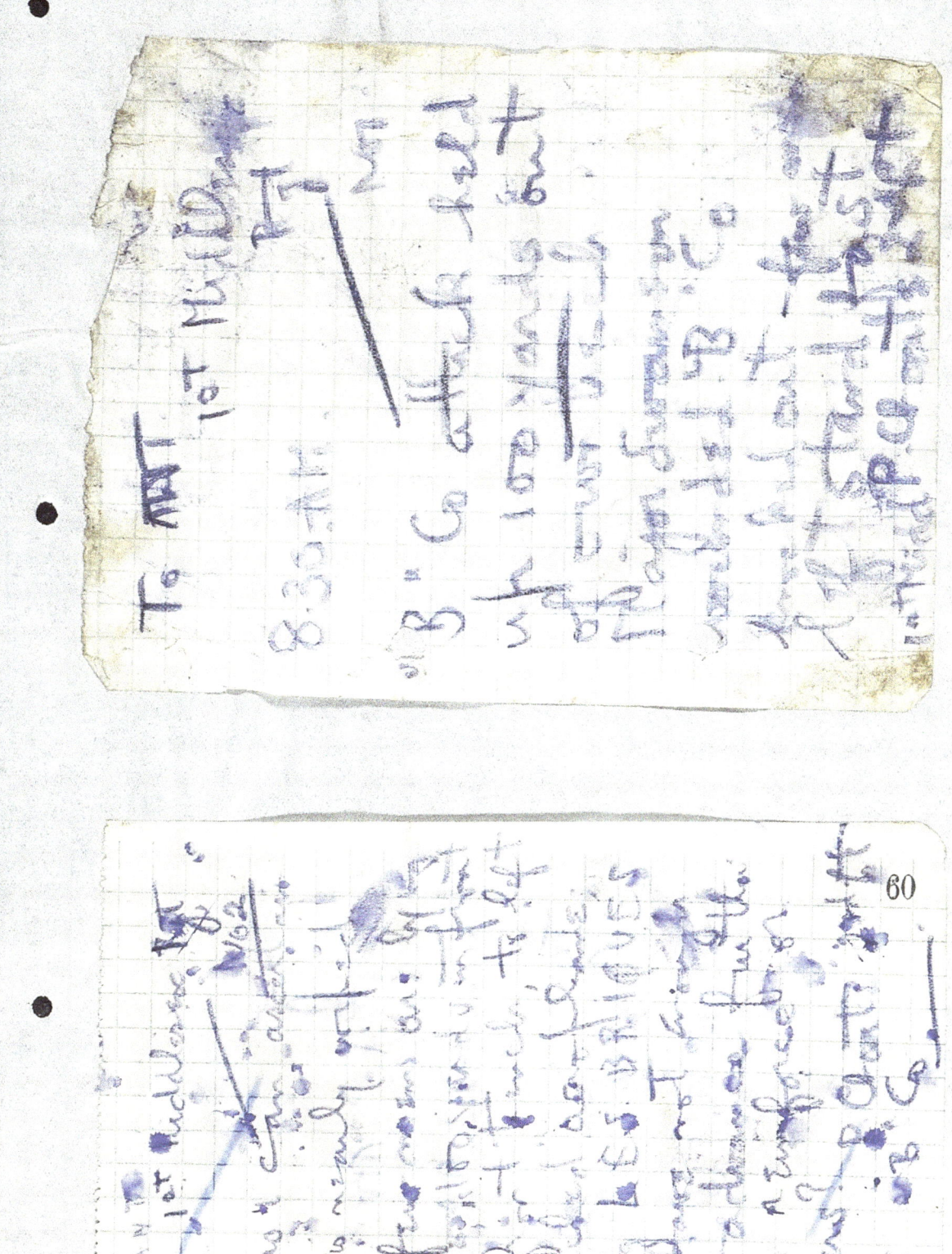

"C" Form (Duplicate)
MESSAGES AND SIGNALS.

To: O.C. Midd. Regt
Sender's Number: M 283
Day of Month: 25

Any news how far have 4th advanced aaa So far returning you are keep me well informed so that artillery barrage may be altered to suit if you want it

FROM: 19 Inf Bde
PLACE & TIME: 6.37 a.m.

MESSAGES AND SIGNALS

To: Middlesex Regt
Sender's Number: BM 488
Day of Month: 25

2nd Division state that reports received state their troops on either side of 19 Inf Bde are progressing as fast as you can

m JB

FROM: 19 J B
PLACE & TIME: 7.15 a.m.

8

To O.C. 4th [?]
C Coy 4th [?]

Enemy in strong force
not in C of R but CC who T
but about 30 or 35 yards
to a mine on account of fire

3½" [?] Haron 75th B⁺ alone
remainder of B Platoon.

Can we have reinforcements
We are on Spring 21 B⁺ Clark
Signed about 60 & Sunley
Just 79.

A Whaley 4th
O.C. Coy
4th
Casualties about 130.

"C" Form (Duplicate)
MESSAGES AND SIGNALS.

Army Form C. 2123.

Service Instructions.	No. of Message.	Office Stamp.
	Charges to Pay. £ s. d.	

Handed in at .... Office .... m. Received .... m.

TO: Middx Regt

Sender's Number	Day of Month	In reply to Number	AAA
No 80	25th		

artillery will fire on
Gateway and LES BR d QUES
trench

FROM: B 19th
PLACE & TIME: 7-50

"A" Form — Messages and Signals (Army Form C. 2121)

Capt 1st Coy

Casualties very heavy
Cannot get communication
with Coy right
Enemy Bge [?] in the craters
A/Col [?] edge firing strong
in front

J. Hill
Lt 1st Coy

"C" Form (Duplicate) — Messages and Signals (Army Form C. 9123)

1st
"D" Coy are in the craters.
Bombers & Sappers of
2nd our own Artillery are
shelling them.

Lt
1st D Coy

"A" Form — Messages and Signals (Army Form C. 2121)

Message 1

TO: O.C. 1/Middx
Day of Month: 25th

Completely held up and heavy casualties

[signature] 33c.

Message 2

TO: Lt CARLESS
Day of Month: 25 Sep
Sender's Number: A.4.14
Time: 8.30 am

Push on. Watson it must go on. They add cook to take over.

The OC intend D company AAA They try must

We had the water improved by Lt Carless

[signed] M/Gurnee

"A" Form — Messages and Signals (Army Form C. 2121)

TO: Middlesex Regt

Sender's Number: B.M. 43 **Day of Month:** 25th

AAA

A fresh bombardment of whole hostile front line opposite to Brigade is being organised this division since will be notified later, and Bns in front will replace Bns in front of latter to reorganise. Welsh Fus will move up to our front trenches on the night. Both Camerons and Welsh Fus will be prepared to assist at the first moment. 51 Cumberland Regt will move two companies up MAISONS WAY

"A" Form — Messages and Signals (Army Form C. 2121)

AAA

To replace Camerons when they advance and two Companies up MAISON ROUGE alley to replace Welsh fusiliers. Ammunition is being sent up to dumps. O.C.s will wire time they estimate new dispositions ordered will take to complete.

19th B.Ge

Time: 8/1/32

"A" Form.
Army Form C. 2121.

MESSAGES AND SIGNALS.

TO { Middlesex Regt

Sender's Number: M 467 Day of Month: 25th In reply to Number: AAA

Where are your machine guns. Can you give one or two of your Lewis [guns]. What are your present dispositions. Address such shall be repeated. G and S His.

From: O. C. 1/8 M'x
Place: S. A. 37
Time:

"A" Form.
Army Form C. 2121.

MESSAGES AND SIGNALS.

TO { Middlesex Regt

Sender's Number: M 508 Day of Month: 25th In reply to Number: AAA

You will not [accept?] with the Welsh Fusiliers but reorganise your Battalion under cover of [bombardment?]

From: O. C. M'x
Place: S. 30.7
Time:

Message 1 (Army Form C. 2121)

TO: Middlesex & Welsh Fusiliers AAA

Sender's Number: BM 57   **Day of Month:** 25th

28th Inf Bde on my right have pushed back the Brigade & are endeavouring to press on & consolidate the line and be prepared for hostile counter attack aaa Dispositions are Glamorgans in support on st to VERMELLES Rd N and OB in support on Churchills Cut and no 4 siding RWF R1 inclusive on SW 5 on STONE & in support in old BOOTS TRENCH Shelling on Middle Keep with Lee in Reserve in Vielines 3 and Cantlee Essex stopping any debouch westwards are

From
Place
Time

Message 2 (Army Form C. 2121)

TO: Middlesex & Welsh Fusiliers AAA

Sender's Number: BM 66   **Day of Month:** 25

Received his message before seen Reference run to 662 on "troops on the South are pressing Very hard they are no further attack will be made by 6th and 19 Bdes at present aaa Situation known South of Cambrin temporarily good Enemy attacking with reinforced Brigade Battn. Am organising attacks and will be ready now attack him nothing will interfere with so intense but later will so advance

From
Place
Time

"A" Form. — Army Form C. 2121. — MESSAGES AND SIGNALS.

TO: 25th Bde (3)

AAA

In case the will attack the line all Coys will be held at will be attached to M.G. Sect. R.E. and one to ammunition and one be carrying the line now occupied. Acknowledge. Released 5th Bn East Anglian Coy R.E.
and 2nd D.L.I.

"A" Form. — Army Form C. 2121. — MESSAGES AND SIGNALS.

TO: All (2)

AAA

Orders issued for Machine Guns and O.C. will be informed. Webb has control. Hold them line sufficiently they can do the advance by one Coy of E.S.R. can help. You will have to hold touch with 25th Bde and ascertain who support are now from 6th Bn can. Chanel attention on Knowles. Use now is of Regt left Ree Co. Keep all the Kings keep will be ginned and Welsh loss could report his position. There will be H.Q.B.

(Z) — Censor.

MESSAGES AND SIGNALS. "A" Form. Army Form C. 2121.

TO: O.C. M. Gun Section 1/5

Sender's Number: A.4.96 Day of Month: 25 Sept In reply to Number: AAA

Our present position will be
taken over by the 2/R.W.F.
AAA You will be under
orders of O.C. 2 R.W.F.
when this is carried out
Number of guns, material AAA
possible to relieve guns and
your personnel to be hostile
before the attack AAA Sgt HEAFEY
will take with him every
endeavour to withdraw the machine
gun now in gun pit AAA
front of your sgt has just
you will withdraw accoutrements
leave his trenches to 2/R.W.F.

From: M Browne Capt
Place: Adjt 1/North'd Regt
Time: 1.15 P.M.

MESSAGES AND SIGNALS.

TO: O.C. No. 13 Platoon D Coy
Grenade Reserve Platoon

Sender's Number: A.4.97 Day of Month: 25 Sept

On relief by 1st Cameronians
of R.W.F. MG you
will relieve via BARBARA
to No 3 siding ALLEY
then await orders AAA and
on No accident you
leave with the to
take MG 1st Cameronians have
MG

W Murray Lgt
Royal Welsh

From: M Browne Capt
Place: Adjt 1/North'd Regt
Time: 1.15 pm
M Browne Capt

MESSAGES AND SIGNALS.

TO — 14 Inf Bde

Sender's Number: A W 4   **Day of Month:** 25 Sept   **In reply to Number:** —   AAA

Much opposition to
Please push on as
to BRIDGES Push
on

From: 0E
Place: 2.40 pm
Time: pm

MESSAGES AND SIGNALS.

TO — 17 IB / OE R.W.F

Sender's Number: Ar.KB 6   **Day of Month:** 25 Sept   **In reply to Number:** —   AAA

Reserve Company then
in on
heavily fired at very

From: OE
Place: 7 pm Tuesday
Time: pm

MESSAGES AND SIGNALS. No. of Message........

Prefix .... Code .... m	Words	Charge	This message is on a/c of :	Recd. at .... m.
Office of Origin and Service Instructions.	Sent		.... Service.	Date
	At .... m.			From
	To			By
	By		(Signature of "Franking Officer.")	

TO 19 Inf Bde

Sender's Number.	Day of Month.	In reply to Number	AAA
* A.466	25 Sept		

[illegible] held up Very heavy [illegible] AAA [illegible]

From	[illegible]	[illegible]
Place		
Time	7.15	Am

The above may be forwarded as now corrected. (Z)

Censor. Signature of Addressor or person authorised to telegraph in his name.

MESSAGES AND SIGNALS. No. of Message........

Prefix .... Code .... m	Words	Charge	This message is on a/c of :	Recd. at .... m.
Office of Origin and Service Instructions.	Sent		.... Service.	Date
	At .... m.			From
	To			By
	By		(Signature of "Franking Officer.")	

TO 19 Inf Bde

Sender's Number.	Day of Month.	In reply to Number	AAA
* A.467	25 Sept		

[illegible] to shell German [illegible] AAA [illegible]

From	OC	[illegible]
Place		
Time	7.2[illegible]	Am

The above may be forwarded as now corrected. (Z)

Censor. Signature of Addressor or person authorised to telegraph in his name.

(illegible handwritten telegraph forms)

MESSAGES AND SIGNALS.

No. of Message ....

Prefix	Code	......m.	Words	Charge		Office of Origin and Service Instructions.			This message is on a/c of:	Recd. at ....m.

Sent
At ....m.
To ....
By ....

Date ....
From ....
Service ....
By ....

(Signature of "Franking Officer.")

TO { OC ARGYLLS AAA

Sender's Number.	Day of Month.	In reply to Number																				
A1/73	23rd																					

*

From ....
Place S.30
Time ....

(Z) | Signature of Addressor or person authorised to telegraph in his name.

The above may be forwarded as now corrected. Censor.

MESSAGES AND SIGNALS.

No. of Message ....

Sent
At ....m.
To ....
By ....

(Signature of "Franking Officer.")

TO { JF HILL Comdg C AAA

Sender's Number.	Day of Month.	In reply to Number																				
A.172	26 Sept																					

*

From ....
Place ....
Time ....

(Z) | Signature of Addressor or person authorised to telegraph in his name.

The above may be forwarded as now corrected. Censor.

MESSAGES AND SIGNALS.

No. of Message..........

Prefix ....Code..........m. | Words | Charge

Office of Origin and Service Instructions.

Sent At ....m. To .... By ....

This message is on a/c of: ....Service.

(Signature of "Franking Officer.")

Recd. at ....m. Date .... From .... By ....

TO	19	Inf	Bde

Sender's Number.	Day of Month.	In reply to Number	AAA
* A. 478	21 Sept		

The	German	[illegible]	nothing	then
[illegible]	[illegible]	[illegible]	H.E.	AAA
[illegible]	Battalion	[illegible]	Suff	[illegible]
[illegible]	Casualties	[illegible]	[illegible]	have
No	own	[illegible]	go	[illegible]
AAA	Shelling	of	front	German
Reinfts	[illegible]	absolutely	Necessary	AAA
and	then	R.W.F	may	be
able	to	get	on	

From .... [illegible] Fusiliers

Place ....

Time ....

The above may be forwarded as now corrected. (Z)

Censor. Signature of Addressor or person authorised to telegraph in his name.

MESSAGES AND SIGNALS.

No. of Message..........

Prefix ....Code..........m. | Words | Charge

Office of Origin and Service Instructions.

Sent At ....m. To .... By ....

This message is on a/c of: ....Service.

(Signature of "Franking Officer.")

Recd. at ....m. Date .... From .... By ....

TO	19	Inf	Bde

Sender's Number.	Day of Month.	In reply to Number	AAA
* A 479	21 Sept	B M 493	

[illegible]	[illegible]			

From .... [illegible]

Place ....

Time .... [illegible]

The above may be forwarded as now corrected. (Z)

Censor. Signature of Addressor or person authorised to telegraph in his name.

MESSAGES AND SIGNALS.

No. of Message..........

Prefix .... Code .... m. | Words | Charge

Office of Origin and Service Instructions.

Sent — At .... m. To .... By ....

This message is on a/c of : .... *Service.*

(Signature of "Franking Officer.")

Recd. at .... m. Date .... From .... By ....

TO — 19th Inf Bde

Sender's Number.	Day of Month.	In reply to Number	AAA
A [illegible]	[illegible]	B.M 497	

[illegible]	[illegible]	[illegible]	[illegible]	to
[illegible]	of	[illegible]	D	AAA
[illegible]	[illegible]	estimate	casualties	AAA
[illegible]	[illegible]	[illegible]	can	passed
back	[illegible]	and	past	and
[illegible]	[illegible]	believed	from	observation
[illegible]	all	those	in	front
mostly	are	wounded	or	killed
[illegible]	officers	including	3	Captain
[illegible]	known	to	be	casualties
AAA	Present	disposition	A. B	and C. D
Companies	lying	out	100 yds	from
our	front	line	And	bombers
with	1 platoon	of	D	and
sapping	platoon	are	in	a
Near	large	crater	at	D.
Frontage of companies from T.1. to T.3				

From — OC [illegible]

Place

Time — 9.20 [illegible]

The above may be forwarded as now corrected. (Z) [illegible signature]

Censor. Signature of Addressor or person authorised to telegraph in his name.

MESSAGES AND SIGNALS.

No. of Message..........

Prefix .... Code .... m. | Words | Charge

Office of Origin and Service Instructions.

Sent — At .... m. To .... By ....

This message is on a/c of : .... *Service.*

(Signature of "Franking Officer.")

Recd. at .... m. Date .... From .... By ....

TO — 19 Inf Bde

Sender's Number.	Day of Month.	In reply to Number	AAA
A 490	25 Sept		

Ammunition	is	[illegible]	[illegible]	[illegible]
[illegible]	unloaded	[illegible]	[illegible]	[illegible]
[illegible]	[illegible]	Bombs	[illegible]	close
[illegible]	R.E	[illegible]		

From — OC [illegible]

Place

Time — 9.10 AM

The above may be forwarded as now corrected. (Z) [illegible signature]

Censor. Signature of Addressor or person authorised to telegraph in his name.

MESSAGES AND SIGNALS. No. of Message..........

Prefix ...... Code ...... m. Office of Origin and Service Instructions.	Words	Charge	This message is on a/c of: ...... Service. (Signature of "Franking Officer.")	Recd. at ...... m. Date ...... From ...... By ......
	Sent At ...... m. To ...... By			

TO 17 Inf Bd

Sender's Number.	Day of Month.	In reply to Number	AAA
* A 441	[illegible]		

[illegible]	[illegible]	guns	[illegible]	[illegible]
[illegible]	[illegible]	[illegible]	D AAA	[illegible]
[illegible]	[illegible]	By	[illegible]	

From [illegible] [illegible]
Place
Time [illegible]

The above may be forwarded as now corrected. (Z) [illegible]

Censor. Signature of Addressor or person authorised to telegraph in his name.

MESSAGES AND SIGNALS. No. of Message..........

Prefix ...... Code ...... m. Office of Origin and Service Instructions.	Words	Charge	This message is on a/c of: ...... Service. (Signature of "Franking Officer.")	Recd. at ...... m. Date ...... From ...... By ......
	Sent At ...... m. To ...... By			

TO 19th Inf Bde

Sender's Number.	Day of Month.	In reply to Number	AAA
* A 492	25 Sept		

Bombardment	should	[illegible]	made	effectually
	[illegible]	[illegible]	opposite	[illegible]
[illegible]	[illegible]	[illegible]	[illegible]	AAA
[illegible]	[illegible]	[illegible]	[illegible]	done
Sufficiently				

From [illegible] [illegible]
Place
Time 9 [illegible] am

The above may be forwarded as now corrected. (Z) [illegible]

Censor. Signature of Addressor or person authorised to telegraph in his name.

MESSAGES AND SIGNALS.

TO: O.C. 2/R.W.F.

Sender's Number: A.498 Day of Month: 25 Sept. AAA

The Os remains at present in front of
our present trench line AAA
Such as can get out during
will you please arrange
No 3 siding owl clark all available to
ATTA after we BEFORE
Semi up to assist will
Person to own Good stretcher
[unmounted] ber it will being
[indecipherable] is then to [indecipherable] from
on top daylight own

From: O.C.
Place: Brigade
Time: 1.20 pm

(Z) Signature: [illegible]

MESSAGES AND SIGNALS.

TO: I.G. —

Sender's Number: A.1418 In reply to Number: A.G.3. AAA

Major 3 Captains 2 subalterns AAA
other ranks
[M.B. Smith] Sgt [wnot] has
how Captain Coe NCOs
Reg [illegible] which Case Officer in
to front [illegible] own stretcher
been wounded bearers very
                                      few

From:
Place:
Time:

(Z)

MESSAGES AND SIGNALS.

TO: OC 2/R.W.F.

Sender's Number: A.501. Day of Month: 25 Sept.

We are on the move now AAA No 3 Platoon moving from BOYAU and went up in extra wounded AAA assistance to will send in addition share the men in Stretcher bearer to

From: OC
Place:
Time: 2.45 p.m.
(Z) MO Capt

MESSAGES AND SIGNALS.

TO: OC ?/ (Signature: 2/L Cunningham RWF)

Sender's Number: A.500. Day of Month: 24 Sept.

Have you platoon AAA Please send our Platoon relieving sending of 13 Platoon and to Sidings No 2 ENCLOSURE ALLEY

From: OC
Place:
Time: 2.25 p.m.
(Z) M.Douglas Lt

MESSAGES AND SIGNALS.

TO: Medical Officer Seine
Grenade NCO RMA Bgd
Sgt Tonkel W.T.M

Sender's Number: A.517 **Day of Month:** 27 Sept

Request AAA prepared to move at 4.30pm AAA if possible before Returns if that time every man to have all be his ready so that 121 can turn out Companies one etc out

M Mouwdey
A/A 1 Munster RHA
(Z)

MESSAGES AND SIGNALS.

TO:

Enemy front very
opened fire quiet
Arty shelling on us
with some shelling
AA very weaker so
strong trenches
very so
wild

(Z)

"A" Form. — Army Form C. 2121.

MESSAGES AND SIGNALS.

TO Camerons Scots
Westminsters
& AFK Highlanders

Sender's Number: RM 567 **Day of Month:** 27

Saw Helena Alps were dispersed
am Galipoli at once aaa
Want Westminster completed as At S Nebs
Highlanders and 5th Scottish Rifles on
to Tower Reserve Trench between BRAINE
ALLEY and BACK Sheet
Trench aaa Remainder with
then until 3.22 D Section
East Gun R.E. will
(C) Boyou 14 and 15 your
be Sure aaa Helena
to be as below
aaa 5th Scout Rifles & ATS Highlanders
to O.C. Commonwealth Trench from
ETNA aaa Earl Dugdon Coy R.E.
from Point D aaa Coleraine

From: 79 **Place:** A.10 P.M.
Time: A.10 P.M.

(Z) W.B.R. Opper

MESSAGES AND SIGNALS.

TO Camerons
Westminsters
AK Highlanders

Sender's Number: BM 570 **Day of Month:** 27

S attack BUA Start
P.M at al operation
up be Shirts off
" 2.25 P.M aaa at S 301
commencement to information SM
to BAA a afternoon aaa
counter to bosh Finish are
kill and push forward British
at strong to attack forward
offensive IVA be
O 2.9 RYANS KEEP A 27 L
through A 21 d 96 FRANKS Trench wo
48. road Image at A.h.C

Priority

From: 19
Place:
Time:

(Z) W.B.R. Opper

"A" Form.

MESSAGES AND SIGNALS.

Prefix	Code	Words	Charge		This message is on a/c of	No. of Message

Office of Origin and Service Instructions.

Recd. at .... m.
Date ....
Sent { At .... m. To .... By ....
Service ....
From ....
By ....

(Signature of "Franking Officer.")

To Col Rowley
    1/Mdx

Sender's Number.	Day of Month	In reply to Number	AAA
BM 570	Sept 22		

Will you please come to Bde
HQ yourself as is to be with
Brigadier to discuss things and make orders
for tomorrow

From Bk 151
Place
Time 5.9 PM

(Z) [signature]

The above may be forwarded as now corrected. Censor.

Signature of Addressor or person authorised to telegraph in his name.

Daily Tactical progress report.

for period in the LAVENTIE sector
of the VIII Divisional line from
1st August 1915 – 15th August 1915

Daily report up to 12 noon, 1st August.

19th Infantry Brigade.

Operations. 1. Enemy quiet and very inactive. He seemed very nervous on our right last night, opening bursts of rapid fire repeatedly: probably disturbed by Black Watch patrol, who were reported to have brought in hat and coat.
This morning, enemy put 17 shells in rear of I.R. and on LE TROU and RUE TILLELOY, N.8.a. He also shelled No. 13 communication trench again. FOLLY post got usual shelling three different times yesterday and today. Battery in direction of 370. Several trench mortar bombs fired at shelter trench line in rear of F.2.

Work. 2. Parapet and parados thickened - dugouts filled in- new traverses put up - fire steps made - two tunnels under parapet dug - wire put out and strengthened - end of Salient and trench X in rear connected by new trench.
520 men working on shelter trench line and communication trenches.
Work much handicapped by lack of material.

Intelligence. 3. Transport.
Heavy transport heard between 9 and 9-30 pm. near 300, moving towards AUBERS. Trolley heard between 368 - 370. Timber heard being thrown out of it. Transport heard between 282 - 307 and on road 282 - 315 - 313.
Working parties.
Some grass cutting parties seen. All work ceased at midnight.
Lights.
At 245, a stationary light seen: it showed for a minute at intervals of 5 minutes. 2 red lights seen at intervals, but nothing happened.
Uniform.
A man seen opposite the right wearing light blue forage cap, light blue band and silver badge in front of cap.
Patrols.
On left met nothing except seeing a few working parties. Patrols on right (of 5th Scottish Rifles) found working parties on wire and listening posts at 316, 319, and 324.
Latter post connected by telephone to trench for patrol was seen by post and fire immediately opened from parapet in rear.
General.
His sniping is improving. Two periscopes hit, and broken by him.

1st August, 1915.

Lieut-Colonel,
Commanding 19th Infantry Brigade.

Daily report up to 12 noon, 2nd August.

19th Infantry Brigade.

Operations. 1. Enemy quiet and fairly inactive. He seemed very quiet on the left up to midnight, when his sniping was fairly frequent until dawn, his working parties having probably finished work at midnight.
Enemy appeared to be very nervous on our right. On our patrols going out, he opened heavy fire and sent star shells up, a dozen at a time.
This morning, at 10 am, the enemy shelled V.C. corner. He put one shell into No. IX's Fort, which exploded some grenades and spoilt some S.A.A.
There was no shelling either on the right or centre.
Enemy sent four trench mortar bombs over 41st Dogras (Bareilly Brigade), on our immediate right, during the night. Opposite our right the enemy were driving in both wooden and metal stakes, for his wire between 319 and 324, up to 2 am.

Work. 2. Parapet and parados thickened, revetted and built up. Dugouts on right filled in and new ones erected.
Traverses put in and old ones repaired. Firing steps made.
Fire trenches deepened in the centre. Wire put out and strengthened the whole way along the line. Communication trenches improved.
Work handicapped by lack of material. 400 men working.

Intelligence. 3. Transport.
Heavy transport heard at 10-30 pm moving along road 306-307-282 from right to left, and again at 11-45 pm returning along same road light.
Our right patrols heard wagons on light railway just behind the enemy's line.
Movement of light and heavy transport heard moving towards AUBERS from 9-30 pm to 10 pm. Again from 8-55 pm to 11-20 pm continuous movement in N.E. direction along RUE DELEVAL.

Working parties.
Our left patrols report enemy working parties very active and working especially behind his 1st line trenches.
Enemy grass cutting parties seen and dispersed by our Machine Gun fire.
All work ceased at midnight.

Lights.
A green flare and a red flare were seen opposite 1.R. at 9-15 pm. last night.
Three red lights were seen opposite the right front of F.2. and were followed by artillery fire at 12-20 am.

Uniform.
5 Germans were seen opposite Q.1. with round khaki caps on. They were fired on.

Patrols.
On left met nothing except seeing a few working parties. They all report enemy very busy noisy and talkative. Trenches appeared to be fully manned. Our centre patrols met no enemy. Patrol on right met nothing, except seeing enemy working parties.

Aeroplanes and balloons.
Usual balloon up from 9-45 am to 10-10 am, and 10-20 am to 11-30 am. Three hostile aeroplanes were observed over our lines during the last 24 hours.

General.
At dusk last night and at dawn this morning the enemy on our right commenced controlled sniping. We replied, and this caused the enemy, in less than five minutes, in each case, to cease firing.

2nd August, 1915.

Lieut-Colonel,

Commanding 19th Infantry Brigade..

Daily report up to 12 noon, 3rd August, 1915.

20th Infantry Brigade.

Operations.
1. Enemy abnormally quiet and very inactive.
The enemy's sniping seems to have diminished in volume, and he hardly sniped at all between 11 pm last night, and dawn, when he carried out the same intermittent sniping as usual. His sniping seems to have slackened off considerably. Enemy has not shelled our line to any extent for the last 24 hours. An enemy trench mortar opened fire on one of Machine Gun emplacements in F.3, whereupon our trench mortars promptly replied, the second round being most effective in not only stopping the enemy's trench mortar, but the moving of his trolley, which appears to be very busy each night. For retaliation purposes more trench mortar bombs are urgently required. 35 pr bombs are of no use as range is too far – only 7 rounds of 18 pr. at present available.

Work.
2. Parapet and parados remade and thickened, strongly revetted and on our right, built up. Dug outs on the right and left were filled in. Traverses put in and old ones repaired along the whole line. Strengthening of wire was carried out along the whole front. Communication trenches were improved behind the centre and right battalion. Fire trenches improved on the left and centre. Battalions now holding the front all complain of the lack of material, which handicaps work on the front line of trenches considerably. 400 men were employed in working under direction of R.E. and Bde. H.Q.

Intelligence.
3. Transport.
Right battalion report heavy transport moving from our right to left along the road 282 – 306 – 307 – from 9-45 pm to 10 pm. Left and centre battalions confirm the above statement about the movement of transport.
An Officer's patrol from our right battalion heard the sound of planks being thrown on to the ground, behind the enemy's trenches, as of a cart were being unloaded.

Working parties.

The enemy did little work in front of his line last night, except opposite O.1., where he was using a grass cutting machine.
Our left battalion reported, about 5 pm. yesterday afternoon the enemy were seen carrying planks in the front of the left of R.1.

Lights.
Right battalion report green light seen in direction of point 201 at 8-40 pm. last night. At 9-50 pm a stationary light was observed as if on a tree or pole about the S.E. corner of wood in H.30.c. At 9-50 pm. a red light was observed in the direction of 201 in the same wood. At 10 pm and at 10-5 pm green lights were observed at point 201.
Centre battalion report 8 red lights seen to the right front of F.3. which were promptly followed by Artillery fire. Left battalion report 3 red lights were sent up opposite O.1., which were answered by one green one further to the right of O.1.

Uniform.
At 5-10 pm. at point 319, a man seen looking over the parapet dressed in khaki, and wearing a motoring cap. At 5-15 pm. a man was observed wearing a grey cap with a green band.

Patrols.
On our right heard a whistle signal on getting 80 yards up the ditch to the left of point 319. It was answered from the

trench, and when about 150 yards out the enemy sent up
2 star shells and the patrol was heavily fired upon.
On the left our patrols were particularly active, but
saw nothing.
The centre battalion reported enemy appeared to be
bricking a trench between points 365 - 368.

Aeroplanes.

Two hostile aeroplanes reconnoitred our line during
the 24 hours.

Miscellaneous.

Right battalion reported having seen a man at point
219 at 5 pm. jump over the parapet and disappear into
the grass - he was not seen to return.
No trace of listening posts could be found between our
right trenches and point 324.

The enemy appear to be using fire fuse trench mortar
bombs opposite our centre.

Left battalion report that a white flag was seen on the
enemy's parapet on the night of P.1.

3/8/15.   Brig-General,

                                        Commanding 19th Infantry Brigade..

Daily report up to 12 noon, 4th August, 1915.

19th Infantry Brigade.

Operations.

1. Enemy fairly quiet. His sniping was very poor, but normal throughout the day.
The enemy sent 18-20 shrapnel shells over trenches last night at 11-30 pm. - a few burst in rear of F.4., but the majority burst near the entrace to No. 17 Communication trench, and the light railway (GREAT NORTHERN) in the vicinity. Three guns were firing from the direction of £.379. No damage was done. A few trench mortar bombs burst in rear of F.3. but retaliation with rifle grenades proved affective in stopping further bombs. Trench mortar bombs are still urgently required by the centre battalion for retaliation. At 4 pm and 4-30 pm yesterday afternoon, the enemy put 14 shells into trench F.1. but no great damage was done. There was no shelling on our left section.

WORK.

2. Work was somewhat hindered by rain. Parapets and parados thickened, revetted, and strengthened all along the line. Trenches were bricked and firing steps were constructed. All battalions had wiring parties out. Work was continued on the shelter trench line. Dugouts were put in and a general thickening of traverses was carried out all along the line. Work was much handicapped by great lack of necessary material for strengthening and rebuilding of front line trenches.

INTELLIGENCE.

3. Transport.
No movement of trabsport was heard last night owing, probably, to the high wind, which was contrary.

Working parties.
No working parties were seen or heard opposite our right. the enemy had a strong working party which was located at 1-20 am in the mine crater, which was disbursed by our machine gun fire. The centre battalion reports that the enemy has, of late, been in the habit of concealing his sandbags with earth. The enemy has been working very hard on his front trenches all day opposite our left battalion P.Q.R.

Lights.
The centre battalion reported last night that one minute prior to the shelling which was commenced at 11-30 pm, three white lights followed by one green were sent up. At 2 am this morning the enemy put up one green light - nothing happened.

Uniform.
At 7 am three Germans were seen in front of our left battalion crawling back to their trench. They were fired upon, and it is believed that none of them got to their trench. No peculiarities in uniforms could be distinguished. The right battalion reported having seen a black helmet with a brass spike lying on the top of the parapet.

Patrols.
All battalions had patrols out last night, but no Germans were seen. A daylight patrol, sent out by the 5th Scottish Rifles at 2 pm yesterday afternoon succeeded in locating an enemy's machine gun emplacement close to point 321. Crawling along parallel to the trenches, they entered the sap. They followed the sap until they struck an advanced fire trench about 10 yards from and parallel to the main parapet. This trench appears to be well within the enemy's wire. The parapet at the apex of the salient is put up very roughly but looks and strong and thick. There appears to be no system of wiring. Their outer wire is strands on wooden posts, knee trip and ground wires only, none of them being taut. The wire along the whole front appears to have been hurriedly done. The enemy's main wire entanglements are about 10 - 15 yards in front of their parapet. The enemy were very talkative and appeared to be working hard on their trenches.

Aeroplanes.
No hostile aircraft was observed.

General.
One of the fuses dug up, of the shells fired at F.1 yesterday afternoon at 4 pm and 4-30 pm was brass and had the following markings on it - H.2.14. AEG.15. 189.
At 10 am this morning a dense cloud of black smoke was seen near point S84 - this continued until 10-20 am.

4/8/15.   Brig-General,

Commanding 19th Infantry Brigade..

Daily report up to 12 noon, 5th August, 1915.

19th Infantry Brigade.

Operations.   1. Enemy has been very inactive during the last 24 hours. He has, however, been very vigilant. Except for occasional outburst of heavy sniping during the night, he has shewn no signs of activity. His machine guns have been more active during the morning.
The enemy has put no shells over during the last 24 hours. He fired 2 rifle grenades which fell short of our left section.
His sniping opposite our right, during the last few days, has improved.

Work.   2. Work was handicapped last night owing to a relief taking place in the centre.
Parapet and parados have been heightened and strengthened. Dug outs have been put in. Traverses have been reconstructed and heightened. Fire trenches were revetted and narrowed all along the line. Strong wiring parties were out wiring last night.

Intelligence.   3. Transport.
No movement of transport has been reported.
Working parties.
The enemy has been wiring in front of his fire trenches, and a good deal of hammering on metal was heard last night at 10-30 pm opposite our right. Only one hostile working party was located last night on their wire opposite F.4., between 12 midnight and 10 am this morning. They were not fired on as the Brigade had many working parties out. The left battalion also located some wiring parties who finished work early.
Lights.
Right battalion reports between 2 am and 3 am. green and red lights were again observed opposite their right front, which were followed by rapid bursts of fire. The enemy seen last night to be signalling to his sap opposite our left section by means of whistles. A green flare almost immediately went up, and a burst of fire opened on one of our working parties.
Uniform.
On the right a man was observed wearing a lightish blue grey tunic and cap. The latter had a single cockade and a whitish band. The tunic resembled a morning coat with two buttons on the tails, as on a tail coat. One or two other men were seen with similar caps, but with broad light blue bands. The men were very young looking and apparently, clean shaven or too young for moustaches.
The centre battalion reported having seen at 8 am this morning a party of 20 Germans moving along the road between points 293 - 292. Also a party of men dressed as far as could be seen in civilian clothes at 9 am. carrying timber at point 332.
Patrols.
An officer's patrol reported that opposite our right battalion the enemy appeared to have sentries posted every 10 to 15 yards. A strong patrol went out from R.1. last night under Lieut. Bucher, The Cameronians, with the object of discovering work the enemy was doing, and also to cover a burying party. Small parties of the enemy were seen. Patrol heard enemy unloading what sounded like corrugated iron sheets from a trolley behind his front line of trenches. Nine dead (killed in the 1st FROMELLES battle) were successfully buried. No identity discs or means of identifying the dead were found.
Balloons.
Balloon went up at 8-45 am this morning - came down at 10 am. It went up again at 10-20 am. True bearing taken from Dead End Corner - 162 degrees.

Miscellaneous.

A German flag was observed on the parapet at point 319 between 5 am and 7 am.
Judging from the volumn of rifle fire against one of our aeroplanes this morning, about 12-15 pm., the enemy's fire thrench is strongly held.

5/8/15.

Brig-General,
Commanding 19th Infantry Brigade.

Daily Report up to 12 Noon, 6th August, 1915.   19th Infantry Brigade.

OPERATIONS: 1. Enemy has been very jovial during yesterday afternoon; very talkative and noisy during the night. Loud cheering was heard at 4.pm and about 20 german flags were stuck on to the parapet. Notice boards were placed on the parapet with the words "WARSCAU in our hands". Otherwise the enemy has been very quiet. His sniping was not very noticeable yesterday. The enemy put 7 H.E. shells just over our right battalion which landed on RUE TILLELOY.
Between 4 and 4.30.pm yesterday afternoon the enemy fired 17 rifle grenades from their trenches between 368 and 370. The usual trolley was heard last night behind the first line trenches and it appears they were unloading some sort of material.

WORK: 2. Parapet and parados thickened. Traverses thickened and revetted. Parapets and parados pulled down entirely rebuilt. Disused trenches filled in. Dug outs put in. Wire repaired and new wire erected. Work handicapped by lack of material.

INTELLIGENCE 3. Transport Opposite our right heavy transport was heard at intervals from 8.30 to 11.pm moving along the road 302 - 287 - 285. At 9.50.pm a light cart was heard followed by the unloading of bricks. Opposite the centre battalion transport was heard moving along ROUGE BANCS - AUBERS Road between 9.30 and 10.5.pm , and again from 10.10 to 10.20.pm. A train was heard between 9.30 and 10.30.pm moving from our left to our right. Left battalion reports that transport heard at 10.15.pm in front of Q.1 moving from right to left, probably on the FROMELLES - LE MAISNEL road.
   Working parties. The enemy seems to have been working more on his front line during the last 24 hours. He is thickening his parapets. There appears to be no parados behind his trenches opposite our right. He was hammering in stakes and brackets (wooden), from 8.30 to 10.pm last night behind his front line. A working party at Point 372 was observed working from 3.pm to 6.pm consisting of 20 men on a communication trench. Supporting batteries opened fire at 4.pm and dispersed the party.
   Lights. Between midnight and 3.am 6th inst. 9 red and 2 green lights were sent up opposite the Brigade on our right. At 1.5.am 1 red light was sent up and after a lapse of 40 seconds one green one followed by two white which remained in the air for 54 seconds and on going out was promptly followed by a burst of artillery fire.
   Uniforms. It is now beyond doubt that several men opposite our immediate front are wearing caps with pale blue bands or bluish grey in colour with a pale blue band round the base. The cap itself seems flat and to have two badges one above the other in front; the lower on the band being either pale blue or white, while the upper badge seems yellow or reddish yellow. The caps as a whole seem fairly new. Opposite our centre battalion however Germans have been seen wearing rounds caps, no peak, and a red band.

PATROLS: 4. Patrols sent out from the Right battalion have nothing to report. The Centre battalion sent out 2 patrols who saw the enemy and dispersed his working patrols by throwing bombs. A strong patrol of the Cameronians went out at 10.pm last night from R.1. They extended and lay down covering a burying party. Six bodies were buried (from the last FROMELLES fight) and crosses were erected. They reported the enemy working very hard on his parapet. The patrol when within 150 yards of the enemy's trench got into a lot of tins which made a noise. A whistle was blown and they were heavily fired at.

BALLOONS AND   Two balloons were up most of the day. At 5.30.pm two
AEROPLANES   German aeroplanes hovered over our lines. One dropped
                a white light when over AUBERS. They were promptly
                joined by a third when all moved off going North.

MISCELLANEOUS   A flag was seen near the wire just opposite the
                Indian sector on our Right. A patrol of the 5th
                Scottish Rifles went out and brought it in at daybreak.
                An inscription had been put on the flag in indelible
                pencil in the following words:-

                    WARSCAU (Warsaw?)

                    IN OUR HANDS

                                            Brigadier General,
                                    Commanding 19th Infantry Brigade.

DAILY REPORT UP TO 12 noon, 7th AUGUST, 1915.   19th INFANTRY BRIGADE.

OPERATIONS: 1. Enemy has been very inactive during the last 24 hours. No shells, rifle grenades or trench mortars were fired. Sniping was active at 8.45.pm and 2.30.am

WORK: 2. Parapet thickened and revetted all along the brigade line. Parados erected and dug outs put in. Wire examined and new wire put up.
Firing steps revetted.

INTELLIGENCE 3. Transport. No heavy transport was heard last night.
Uniforms. More men were seen wearing caps as described in yesterday's report.
Working parties. The enemy seems to be putting up wire behind his first line and a patrol reports that it heard iron stakes being driven in. A small party of about 8 men was observed at work on a communication trench near point 371 between 2 and 6.pm
Three men were observed just in rear of enemy's front line, they were fired on and one was seen to drop. A working party was also located working on their parapet and wire at 9.20.pm but owing to a patrol being out at the time they were not fired on.
Lights. One Red light was sent up in front of Bareilly Brigade at 10.30.pm. A small trench searchlight appeared at 11.45.pm

PATROLS: 4. Patrols from Right and Left battalions have nothing to report.
A patrol of 1 N.C.O and 2 men went out from Centre Section and reported that the enemy had no working parties out between front 323 and 324. They found a large empty acid bottle about 40 yards in front of the German wire, which they brought in.

BALLOONS AND AEROPLANES: 5. No hostile balloons or aeroplanes were observed.

MISCELLANEOUS: 6. The enemy put up a flag opposite front 324. This was brought in by a man of the 5th Scottish Rifles in daylight. It was white with following inscription in red

      WARSCAU HAS BEEN

         FALLEN

                        Brigadier General,
                Commanding 19th Infantry Brigade.

DAILY REPORT UP TO 12 noon 8th AUGUST, 1915.   19th INFANTRY BRIGADE.

OPERATIONS: 1. Sniping has been more active during the past 24 hours. The enemy fired 9 shells from a trench mortar into trenches occupied by centre section at 6.pm and our supporting batteries retaliated on to enemy's fire trench.

WORK: 2. Parapet and parados thickened and revetted all along the line. Wire put out and dug outs put in. Latrines improved.

INTELLIGENCE 3. **Transport.** No heavy transport was heard last night.
Uniforms. Three men were seen working behind enemy's trenches wearing green caps with white badge, green tunics with vest and 2 brass buttons, and darker green trousers. Opposite R.1 a german was observed wearing grey uniform with black band on cap and black on sleeves.
Working parties. A working party was located between 368 - 370 at 2.pm and also at 5.pm and 6. m. There appears to be a good deal of work going on between these two points. A small working party was observed near point 323. The enemy appears to be erecting a parados to his parapet between 319 and 321 and he has also made considerable additions of earth in front of parapet at these points.
Lights. Shortly after midnight what appeared to be a revolving light was observed bearing 149 degrees from M.13.a 7.0 distant about 8 or 10 miles. The light itself was not visible but the reflection on the low lying clouds was quite clear. The motion of the light was anti clockwise and time for a complete revolution one minute. At 2.30.am a red and green light was observed opposite R.1.
At 8.50 and 9.10.pm one red flare was sent up from Point 321. No hostile action seemed to follow. All units report that enemy fired a great many more flares than usual.
Trench Mortar Shells. One trench mortar shell fired at our trenches did not explode. It consisted of a thin black tin can, 4" in diameter, 15" long, about 6 lbs in weight, with a fuze similar to a double cylinder bomb.
Telephone. There is a high telephone wire on a pole near point 370. The pole appears to be about 8' high.

PATROLS 4. A patrol of 1 officer and 1 N.C.. went out from centre section at 9.pm with the object of locating a listening post and with the further object of capturing a prisoner. They reached the german wire along the front of which they proceeded. The wire consisted of low diamond wire and they estimate its depth at about 50 yards and it appeared to be strong. They heard someone moving about in front of the wire. The officer(Lieut.Mostyn 2nd R.W.Fusiliers) proceeded towards the spot and when about 5 yards from it he was fired at and wounded in the arm. He fired his pistol when 2 men got up and ran into the German trench. He then crawled up to the spot and found a trench capable of holding 3 men, then rejoining the Corporal he returned to the trenches.

BALLOONS & AEROPLANES 5. No hostile balloons or aeroplanes were observed.

PRISONERS 6. The 2nd Argyll and Sutherland Highlanders report that at 12.45.pm, two lance corporals were in front of R.1 trench and burying a dead body. They saw two Germans to their left front and went forward to capture them. A hand to hand struggle ensued one German escaping, the other showed good fight but was captured. Both sides were unarmed.
The prisoner in question was sent to Headquarters 8th Division.

8/8/15.

Brigadier General

Commanding 19th Infantry Brigade

DAILY REPORT UP TO NOON, 9th AUGUST, 1915: 19th INFANTRY BRIGADE.

OPERATIONS: 1. The enemy was very inactive all day, hardly answering the fire of our snipers. At dusk he kept up some vigorous sniping and continued to fire bursts of rapid fire at intervals during the night.
The enemy last night at 8.30.pm traversed the RUE TILLELOY in rear of F.4 with machine gunfire. This gun was located at a point 150 yards N.E. of Point 370. Another gun was located at a point 100 yards S.W. of Point 368.
The enemy put 12 shells in to 1.A Fort at 2.15.pm today.

WORK: 2. Work was greatly handicapped by lack of material. No stakes were available for wiring.
Parapet thickened, trenches narrowed, parados erected. A little wire was put up. Dug outs and loopholes put in. Traverses were thickened and heightened..

INTELLIGENCE 3. Transport. Right Battalion reported that a light cart was heard about 9.pm coming close up to the trench and the sound of metal sheeting was distinctly heard. The centre battalion reported that a trolley was heard moving between Points 370 - 334 at 1.am. and a sound of iron bars being unloaded was heard. Left battalion did not hear any movement of transport last night.

Working parties. The enemy have been doing a great deal of work during the past 24 hours. A party working with wood was observed 50 yards S.W. of and 100 yards to the rear of 321. Probably sinking a mine shaft.
Working parties were also observed in communication trench 100 yards S.W. of Point 371 between 12 noon and 6.pm, also in the fire trench immediately in front of Point 371 work was being carried on between 12 noon and 3.pm.
A small party was observed working in front of Point 333 at 12.35.am on their wire. Rifle fire was immediately opened and the party was dispersed. A great deal of shouting was heard on the rifle fire opening.
About 20 men were seen running along the road 150 yards N.E. of Point 299 when our artillery were firing between 5 and 6.pm
A great deal of work is being done between Points 368 - 370. The enemy's wire after very careful observation appears to be very irregular and of varying density. Along practically the entire front wire is put on iron standards broken at intervals by low trip wire and "chevaux de frise" Enemy has been wiring with thick coils opposite our trenches at Point 333.
Lights. On the right one red star shell was seen at 8.25.pm Also 2 green lights about the same place at 8.40.pm
It appears that a whistle often precedes a star shell.
At 10.30.pm a lamp was placed on the German parapet, true bearing from the RED LAMP Corner 195 degrees.

PATROLS 4. Patrols from all three battalions in the trenches worked all along the front, but nothing unusual happened. Two patrol reports are attached.

BALLOONS 5. Three balloons were up today and remained up until dusk. An enemy aeroplane flew over our lines at a great height at 6.30.pm last evening.

MISCELLANEOUS 6. Three white wires were seen together on short stakes (probably insulators). These extended along the enemy's parapet for a number of yards.
From a report it appears that an explosive bullet struck the ground close to one of our listening posts at 1.30.am this morning.
It appears that the Germans have some checked Blue and White sandbags which render the German loopholes in the parapet almost invisible.
At 2.10.am this morning the enemy shouted out "Come on English"

Brigadier General,
Commanding 19th Infantry Brigade.

DAILY REPORT TO 12 NOON 10th AUGUST, 1915.   19th INFANTRY BRIGADE.

OPERATIONS: 1. Enemy fairly quiet and inactive. His sniping was fairly heavy at periods especially opposite our right and left between 11.30.pm and 3.30.am
Yesterday the enemy fired 4 trench mortar bombs between 2.50 and 3.pm all of which exploded. These fell behind our front line opposite No: 13 communication trench. Two more bombs were fired at 6.30 pm. and fell in more or less the same place. On neither occasions was there any damage done.
At 7.15.pm a machine gun opened heavy fire from a point 150 yards N.E. of Point 370. As this gun had fired from the same position on the previous evening, arrangements had been made with the supporting batteries to fire on this gun. A salvo was fired and all 4 shells struck the german parapet. The machine gun at once ceased fire.
An explosion was heard in the direction of Point 327 at 8.50.am but owing to the heavy mist it was difficult to loacte.
The enemy's snipers devoted their attention yesterday afternoon to sniping the cross roads and road junctions at odd intervals along the RUE TILLELOY.

WORK: 2. Owing to the mist a good deal of work was done. Battalions had the opportunity of examining the thickness of their parapet. In most places especially on the left the parapet at the top is now 8 feet thick. Parapets have been built up and trenches narrowed. Parados were built, dug outs were put in. Traverses were also thickened and revetted. A good deal of wiring was done.

INTELLIGENCE : 3. Transport. All battalions in the line report the moving from right to left of heavy transport last night, along the road 282 - 307 - 306 from 10.pm until 2.am From the noise it appeared that the wagons were very heavily loaded. The unusual amount of heavy transport heard rather points to the fact that a relief was being carried out. The trolley was again heard at 9.30.pm approaching from S.E. It stopped about 50 yards S.W. of Point 324 and was unloaded at this point. Judging from the sound it appeared to contain slates or pipes. A horse was heard to neigh when the trolley stopped, and it is surmised that the trolley is brought up nightly by horses.

Working parties. An enemy working party was observed working on communication trench 100 yards S.W. of point 371. At 2.30.pm 8 men were seen carrying timber up to the trenches at point 371. It was dropped in rear of the fire trench. Last night enemy had working parties driving in stakes about 150 yards N.E. of Point 370. The noise of hammering was very loud and it sounded as if metal was being struck.

Lights. At 9.30.pm 2 lights were observed resembling lamps, these appeared to be very high in the air and were on the line from our trenches through points 370 - 343. The distance away could not be estimated.

Patrols. All battalions patrolled between the trenches last night. Only one hostile patrol was seen opposite P.1 and when fired on by us a whistle was heard in the German trenches opposite. Patrol report attached.

BALLOONS: 4. Usual two balloons were up all day.

GENERAL: 5. Observation has been difficult owing to the misty day.

Brigadier General,

Commanding 19th Infantry Brigade.

Daily report up to 12 noon, 11th August.

19th Infantry Brigade.

Operations. 1. The enemy was inclined to be a little nervous last night, and, except for a little sniping during the night, he was inactive and fairly quiet. The enemy kept on sniping our working parties on the right the greater part of the night. He fired four large H.E. shells between Forts 1.A and 1.X. about 2-45 pm. Opposite the centre battalion, the enemy's wiring parties were located near points 370-324 - 319. These were dispersed by Machine Gun fire. A trench mortar was used against F.3. and F.3. shelter trench last night between 10 pm and 1 am. Some effective means of retaliation is urgently required.

WORK. 2. Work is greatly hindered by sheer lack of necessary material. Parapets rebuilt and parados erected and improved - traverses were heightened. Machine Gun emplacements were reconstructed. Firing steps erected. A good deal of new wiring was done, especially on the left, and wire was repaired almost along the whole front.

INTELLIGENCE. 3. Right battalion report no movement of transport during the night. Centre battalion reported movement of heavy transport was heard last night. The usual trolley was heard moving up until 12 midnight near point 324 and rubble and iron bars appeared to be unloaded. The left battalion confirm this report.

Working parties. 4. An Officers patrol from right battalion reported working parties and wire parties out up till midnight. At 1-30 am a working party was heard running out wire about 100 yards N.E. of point 319. At 10 am this morning an enemy's working party was observed working at their parapet opposite our right which was dispersed by our rifle fire.

Lights. 5. At 10-55 pm. a red rocket was sent up in the direction of 35D. On the enemy sending up, at 10 pm some green star shells, heavy sniping immediately followed. The left battalion reported that an unusual number of flares were put up during the night opposite them. A light was observed opposite our left which is believed to be some method of signalling used by the enemy. Bearing 320 degrees Magnetic from the right of R.1.

Balloons. 6. At 11-55 am a balloon rose half right from our trenches & it is still up.

Miscellaneous. 7. A scrap out of a German newspaper was sent over to our trenches yesterday evening. It was fired over, attached to a rifle grenade. (paper enclosed).

11/8/15.

Brig-General,
Commanding 19th Infantry Brigade..

Daily report up to 12 noon, 12th August, 1915.

19th Infantry Brigade.

Operations. Sniping was a little more active last night between 12-30 am and 2 am. A trench mortar fired on our trenches at F.3 between 11-30 pm. and 12-30 am. Every time it was fired a star shell was fired simultaneously.

Work. Parapets were thickened, firing steps repaired, parados and traverses continued. Wire put out and improved all along the line. Communication trenches improved.

Intelligence. A sniper was located firing from a shell hole in a house behind the German lines opposite R.1. He was fired at by a machine gun, and did not fire again.
Light transport was heard last night between 9 and 10 pm. moving on RUE DELEVAL.
A man was observed in observation in a tree reports wire between enemy's front line and support line trenches.

Working parties.
Working parties were located near points 324 & 333. They were dispersed by rifle grenades and machine gun fire. Opposite F.4, 6 of the enemy were observed tracing out a work in rear of 2nd line. This was noticed from an observation post in rear of our line.
At 11-30 pm a working party was working on parapet 100 yards West of point 324.

Lights. A signal lamp was working near point 363 from 8-30 pm to 9 pm, and several red and green lights were observed by the centre battalion but no results noted.

Patrols. An officer's patrol was out from the right battalion between 9-30 pm. and midnight. During this time, our guns were shelling the enemy's trenches. Each time the flash of ours guns was seen, the sentry was heard to shout a warning. The first word was indistinct, but the 2nd word seemed to be FEUER.
No hostile parties were met or seen.

Balloons. Two observation balloons were up throughout the 11th.

12/8/15.
Brig-General,
Commanding 19th Infantry Brigade.

19th INFANTRY BRIGADE. DAILY REPORT UP TO 12 NOON, 13th AUGUST, 1915

1. OPERATIONS: Enemy quiet. Sniping active between 12 and 2 am and very heavy on the right between 11.30.pm and 1.30.am Trench mortar very active again against F.2. Our trench mortar retaliated with effect. Rifle grenades were fired by enemy against F.4 and burst on parapet. This is the first time this has happened at this range.

2. WORK: Work continued on thickening parapet, building parados and putting in new traverses. Wire strengthened and extra entanglements added. Firing steps and dug outs constructed. Communications improved. New sap trench dug. Borrow pit filled with wire. Fort F.5 bricked and parados revetted and thickened.
440 men working under R.E. on shelter trench and support lines and communications.

3. INTELLIGENCE: Hostile working parties were located between during night near 334 behind the trenches - at 368 and 370 driving in stakes, and at 324. All of these were dispersed by rifle grenades and trench mortar bombs. Working parties seen by patrol at 319 and 321, latter moving large planks and pickets.
Near 323 a great deal of new earth has appeared in front of parapet.
Transport None heard. Trolley was working as usual.
Trench mortars fire from alternative positions near 324 and 370. The fuze is not altered for range as when fired at shelter trench line bombs burst in the air, and when fired at front parapet bombs roll some feet before exploding.
Balloons. 2 hostile balloons were up all day.
Lights. Several coloured lights observed but no reason for them yet discovered. Signal lamp working near 363 from 8.30 to 11.45.pm
Explosions. Right battalion report heavy explosion heard at 2.45.am some distance behind enemy's lines due South of F.1. Left battalion report a very heavy explosion seen at 3.am opposite 1.R; report was heard 3 to 4 seconds after flash seen. These reports are probably of the same explosion.

4. PATROLS No hostile patrols met. Wire at 321 examined which consisted of round iron posts 3 feet high with 3 strands of wire.

13/8/15.

Brigadier General,
Commanding 19th Infantry Brigade.

14th August, 1915.   19th Infantry Brigade.

DAILY REPORT

OPERATIONS 1. Quiet. Sniping active between 2 and 4 am. It is believed that enemy stands to arms at about these hours and practices fire discipline and fire control. Hostile trench mortar active on 2 occasions against F.2 firing from 323, 324. Our trench mortar retaliated with effect, groans of wounded heard in trench. R.E. blew in a small gallery causing smoke to rise from hostile mine crater - Germans seen running out. Unfortunately no warning was given of this and several good targets were lost.

WORK 2. Thickening parapets, erecting parados, putting out wire, making fire steps, improving communications, building dug outs, narrowing fire trenches, new traverses put up, new sap dug. Filling up old dug outs. 560 men worked under R.E. during night.

INTELLIGENCE 3. No sound of transport heard but trolley still busy near Point 324. Working parties located at 323, 324, 370, 333, all dispersed by our machine gun fire.
Parties also seen and heard working opposite 1.R,1Q and at 327.
A winch was heard working near 370 and another trolley heard near same spot. Machine gun fired from 370.
No hostile patrols met anywhere. A patrol of 5th Scottish Rifles was heavily fired on from trenches with rifle and machine gun fire - losing one man killed. They discovered a listening post close to enemy's wire.

14/8/15.   Brigadier General,
                                        Commanding 19th Infantry Brigade.

15th August, 1915.   DAILY REPORT   19th Infantry Brigade.

OPERATIONS: 1. Quiet - usual active sniping before dawn and between 10.pm and 12 midnight. Hostile trench mortars active last night opposite Salient - fired in retaliation for our rifle grenades. Our trench mortar ammunition ran out and our guns were finally turned on to trench mortar position about 324.

WORK: 2. Parapets thickened - parados rebuilt and new ones put up Dug outs made Wire strengthened Firing steps added New traverses put in 2saps revetted part of trenches floored with bricks. Posts I.A I.X and I.B repaired and revetted and trenches bricked Incinerators built. Advanced Head Quarters' dug out of left battalion built.
400 men working under R.E. all night.

INTELLIGENCE 3. <u>Transport</u> : Light horse transport heard distinctly for 8 minutes at 5.10.am moving away from trenches on FAUQUISSART - AUBERS Road. No other transport heard except the indefatiguable trolley.
<u>Working parties</u> : None opposite Right battalion, owing probably to our shell fire on previous nights. Other parties heard at 321 333 and 372 . They were dispersed by our rifle and machine gun fire.
<u>Aeroplanes</u> Hostile aeroplane reconnoitred our lines yesterday afternoon.
<u>Lights and signals:</u> Great use is made by enemy of coloured lights-their number and variety make it quite impossible to grasp any meaning, if any, that they may convey. Some of the lights seem to be hung on frames and look like Earl's Court on a Saturday night.
A motor horn of sorts seems to be a regular signal opposite No: 1 Section. The blast heard last night was followed by working parties behind enemy's trenches starting work.
<u>Patrols.</u> No hostile patrols were seen or heard last night. Look outs opposite right battalion were very vigilant and our patrols there were heavily sniped. A patrol of 2 men under a Corporal, went out at 6.45.pm yesterday to waylay a listening post opposite junction of F.1, F.2 but apparently no listening post came out.
An officer's patrol reconnoitred the front of 321. Nothing special was seen but patrol reports trenches were strongly held.
<u>Reliefs</u> Relief opposite Right battalion believed to have taken place on night of 13th - 14th August.
<u>Machine guns.</u> Machine gun at 370 fired again last night.

15/8/15.

for Brigadier General,
Commanding 19th Infantry Brigade.

Daily reports

19th Infantry Brigade
for the period in the CUINCHY sector of
the IIIrd Division line of trenches
from 26th August 1915 - 4th September
1915.

DAILY REPORT UP TO 12 NOON, 25th AUGUST; 19th INFANTRY BRIGADE.

OPERATIONS: 1. The 19th Infantry Brigade relieved the 6th Infantry Brigade on the 24th and the relief was completed without incident.

Opposite A.1
The enemy were quiet and inactive during the night. Our machine guns opened heavy fire at dusk which apparently silenced the enemy for the night.
The enemy at 11.am put over one H.E. shell in front of the MARYLEBONE Road.

Opposite A.2
At 6.40.pm the enemy fired a few trench mortar bombs on the right of our sub section. Our howitzers replied at 6.53.pm.
At 8.pm the enemy traversed our front parapet with a machine gun from the North side of the Canal.
From 7.pm to 9.30.pm enemy's small trench mortars were active.
At 8.50.am the enemy fired three shells on the railway in rear of the left of the subsection.
At 9.30.am a man was observed digging in a small trench in front of JERUSALEM Hill. Our snipers failed to hit him but the field guns got a direct hit and stopped the work.
The attitude of the enemy opposite A.2 subsection has been very passive during the last 24 hours.

Opposite A.3
Enemy reported very quiet, only a little sniping along the canal bank opposite right company.
No shells have been sent over.

WORK: 2. A.1. All the machine gun emplacements in the line were improved.
A.2. Clearing up communication trenches. Connected saps 7 and 10. Continued new communication trench between GERMAN LANE and HANOVER STREET.
Sapping was carried out to 15 and 16 craters.
Parapet repaired, firing steps erected. Wire erected.
A.3. Wire was thickened along the whole front. The front parapet was strengthened considerably and thickened to over 5 feet where completdd. Parapets in the support line were heightened and improved.

INTELLIGENCE: 3. Transport: A.2 report 3 light carts were heard at 8.45.pm to 8.55.pm. They halted at the station in A.17.c and unloaded either planks or boxes.
Empty carts were heard going North at 12.10.am to 12.15.am near the cross roads at A.16.b.9.4
A trolley was heard moving in rear of the enemy's line.

ENEMY'S WORK: 4. From 10.pm till 12 midnight the enemy were working on their own wire opposite JERUSALEM HILL (A.15.d.9.2.)
The enemy were heard working underground in front of No: 6 sap. O.C. miners has been informed.

LIGHTS: 5. A red flare was fired just North of the railway on the left of sub section A.2. This was followed by a white flare which in its turn was followed by a trench mortar bomb.

MISCELLANEOUS: 6 At 6.pm last night a rifle grenade was fired into sub-section A.2. It appears to have a message attached. The rifle grenade did not explode. The grenade is being investigated by the Grenade Bomb Officer, and particulars will be forwarded. The message marked X taken from the rifle grenade is forwarded with this report.
Another grenade was found by a working party in front of the left of sub section A.2. with a paper and message attached. Both are enclosed. The grenade had evidently been sent over a month or two ago.

At 10.pm last night the enemy called over to A.3 saying that they perceived that a Highland Regiment was opposite to them and asked whether the regiment was the BLACK WATCH. No reply of any kind was given.

25/8/15.

Brigadier General,
Commanding 19th Infantry Brigade.

TRENCH MORTARS IN ACTION 12 noon 24/8/15 to 12 NOON 25/8/15.

No: 6 TRENCH MORTAR BATTERY.

No of rounds and time.	TARGET	REMARKS.
12.30.pm	Trench between	(1) Heavy bomb - Good burst behind trench.
2 rounds.	A and B Stacks.	(2) Shortened range slightly. Good burst apparently in trench. Pieces of sand bag rose in the air. These were in response to rifle grenades which promptly ceased.
3.45.pm	Trench opposite	(1) Light bomb. Effective burst - unobserved.
2 rounds.	B Stacks.	(2) Light bomb - blind. In response to rifle grenades.
5.pm	Behind A Stack	(1) Heavy bomb - blind.
2 rounds.	German Mortar.	(2) Heavy bomb. Effective burst behind stack.

DAILY REPORT TO 12 noon, 26th AUGUST.   19th INFANTRY BRIGADE.

OPERATIONS: The enemy has been fairly active during the past 24 hours. He appears to be very jovial and has been shouting and loud talking has been heard.

Opposite A.2
At 8.30.am a working party was observed in front of the Brickstack A. This was immediately dispersed by our trench mortar battery.
At 11.30.am, the left company observation post located two hostile snipers on the South side of the embankment in front of the left side of the subsection. One of them was shot by O.C. left company.
At 7.30.pm, two hostile machine guns traversed along our lines from positions in rear of the enemy's front line. Up till now they have not been located.
From 7.30 to 8.pm the enemy fired 7 rifle grenades into No: 13 brickstack. Our trench mortars retaliated.
From 8.30 to 9.pm, the enemy fired 3 trench mortar bombs in to the right of the subsection. Our trench mortars retaliated.
At 11.50.pm, working parties were located on enemy's side of the crater about A.15.d.9.8 They were fired on by our supporting Field Battery. The party dropped their tools and fled.
At 12.45.am they returned to pick up their tools or to work when they were again dispersed by the battery.
A machine gun has been located at A.16.c.8.5

Opposite A.1
The enemy has been very quiet opposite A.1 subsection during the past 24 hours. One sniper has been very active near the enemy's brickstack. Our snipers are trying to locate him. The enemy put a few shells behind our front line at 1.40.pm No damage was done.

Opposite A.3
Two machine gun emplacements were located at A.16.c.1.1 and A.16.c.9.5 . On firing from the SPOIL BANK our machine gun silenced the one located at A.16.c.1.1, but the latter continued intermittent fire during the night.
Four H.E. shells were fired on the left front trench and 7 H.E. on the left support trench at about 12.50.pm.
An intelligence patrol on the right of A.3 reported the enemy working on his parapet near the FORT on the CANAL BANK. At 11.15.pm our artillery fired two rounds at the FORT whereupon the enemy ceased work.
CUINCHY POST was shelled at 6.20.pm and at 2.5 am.
Shrapnel, H.E. and small common shrapnel were used - 20 in all. No damage was caused.

WORK: A.1: Harrowing and revetting of CONDUIT Street was carried out.
Barbed wire balls were made. Parapet in PRAED Street and MARYLEBONE Road repaired where knocked down by shells.
A wash house in SEVENTH Street was repaired. A new machine gun emplacement in GIVENCHY support trench was made. PARK LANE and STAFFORD Redoubt were cleared of all refuse on the parapets and parades.

A.2: Fire trench between 5 and 7 saps continued which is now fit to hold.
Wiring parties were out. Loopholes were made. Parapet was strengthened and firing steps constructed. Sapping to No: 15 crater was continued. Latrines were dug. The BULGE and WORCESTER Terrace were wired. Work on the three saps opposite left company is progressing.

A.3: New apron wire was erected in front of the left company and 550 yards in front of the right company.
Parapets were thickened and traverses were improved.
Firing steps were made in places and general improvement was carried out.

Page 2

TRANSPORT: A hand cart was heard last night at 10.pm moving near the Brickstacks B.F.H. Our field guns fired on them and all disturbance ceased. From 8.10.pm to 1.am. transport was reported by all three companies in A.2 moving in all directions. in the neighbourhood of AUCHY.

LIGHTS No lights have been seen.

UNIFORMS Three Germans were seen when our artillery were shelling running towards the railway dressed in dark blue uniforms with forage caps.

PATROLS No patrols went out from A.1.
A patrol report is attached from A.2 with sketch.
Last night an officers' patrol went out in front of the right company of A.3. An enemy working party was observed on parapet. The patrol ran into a large covering party and were fired on, and forced to return. One man was badly wounded and was carried in, in spite of the heavy rifle and machine gun fire brought to bear on them.
No enemy's patrols were reported to be out.

MISCELLANEOUS The enemy last night were very cheerful, singing, whistling and shouting. They shouted across to A.2 to ask if they were the WELSH FUSILIERS.

A report of work done by O.C. No: 6 Trench Mortar Battery is attached.

26/8/15.

Brigadier General,
Commanding 19th Infantry Brigade.

DAILY REPORT TO 12 NOON 27th AUGUST, 1915.   19th INFANTRY BRIGADE.

OPERATIONS: The enemy has been fairly quiet except for occasional violent outbursts of hand grenades, trench mortar bombs and rifle grenades. His sniping has decreased in volume.

Opposite A.1
 About 9.pm the enemy shelled the neighbourhood of OXFORD STREET with field guns.
Six trench mortar bombs fell between the front line and OXFORD STREET at about midnight.
No hostile working parties were seen.
The enemy put one shell into STAFFORD Redoubt without doing any damage

Opposite A.2.
 At 8.30.pm the enemy fired several grenades at our working parties in No: 15 saphead. These were replied to with trench mortars and hand grenades, whereupon the enemy retaliated with rifle grenades, trench mortars (located at A.15.d.9.1) and hand grenades. The supporting howitzers then fired and silenced the enemy.
From 10.15 to 11.15.pm, 26 shells fell in the immediate rear of the right of the subsection.
At 4.30.am, 40 small trench mortar bombs fell around OLD KENT ROAD and JERUSALEM HILL.
Between 1.45 and 2.pm the enemy burst five shells, 200 yards in rear of No: 2 Brickstack. No damage done.

Opposite A.3
 The enemy's machine guns opened heavy fire last night from points located A.16.b.9.5 and A.10.c.4.4. On our machine guns opening fire from SPOIL BANK the enemy ceased firing. At 12.30.am our machine guns in front line opened fire and stopped enemy's working parties along the whole front opposite 13.
No shelling reported from A.3
At 8.20.pm one trench mortar bomb was sent into the saphead of the right company.
A magnetic bearing has been taken to some German howitzers which was found to be Magnetic 130 degrees from A.15.d.6.9

WORK: A.1
Trenches bricked. Supporting points wired, traverses reconstructed. Parados repaired and redoubts wired. Two machine gun emplacements made.

A.2
Trenches deepened. Loopholes put in. Parados built up in BRICKFIELD Terrace. Wire was repaired. Parapet in Sap 6 built up. Firing steps continued. Parapet in centre company improved. The BULGE strengthened. Work begun on Sap No: 2.

A.3.
Alternative machine gun emplacements in ARTILLERY ROW completed and some machine gun emplacements in BAYSWATER Road begun. Parapets and parados were heightened and thickened. Some wiring done.

R.E. WORK: No: 1 section with 3 platoons 5th Kings continued work on the BRADDELL POINT. 2 platoons 5th Kings with part of No: 2 section continued to work on the CUINCHY SUPPORT POINT.
No: 2 section put in dug outs in A.1 and A.2
No: 3 section worked on H.Q. dugout in siding 6 and on ~~insidings~~ dug outs in TOURBIERES.
No: 4 section worked on dugouts in A.3 (Battn. H.Q.)

Page 2.

INTELLIGENCE:

Transport: Light transport was heard arriving in squares A.17,18,22,23 in all directions between 7.50 and 11.pm The noise as if the carts were returning empty was heard between 11.45.pm and 12.15.am A small hand cart was heard moving about STACK D between 9 and 11.pm.
A.1 report an unusual amount of transport was heard moving from right to left between 7.30 and 10.30.pm

Enemy's working parties.
The enemy put up some new wire on the embankment on the night of 26th - 27th August.
At 1.40.pm the enemy was heard driving in timber in front of No: 14 sap.
The enemy has been observed to be working in his trenches at HOILANES - LA BASSEE shed, A.21.b.7.5 with corrugated iron sheets.

Lights.
A red flare was seen at 4.45.am but nothing followed.
At.1.30.am a red flare was sent up bear the railway embankment but nothing followed.
At 2.pm the enemy fired two flares between the fire trench and BOND STREET setting fire to the grass.

Uniforms.
At 5.am this morning two men were seen on the embankment They were fired on and disappeared into what looked like sniper's shelters. Owing to the mist,no distinguishing mark of their uniforms could be noticed.

Miscellaneous.
At 6.pm a hostile aeroplane flew high over the lines and then turned back. Again at 8.45.am two hostile aircraft flew over the lines at a great height and then disappeared on being engaged by our anti-craft guns.
Yesterday afternoon at 3.45.pm a dog came over from the German lines with a message attached.
The message contained the following words:-

"125,000 Russen gefangenen
"Petersburg besetzt
"Nicholas strassenfeger in BERLIN .
"King Edward folgt
"Gruss Gustav Wilhelm".

Opposite A.3 a flag 18 inches square on a four ft pole was discovered by a patrol twenty yards in front of a listening post of the left company. It was brought in. There are no marks of anykind on either the flag or the pole. A german periscope was broken by one of our snipers yesterday.
This periscope, which was a large one, was thought to have belonged to the german artillery observation post as it was seen whenever the german guns commenced to fire. This periscope was an easy target as it was against the sky line on the embankment opposite A.2.

The position of some enemy's trench mortars has been located but the officer could not describe it.
Herewith rough sketch attached.

27/8/15.

Brigadier General,
Commanding 19th Infantry Brigade.

DAILY REPORT UP TO 18 HOON, 24th AUGUST, 1916.

Tenth Infantry Brigade.

OPERATIONS: The enemy has been more active during the last 24 hours.
His artillery he has been fairly heavy, but on our snipers reprisals
between 9.50 am and 10.50 am there appeared more
aeroplanes than usual. Verbal enquiry from this Headquarters
yielded the answer, "Fully OUTING X
has been little or no sniping. The enemy shelled OUTINO Y
SUPPORT POINT as usual, at 10.15 a.m. but made no impression
or did any damage.

A.2:
    work enemy exploits shells more thinly in the
neighborhood of OUTINO Post at 7.50 pm and again at 8
pm. Enemy very heavy and sniping and snipers worry rifle between
6 and 4 am but no damage was done. Our guns retaliated with
the usual shots on more enemy morter bombs over.
The enemy's trench morter bombs appear to do little damage
to our trenches. Which have been well strengthened. The
mortars of the trench bombs over snoot their mark,
and do not affect the front line of trenches to any extent.

A.2:
    Opposite this subsection the enemy kept up very heavy
rifle and machine gun fire throughout the night. Our
infantry our morter parties and parties consolidated.
Recommenced. No shots were made over this subsection.
A hostile telephone wire over our lines this morning at
11 am it was fired a machine gun battery upon shower in a
dug out.

A.1:
    CONDUIT Street
Machine Gun emplacements were improved. Wire was put one in front of 10ft. Saps were
thrown. Wire was our one in front of IN PASSE Road. Parapets and
traverses were repaired and built up.

A.2:
    parapets strengthened.
All subsections were consolidated. Wiring was carried out on
the left. Wiring steps were improved and built up. Parapets
and parados further strengthened. Men in reserve worked
under M.E. supervision.

A.3:
    Outing to the heavy machine gun and rifle fire little
Wiring of work in front of the parapets was carried out.
parapets were shortened on right last in places. Firing steps
were erected. Dugouts and revolving of OXFORD TERRACE.
Position and blocking communication trenches.

A.E.WORK:
    No I section with 2 platoons of 4th Rifles continued to work
on PARADEL POINT. 2 platoons 4th Rifles continued work
CONDUIT SUPPORT POINT.
No. 2 section continued deep dug outs throughout A.1 and A.2
sectors.
No. 3 section continued and deep at OUTINOIRS and deep throughout
for Brigade Headquarters No: 6 stable.
No 4 section continued Battalion Headquarters, dug out in
A.2 IN the SPOIL BANK.

INTELLIGENCE:
    Trenchard
A's Report Lieutenant was heard arriving at 10.50 p.m.
Enemy post on no side are of be seen from the two sapes
10.50 a.m. and 1.00 a.m. As able are to see the two pumps
Re: points 34, 84, 88 H, of the canal (reference VCLINAS,-
IN PASSCHENDAG.

Enemy's working parties

The enemy are still working with corrugated iron at point 75. D. 21 (VOILANES - LA BASSEE Sheet).
A working party was located on the Railway near point 88 near the barrier. It was a very noisy party and much shouting was heard. It was dispersed by our fire at 11.30.pm.

PATROLS: Patrolling was very difficult last night owing to the enemy's heavy fire.
A patrol went out from A.1 at 7.45.pm to watch the point 21.B.75 (mentioned above) It reported that from this point a German sap runs along the ditch on the North side of the LA BASSEE road to the tree East of the B on the map. While they were out a red light was sent up and after that there was complete absence of any firing by the enemy. The enemy's sap was occupied and talking was distinctly heard and a flare was sent up from the saphead. The enemy appear to do little patrolling. His saps which run well out towards our lines are strongly held at night.

MISCELLANEOUS: At 8.pm last night the enemy called over to No: 17 sap listening post and said "Is that the Middlesex". The reply sent was a rifle bullet. The Germans appear to be using very large periscopes for observing the effects of their artillery fire. Two or three of these have been successfully hit by our snipers.

28/8/15.

Brigadier General,
Commanding 19th Infantry Brigade.

DAILY REPORT UP TILL 12 NOON 29th AUGUST, 1915. 19th INFANTRY BRIGADE.

OPERATIONS:- The 2nd Argyll and Sutherland Highlanders were relieved by the 5th Battn Scottish Rifles yesterday afternoon without incident.

The enemy has been exceptionally quiet during the past 24 hours. He has no done much shelling or sniping as usual. The Brigade has been most active in replying at once to any heavy sniping both with rifle and machine gun fire.

A.1

At 6.10.pm last night the enemy opened a very heavy fire on our aeroplanes both with machine gun and rifle fire. It appears that the enemy on seeing our trench mortar bombs coming over blow a horn so as to warn all men in the vicinity. This blowing of a horn has been frequently heard. Opposite this subsection from 12.30.am onwards the enemy has been very quiet and has not sniped at all.

A.2

Opposite this subsection between 2 and 4.am the enemy's snipers were very busy. CUINCHY SUPPORT Post was shelled as usual during the night. Sniping, however, was less than usual in this subsection during the past 24 hours. The enemy sniped at the Crater near the railway during the day. At about 10.pm last night the enemy pitched " 3 Chevaux de frises" over his parapet at point A.15.d.8.2 CUINCHY Post received 8 shells during the day which did no damage.

A.3.

Between noon and 12.30.pm today the enemy sent over 12 rifle grenades which landed well in rear of our trenches. Sounds of a small winch were heard on the right front of A.3 left company working from 11.pm to 12 midnight, last night. About 3.am a searchlight appeared on our front directed towards the left of A.3

At 6.45.pm. an explosion of a mine was heard on the left of A.3. Sniping was active at certain points on the parapet between 7.45 and 8.pm 45.pm Bursts of rifle fire were opened on A.3 between midnight and 2 am.

WORK: A.1.

Trenches revetted, work on Sap No: 10, continued. Brick s flooring carried out. Redoubts revetted and improved. Trenche narrowed. Machine gun emplacements improved.

A.2.

Firing steps constructed, traverses repaired. Chevaux de frise put out. Parapet relaid on top. Construction of parallel between No: 7 and No: 10 saps continued. Overhead cover in No: 17 sap put up. Strengthening work continued. The BULGE repaired. LOVERS Redoubt and PUDDING Lane strengthened and traverses heightened.

A.3.

Wire overhauled. Parapet raised and thickened. Repaired damage done by shell fire. The communication trench from the fire trench to STRATHCONA Walk continued.

R.E.WORK: No: 1 section continued work on BRADDELL Redoubt.
Part of No: 2 section continued dug outs (concrete) in CUINCHY SUPPORT POINT.
No: 2 section continued deep dug outs in A.1 and A.2.
No: 3 section continued deep dug outs for Brigade Head Quarters and in TOURBIERES.
No: 4 section continued Battalion Headquarters' Dug outs in SPOIL BANK (A.3)
Last night 3 parties were detailed to work under the R.E.
No: 1 party 160 men (Brigade Sapping Platoons) worked between HERTFORD STREET North of the CEMETERY to EDGEWARE ROAD (A.1)
No: 2 party 400 men of the 5th King's worked between the SCHOOL and HARLEY Street and BANBURY CROSS (A.2)

No: 3 party 5th Scottish Rifles worked on ground from road junction of GLASGOW Street and CAMBRIDGE Terrace to the West end of CORUNNA Road (A.3).

INTELLIGENCE: Transport

At 7.pm light transport was heard moving behind the enemy's line. The sound lasted about 20 minutes and was intermittent and seemed far off. The transport sounded like horse transport. Transport was again heard moving from the left to right at 8.45.pm and practically continuous from 10.pm until 12 midnight. Wood was heard being unloaded at various points. A considerable amount of transport was heard between 9 and 11.30.pm on the road at point 69 - CANTELOUX and from point 84 to LA BASSEE. Timber was heard being thrown out at point A.16.b.8.4 and also near the Canal bank.

Lights.

The enemy fired a red flare from the Railway North of point 97 and at 11.20.pm a white flare was fired perpendicularly from the German line just South of the Railway.
At 8.15 and 9.45.pm the enemy sent up two red flares opposite A.3 but nothing happened.

Patrols

No hostile patrols were met during the night.
A patrol from A.3 worked along the front of the line at about 200 yards out and found all quiet. No enemy working parties were seen. The patrol report that the grass is fairly long in front and there are numerous little hollows which could provide excellent cover for small parties.
A patrol from A.2 heard the enemy whistling and singing in their trenches from up till 11.pm.

Miscellaneous

From the extraordinary quietness and inactivity which reigned throughout the day and night it was presumed that the enemy were carrying out a relief. At 2.45.am the sound of singing was heard coming from behind the enemy's trenches which seemed to get fainter and fainter and if the relieved enemy were marching back to billets. The sound of the tapping of a drum was distinctly heard as if accompanying the party.
The enemy did not attempt yesterday to reply to our gunfire nor was he in the least bit aggressive. From all appearances it would seem that we have got the upper hand of the enemy.
In front of A.3 there is an old disused trench about 20 yards in front of the left company. It is concealed from view by a slight rise of In front of this trench there are four rows of concertina wire. The trench stands quite apart from any portion of the German front line.

29/8/15.

Brigadier General,
Commanding 19th Infantry Brigade.

DAILY REPORT UP TILL 12 NOON, 30th AUGUST, 1915.   19th Infantry Brigade.

OPERATIONS: On the whole during the night the enemy were fairly quiet. They were a little more aggressive opposite the centre battalion (A.2)

A.1.
At 7.30.pm the enemy fired a few field gun shells at the support trenches to the North of the LA BASSEE Road. No damage was done. From 10.30 to 11.30.pm the enemy's snipers were busy very active and they fired some rifle grenades into our trenches. These were promptly replied to. The enemy put over a few trench mortar bombs which fell just South of the LA BASSEE Road. No damage was done.

A.2. The enemy has shown more activity opposite this subsection during the past 24 hours. His sniping was particularly heavy from 3 am until 9.am. He sniped our working parties and traversed our trenches with heavy machine gun fire at 12.30.am. The gun was located as firing from Brickstack L.
A German sniper was located in a Brickstack opposite the right company. He had been worrying our snipers. He was hit at 8.pm. Two small H.E.shells dropped 50 yards in rear of No: 2 brickstack. At 5.10.pm 2 small percussion shells struck near the Cabbage Patch Redoubt. At 10.25.am 6 small percussion shells landed in the RAILWAY HOLLOW, but no damage was done.

Trench mortars. The O.C. No: 10 Trench Mortar Battery had no occasion to fire his guns yesterday.

WORK:
A.1.
The bricking of CONDUIT STREET is complete and it is now being revetted. OXFORD STREET is now being bricked. Dugout floorings repaired. PRAED STREET was narrowed and GLASGOW Road was refloored.

A.2.
Parapet remade on the right. Firing steps erected. Some wiring was done, and some concertina wire was put out in front of saps 7 and 10. 8 "Chevaux de Frises" were made and erected round the KEEP. The BULGE was improved, and 14 feet of the new sap was excavated. LOVERS REDOUBT and PUDDING LANE improved.

A.3.
Communication trenches improved and deepened. Traverses in CHEYNE WALK were cut so as to allow stretchers to pass along. New wire was put up by both companies in the front line. Firing steps were made.

R.E.WORK. No: 1 Section continued work on BRAMDELL POINT.
Part of No: 2 section worked on concrete dug outs in CUINCHY SUPPORT POINT.
No: 2 Section worked on Dug outs in A.1 and A.2.
No: 3 Section continued working on Advanced Brigade Head Quarters' Dug outs and the roofing of the dugout in TOURBIERES.
No: 4 Section worked on DEEP dugouts for Battalion H.Q. A.3 (in reliefs) in the SPOIL BANK.
The same working parties for the communication trenches were found as on the previous night.

INTELLIGENCE: Transport:
Yesterday afternoon at 2.30.pm a train was heard from the direction of LA BASSEE. Transport was heard at intervals between 9.pm and 11.pm, but the weather being bad it was impossible to locate its whereabouts.
Enemy's working parties:
The enemy last night worked on his wire at points 96 and 97 (A.15.d.). He was frequently compelled to cease working and eventually finished work at 12.45.am The enemy then opened heavy fire on our trenches working parties and compelled our men to cease work. A party of the enemy also worked on their trenches just North of the Railway but were stopped by rifle fire. It is thought that this party were working on a sap.

New earth appeared on the German parapet just South of the Railway.
At 2.30.am an enemy's wiring party was located on our left in A.3.

Lights.
At 9.30.pm and 12.30.am the enemy put up two red flares. No action of any kind followed.

Patrols.
All battalions patrolled last night and no hostile patrols were met.
A patrol from A.3 went out last night but owing to the vigilance of the enemy's bombers could not get near enough to obtain any useful information. One man of the patrol was slightly wounded by a grenade.(hand)

Aeroplanes.
Two hostile aeroplanes passed over our lines at 9.am. They were hotly engaged by our anti-aircraft guns. Another appeared over at 8.45.am very high up which was also engaged by our guns and then made back.

30/8/15.   Brigadier General,
                                    Commanding 19th Infantry Brigade.

DAILY REPORT UP TILL 12 noon, 31st AUGUST, 1915: 19th Infantry Brigade.

21st Brigade

OPERATIONS: The 2nd Wiltshires relieved the 5th Scottish Rifles yesterday afternoon without any incident.
The general attitude of the enemy seems cheerful. He has not been very active during the past 24 hours. His snipers have been very quiet and inactive.

A.1
At 7.pm last evening we fired a few rifle grenades at the enemy. He did not retaliate. Otherwise all has been quiet in this subsection.
Yesterday at 1.30.pm the enemy fired 10 rifle grenades at our trenches, no damage was done. The enemy sniped at our periscopes yesterday afternoon.

A.2
At 5.pm and 6.pm the enemy fired on one of our aeroplanes with a machine gun which was located as being close to Brickstacks F G & H.
At 6.am the enemy had a small working party on their sap to the crater in front of our No: 6 sap. Our bombers threw four bombs at them from No: 6 sap all of which exploded. Shrieks were heard coming from the German saphead. Rifle and machine gun fire was directed at our working parties at intervals during the night.

WORK

A.1.
In STAFFORD Redoubt dugouts were repaired. Parapets and parados were repaired. EDGWARE Road was revetted. Some wiring was done. CONDUIT STREET was revetted and refloored. Saps were worked upon.

A.2
Parados and parapets strengthened and repaired in BRICKFIELD Terrace. Continuation of saps round the craters carried out. Wire was put out in front of 1st and 2nd lines. LOVERS LANE was deepened. BULGE was strengthened and traversed.

R.E.WORK: No: 1 section continued work on BRADDELL POINT.
Part of No: 2 section finished the walls of the dugouts in CUINCHY SUPPORT POINT.
No: 2 section worked on dugouts in A.1 and A.2.
No: 3 section on Advanced Brigade Headquarters' dugout and dugouts at TOURBIERES.
No: 4 section revetted steps of dugouts in A.1.
During the night 140 men (Brigade Sapping Platoons) dug GRAFTON STREET a new communication trench connecting GLASGOW Road, HERTFORD Road, MARYLEBONE Road and EDGWARE Road. Three companies 5th Kings dug DAWSON STREET new Communication trench connecting HARLEY STREET and SACKVILLE STREET. One company 5th Kings is working on SACKVILLE STREET a new communication trench connecting HARLEY STREET and BANBURY CROSS.

INTELLIGENCE: Transport.
Light transport was heard from 9.pm to 11.pm moving in squares A.17.18,23.24.

Lights
At 1.am two small red flares and one large red light were seen behind the enemy's lines opposite to centre of subsection A.2. The enemy guns immediately opened fire sending 6 shells which landed near our trenches just North of the railway. This is the first case of any action following the appearance of red lights since the 19th Infantry Brigade has held this line.
At 2.30.am a white light appeared from the same place, but no result followed.

Enemy's works.
During the last 3 days, the enemy has done considerable work along the Canal and the railway embankment and a great quantity of wire has been put up in front of this work. It is suspected that a strong work is being made at this point and a machine gun position is also suspected.

This work commands the crater just South of the Railway and is likely to be a menace to the new saps which are being pushed forward.
No working parties of the enemy were heard during the night except at No: 6 Crater.

Miscellaneous.
The enemy appear to be very cheerful and shouted across to A.2 at intervals during the night. One of their remarks was "What about CALAIS"
It would appear from this remark that the German soldiers had received a little encoiragement of late with the news that CALAIS had been taken from the English. No answers, ~~other than bullets,~~ were returned.

31/8/15.

Brigadier General
Commanding 19th Infantry Brigade.

DAILY REPORT UP TILL 12 NOON, 1st SEPTEMBER, 19th INFANTRY BRIGADE.

OPERATIONS: The Cameronians in A.1 were relieved by the 5th Scottish Rifles this morning, relief being completed by 11.50.am
The enemy were very quiet during the day, but were inclined to be "jumpy" during the night.
Sniping has not been very active, except at odd intervals during the night.

A.1
At 11.30.pm the enemy opened fire on our front line of trenches, with rifles, trench mortars, and rifle grenades. Two men were killed and three severely wounded. The enemy as usual shelled STAFFORD Redoubt, but did no material damage. Otherwise all was quiet opposite this subsection.

A.2
An enemy's working party near point 88 was heard working on the railway embankment at 9.45.pm. They were dispersed by two rounds from the 50th battery, R.F.A.
Again at 11.15.am they were observed working and were again dispersed by 3 shells.
The enemy sent over several small shells, and rifle grenades between 2 and 3.15.pm into our trenches near the railway embankment. No damage was done and no casualties were caused.
At 11.pm the enemy fired rifle grenades trench mortars and very heavy rifle fire on the right of subsection A.2
Our trench mortar promptly retaliated with good effect.
At 1.15.am the enemy again fired 5 small trench mortars into our trenches. No damage was done. He quietened down again at 1.30.am

WORK A.2
Chevaux de frise put up in front of the fire trench. Brickfield Terrace was wired. Loopholes were made. Sapping continued to sapheads 15 and 16. Traverses were rebuilt. Fire steps bricked and revetted. The trench joining saps 7 and 10 was strengthened. Wire was put up in front of Worcester Terrace. Fire positions and splinter proofs were built in the crater nearest the railway embankment. It was then connected up by telephone.

R.E.WORK: No 1 section continued work yesterday morning on BRADDELL Point.
No: 2 section continued work on the dugouts.
No: 3 section worked at the Brigade Headquarters' dugouts and on the dugouts in TOURBIERES. The house for the use of the R.A. in TOURBIERES was strengthened.
No: 4 section worked all day and No 1 section worked all the afternoon in conjunction with 186th Company R.E. One company of the 5th King's by day and 2 companys by night continued the new communication trenches.
The 19th Inf.Bde.Sapping Platoons have practically completed GRAFTON Street communication trench.

INTELLIGENCE Transport No transport was heard last night probably owing to the high wind which was contrary.
Lights The enemy put up red and green lights at odd intervals during the night but no action followed.
Miscellaneous.
Train whistles in rear of the enemy's trenches were heard frequently during the 24 hours. The enemy were heard blowing whistles in answer to the whistle of the trains
Two hostile aeroplanes came over from an Easterly direction, one at 4.10.pm and the other at 7.45.am this morning.
A searchlight was observed in rear of the enemy's lines just North of the Canal. The Germans sent over a newspaper in a rifle grenade into subsection A.1. The paper is forwarded with this report.

NOTE WORK continued: A.1. CONDUIT STREET repaired and rebuilt. Parapet and parados of EDGWARE Road repaired. STAFFORD REDOUBT and PARK LANE redoubt improved.

1/9/15.

Brigadier General,
Commanding 19th Infantry Brigade.

DAILY REPORT UP TO 12 NOON, 2nd SEPTEMBER: 19th INFANTRY BRIGADE.

OPERATIONS: The 1st Battn. South Wales Borderers (3rd Infantry Brigade) were relieved by the 2nd A. & S.Highlanders yesterday evening. The relief was completed with no casualties. On the whole the enemy has been fairly quiet except for some slight shelling and bombing. His sniping has not been very active.

A.1
Opposite the right centre company the enemy kept up intermittent bombing throughout the night. This was effectively replied to by our bombers and some rifle grenades sufficed to silence the enemy. About 11.pm the enemy threw 2 bombs at our listening post in the right company opposite the minecrater D. Our bombers promptly retaliated and prevented the enemy from entering the crater. The enemy made several further attempts to enter the crater during the night but without success. They attempted on more than one occasion to enter the crater under cover of heavy rifle fire from the main fire trench. None of their efforts were successful. Between 10.am and 1.pm the enemy burst 10 shrapnel and H.E.shells 50 yards behind TOWER RESERVE. Trench. At 10.pm last night the enemy sent over 8 light H.E. shells near A.1 Battalion Headquarters. The enemy were very quiet opposite the left Company of A.1.
The 1st South Wales Borderers reported that the D mine crater was held by the enemy with machine guns. A careful reconnaissance was carried out at 11.am this morning which showed no men or machine guns in the crater: further investigations are being made as to the possibility of its occupation by us.

A.2
The Germans have been very quiet opposite this subsection. The sniping increased slightly towards midnight, but soon after he settled down for the night. At 12.45.pm a few percussion shells were sent over and all burst in the vicinity of PARK LANE REDOUBT. No damage was done. The enemy's wire opposite this subsection appears to be very poor. Further information will be forwarded concerning this.

A.3.
No enemy's working parties were heard during the night. At daybreak this morning mallets were heard and timber and sandbags were seen being used on the new work near the embankment. The enemy is still working very hard on his new work. He is connecting up a sap with the embankment, und under which he is tunnelling. The earth dug out of the embankment is used to form and thicken the parapet of the connecting work. Two strong traverses can be clearly seen, one of them not yet complete. A long ladder is also being used, the end of which was showing over the parapet. This new trench now being made runs obliquely into the original trench having joined the sap. A small plan sketch is attached.
At 7.45.pm about 10 men were seen carrying planks up various communication trenches. More wire has been put up in front of the work on the embankment.
A report on the firing of the 95 mm guns in subsection A.3. is attached. This should have been sent in with yesterday's daily report.
O.C.No: 10 Trench Mortar Battery had no occasion to fire his guns during the last 24 hours.

WORK: A.1
Parapet repaired and strengthened. Firing steps improved. Some wire balls made. A reconnaissance of trenches on work required was carried out this morning.
A.2:
Parapets and parados improved and repaired. Three sapheads continued. Various repairs and improvements carried out at CAMBRIN Post. Dugouts at STAFFORD REDOUBT repaired and old disused trench wired.

WORK contd.   A.3.
Traverses rebuilt and strengthened. Parapet and parados thickened and relaid. Completion of parapet parados and traverses connecting saps 7 and 10. Wire was put out. Loopholes put in. Heights Heightening and revetting, LOVERS WALK. The three saps in the left company have been continued and are now each 25 yards long. The BULGE was strengthened. Machine gun emplacements were repaired.

R.E.WORK: Nos: 1 and 4 section worked in all 3 subsections, in conjunction with 186th Company R.E.
No 3 section continued Brigade Headquarters' dugouts in Siding No: 6. Also dug outs in TOURBIERES. Strengthening the house for two guns in TOURBIERES.
No: 2 section continued dugouts in A.2 and A.3.
One of the Brigade Sapping Platoons continued GRAFTON Street.
5th Kings continued SACKVILLE Street and DAWSON Street. (GRAFTON Street is nearly finished, and should be completed today)
The remaing remaining 3 brigade sapping platoons dug the West end of DAWSON Street.

INTELLIGENCE: Transport
No movement of transport has been heard during the past 24 hours.
Lights:
At 8.30.pm, 10.pm and 12.20.am red lights were shot up by the enemy. No results followed. At 11.45.pm a rocket shot up into the air with silver and light blue stars. No action followed. Probably the enemy were carrying out some experiment.
Miscellaneous:
Cooking was observed going on behind the German lines today, behind Brickstack B.
A board which looks like a slide was observed in Brickstack G.

2/9/15.

Brigadier General,
Commanding 19th Infantry Brigade.

DAILY REPORT UP TILL 12 NOON 3rd SEPTEMBER, 1915: 19th INFANTRY BRIGADE.

OPERATIONS: The 2nd Royal Welsh Fusiliers were relieved by the 1st Middlesex Regiment yesterday.
The enemy have been aggressive at odd intervals during the past 24 hours, but on the whole he has been fairly quiet. There was some heavy firing directed against the working parties of the Brigade on our right last night. Brisk rifle fire was directed against the battalion North of the canal also last night, but nothing happened.

A.1
During the night the enemy fired several trench mortars and numerous bombs at our left centre companies. Our grenadiers replied with 3 or 4 bombs to every one the Germans sent over which succeeded in silencing them. The enemy were seen working in front of their trenches in what looked like a sap to a mine crater in front of BOYAU 19. A reconnaissance of the mine crater D during the night was carried out and showed it to be empty. This crater is commanded by 3 of the enemy's loopholes, the centre one of which is directly opposite our listening post. Efforts to destroy this loophole by bombs have so far been unsuccessful.

A.2
The enemy have been very quiet opposite this subsection during the past 24 hours. Although his grenades were bursting on the right of the LA BASSEE Road and on the left of RIDLEY Street, none were fired at this subsection, and 3 bombs fired at 11.30.am this morning failed to provoke any reply. There was occasional sniping by the enemy during the day. Observation through a telescopic periscope was very difficult owing to the bad wet weather. A small party of the enemy were observed yesterday morning moving into trenches by a communication trench leading from behind the first brickstack immediately North of the LA BASSEE Road. The enemy's parapet was registered by our catapults and rifle grenades yesterday afternoon. This failed to rouse the enemy.

A.3
The enemy were quiet all along this front. Sniping was active between 1 and 1.30.am and again at dawn. The enemy shelled the railway hollow between 10 and 10.30pm but no damage was done. Between 10.10 and 11.20.pm eight shells burst 100 yards in front of LOVERS R DOUBT. Only 15 pdr. percussion shells were used and our own artillery retaliated at once on each occasion. Between 12 midnight and 1.am 12 rifle grenades were fired at No: 18 listening post. Our trench mortars retaliated.
A German working party was located near the railway and were dispersed by the supporting battery.

WORK: A.1
A general repairing of trenches was carried out in this subsection. Some wire was put out. The parapet and parados were heightened and strengthened more especially in BROOK STREET and BACK STREET.

A.2
Parapet and parados of the fire trench improved. Traverses in CONDUIT Street which were damaged were rebuilt. Wire was put up in front of WATERLOO PLACE. Work on saps continued. Various minor repairs were carried out such as cleaning up communication trenches.

A.3
Parapet and parados, relaid and rebuilt. Wire balls were made and put out. Some concertina wire was also put up. Fire steps were raised, repaired and levelled off all along the line. Three dugouts were excavated. Saps were continued.

R.E.WORK: No: 1 and 4 sections continued work in conjunction with 186th Field Company, R.E..
No: 3 section worked on Brigade Headquarters dugouts in Siding No.6 also on dugouts at TOURBIERES.
Strengthening of the cottage for the artillery in TOURBIERES was continued.
No: 2 section worked on dugouts in PARK LANE, CONDUIT Street, STAFFORD Redoubt and BRICKFIELD Terrace.
Two 19th Inf.Bde.Sapping platoons finished GRAFTON STREET
The remaining two dug DAWSON STREET (West end)
5th Kings (400 men) deepened and broadened DAWSON STREET and SACKVILLE STREET.

INTELLIGENCE: Transport
Owing to the bad night no movement of transport was heard.
Enemy's works
Hostile work is being continued on the parapet 20 yards North of the point 97 and much new earth is visible at this point.
Lights
Numerous lights went up last night but no action followed The hostile flares opposite subsection A.3 are excellent and give a most brilliant light.
Patrols:
Last night at about 10.25.pm two Germans who gave themselves up were caught just outside the fire trench between BOYAUS 17 and 18. The company wire cutters of subsection A.1 were out in front of the fire trench putting up wire when the enemy threw about 8 bombs and opened rapid fire. The sentry in the fire trench saw and challenged a man and 2nd Lieut.Fraser (2nd A. & S.Hrs) who was near went out to see who it was and brought in a German. About the same time two men of the 2nd A. & S.Hrs. saw a man struggling in the wire in front and thinking he was one of our own men went out and brought in a wounded German who had been hit in the thigh and the ankle, under heavy bomb and rifle fire. Both men belonged to the 16th regiment of PRUSSIAN Infantry. The unwounded prisoner belonged to the 1914 class and was a young man of 21, and seemed or pretended to be "fed up" with the war.
Miscellaneous
Between 5.15 and 5.45.pm a hostile aeroplane reconnoitred the GIVENCHY Section after repeated attempts to get further over our lines, it was driven off by our anticraft guns
A hostile sausage balloon was up in the direction of LA BASSEE between 3.30.pm and 5.pm

3/9/15.

Brigadier General,
Commanding 19th Infantry Brigade.

TRENCH MORTARS IN ACTION   3/9/1915.

No. of Battery	Sub-sect.	No. of rounds	Target	Remark.
10th T.M. Bty	A1-A3			
No 3 gun	A1	3	German firing trench	One round carried away several yds of parapet. Two rounds were made to burst as shrapnel over the German trenches.
No 4 gun	A1	3	German firing trench	One round carried away several yds of parapet. Two rounds were made to burst in air as shrapnel. All bursts were good.

Brigade Major,
Brigade.

Brigade Major
19th Inf. Brigade.

DAILY REPORT UP TILL 12 NOON, 4th SEPTEMBER, 1915: 19th Infantry Brigade.

OPERATIONS:

A.1

Enemy were active with bombs and trench mortars especially with the former opposite the Crater D and ETNA. The enemy's bombs from the Crater just to the right of BUNTY SAP wounded 6 men including one officer. This crater was afterwards bombed by us and the enemy were silenced. Groans were heard coming from the trenches when our trench mortars ceased firing.

A.2

The enemy fired one rifle grenade last night which landed to the left of No: 4 sap at 9.50.pm.
Between 8 and 9.pm sounds as if the enemy were driving in iron stakes were heard. He is apparently driving them in well in rear of his front line trenches, probably in front of his second line, as it appears that this line is wired very strongly; the wire being attached to iron stakes.
Again beyween 5 and 6.pm sounds as if he was driving in small iron stakes were heard.
The enemy was inclined to be noisy during the night and there was a certain amount of sniping and loud talking which however ceased after 2.am

A.3

The enemy were noisy opposite this subsection during the night. They were singing and shouting up till midnight. No hostile patrols were met last night.
At 10.pm, 10.45.pm and at 12 midnight the enemy's working parties were dispersed by our artillery from the new work on the Railway embankment.

WORK:

A.1

Barbed wire balls were put out. Parapets were repaired and improved in places. General cleaning up and repairs to trenches were carried out.

A.2.

The front line of trenches has been drained in this subsection. Traverses in CONDUIT Street put up. Saps were continued by working parties last night.

A.3.

Saps pushed forward. Wire was put out. Firing steps repaired. Various repairs were done to the trenches in general such as repairing traverses, communication trenches, etc.

R.E.WORK:

No: 1 and 4 sections made M.G. emplacements in the front line
No: 2 section continued work on the deep dugouts in the front line trenches.
No: 3 section continued Advanced Brigade Headquarters' dugouts. Also boarded the Eastern end of DAWSON Street.
1 Section of East Anglians roofed the dugouts in CUINCHY SUPPORT POINT (concrete).
2 sapping platoons finished the East end of DAWSON Street.
2 sapping platoons dug the CEMETERY Trench.
5th King's Regt finished new parts of SACKVILLE Street and DAWSON Street and started deepening SACKVILLE Street between QUEEN'S Road and PONT FIXE.

INTELLIGENCE:

Transport:

Sounds of light transport were reported frequently last night especially between 9 and 10.pm from the direction of the LA BASSEE Road. It was difficult to detect which direction it was proceeding, but probably from left to right. A small light cart was heard moving on the cobble stones on the LA BASSEE Road. A.3 report light transport was heard moving in the direction of AUCHY - LA BASSEE at 9.30.pm last night.

Page 2.

Enemy's works:
The enemy's wire in front of subsection A.2 is very poor.
The wire consists of several rows of short wooded posts
apparently not more than 3 feet high (long grass makes
observation difficult).
There is a distance of about 3 to 4 feet between the rows
and the intervals from post to post is 6 to 8 feet.
At several places rolls of barbed wire in concertina form
are lying near the parapet as if they had been tossed over.
There seems to be no recognised system of wiring in front
of this subsection. No iron stakes were seen. There are
no "chevaux de frise" and generally the wire appars to be
old and not very thick.

Miscellaneous:
At 3am a pulley was heard working in the hostile trenches near
the Railway Embankment probably raising earth to repair
the parapet at this point where much new earth has been
noted of late. ~~Between~~ Last night at 11.30.pm the sluice
gates in the German lines were opened slightly and water
was heard running through. It was noticed that there is a
dam in the Canal where the German line crosses it. No
other information could be got.

4/9/15.   Brigadier General,

                                            Commanding 19th Infantry Brigade.

TRENCH MORTARS IN ACTION   4th Sept 1915.

No. of Battery	Sub-sect.	No. of rounds	Target	Remarks
10th T.M. Bty	A1-A3			
9.0 pm	A1	2	Enemy firing trench	Two rounds were fired. One burst in trench effectively
12 mn	A1	3	Enemy firing trench	Three rounds fired. One burst in trench effectively. Two were blinds.

Brigade Major,
Brigade.

To Miguelle Mejor

Summart of Daily operation, Work and Intelligence reports from
25th August, 1915 - 4th September, 1915. 19th Infantry Brigade.

Operations. On the whole the enemy have been quiet and inactive. At times his
trench mortars have been active but during the last five days they
have hardly fired at all. He has worried A.3. (formerly A.2.) with
rifle grenades but promt retaliation on our part has invariable
silenced the enemy. During the past week, the enemy has done little
shelling. CUINCHY SUPPORT, STAFFORD REDOUBT, the Railway Hollow,
the Brickstacks and all round OXFORD STREET have been shelled
almost every day, but to no extent. The following M.G. emplacements
have been located at A.16.c.11., A.16.c.95., A.16.c.85., A.10.c.44.
Brickstack L. and one near Brickstack F.G.H.
The enemy's sniping has considerably decreased in volumn and there
is practacly no sniping ablday. The enemy occasionaly opens heavy
rifle and M.G. fire at our working parties at odd intervals during
the night. To all appearances he wants to be left alone to work
on his trenches.

Work. A considerable amouht of work has been done. Three communication
trenches have been dug. SACKVILLE STREET, DAWSON STREET and
GRAFTON STREET. Parapets and parados have been rebuilt and
strengthened. Firing steps have been repared, relaid and leveled
off. More bricking of trenches and communication trenches has
been carried on. The BULGE has been strengthened. Some wiring has
been done. Saping has been conyinued to the various sapheads and
craters. All the craters have been stregthened. Loopholes have
been put in.

Intelligence. Transport.
Enemy's transport has been heard almost every night up to midnight.
    Enemy's Works.
The enemy has commenced and almost finished a new work close to the
railway embankment. This work is being made very strong. This
work joins up two of his saps near the embankment. The enemy is
also tunneling underneath the railway and is using the earth to
strengthen the parapet. This new work has been wired and is very
obvious. It is about 100 yards from the mine crater nearest the
embankment and about 200 yards from the parapet of the left
company.
The enemy's wire in front of A.2. (late A.1.() is very poor stuff,
and he seems to have made no effort to repair it. Almost continuously along the enemy's second line there is high and low
entanglements interwoven on iron stakes.
    Patrols.
No hostile patrols of any description have been met. He holds his
saps strongly at night and worries our front line of trenches in
A.1. (formerly A.2.) with bombs, trench morters and rifle grenades,
more especially near ETNA and VESUVIUS.

Miscellaneous.
At times the enemy has been very jovial. He shouted across to our
men on two or three occasions. He has been very quick in finding
out who is in front of him, and has already detected the 2nd Royal
Welsh Fus: and the 1st Middlesex. Presumably he has some means of
taping our wires. On the whole all has been very quiet.

                                        Brigadier General,
4th September, 1915.   Commanding 19th Infantry Brigade....

Daily Tactical progress report.

For period in the GIVENCHY section of the
II Divisional line, from 13th September
– 17th September 1915.

H Whitfoot Lt.
1/Middx.
Brigade Intelligence Officer

Weekly report shewing areas shelled by the enemy.

19th Infantry Brigade.

September 9th	No shelling.
September 10th	The enemy shelled GUNNER SIDING for 10 minutes, and KINGS ROAD near PICCADILLY for 10 minutes. PONT FIXE for half an hour.
September 11th	No shelling.
September 12th	Area between ARTILLERY HOUSE and GIVENCHY Church for 5 minutes.
September 13th	No shelling.
September 14th	PONT FIXE shelled for an hour and a half. 40 shells were put in. The enemy were probably registering the bridge and PONT FIXE - WINDY CORNER road. Area between HAMILTON ROAD and GALLOWGATE deliberately shelled for one and a half hours. Enemy shelled front trenches, crater and support trenches there.
September 15th	Enemy shelled area round GIVENCHY Church and ORCHARD for 5 minutes.

Lieutenant,

16th September, 1915. 1st Middlesex Regiment......

Daily report up to 12 noon, 14th September, 1915.

19th Infantry Brigade.

OPERATIONS. The 19th Infantry Brigade relieved the 5th Infantry Brigade yesterday afternoon. The relieve was completed without any incident. The enemy has been fairly active during the past 24 hours. His sniping as not been heavy, but he has been very aggressive with a certain amount of shelling and heavy bombing, and trench mortaring.

Opposite A.3. The enemy have been fairly quiet, and practically no sniping. The enemy fired two shells over B.1. at 10-12 pm one going well over towards QUINCHY and the other about Orchard Road. No damage done by latter.
From 4-30 am to 6 am the enemy fired 40 shrapnel shells in the vicinity of PONT FIXE. No damage was done.

Opposite B.1. The enemy sent over occasional trench mortars during the night. There was very little sniping during the past 24 hours. From 6 to 7-30 am the enemy registered along the Southern half of PONT FIXE - WINDY CORNER Road with H.E., shrapnel. from 7 pm to 9 pm last night about 50 hand grenades were thrown at the enemy from one the craters. From 11-15 pm till 1 am the enemy fired trench mortars and rifle grenades at our wire parties.

Opposite B.2. At 7-10 pm the enemy's machine guns opened fire on WINDY CORNER and continued at intervals throughout the night. From 8 pm to 1 pm the enemy's trench mortars were very active. Our mortars retaliated. At 4-47 am this morning the enemy blew up a small mine between the warren WARREN and RIFLEMAN'S REDOUBT and opened heavy rifle and machine gun fire. There were no casualties. AT 7-45 am the enemy's trench mortars blew in a machine gun emplacement, slightly wounding five men. We retaliated with trench mortars and gun fire, whereupon enemy ceased firing. From 9-30 am to 11 am the enemy shelled our fire trenches and support trenches between HAMILTON ROAD and GALLOWGATE. Five men were killed and one Officer wounded. Considerable damage was done to the trenches. Our guns retaliated The enemy put in 30 5.9 inch shells.

WORK. A.3. Cleaned and cleared communication trenches, deepening sap on the SPOIL BANK. Worked on a new dressing station.
B.1. General clearing up of trenches and repairing parapets and parados. Continual work on 8 saps done in reliefs. Some wire was put out. Saps into the craters were wired and blocked.
B.2. Parapets and parados repaired. Wire was put out. Cleaning up communication trenches.

INTELLIGENCE. Transport. No sound of transport was heard.
Patrols. An officer's patrol from A.5. went out from the sap near the canal at 8-15 pm and moved along the front, returning by the centre of the left company. They met no patrols or heard any pumping of water. A patrol went out from LONE TREE sap at 8-15 pm but owing to the frequent explosions, listening was difficult. The enemy had no working parties or patrols out. Two officers from B.2. reconnoitred the new crater found by Ox. & Bucks L.I. between 3 and 4 craters and decided the line for a new sap to it. They heard the enemy driving in stakes apparently in their trenches near A.9.a.7.7.
Lights. The enemy sent up several red and green lights during the night.
At 2 am the enemy opened heavy rifle fire, immediately after having sent up two red lights, which lasted 10 minutes.

<u>Uniforms</u>. Yesterday morning, two Germans were seen. One in a sap at the DUCK'S BILL, the other in the front line at A.9.d.3.9. The German in the sap was wearing a hat with a khaki cover and a black shiny peak. The Herman in the front line, who was on the look-out, was wearing an all grey cap with a similar peak. There was no decoration of any description on the cap.

MISCELLANEOUS. It is thought that from the smallness of the explosion of the mine that the enemy were obstructed by loose earth, and blew up a small charge to clear it.

The canvas screen at PONT FIXE has been partially shot away.

Reference the rise and fall of the canal, a measurement was prepared. At 8 pm last night about midway along CHEYNE WALK, It was checked at 6 am this morning and a FALL of exactly 6 inches was recorded (6 inches in 10 hours). Between 6 am and 9 am a fall of 2 1/8th inches. Between 9 am and 12 noon a fall of 1¼ inches. Total fall from 6 am to 12 noon was 3 3/8th inches.

14/9/15.

Brig-General,

Commanding 19th Infantry Brigade.

TRENCH MORTARS IN ACTION.

12.9.15 to 14.9.1915. 12 noon.

No. of Battery.	Sub-sect.	No. of Rounds.	Target	Remarks
Battery of 95mm Guns in B.1.	B.2	4	At 5pm at German trench.	Fired to test range. all exploded.
"	"	3	Fired from OXFORD ST at German trench at 6.30pm.	One short and 2 failed to explode.
"	"	1	Fired from HIGH ST at German trench at 7.30pm.	Exploded behind 1st line of enemy trench.
"	"	4	from DUCKS BILL at same target	All exploded. Germans ceased firing.
"	"	2	from OXFORD STR at 10.0pm at enemy trench	Both exploded. results could not be seen.
"	"	4	From Ducks bill at the enemy trench and bombers at 7.15am	All burst and timber was seen to fly up.

Brigade Major,
Brigade.

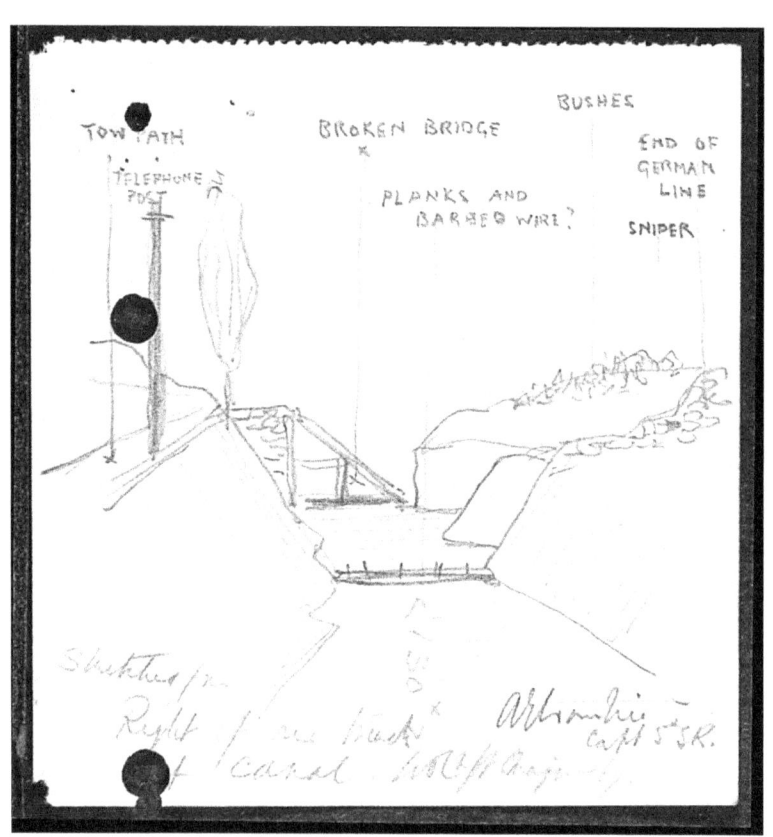

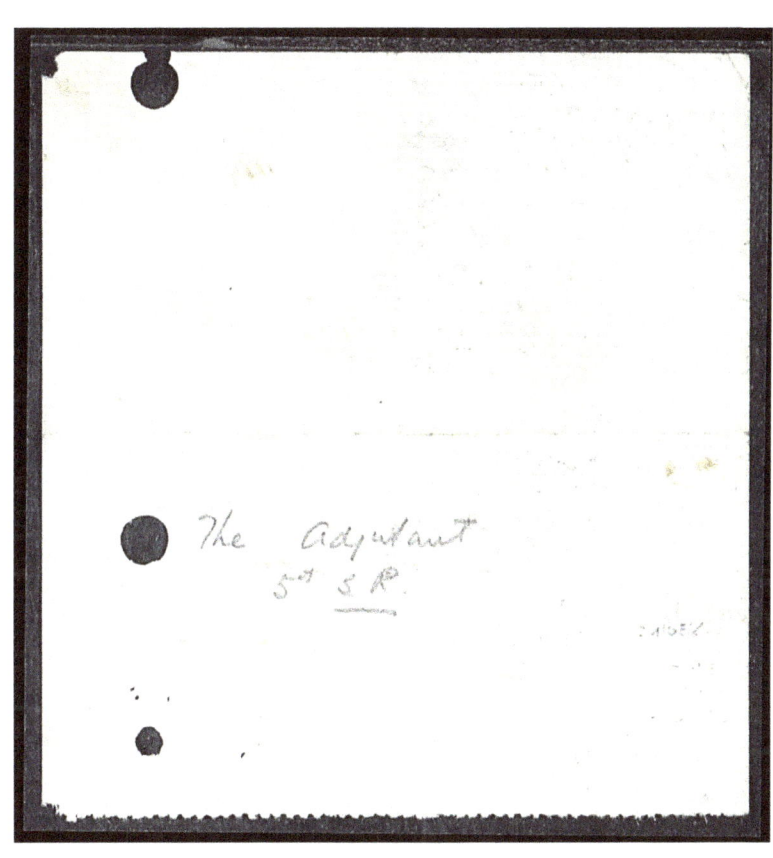

The Adjutant
5th S.R.

Daily report up to 12 noon 15th September, 1915.

19th Infantry Brigade.

OPERATIONS.

The enemy have been quieter since yesterday. Except for intermittent bombing, and a few rifle grenades, and trench mortars, at intervals during the night, and early morning, nothing unusual has happened.

Opposite B1. The enemy have been active at times opposite this subsection, his sniping being more vigorous. He has also put over 4 rifle grenades, fired from his redoubt close to the South bank of the Canal. They all fell near the CANAL POST. These rifle grenades, and his heavy sniping were however stopped by prompt retaliation from our guns. At 1-30 pm he fired 6 rifle grenades which landed on the right of the right Company. No damage was done. Again at 11-20 am he sent over 18 rifle grenades (6 of which failed to explode). All were fired from the South bank of the Canal and all landed near CHEYNE WALK. One man was killed. Our guns retaliated which silenced the enemy.

Opposite B2. Up to 9-15 pm last night the enemy became very very quiet. At that hour his sniping became more active, but decreased at 10-15 pm after which, only occasional mortars were fired until midnight, when all was quiet. A Machine Gun was located (reference Trench Map 36 c N.W.1.) at 9.B.1.1. in the sap behind the crater.
At 12 noon yesterday the enemy put one very large mortar into the trench opposite the DUCKS BILL. We retaliated with rifle grenades. The bombers of this subsection have had several grenade fights with hostile bombers in the new crater in all of which we have gained the ascendency.
At 8-30 am this morning the enemy sent over 5 minenwerfer on the DUCKS BILL. At 9-30 am he blew in a short length of parapet with a minenwerfer causing no casualties. A few shrapnel shells were sent over doing no harm.

Opposite B3. At 10-45 am the enemy fired 5 heavy shells which fell on the subsection to our right. Three of them fell on GIVENCHY Church and two to the right of it.
At 9-40 am three small shells fell on the right of this subsection. There has been an exchange of rifle grenades, hand grenades and trench mortars at intervals during the night and morning.
A Machine Gun was located on the North slope of the crater, A.9.a.6.7. A fresh crater appears to have been made by the explosion of the mine of the 14th instant.
The enemy were heard driving in stakes about 10 pm near A.9.a.7.7. They were bombed and promptly ceased work.
An anti-aircraft Machine Gun was located this morning. The F.O.O. was informed and our trench mortars are engaging it.

WORK.

B.1.
Work on the dressing station was continued. All communication trenches were widened to admit stretchers being taken down. Work on sap continued.

B.2.
Saps continued. Sapping round right-hand crater continued. Parapets and parados repaired and revetted. Firing steps and traverses repaired and remade. General clearing up of trenches. Assisting R.E., in HILDERS REDOUBT.

B.3.
Damage done to trenches and parapets by the heavy shelling of the 14th instant has been repaired. Wire was put up in front of fire trenches. No.2. Sap has been cleared. A branch sap from Sap No.4 has been begun. 60 yards of COLDSTREAM LANE revetted.

Sheet 2.

Re work.
(a) Continued work on SIDBURY.
(b) Continued wiring the MOAT HOUSE.
(c) Continued O.P. for 33rd Battery.
(d) Continued platforms for 15th Battery R.F.A.,
(e) Continued bridge of the CANAL near the Lock. This will be completed by the 16th instant.
(f) Making bridges for new cuts on the PONT FIXE - WINDY CORNER road.

Intelligence.   Miscellaneous.
At 5-55 am ten large fires probably for cooking purposes were seen at intervals of 40 yards from A.9.a.8.7. to A.3.d.1.5.

Between 3-30 pm and 4-pm yesterday afternoon a British aeroplane was very heavily fired upon by the German's. Ani-aircraft,Machine Guns were observed being used.

Reference the canal readings. Readings have been taken early and register a precise and average fall of 3/8 inches per hour. At 7-45 pm the Adjutant, 5th Scottish Rifles waded across the canal near our trenches (on the enemy's side of the lock) and also up and down the centre of the canal bed for some distance. He found that the maximum depth is four feet. The centre of the bed is a sound gravelly bottom. There is about 3 inches of mud silt on the sides. Soundings at 9-30 pm at the lock on the enemy's side were taken and found to be 3 feet.

The following is a table of fall taken from 5-30 am this morning :-

5-30 am to 6-30 am	1/8 inch.
6-30 am to 7-30 am	1/4 inch.
7-30 am to 8-30 am.	1/8 inch.
9-30 am to 10-30 am	1/8 inch.
10-30 am to 11-30 am	1/8 inch.
11-30 am to 12-30 pm.	1/16 inch.
12-30 pm to 1-30 pm.	1/8 inch.

From 5-30 pm yesterday afternoon to 5-30 am this morning fall was 2½ inches.

From the above it will be clearly seen that there is a decrease in fall and that the average is 1/8th inch as against 3/8th inch yesterday.

Reference the bridge which connects the German front line trenches. A careful observation seems to indicate a strong wire entanglement. A small sketch is attached.

Patrols.
An Officer's patrol went out from B.1. between 8-30 pm and 11 pm. and reported sounds of a rotary pump behind the German front line near the canal..

An Officer's patrol from B.2. went out at 9-15 pm and were out until 10-30 pm. They reported enemy were doing no work and had no one out. Every thing in the German trenches was quiet.

At 10 pm last night, the enemy shouted across to our left company of sub section B.1. something about the London Scottish.

At about the same time they shouted "Good shot Tommy" and "Hindenburg is coming" to our right company of the same subsection.

15/9/15.

Brig-General,
Commanding 19th Infantry Brigade..

~~Trench~~ Mortars in action.

15th September 1915

No. of Battery	Sub. Sect:	No. of rounds	Target.	Remarks.
19th Inf. Bde. Trench Battery. (95mm)	B2.	6.	Fired from High Street at German front line 3.30 pm.	These rounds were fired in answer to rifle fire on one of our aeroplanes. 4 exploded
"	"	4.	Fired from HIGH ST. at German MG firing on one of our aeroplanes. 6 pm.	2 rounds fell near trench 2 " " 30ˣ N of the target aimed.
"	"	2.	Fired from HOPE STREET at German fire trench at 6.30pm.	Both fell just in rear of front line.
"	"	30	Fired from High Street and Woodstock road at same target.	Fired in retaliation to enemy's trench mortars. 10 out of 30 failed to explode. These bombs had already been prepared and fitted up with wax. It is believed that where the wax had not sufficiently been used, the plug fell out and so bomb did not explode. During the night the Germans were quiet at DUCKS BILL

H W McPaul Lt.
1/ Middlesex. for.
Brigade Major
19th Inf Bde

Daily report up to 12 noon 16th September, 1915.

19th Infantry Brigade.

OPERATIONS. On the whole the enemy have been fairly quiet. The usual exchange of trench mortars, rifle grenades and bombs took place opposite B.2. and B.3.

B.1. This morning the enemy tried to shout over to the 5th Scottish Rifles but were promptly replied to by bursts of fire from B.2. and also from this subsection. At 9-35 pm 17 rifle grenades landed on the right of this subsection yesterday. Two of them failed to explode. All the saps running out from this subsection were rifle grenaded about 10-30 pm. The Germans opened heavy sniping at 11-0 am this morning.

B.2. The enemy shelled Picadilly and WHITEHALL with light shrapnel this morning. They had seen a working party at work in these places. There was no damage done and no casualties. A few rifle grenades and trench mortars were sent over which did no damage. These were replied to which caused the enemy to cease firing. Early this morning the enemy appeared to be very nervous opposite this subsection. He is reported to have manned his trenches.

B.3. The enemy have been particularly quiet opposite this subsection. Nothing except the intermittent exchange of bombs, trench mortars and rifle grenades, which did no damage, has happened.

WORK. B.1. Trench pits were worked on. New dressing station continued. OBSERVATORY DRIVE deepened. Machine Gun positions repaired and arranged to graze the surface of the Canal.

B.2. Parapet rebuilt where blown in. Latrines dug. CURZON STREET, PICADILLY, WHITEHALL and SHAFTSBURY AVENUE all worked on rebuilding parapets. KINGS ROAD built up. Wiring up the craters. 8 saps pushed up to from 25 - 30 feet.

B.3. Bomb proof shelters erected in Nos. 2, 3 and 4 saps and in RIFLEMANS REDOUBT. Sap dug through from No. 4 sap to the new crater between Nos. 3 and 4 saps. (This sap is now right through; but wants deepening). Wire parties worked in front of the fire trenches. 30 yards of apron wire were put up. Work on advanced Battalion Headquarters continued.

INTELLIGENCE. Patrols.
A covering party for a wire party visited DEADMAN'S TRENCH yesterday and brought back a British Officers cap and a rifle belonging to the Wiltshire Regiment.
A patrol is being sent out today to visit the trench by day and further details will be forwarded.
An officer's patrol from B.1. left the trench sap at 10-30 pm and worked out to the right towards the canal bank, till they could hear the men in the enemy's sap coughing. They lay still and listened for some time but could hear nothing (no pumps working) The enemy's listening post was very quiet No sounds of working or any sign of wire parties could be heard or seen. The patrol were unable to get closer here as the grass was very dry and made a loud noise when one moved. The patrol then worked across to the left and then came in at 11-40 pm. A personal reconnaissance of the enemys sap wire by the Adjutant, 5th Scottish Rifles (B.1.) showed a little concertina wire which is practically no obstacle.

Sheet 2.

INTELLIGENCE. Canal.
Yesterday from 5-30 am - 5-30 pm the fall was 1¾ inches.
5-30 pm yesterday to 5-30 am this morning, 16th instant, a
fall of ~~XXX~~ 1 3/8 inches.
This shows a fairly regular drop of 1/8 inch per hour.
Readings are taken hourly and at 12-30 pm - 1-30 pm today
no fall is shown.

Uniform.
At 6-30 am a man was seen wearing a grey cap with a red band,
in front of No. 4 sap. He shouted "Good morning, how are
you". Several bombs were thrown at him and he did not appear.

MISCELLANEOUS.
A party of the enemy numbering about 50 men were observed at
11-35 am this morning, marching to right in square S.28.6.
4.6. This party was seen from an observation post near
WINDY CORNER. They had dissapeared before the F.O.O. could
be informed. At 5-35 am several large fires, probably for
cooking purposes were observed in the enemys trenches.
At 10 pm a very drunken Prussian was shouting from the
German parapet opposite the right Company of B.1. for about
half an hour. There was also a good deal of shouting all
along the German line opposite this subsection, which was not
checked at all by any of the officers. Frequent references
to Cognac were made by the enemy, which was clearly heard from
our saps. One of the Germans shouted "Are you the Guards?"
No responce of any kind other than increased sniping was
given.

                                                      Brigadier General,

16th September, 1915. Commanding 19th Infantry Brigade....

Trench Mortars in action

16th September 1915

No of Battery	Sub Sec	No of rounds	Target	Remarks
19th IB. Trench Mortar Battery 9.5 m.m.	B2.	12	Fired from Shaftesbury Avenue, Hope street and Oxford Street at German trench 7.15 am. 15-9-15	3 failed to explode. All the others exploded well.
"	"	3	Fired from Shaftesbury Avenue at 10.30 am at same target.	In retaliation to 2 enemy trench mortars. All took effect.
"	"	2	Position Oxford street fired at German parapet at 2.25 pm.	In answer to rifle grenades one failed to explode
"	"	1	Fired from Oxford street at Enemy's trench 4.30 pm	In retaliation to rifle grenades. The round exploded.
"	"	4	Fired at German trench from Hope street and Shaftesbury avenue at 6.45 pm.	2 failed to explode 2 exploded well.

H W St Paul, Brigade Major
Lt 1/Middx for Brigade.

19th Infantry Brigade.

Summary of operations, work and intelligence from 13th September until 12 noon, 17th September.

OPERATIONS.

The enemy have on the whole been quiet. Except for one morning's heavy shelling, which was directed against the fire trenches, crater and support trenches, between HAMILTON ROAD and GALLOW GATE, and the almost intermittent exchange of rifle grenades, trench mortars and hand grenades-nothing unusual has happened.

The enemy have shelled PONT FIXE - WINDY CORNER ROAD, and GIVENCHY Church, but did no damage.

The following Machine Gun emplacements were located (reference Trench map, 36.c. N.W.1.) one at 9.B.11. another at A.9.a.6.7.

He blew up a small mine between the WARREN and RIFLEMAN'S Redoubt on the 14th instant, which did no damage.

WORK.

All the saps have been pushed forward and are well out. Communication trenches have been widened to admit stretchers being taken down. Parapets and Parados have been repaired and revetted. Firing steps have been remade, and traverses thickened and heightened. New dressing station worked on in SPOIL BANK.

INTELLIGENCE.

Miscellaneous.

Many fires have been seen in the German trenches, each morning at about 5-55 am.

The canal has been steadily falling at an average of 1/8th inch per hour.

A man was seen in front of No. 4 sap wearing a grey cap with red band yesterday morning at 6-30 am.

The enemy on the whole have been quiet, but very communicative. He has, on several occasions, shouted across to our men, more especially to the right battalion subsection B.1.

The Germans opposite are very jovial and a greater part of them appear to be drunk almost every other night. It is presumed that, from the frequent references to COGNAC, the enemy receives his ration of liquor every other night.

No working parties have been seen or any patrols met.

He is, nevertheless, almost always on the alert, and keeps a sharp look out.

17/9/15.

Lieut.,

Intelligence Officer, 19th Inf. Bde.

19th Infantry Brigade.

Daily progress report up to 12 noon, 17th Sept., 1915.
===

OPERATIONS. The enemy have been fairly quiet. The usual intermittent bombing continued during the night. A little shelling.

B.1. A 8 pm a working party of Germans were heard at Sniper's Post on the South bank of the canal. The Artillery were informed, and the party was dispersed by Artillery and rifle fire.
   At 12-15 am heavy sniping from the South bank of the canal against the CANAL post was silenced by Artillery fire.
   At 1-30 am the enemy commenced firing rifle grenades at the CANAL Post, but were at once stopped by the Artillery.
   Our snipers in this sub section have certainly gained the upper hand of the enemy's snipers. Any attempt on his part to commence sniping is at once stopped by our accurate sniping.

B.2. The enemy has been fairly quiet opposite this sub section during the past 24 hours. He sent over a few rifle grenades which caused no damage. Two Mininwerfers were sent over, which fell at the junction of OXSFORD STREET and HALF MOON STREET and demolished 15 yards of parapet. Our guns at once retaliated, which silenced the enemy's trench mortars.
   The enemy again shelled our working parties in WHITEHALL and SHAFTESBURY AVENUE, but did no damage.

B.3. Two of the enemy's snipers were shot from the high ground at the back of the WARREN on the 16th instant. Enemy's owrking parties on the East side of the craters in A.9. were bombed continually through the night. At 3-15 pm 6 small shells fell in A.8.d. near the BREWERY. At 10-15 am 2 heavy shells fell A.21.a. and again at 10-30 am 6 shells fell in A. 9. c. During the night of September 16/17th 5 enemy machine guns opened fire almost simultaneously on a frantage between the points A.9.a.8.4. and A.9.a.6½.7. Owing the the craters between our lines and the enemy's it was only possible to locate them by sound.

WORK. B.1. General work was carried on in this subsection under R.E. supervision. The new dressing station in the SPOIL BANK is nearly complete.

B.2. Sapping to the centra crater was continued. Eight of the saps which have been worked upon night and day have now reached over 40 feet. Repairs to parapet carried out. PICADILLY, WHITEHALL, and KING'S ROAD repaired.

B.3. Bomb proof shepters, built in saps 2, 3 and 4, and in RIFLEMAN'S REDOUBT. Sap to new crater between saps 3 and 4, completed. General repairing.

R.E. WORK. Work. (a). Continued MOAT AND SIDBURY.
   (b) Continued O.P. for 33rd Battery, R.F.A.
   (c) Continued bridge for 48th Battery, R.F.A.
   (d) One additional siding of WOLFE'S ROAD has had two reliefs on.
   (e) Dug outs continued.
   (f) Dressing station near ALBANY and machine gun emplacements in SPOIL BANK are in progress.

(2)

INTELLIGENCE. It appears that 30 yards back from the firing line along CHEYNE WALK is under observation by the enemy. Whenever a party moves along this bit rifle grenades are sent over. The only possible explanation of this is that the enemy must have some sort of periscope on the top of a the telegraph pole on the railway embankment.

Canal. Fall 5-30 am to 5-30 pm. 16th inst. = 15/16th inch.
          5-30 pm to 5-30 am. today (17th)= 1 1/8th inch.
          5-30 am to 10-30am today (17th)= 1/2 inch.

At 4-25 pm yesterday afternoon 15 Germans were seen carrying timber along the trench which passes point 94, 34, 05 in square A.3.d. The timber was deposited in the fire trench at A.3.d.1.6.

The party, to all appearances, was under the charge of an Officer who had a peak to his cap, the others had round caps with non peaks. 5-20 pm to 6-40 pm 3 working parties were observed between A.3.d.0.8. and SUNKEN ROAD, A.9.b.1.9. At 10 am a loud explosion took place behind the German lines. Smoke was seen rising east of the Ruined farm, burning at point A.39.34, and pieces of timber were seen going up into the air. Again at 9-15 am this morning an explosion was heard in the enemy"s second line near A.9.d.2.6. a large quantity of timber was seen in the air.

NOTE. An enemy's mine was exploded at 12-35 pm. ten yards in front of the left of RIFLEMEN'S REDOUBT. No damage was done to our trenches, and no casualties

17/9/15.   Brig-General,

                                        Commanding 19th Infantry Brigade.

Trench Mortars in action.

17th September 1915

No of Battery.	Sub. section	No of rounds	Target.	Remarks.
19th IB. 95.mm guns	B2.	10.	Fired at German parapet at 9.40 am from HOPE STREET.	All burst well.
"	B3	7.	From SANDBAG alley at Enemy's trench.	All but one exploded well. Two exploded in the German trench.
"	B3.	8.	Fired from High Street at the German side of the Crater N of R.flemans redoubt.	Two failed exploded. Remainder exploded well.
"	B2	2.	At 4.0 pm from Oxford Street at Enemy's trench.	Landed well and exploded behind the trench. No reply.
"	B2.	3.	German trench fired from Shaftesbury Av.	In retaliation to two German trench mortars. 1 Exploded.

This morning at 9.40 am a German trench mortar exploded opposite OXFORD St. There has been little trench mortaring during the last three days in front of 152

H W McPaul Lt.
1/Middx.
to Brigade Major
19th Inf Bde

Daily progress report up till 12 noon 18th September, 1915.
19th Infantry Brigade.

OPERATIONS.

The 19th Infantry Brigade relieved 1 Battalion of the 28th Brigade and 1 Battalion of the 6th Brigade yesterday. The relief was completed without any casualties.
The enemy have sent over a few rifle grenades and minenwerfers and have done a little shelling, but have been fairly quiet.

Z.1.
Sniping was fairly active opposite this subsection throughout the night and the enemy have fixed rifles laid on the VERMELLES ROAD.
Hostile parties were observed busy working near point 87 from 9 pm until 12 midnight. It appears that hostile trenches are strongly held by night from the volume of fire and noise which came from his front line.

Z.2.
A few trench mortars and minenwerfers fell between the N. end of HOLLOWAY and BOYAU 18, between 10 pm and 12 midnight. No damage was done, and our guns retaliated at once on the minenwerfers, who immediately ceased. The enemy put 6 small howitzer H.E. shells at the junction of BOYAU 17 and the fire trench, at 6-30 pm yesterday.
The enemy were fairly active with rifle grenades opposite MOUNT VESOVIUS at 4-30 am

WORK.

Z.1.
Work was confined to improvements of fire steps and BOYAUX; but few men were available as all stores and ammunition etc had to be brought into the trenches.

Z.2.
New trench in rear of the firing line from BOYAU 18 to 19 was continued. BOYAU 17 was cleared for traffic. HIGH STREET was improved. Parapets in the fire trenches were thickened and improved.

INTELLIGENCE.

Between 1-30 am and 3 am a searchlight played on the left Company of Z.1. for 5 minutes each time. The light was a particularly good one. It was not on long enough to be able to locate it.
At 11-20 pm a flashlight opposite right Company of Z.1. signalled to the rear and was answered by a green light, which seemed to be a signal for 4 trench mortar bombs to be fired at the Z.2. trenches.
A hostile aeroplane reconnoitered our line at 8-30 am this morning for an hour.
An enemy's fire was observed opposite BOYAU 15a a thousand yards behind the enem's front line at 9-30 pm last night.
The enemy appeared to be working opposite BOYAU 18 driving in stakes from 8 pm until 9 pm last night.

Brigadier General,
18th September, 1915. Commanding 19th Infantry Brigade....

Daily report up till 12 noon 19th September, 1915.

19th Infantry Brigade.

OPERATIONS.

The enemy have been unusually quiet during the past 24 hours. His sniping has been heavy at times but nothing very aggressive. He bombed and sent over some rifle grenades at intervals during the night.

Z.1.

The enemy were quiet last night opposite this subsection. In the early part of the night there was no sniping at all, but it became very active between 4 am and dawn. The enemy opposite this area usually man their trench about this time. The fixed rifles laid on the VERMELLES road were not fired at all last night. Between 10 pm and 1 am hostile working parties were located at points 97 and 93. These were dispersed on many occasions by our machine gun fire. Since we have occupied this subsection the enemy have hardly ever fired their Machine Guns. No positions have so far been located. This morning about 11-30 am our big guns exploded what appeared to be an explosive store. A very large column of white smoke went up. The explosion was a loud one.

Z.2.

Between GUN STREET and BOYAU 18 the enemy were fairly active throughout the night. The enemy fired several trench mortars and rifle grenades into the left company almost continuously throughout the night and especially between 6 am and 7 am. No damage was done. Our Artillery retaliated, and each time stopped the enemy and kept him quiet for a short period. Our grenadiers also retaliated but could no do so to any extent owing to the shortage of bombs. The enemy fired 5 light H.E. howitzer shells between GUN STREET and the North end of HOLLOWAY.

WORK.

Z.1.

Work was continued on the wire between the front line and the rear trenches. Sap T.1. and the BOYAUX 11 and 13 were widened. Firing steps and parapets were repaired and revetted. New latrines and new refuse pits were dug where necessary. A general widening of the Boyaux is being carried out where necessary.

Z.2.

The parapet and traverses in HIGH STREET was strengthened and completed. A new trench between Boyaux 17 and 18 was begun, and dug down to 4 feet deep. General improvements were carried out.

INTELLIGENCE. Transport.

Both motor and heavy horse transport was heard crossing our front moving towards HAISNES between 8 and 10 pm last night. The transport was unusually heavy.

Patrols.

No hostile patrols were met by our patrols. They saw no enemy at work on his wire, but reported having heard the enemy hard at work on his trenches between point 79 and 97.

MISCELLANEOUS.

From careful observations from Boyau 16 there seems to be a good deal of enemy's wire behind the craters opposite Z.2. but not much can be seen in the open grass. There is, however, a great deal of wire in front of the enemy's support lines.

On one of our bombs lading inside the crater opposite VESUVIUS a spray of water was observed, probobly used for extinguishing the fuse.

Brig-General,
Commanding 19th Infantry Brigade.

19/9/15.

Trench Mortars in action.

19th September 1915

No. of Battery	Sub section	No of rounds	Target	Remarks
95mm.	Z2	1	Fired from BOYAU 15 at 6.20pm at German fire trench.	This was a ranging shot and fell and exploded 10x in rear of the trench.
"	"	4	Fired from BOYAU 17 at 7.0pm at enemy's trench.	Two failed to explode. Two others exploded on German trench.
"	"	1	Fired 11pm from same place at enemy's place.	In retaliation to rifle grenades. Exploded well.
"	"	18	Fired at 5.30am from BOYAUX 15 and 17, at German trench	In reply to rifle grenades which stopped the enemy. Two failed to explode.
"	"	6.	Fired from BOYAU 15 at 10.7 AM.	Three failed to explode. The remainder exploded well on the German trench.

Brigade Major
19th In/Bde

19.9.15:

19th Infantry Brigade.

Daily report up to 12 noon, 20th September, 1915.

OPERATIONS. Opposite Z.1. the enemy have been very quiet during the past 24 hours. Z.2. has received its usual bombing and rifle grenading.

Z.1. The enemy have been quiet opposite this front, Sniping was particularly active between 4 and 5 am after which it ceased. Sniping was continuous from dusk to midnight. A hostile sniper who has been rather troublesome was silenced and believed to be hit, after his iron loophole was hit five times. A dummy periscope was put up and while he was sniping at it, he was sniped from a flank. Scouts reconnoitred the hostile wire opposite the right centre company of Z.1. They reported that it is from 3 to 4 feet high and very broad.

Z.2. Between 12 noon and 3 pm the enemy threw over several rifle grenades and bombs on the left company without doing any damage. At 7 pm. about 8 Germans were observed to enter VESUVIUS. They were bombed but the effect was unknown. During the night the enemy were active on the left company with mortars and bombs, but ceased on our guns firing. Four light H.E. shells fell close to battalion Headquarters about 11 pm doing no damage. Opposite Boyau 17 there is a long loop in the enemy's trenches which looks like one used for a machine gun.

WORK. Z.1. The following Boyaux were widened and improved 7,8,9,11,12,13, and 13a. Emplacements were deepened and widened along this front. Some alterations were carried out in the wire. T.1. was improved.

Z.2. A bomb proof in NEW trench between boyaux 18 and 19 started. New trench between boyaux 17 and 18 deepened but not completed. Work on HIGH STREET parapet continued.

INTELLIGENCE. Light transports was heard moving between 7-30 pm and 11 pm last night on the HAISNES - DOUVRIN Road. Lights. At 2 am a light in the enemy's front line opposite the left company of Z.2. resembling a magnesium flare, was seen. At 9-30 am a German aeroplane dropped a white light breaking into stars. No result was observed.

MISCELLANEOUS. Hostile working parties were active up to 12 midnight between point 79 and 97. A German aeroplane reconnoitred Z.1. line between 7-30 am and 7-45 am, but successfully driven off by our anti-aircraft guns. The enemy have been communicative opposite Z.2. and have been asking our men whether they were coming across on the 25th. No reply of any description of any discription was given.

20/9/15.

Brig-General,
Commanding 19th Infantry Brigade.

Trench mortars in action

20th September 1915.

Battery	Sub section	No of rounds	Target.	Remarks.
95mm	Z2	3	German trench at 6 pm	In reply to snipers and rifle grenades. All three burst well and stopped the enemy.
"	Z2	8	German trench 11.30pm	In reply to mortars and grenades. Two failed to burst. Remainder burst well, Germans were heard yelling.
"	Z2	8	ditto 10.30am	In retaliation to trench mortars etc. All exploded except one.

H W ...... Lt for
Brigade Major.
19th L.f.Bde.

28.9.15.

19th Infantry Brigade.

Daily report up to 12 noon, 21st September, 1915.

OPERATIONS. The enemy have not been very aggressive during the past 24 hours. Occasional burst of rifle and machine gun fire and rifle grenades. During the bombardment, which commenced at 6 am, the enemy has done little retaliation mostly with field guns and howitzers, which have done little or no damage to our trenches.

Right battalion of Z.2.

Rifle fire and rifle grenades and trench mortars were active during the night, especially on the right of the sub section. The enemy have replied to our bombardment in this subsection with short bursts of field gun and howitzer fire, at irregular intervals with little effect.

Left battalion.

Up to 12 midnight, the enemy was fairly quiet. He bombed our trenches but was vigourously replied to by the grenadiers.

Opposite the left company the enemy put some trench mortars over but no damage was caused. He also put a few shells behind the fire trench, which made no impression.

Our guns have caused considerable damage to the enemy's trenches. Opposite the centre, hostile grenadiers worked up a sap, but were bombed out of it.

It is particularly difficult to observe the enemy's wire opposite this subsection, owing to the long grass.

WORK. CORPORATION Street was filled in. Lateral trenches widened and deepened.

General fatigues were found, to work under Brigade arrangements.

Strengthening of trenches was carried on almost the whole way along the front..

INTELLIGENCE. About 3 am the enemy called out to the left battalion and asked many questions. No reply was given.

A hostile aeroplane was seen behind the enemy's lines at 9-15 am.

At 9-45 pm a building was seen to be on fire in square A.22.c. The fire lasted until 12-45 pm.

PATROLS. A patrol of 2nd R.Welch Fus. was sent out with the object of reconnoitring the barbed wire in front of the German trenches.

The patrol went out at 9-20 pm. and made for Railway trench, point 97. On the way the patrol crossed an old communication trench running about 120 yards in front of the German lines. There is a field of growing wheat on the East side of the communication trench.

The ground in the immediate front of the German trenches is cleared for cover.

The wire was old and pegged down to the ground with low stakes. It was carelessly put up, and unlikely to form a serious obstacle to attacking troops. A few men were working on the wire as if patching it up. A great deal of talking was heard. Another patrol from the right centre company reported that the enemy's wire was fairly strong but patchy. The only obstacle encountered was an old trench 60 yards from our parapet about 2 feet deep and 1 foot wide evidently an old trench constructed in a hurry.

21/9/15.

Brig-General,
Commanding,19th InfantryBrigade.

Trench Mortars in action

21st September. 1915

Battery	Sub-section	No. of rounds	Target	Remarks
95mm	Z.2.	3.	Fired from BOYAU 15 into the German Sap	One failed to explode.
"	"	6	Ranged on German front line.	3 failed to explode. All the others exploded well.

H W M Paul Lt.
for Brigade Major
19th Inf Bde.

Daily report up to 12 noon 22nd September, 1915.
19th Infantry Brigade.

OPERATIONS. There is nothing very much to report except that the enemy have returned occasional Machine Gun and field and howitzer gun fire to our bombardment.
From time to time the enemy has increased the volum of his retaliation more especially between 10 and 11 am this morning, when our artillery were not firing so intensely. His artillery have done no great material damage, and our trenches have stood the retaliation well. Whenever the enemy has retaliated his shooting has on the whole been good.
The enemy replied from time to time with his Machine Guns last night; but it was very half hearted.

Z.2. It has been very difficult to see if the wire has been cut in front of the enemy's trenches, owing to the very long grass and the heap of craters. The shooting of our guns was on the required frontage and should have cut the wire; but it is very difficult to see. Last night during a slight lull in the bombardment the enemy was sending up flares at intervals, shot from his second line. At 10-0 am this morning, an enemy's howitzer battery was located from the top of BOYAU No. 11. The Magnetic bearing from this point is about 98 degrees. The rough direction from the above point was the trees N.E. by E. of HAISNES Church.

WORK. General work was carried on as usual. A considerable amount has been done during the past five days. Three new communication trenches have been dug, viz:- ROBERTSONS ALLEY, BRAINES TRENCH and CHURCHILL'S CUT. Also six sidings have been dug connecting up WILSON'S WAY, BURBURE ALLEY and MAISON ROUGE ALLEY.
These sidings are capable of holding 2 Battalions in support.
BRADELL TRENCH and the trench under the bank connecting up MAISON ROUGE HOUSE and the commencement of WILSON'S WAY have been strengthened and dug out to accomodate one Battalion.
(Small rough sketch of trenches attached).

MISCELLANEOUS. Practically nothing has been seen of the Germans in front of us. He has been fairly quiet, and has not shouted over as on previous nights.
A few of the enemy were seen trying to work opposite the right of the left Battalion; but were stopped at once by Machine Gun fire.

Brigadier General,
22nd September, 1915.   Commanding 19th Infantry Brigade......

Trench Mortars in action.

22nd September 1915

Battery No.	Sub-Section.	No of Younds	Target.	Remarks.
95mm	Z2	2.	German lines	Both good. Ranging.
"	"	3	" .	In retaliation to the enemys fire. All Exploded well on the German parapet. A flame was seen to shoot up about 20ft after the explosion of the first shell. After this the enemy were quiet.

H W T M Pauldt
1/Middx for.
Brigade Major
19/9/15

13. To The Officer Commanding 2nd Batt R. W. F.

Report on patrol night 20/21 Sep.

Patrol Lieut H.M. BLAIR
        10108 L/c E. Chatfield
        4361 Pte T. Davies (Bomb-thrower)

Object of patrol. to reconnoitre the barbed wire entanglements in front of the German trenches.

The Patrol left at 9.20 p.m. making for "Railway Trench 97". We reached the German entanglements at 1.30 A.M. On our way out we crossed an old communication trench running about 120 yards in front of the German lines. There is a cornfield of growing wheat on the East side of the communication trench. The ground in front of the German trenches is cleared of cover for forty yards. The barbed wire was old and was pegged down to the ground with

15. low stakes, it appeared to be carelessly done and unlikely to form a serious obstruction to advancing troops. I was unable to ascertain the width of the entanglement as the enemy were working on the parapet and were keeping a good look out down the line. The German working party were about twenty yards in front of me, the parapet appeared to be a high one. My observation of the entanglements lasted several minutes but I was unable to patrol along the line of barbed wire as there was no cover and the brightness of the moon would probably have disclosed our position to the enemy. The enemy sent up flares which fell close to the patrol and also fired on us.

Lance Corporal Chatfield and Private Davis worked with great patience and coolness, particularly Private Davies. I regret to inform you that L/C Chatfield was killed on the return journey.

I heard a lot of talking on both sides of me when we were in front of the German entanglements.
The patrol return to opr [lines] at 2.55 AM

H. M. Blair.

Lt 2nd R.W.F.

THE. ADJT.
2/ R.W.F.

Report on enemy's wire and intervening ground

Patrol consisting of
    Lt P. Mordy
and Pte. 10714 Brazier

The enemy wire seemed to be fairly strong but patchy. A small party consisting of 3 men were seen working in front of parapet working on the wire.

There are no obstacles in the intervening ground except a small trench 60 yds from our parapet about 2ft wide and 1ft deep. This appears to be the beginning of a trench it extended about 30 yds parallel to our front trench.

8.20 am   J. Childe-Freeman Capt
                        B Coy. R.W.F

DAILY REPORT UP TO 12 NOON, 23rd SEPTEMBER, 1915.

19th Infantry Brigade.

OPERATIONS. There has been no sniping at all during the past 24 hours opposite the left battalion. Very half hearted machine Gun fire was directed against our front trenches last night. This was hotly replied to by our machine guns. As on the previous days of bombardment, the enemy have only retaliated intermittently on our trenches, more especially on the support trenches, but it has done no harm. A few casualties have resulted from this shelling.

2.2. Opposite the left battalion the enemy have sent over trench mortars and rifles at intervals, especially between 1 and 2 am. There has been hardly any sniping.
The wire opposite Boyau 17 and 19 has been very successfully cut. Fresh rolls were thrown over during the night, but these have been dealt with. The wire has not been cut to the right of boyau 17.

Opposite the right battalion between points A.21.d.5.1. and A.27.b.9.4. the wire has been successfully cut. There still remains a little to be cut at the Northern and Southern ends of the subsection.
The enemy's retaliation has increased in volume on this subsection and heavier guns than previously reported have been firing on the support trenches and round battalion headquarters. No damage has been done.
Enemy's snipers were active opposite this subsection during the early part of the night.
The enemy appears to have few guns opposite. He has not retaliated to any great extent, except occasionally opposite our right battalion.

MISCELLANEOUS. No enemy were seen during the night. He does not appear to show any signs of activity.
Three men wearing helmets were observed in the enemy's front line of trenches opposite the right centre company of the left battalion at 6-45 am. No distinguishing marks were seen.
At intervals during the night the enemy shouted over to our men of the left battalion and asked them "When were they coming". No reply was given.
At about 5 am this morning smoke was seen in rear of the enemy's front line of trenches, opposite boyau 17. These were probably cooking fires.

23/9/15.

Brig-General,
Commanding 19th Infantry Brigade.......

TRENCH MORTARS IN ACTION.

23rd September, 1915.

No. of Battery.	Sub-Section.	No. of rounds.	TARGET.	REMARKS.
95 mm	Z.2.	6.	Fired from Boyau 17 at 11-45 pm at enemy's lines.	One failed to explode. Three exploded in the air and two inside the German trench.
-do-	Z.2.	10.	Fired from same place at 8-30 am.	One failed to explode.

25/9/15.

Major,
Brigade Major, 19th Infantry Brigade..

Daily report up to 12 noon 24th September, 1915.
19th Infantry Brigade.

OPERATIONS.

There is nothing much to report other than the reports sent in this morning. The enemy are still retaliating at intervals. Last night the enemy's guns retaliated in greater volume oppposite the right battalion especially between 10 pm and 12 midnight.

Right Battalion. The enemy shelled the right battalion this morning especially on the VERMELLES road, most of the shells falling about 200 yards behind the HEADQUARTERS KEEP RESERVE Trench. Some fell at the jonction of BOYAU 9 and the support trench. The enemy were using small howitzer and percussion field gun shells.

Left Battalion. Yesterday afternoon at 4 pm the enemy shelled the junction of BOYAU 16 and HIGH STREET with three salvoes of small shells. The sniping has been more intense opposite the left battalion.
With one of his shells the enemy blew in one of the saps on the left of the line burying two men whom were successfully dug out.
The enemy still persists in sending over a few trench mortars and some H.E. shells at intervals. His chief target seems to be HIGH STREET.

GENERAL.

Intelligence.
The enemy failed to be roused by our feint yesterday afternoon. A Machine Gun fired across the right battalion's front, and apart from a few small shells, the enemy remained quiet and nothing was seen of him.
The weather and mist has made observation very difficult and it was almost impossible to distinguish the enemy's wire in front of his support lines this morning. Most of it appears to have been cut successfully. There is a fair amount of wire round RYAN'S KEEP and along the HEDGE on the railway.
A patrol from the 1st Middlesex R. went out last night and reported that the wire behind the hostile craters was little damaged and that the wire was about 25 yards thick. Otherwise opposite the right battalion's front the wire has been well cut.
From this morning's bombardment opposite the left battalion the German trenches appear to be pretty smashed about and it is thought that some emplacements have been damaged. The gap in the wire is slowly increasing, the shooting of our artillery being excellent. No enemy have been seen working on the wire, and on the whole he was very quiet during the night.
Neither the Trench Mortar or the 95 mm guns have had the opportunity of firing their guns.

Brigadier General

24th September, 1915.   Commanding 19th Infantry Brigade.

Reconnaissance of wire in front of the German support lines.

Right battalion report

The atmosphere has made observation very difficult and almost impossible of any points where fresh work has been carried out. Heavy rain has also washed away any appearance of such work. The Commanding Officer of the right battalion considers that the following points require special attention.

① LES BRIQUES FARM.
② Junction of DOOR ALLEY and LES BRIQUES trench and generally the vicinity of point 85.
③ RYANS KEEP and if possible the Craters round MINE POINT.
④ Works at A 27 b 93
⑤ " " A 27 b 95
⑥ Houses W of AUCHY also should be bombarded.

A patrol from the left company report that the wire behind the hostile Craters is both damaged and is about <u>25</u> yds thick.

24.9.15

H.D.M.Paul Lt
1/Middx R for

Left battalion report

The enemy's wire in the support line was visible at 6.0 am. Wire was also visible at RYANS KEEP, point 19. and the HEDGE on the railway. Owing to the mist it is impossible as yet to make out the wire distinctly.

The Hostile wire looks intact at A21 D 55 opposite BOYAU 18.

H.Q., 2nd Division.

SUMMARY OF OPERATIONS, 25th SEPTEMBER, 1915.
☸☸

1. After the gas attack the right battalion (1st Middlesex Regiment) attacked on a four platoon front with three companies in front line, the fourth company being in reserve.

The left battalion attacked with two companies on a 2 platoon front, remaining two companies in support.

The right battalion attacked between R.1 and VERMELLES Road on about 240 yards front with a fairly clear run in.

The left battalion on an 80 yard front through a gap between a mass of craters, 60 yards wide.

Both battalions were protected by strong flanking parties of grenadiers, except on the right, where there were no craters, and which was protected by the advance of the 28th Infantry Brigade.

2. The gas attack had no effect on the enemy. They were seen using sprayers in many places in rear, and burning a line of bon-fires along their parapets, over which the gas passed. Some men were seen wearing smoke helmets as soon as the gas started. As soon as the smoke screen lifted, no men were seen wearing helmets.

The pace of the gas retarding the advance of both battalions and on the left blew back on to our own men.

It is not known how many of the cylinders are still intact. It has been reported that some of the men operating the gas were gassed but this cannot be verified.

3. The right Battalion's advance under the smoke screen was not checked at first. As soon as the screen lifted the assaulting troops came under heavy rifle and machine gun fire when 120 yards from the parapet. The rifle fire was accurate and steady - more accurate and steady than has been usual - and it was heavy, being delivered from a thickly lined parapet. The communication trenches seemed packed with men. It would seem the enemy fires from his support trench at the first assault while other troops rush up to the front line.

Machine gun fire came from the left - from the MINE point salient. The gun or guns was sited low down as many of the wounded were hit in the lower part of the legs or ankles.

As soon as these companies were checked, the reserve company was put in and suffered heavily in getting over the parapet.

The 2nd Royal Welsh Fusiliers who were filed into the vacated front trenches then tried to retrieve the situation but lost 150 men immediately on getting over the parapet, this was out of about two companies or less.

The remnants of the Middlesex Regt. were unable to advance and dug them-selves in as best they could and crawled back later under cover of the artillery barrage which was ordered to stop moving eastwards or concentrate on the German front trench and trenches in rear.

4. The left battalion's advance was also somewhat retarded by the slow pace of the gas, and on reaching the gap which was the only place available to attack through, were held up by heavy machine gun and rifle fire. The gap being the only obvious place to push through was well covered especially by flanking machine gun fire cleverly concealed behind the craters. Covering fire was impossible down to the craters. The wire in this gap though cut was very broad and thick in its scattered state. One platoon was able to get through and into the German trench. It has not been seen since. The others suffered heavy casualties trying to remove the wire. The remnants eventually withdrawing to their own trenches.

5. The Brigade was re-organised with a view to a further assault and a bombardment of the front was arranged. The Royal Welsh Fusiliers took the place of the Middlesex Regt. on the right and the Cameronians on the left, that of the A. & S. Highrs.

6. Instructions were received from the 2nd Division that a heavy bombardment was being arranged for from 9 am to 9-30 am.

7. As it was very improbable that the first assaulting troops would be ready by that time, a posponment was asked for, and the Division arranged for the bomardment to continue until the brigade was ready.

8. This order was later cancelled and the Brigade ordered to consolidate but to be prepared for offensive action if a favourable opportunity occurred.

9. Orders were then issued to hold the line (and consolidate it) as follows:-
    GUN STREET - VERMELLES ROAD   - 1st Cameronians.
    VERMELLES ROAD - R.1.   - 2nd R.Welsh Fusiliers.
    In support of R.Welsh Fus.   - 5th Scottish Rifles.
    (2 companies in close support)
    In support of 1st Cameronians.   - 2nd A. & S. Highrs.

    Brigade reserve   1st Middlesex Regt.
    (MAISON ROUGE).

10. After the action, the enemy were seen to thin their front line and move back to their support trenches.

Daily report up till 12 noon 30th September, 1915.
19th Infantry Brigade.

OPERATIONS. General.
The enemy have calmed down considerably during the past 24 hours and has not worried the Brigade beyond a few rifle grenades and trench mortars. Although he has not been very aggressive, he has nevertheless been on the alert and has worried our collecting parties for the dead considerably by groaning so as to attract our stretcher bearers. He has shelled our back support lines, more especially BACK and HIGH STREETS. On each occasion, however our guns have retalliated at once and have silenced the enemy's guns and snipers.
From the amount of fire our aeroplanes draw, it is to be presumed that his trenches are still very strongly held. Most of the fire seems to come from his second line of trenches. During the past few days he has not employed his anti-aircraft guns against our aeroplanes.

Z.2. The enemy has commenced digging an open sap running at an angle with his fire trench. This sap is immediately opposite the right of the left battalion. They were digging very energetically up till 4-15 pm yesterday afternoon.
Last night the Germans started shelling their own lines opposite the left company of the right battalion, and after a few shells had landed, a green light was sent up towards their rear, whereupon the guns lengthened. As near as could be judged, the line of the guns seemed to be in the direction of the road and railway junction in square A.29. c.2.6.
The enemy have thrown out some loose wire near the crater ETNA. Our grenadiers bombed the crater opposite the left company of the left battalion last night from 6-30 pm - 9-30 pm.
On the whole he was fairly quiet last night.

WORK.
Much work has been confined to removing cylinders and generally clearing up. Some parts of the front line trenches have been badly blown in and a great deal of labour has been expended in order to get everything into proper order. Firing steps have been improved and a general strengthening all along the line has been carried out. Some of the communication trenches and BOYAUX have been cleared out where blown in by the R.E.
Many men have been engaged nightly in fetching in dead and wounded.

INTELLIGENCE. There is nothing to report under this heading. Behind his line the enemy has been very quiet. No sound of transport have been heard.

Brigadier General,
30th September, 1915. Commanding 19th Infantry Brigade.

PLANS AND SKETCHES.

THE LANE
TOWER RESERVE TRENCH
BRAINES WAY
WILSONS WAY
RUSSELLS KEEP
BURBURE ALLEY
MAISON ROUGE ALLEY
ARTHURS KEEP
OLD BOOTS TR.
HEADQUARTER
HQ
SIMS KEEP
KEEP RESERVE TR.
THE PARADE
ETNA
VESUVIUS
JUNCTION
SHORT CUT
TOWER TR.
QUARRY TR.
GUN ST.
Keep

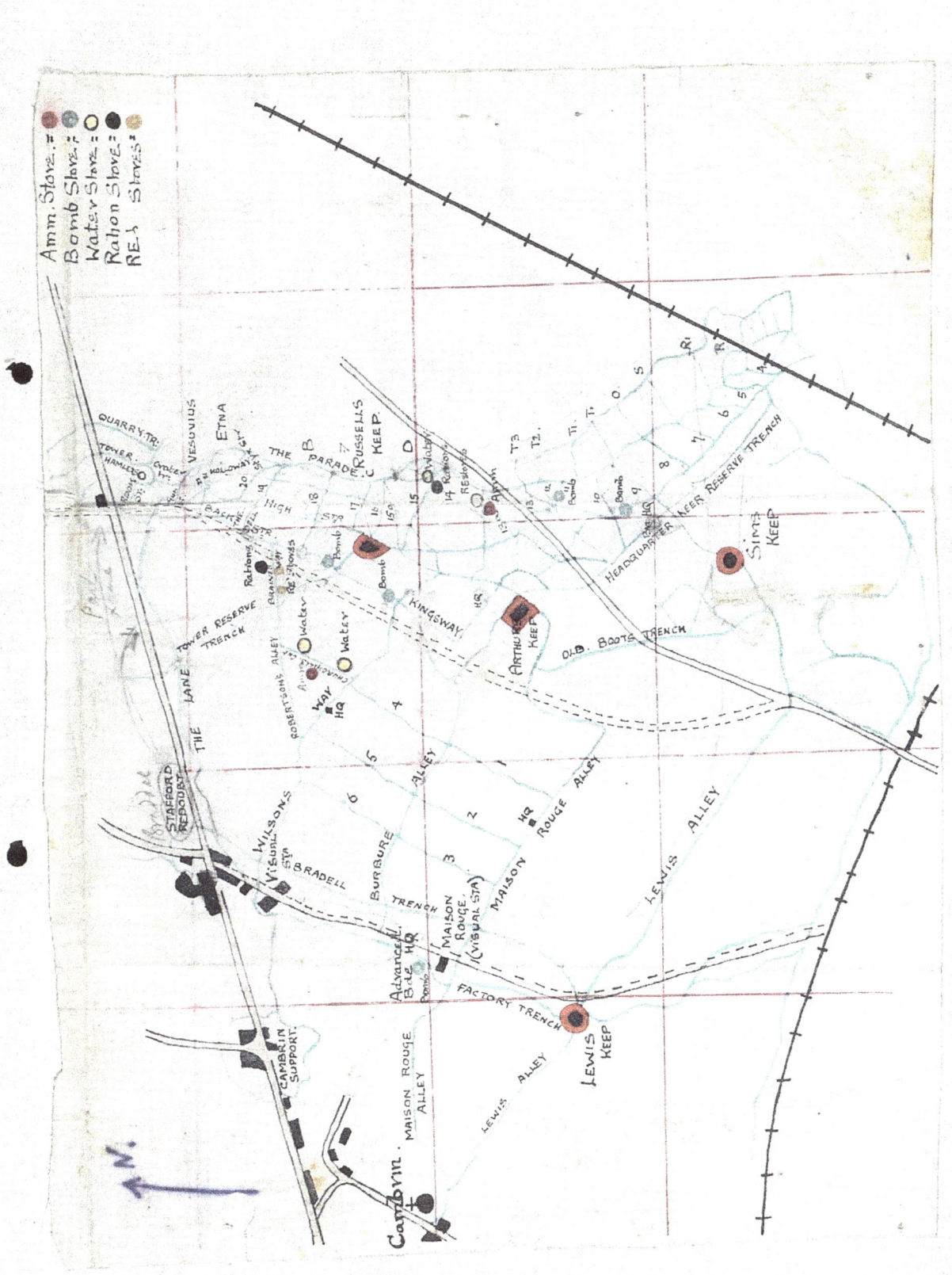

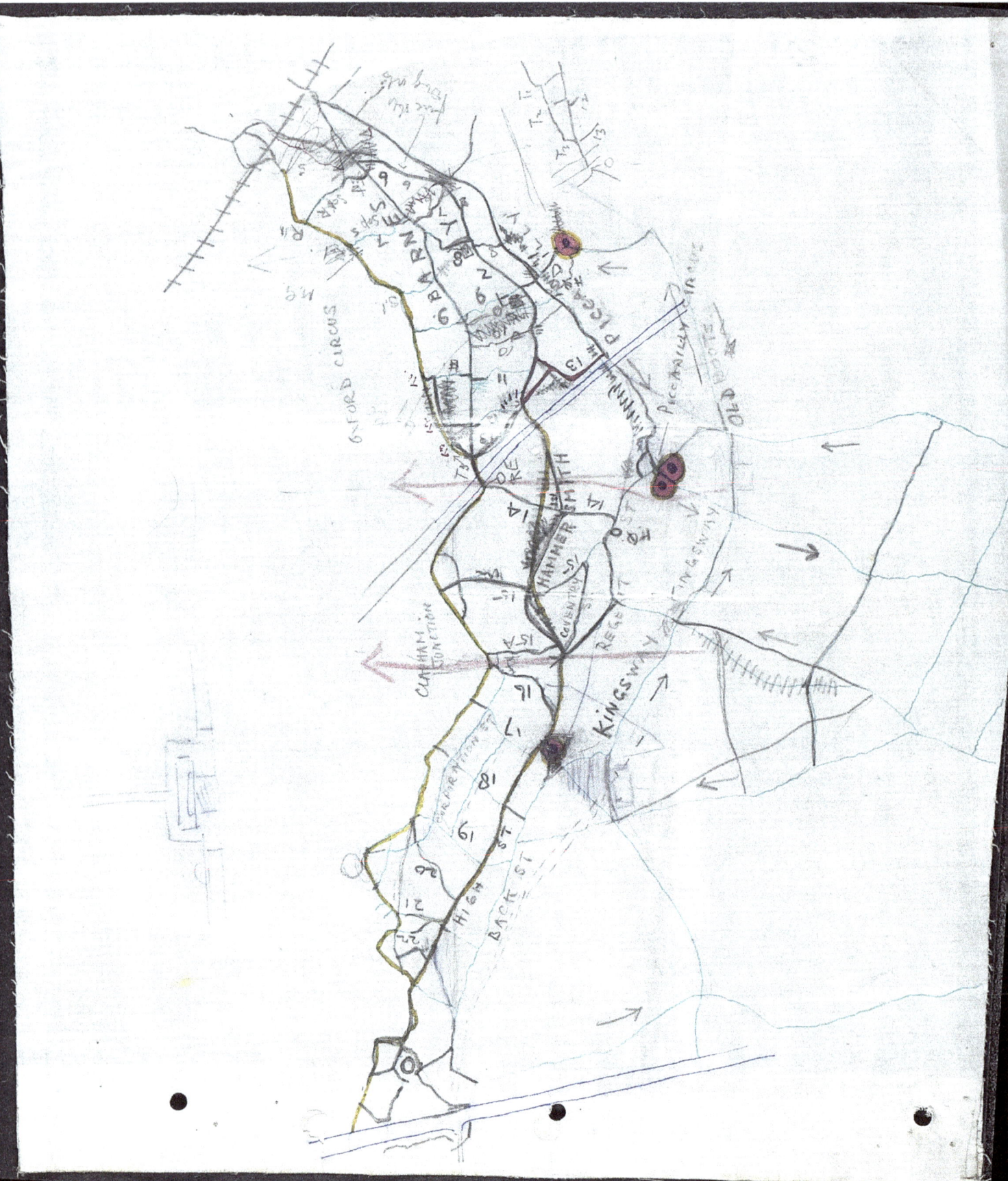

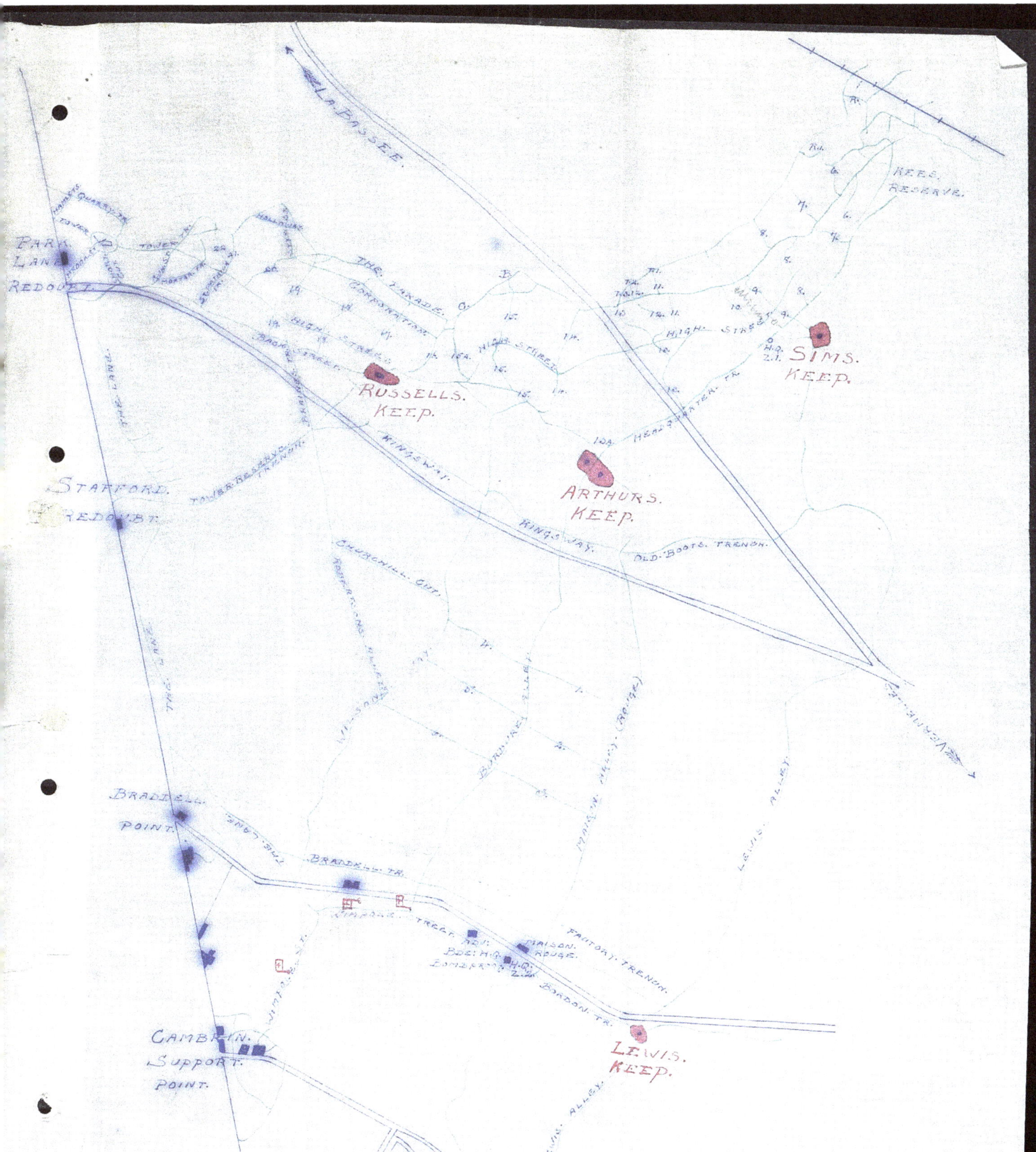
LA BASSEE
PARK LANE REDOUBT
STAFFORD REDOUBT
BRADDELL POINT
CAMBRIN SUPPORT POINT
RUSSELLS. KEEP.
ARTHURS. KEEP.
SIMS. KEEP.
LEWIS. KEEP.
KEES. RESERVE.
THE PARADE
CORPORATION
HIGH STREET
BACK STREET
KINGSWAY
TOWER RESERVE TRENCH
OLD BOOTS TRENCH
HEADQUARTER TR.
CHURCHILL CUT
BRADDELL TR.
FACTORY TRENCH
MAISON ROUGE
BDE: H.Q.
BORDON TR.
LEWIS ALLEY
VERMELLES

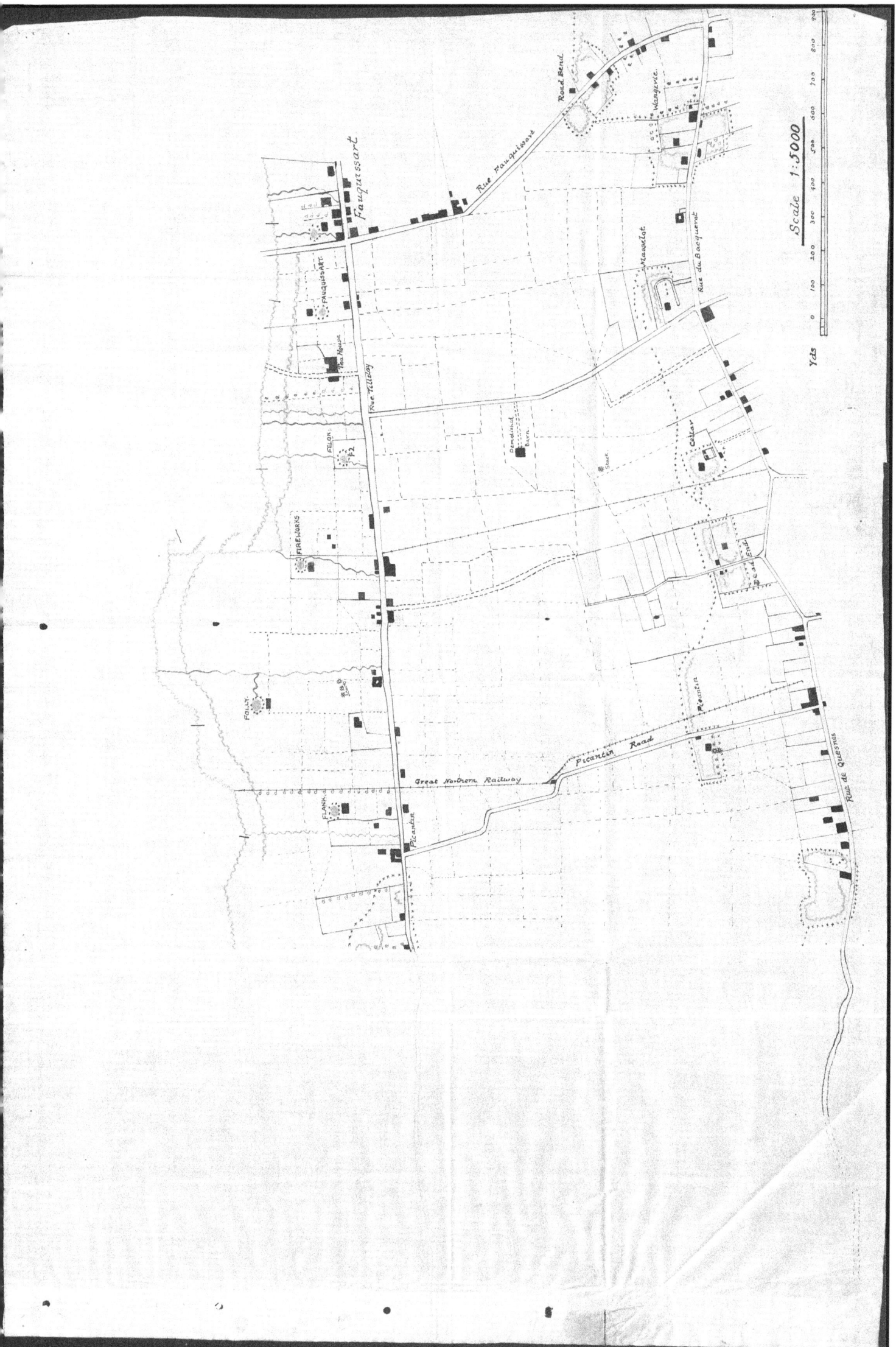

PANORAMA SKETCH OF ENEMY'S LINES IN FRONT OF TRENCHES 58 & 59.

← Escobecques Spire 1480°

← Le Quesnes Farm 1180°

← Low Wire Trips in rear Enemy's 1st Line 15'x

→ Enemy's Communicating Trench.

← La Houssoie Farm 1130°

← Low Wire Entanglement immediately in rear of Enemy's 1st Line

← Long Low Shed with Loopholes facing our lines & apart for use when standing, with Low Wire Entanglement 30' in front   1000' 350'

→ Lavender Coloured Crops

← Single Line to Wavrin

← Chevaux de Frise Entanglement Protecting 2nd Line 1180°

← La Houssoie Station 1250°

← La Houssoie Goods Shed 1175'

← Emmeterres Spire 1150°

Headquarters,

19th INFANTRY BRIGADE.

(2nd Division)

O C T O B E R

1 9 1 5

Brigade Operation Orders
Nos. 53 to 59 inc.
Daily Reports.

WAR DIARY or INTELLIGENCE SUMMARY.

(Erase heading not required.)

Instructions regarding War Diaries and Intelligence Summaries are contained in F. S. Regs., Part II. and the Staff Manual respectively. Title pages will be prepared in manuscript.

Army Form

Hour, Date, Place	Summary of Events and Information	Remarks and references to Appendices
SAILLY LABOURSE	A quiet day. 19th Infantry Brigade sent notes to be relieved by	Casualties
		Killed. Officers O.R.
		Wounded. — —
4th September 1915	The 26th and 23rd Bde (7th Div.) Relief commenced at 3 p.m.	Total 2 O.R.
	Bayond relieved 1st R.B. and 2nd R.B. as usual.	
	3rd Royal Welsh Fusiliers and 1 Bn Argyll in SAILLY LABOURSE	
	2nd Argyll & Sutherland Highlanders and 5th Scottish Rifles in FOSSE	
	No 9 BETHUNE billets and in Carissoires were in bey-ends	
	E of FOSSE No 9. Bde. H.Q. in SAILLY LABOURSE.	
6th September		Wounded 4. O.R.
SAILLY-LABOURSE	Sr. Relief at SAILLY-LABOURSE in present Possn.	
	Brigade received orders to march to BETHUNE	
6th October 3rd		
BETHUNE	II Bavord Bde. moved to BETHUNE as Corps Reserve.	Wounded 3 O.R.

Army Form C. 2118.

WAR DIARY
or
INTELLIGENCE SUMMARY
(Erase heading not required.)

Instructions regarding War Diaries and Intelligence Summaries are contained in F. S. Regs., Part II. and the Staff Manual respectively. Title pages will be prepared in manuscript.

Hour, Date, Place	Summary of Events and Information	Remarks and References to Appendices
Oct 4th BETHUNE	In Billets. Programme of training drawn up. 2nd R.W.F. at ANNEZIN. Divisions at CEMETRY near BETHUNE. 1/Installion at VENDIN, 2&3/H. BETHUNE. 5. S. R. BETHUNE.	Casualties
October 5th BETHUNE	In Billets Training	✱
October 6th BETHUNE	In Billets Training	
October 7th BETHUNE	In Billets Training	
October 8th BETHUNE	In Billets Training	

Army Form C. 2118.

WAR DIARY
or
INTELLIGENCE SUMMARY.
(Erase heading not required.)

Instructions regarding War Diaries and Intelligence Summaries are contained in F. S. Regs., Part II. and the Staff Manual respectively. Title pages will be prepared in manuscript.

Hour, Date, Place	Summary of Events and Information	Remarks and references to Appendices
October 9th BETHUNE	In Billets Training.	
October 10th BETHUNE	In Billets. Orders received for two battalions (2RWF & 1 Middlesex) to move to BEUVRY to support 5th Bde. in the trenches. Order was however cancelled at 2.30 pm.	
Operation order No 15 (subsequently cancelled) attached.		
Oct 11th BETHUNE	In Billets Training.	
Oct 12th BETHUNE	In Billets Training.	
Oct 13th BETHUNE	Operation orders received. Attack by 11th Corps to begin at 2 pm. 2nd Division (less 5th & 6th Bde) to be prepared to move at 3 hours notice if required.	
Oct 14th BETHUNE	Order issued to move at 2 hours notice cancelled. Brigades continued training in respective areas.	

Army Form C. 2118.

WAR DIARY
or
INTELLIGENCE SUMMARY.
(Erase heading not required.)

Instructions regarding War Diaries and Intelligence Summaries are contained in F.S. Regs., Part II. and the Staff Manual respectively. Title pages will be prepared in manuscript.

Hour, Date, Place	Summary of Events and Information	Remarks and references to Appendices
October 15th BETHUNE	Gn. Lillle, General Gough came round to see C.T.O's. Training was carried on.	Casualties. O.R. 1 3
October 16th CAMBRIN	The 13th Inf. Bde. relieved the 20th Inf. Bde. (7th Div.) The Middlesex relieved the 2nd Gordons and half the 9th Devons from R1 - point D inclusive. The 2nd A.'s S. Highlanders relieved the 2nd Border Regiment and half the 9th Devons from point D exclusive to the LA BASSEE - BETHUNE road inclusive. The 22nd Brigade was on our left and the 5th Bde. on our right. Communications were in support at ANNEQUIN. 5th Scott'sh Rifles were billetted at BEUVRY and the 2 R.W.F. were billetted in BETHUNE. The relief was completed without incident.	killed wounded
H.Q. CHEMISTS SHOP		
(Appendices only) Nos 5 & 6 attached		

WAR DIARY
or
INTELLIGENCE SUMMARY.
(Erase heading not required.)

Army Form C. 2118.

Hour, Date, Place	Summary of Events and Information	Remarks and references to Appendices
		OR.
Oct. 17th CAMBRIN	Enemy narrow and jumpy. Persistent sniping throughout the night. Enemy did not shell all day. Work were carried on. (Reof Report attached).	Wounded — 4
Oct. 18th	Quiet in the Brigade front	{ Killed — 1 Wounded — 2
Oct. 19th	ditto	
Oct. 20th	ditto	Wounded — 6.
Oct. 21st	This morning the 1/Middlesex were relieved by the 2.R.W.F. from R1 – Bayonne 15 and the connections were relieved by the 2nd Argyll and Sutherland Highlanders on the left to the BETHUNE – LA BASSEE road. The morning we were relieved by the 6th Infantry Brigade of the trenches between GUNN STREET and the main road. The enemy was quiet but our snipers were active and succeeded in shooting some German gunners	Killed — 1 Wounded — 1
Opening Cond. A. 57 attached.		

Army Form C. 2118.

WAR DIARY
or
INTELLIGENCE SUMMARY.
(Erase heading not required.)

Instructions regarding War Diaries and Intelligence Summaries are contained in F. S. Regs., Part II. and the Staff Manual respectively. Title pages will be prepared in manuscript.

Hour, Date, Place	Summary of Events and Information	Remarks and references to Appendices
CAMBRIN October 22nd	There was a fine attack with hand rifles, also machine guns, rifle grenades and West Bomb throwers. In an operation with the old battery fire was opened at 11pm for two minutes	Casualties S/S. O.R. { killed — 1 { wounded — 1 wounded 1 2
" October 23rd	There was another fine attack at 4pm tonight but owing to the fog the result could not be observed. The trenches are steadily being improved	wounded — 1
" October 24th Operation Order No 58 attached.	The enemy shelled more than usual this afternoon, probably owing to our bursts of fire on the late previous nights.	killed — 1 wounded — 1
" October 25th	The 3rd Royal West Surreys were relieved this afternoon by the 1st Middlesex without incident. The inner companies were relieved by the 2nd Argyll and Sutherland Highlanders. The enemy was exceptionally quiet today.	
" October 26th Operation Order No 59 attached.	Nothing of interest took place today. Work is being done on the trenches	wounded — 1.

Army Form C. 2118.

WAR DIARY
INTELLIGENCE SUMMARY.
(Erase heading not required.)

Instructions regarding War Diaries and Intelligence Summaries are contained in F.S. Regs., Part II. and the Staff Manual respectively. Title pages will be prepared in manuscript.

Hour, Date, Place	Summary of Events and Information	Remarks and references to Appendices
27th October CAMBRIN	The enemy is still comparatively quiet, but some machine guns have been located by observation of flashes	Casualties: Off — OR 3 Wounded
28th October CAMBRIN	The enemy shells the LA BASSEE road with light howitzers. There were two casualties	1. Wounded
29th October CAMBRIN	The Brigade was relieved by the 5th Infantry Bde today and moved back to Nillik in GONNEHEM	1 3 Wounded
30th October 31st 1st November 2nd 3rd 4th 5th GONNEHEM	In Nillik training	Operation Order No 60 attached

E. Wilson Capt
for Lt Col Bn kiefsmed
Commanding 5 to Brigade

BRIGADE OPERATION ORDERS NOS.

53
54
55
56
57
58
59

Copy No......1....

19th Brigade Operation Order No. 53

1st October, 1915.

Reference BETHUNE combined sheet, 1/40,000
and trench Map 36 c N.W. Sheet 1.

1. The Brigade will be relieved today by 20th and 22nd Infantry Brigades of 7th Division and will be in Divisional Reserve.
   The 5th and 6th Infantry Brigades are today taking over that portion of the front line between G.18.b.4.4. and G.5.c.8.5.

2. The relief will take place as below:- details of which have already been telegraphed out to battalions.

22nd Infantry Brigade

Unit.	Relieved by.	Billets after relief.
1st Middlesex R.	1st R.Welch Fus.	SAILLY LA BOURSE.
5th Scottish Rifles.	2nd Queens.	ANNEQUIN (F.29.d.)
2nd R.Welsh Fus.	(2nd Warwicks & (1st South Staffords)	SAILLY LA BOURSE.

20th Infantry Brigade.

2nd A. & S.Hrs.	(9th Devon Regt. (2nd Gordon Highrs. (6th Gordon Highrs.	Dugouts in LANCASHIRE TRENCH. North of VERMELLES (G.2.b.)

1st Cameronians will move from ANNEQUIN into the NOYELLES line of dug outs about G.1.b.

3. Officer Commanding 95 mm Trench Mortar Battery will hand over his 6 remaining mortars to O.C. 9th Devonshire Regiment.
   The personnel will be billetted in SAILLY LA BOURSE
   Officer Commanding section No. 6 Trench Mortar Battery will bring out his Mortars and go into billets at SAILLY LA BOURSE.

4. The usual trench stores will be handed over.

5. Transports will be on BEUVRY - SAILLY LA BOURSE Road.

6. On completion of relief Brigade Headquarters will be at SAILLY LA BOURSE.

Major,
Brigade Major, 19th Infantry Brigade.

Issued at 4 pm.

Copy. No.	1 Office.	Copy No.	7 20th Infantry Bde.
"	2 2nd R.Welsh Fus.	"	8. 22nd Inf. Bde.
"	3 1st Cameronians.	"	9 Adv. 2nd Division.
"	4 1st Middlesex R.	"	10 Bde. Transport Officer.
"	5 2nd A. & S. Hrs.		
"	6 5th Scottish Rifles.	"	11 Spare.

Copy.No...... 12

19th Infantry Brigade Operation Order No.54.

Reference 1/40,000 Bethune Combined Sheet.   3rd October, 1915.

1. The 2ndv Division will be relieved by the Guards Division today and will be withdrawn into Corps Reserve. It will be billetted in the area BETHUNE - BEUVRY.

2. The Brigade will move as per attached March Table.

3. Section No. 6 Trench Mortar Battery and the 95 mm Trench Mortar Battery will move to billets in BETHUNE with Brigade Headquarters at a time to be notified later.

4. Arrangements are being made for the transport in lorries of those parties of 5th Scottish Rifles and 2nd Argyll & Sutherland Highlanders who are detailed as carrying parties for 7th Division.

5. Transport (Boss 1st Line alrrady with units) will move independently under battalion arrangements. It must be clear of Road Junction F.20.a.9.5. by 12 noon.

6. Brigade Headquarters will be established in Bethune Exact locality will be notified later.

                                     Major,
                    Brigade Major, 19th Inf. Brigade.

Issued at 1-20 am.
  Copy No. 1 2/R.Welsh Fus.   Copy No. 7. Bde. Transport
        2. 1/Cameronians.   Officer.
        3. 1/Middlesex R.   8. Sec.No.6 T.M.
        4. 2/A. & S. Hrs.   Battery.
        5. 5th Scottish Rifles.   9. 95 mm T.M.Battery
        6. Adv. 2nd Div.   10. Office.
                                              11. Staff Captain.
                                              12. Spare.

MARCH TABLE.

To be attached to
19th Brigade Operation Order No. 54.

19th Infantry Brigade.

UNIT.	STARTING POINT.	TIME OF PASSING STARTING POINT.	ROUTE.	BILLETS.
2nd R.Welsh Fus.	Cross Roads F.27.c.8.2.	1-20 pm.)	) BEUVRY - BETHUNE	ANNEZIN (E.9).
1st Middlesex Regt.	--do--	1-30 pm.)		VERDIN - LEZ - BETHUNE (W.27)
2nd A. & S. Highrs.		1-45 pm.)		
5th Scottish Rifles.	Road Junction F.29.b.4.6.	2 pm.)	) BETHUNE - LA BASSEE) ROAD.	BETHUNE. Each locality will be notified later.
1st Cameronians.		2-15 pm.)		

3rd October, 1915.

Major,

Brigade Major, 19th Infantry Brigade.

Copy No... 10

19th Brigade March Order No. 55.

10th October, 1915.

Reference BETHUNE Combined Sheet 1/40,000
& Trench Map Sheet 36.c.N.W.1.

1. The 5th Infantry Brigade is today taking over the front line trenches from G.4.a.7.4. to the VERMELLES - AUCHY - LEZ - LA BASSEE Road exclusive.

2. The Brigade will remain in present billets except that 2nd Bn. Royal Welsh Fusiliers and 1st Bn. Middlesex Regt. will move to BEUVRY this afternoon as follows :-

   (a) 2nd R.Welsh Fus.

Starting Point.	Road Junction E.10.a.4.5.
Time of passing.	3-15 pm.
Route.	E.10.d.4.4. - E. 11.c.9.5.

The battalion will be clear of the cross roads F.14.c.4.4. by 4-30 pm.

   (b) 1st Middlesex Regt.

Starting point..	Road Junction E.4.a.4.4.
Time of passing.	3-40 pm.
Route.	RUE D'AIRE - E.11d.2.9. - E.11.c.9.5

3. Transport will move under battalion arrangements.

4. Brigade Headquarters will remain at E.4.a.8.4.

                                         Major,
Brigade Major, 19th Infantry Brigade.

Issued at 11 am.

   Copy No. 1 Office.
         2. Staff Captain.
         3. 2nd R.Welsh Fus.
         4. 1st Cameronians.
         5. 1st Middlesex Regt.
         6. 2nd A. & S. Highrs.
         7. 5th Scottish Rifles.
         8. 2nd Division.
         9. Brigade Transport Officer.
       10. War Diary.

Copy No. 12

19th Infantry Brigade Operation Order No. 56.

15th October, 1915.

Reference tracing of trenches and
BETHUNE Combined sheet, 1/40,000.

1. The Brigade will, tomorrow morning, relieve the 20th Infantry Brigade of the 7th Division in the trench line from R.1 inclusive (A.27.d.8.10.) to BETHUNE - LA BASSEE Road exclusive (A.21.b.4.3.)

2. The relief will be carried out as per attached March Table.

3. Sapping Platoons will be detached from units and assemble at Brigade Headquarters, E.4.a., at 10 am tomorrow.

4. Instructions for machine guns will be issued later through Brigade Machine Gun Officer.

5. List shewing trench stores handed over will be sent into Brigade Headquarters as soon as possible after relief is completed.

6. No. 6 Trench Mortar Battery and 2 Sections 5th Company R.E. will be attached to the Brigade. O.C., No. 6 Trench Mortar Battery and O.C. 19th Brigade Trench Mortar Battery will select positions along the front VERMELLES - LA BASSEE and BETHUNE - LA BASSEE Roads, reporting to Brigade Headquarters and to O.C. Battalions in front line concerned what their final dispositions are.

7. Disposition of Artillery supporting batteries will be notified later.

8. Further orders as to move and billets of Battalions in Brigade reserve and Transport lines will be issued later.

9. Present Brigade Headquarters will close at 12-30 pm. tomorrow and open at the CHEMIST'S SHOP (A.19.d.5.2.) at the same hour.

H. E. Browne
Major,
Brigade Major, 19th Inf. Bde.

Issued at 8 pm.
Copy No. 1 2/R.Welsh Fus.   8. Bde. Transport Officer.
        2 1st Cameronians.   9 20th Infantry Brigade.
        3 1st Middlesex R.   10 2nd Division.
        4. 2/A.& S.Hrs.   11 Office.
        5 5/Scottish Rifles.   12 War Diary.
        6 No.6 T.M.Battery.   13 Staff Captain.
        7. O.C. 19th Bde. T.M.   14 Spare.
           Battery.

To be attached to Operation Order No. 53.

RELIEF TABLE.
****

UNIT.	Frontage in the line or billets.	Unit relieved.	Rendezvous for guides.	Time.	Remarks.
Middlesex R. (R.19th Br.)	R.1 (inclusive) – Point "E" (inclusive)	2nd Gordon Highrs. Part of 9th Devon Regt.	CHEMIST'S SHOP (A.19.d.5.2.)	11-30 am.	Battalion will find 1 N.C.O. & 25 men as garrison of ARTHUR'S Keep.
1d A.& S. Hrs. (Left Br.).	Point D (exclusive) – LA BASSEE Road (exclusive)	Part of 9th Devon Regt. and 2nd Border Regt.	---do---	10-30 am.	3 Companies front line and Support including 1 N.C.O. & 25 men as Garrison of RUSSELL'S KEEP. 1 Company Battalion Reserve at MAISON ROUGE Dug-outs.

H. E. Noume
Major,
Brigade Major, 19th Infantry Brigade.

15/10/15.

Copy No. 10

19th Infantry Brigade Relief Order No. 57.

Reference trench map and
BETHUNE Sheet, 1/40,000.

20th October, 1915.

1. (a) From tomorrow inclusive the Brigade will hold the line from R.1 inclusive to GUN street inclusive.
   The 2nd Guards Brigade will be on the right and the 6th Infantry Brigade will be on the left.

   (b) Southern boundary of the Brigade area will be :-
   R.1 - HEADQUARTERS TRENCH - LEWIS ALLEY (all inclusive to 19th Infantry Brigade) - along road in A.25.d. - road junction F.30.a.4.0. - then to main road at F.29.b.0.7.

   (c) Northern boundary of Brigade area will be :-
   GUN Street - THE LANE - Bridge at A.20.c.8.5. - cross roads F.30.a.2.8. - thence in a straight line to road junction F.29.a.

   THE LANE will be used by both Brigades.

   (d) Dividing line between right and left battalions will be Boyau 15, which will be used by both.

2. (a) 5th King's Liverpool Regiment of 6th Infantry Brigade will take over trenches from GUN STREET (exclusive) to LA BASSEE ROAD from 1st Cameronians tomorrow. Relief commences about 10 am.

   (b) 2nd Royal Welsh Fusiliers will take over SIMS KEEP and LEWIS KEEP from 5th Infantry Brigade at 2 pm tomorrow. Garrisons - 1 platoon for each keep.

3. Brigade reserve battalions will be billetted as follows:-
   One along LA BASSEE ROAD between A.20.c. & F.29.b.(One
   One at BEUVRY.   Company at BEUVRY)
   One at BETHUNE (RUE D'AIRE).

4. Artillery support will be given by two batteries 41st Brigade R.F.A. and two batteries 36th Brigade R.F.A. under O.C., 41st Brigade R.F.A.
   Further details will be given later.

H. E. Braine
Major,
Brigade Major, 19th Infantry Brigade.

Issued at 8 pm.

Copy No.1 2nd R.Welsh Fus.	Copy No.6. 2nd Division.
2 1st Cameronians.	7 6th Infantry Bde.
3 1st Middlesex R.	8 5th Infantry Bde.
4 2/A. & S. Hrs.	9 Office.
5 5th Scottish Rifles.	10 Diary.
11. Staff Captain.	

Copy No........... 11

19th Infantry Brigade Relief Orders No. 58

24th October, 1915.

1. The following reliefs will be carried out tomorrow :-

   (a). 1st Middlesex Regt: - BETHUNE to Subsection Z.1.
   2nd A. & S.Hdrs: - CAMBRIN-ANNEQUIN to Subsection Z.2.

   (b). 2nd Royal Welsh Fusiliers: Sub-Section Z.1 to CAMBRIN - ANNEQUIN.

   1st Cameronians: Sub-section Z.2 to BETHUNE (Rue D'AIRE)

2. (a) Relief of sub-section Z.1. to commence at 3 pm from CAMBRIN Church, where guides will be met.

   (b) Relief of sub-section Z.2. to commence at 11am from Brigade Headquarters where guides will be met.

3. List showing S.A.A., grenades and trench stores handed over will be given to relieving units, copies being sent to Brigade Headquarters.

4. Transport will move under battalion arrangements as follows:-

   1st Cameronians: BEUVRY to BETHUNE.

   1st Middlesex Regt: BETHUNE to BEUVRY.

H E Prewis
— Major,

Brigade Major, 19th Infantry Brigade.

Issued at 2 pm.

Copy. No. 1 2nd R.Welsh Fus.
2. 1st Cameronians.
3 1st Middlesex Regt.
4 2nd A. & S. Hrs.
5 5th Scottish Rifles.
6 6th Inf. Brigade.

Copy No. 7. 3rd Guards Brigade.
8. 2nd Division.
9. Brigade Transport Officer
10. Staff Captain.
11. War Diary.
12. File.

19th Infantry Brigade Operations Order No. 59

Reference 1/40,000 BETHUNE SHEET.

28th October, 1915.

1. The Brigade will be relieved by the 5th Infantry Brigade on Friday, 29th October, as per Relief and March Table attached.

2. The relief of machine guns will commence at 10 am under arrangements made between Brigade Machine Gun Officers. On relief sections will rejoin their units in their new billets

3. 5th Brigade Trench Mortar Battery (95 mm) and 15th Trench Mortar Battery will be at Brigade Headquarters at 12 noon where guides will be provided by Officer Commanding 19th Brigade Trench Mortar Battery and 6th Trench Mortar Battery, respectively.

   6th Trench Mortar Battery will remain in the trenches and be attached to 5th Infantry Brigade.

   Four Mortars of 19th Brigade Trench Mortar Battery will be brought out, and four mortars handed over to 5th Infantry Brigade.

4. Transport will move under battalion arrangements.

5. All S.A.Ammunition, grenades and trench stores will be handed over, except Vermorel sprayers and sniperscopes, all of which must be brought out.

   Lists of stores will be given to relieving units, copies being sent to Brigade Headquarters.

6. The two officers and 100 other ranks attached to 180th Tunnelling Company, R.E. will be relieved by a similar party from 5th Infantry Brigade.
   Time of relief will be notified later.

7. Commanding Officers and Company Officers of 2nd Highland Light Infantry and 1st Queen's Regiment, Officer Commanding 15th Trench Mortar Battery and 5th Brigade Trench Mortar Battery will visit trenches at 10 am on 29th October. Guides will be furnished by Brigade Headquarters.

8. Brigade Headquarters, on completion of relief, will be established in GORRE (V.18.a.)

Major,
Brigade Major, 19th Infantry Bde.

Issued at 7-30 pm.

Copy. No.		Copy No.	
1.	Office.	9.	6th T.M.Battery.
2.	War Diary.		
3.	Staff Captain.	10.	19th Bde. T.M.Btty.
4.	2nd R.Welsh Fus.	11.	180th Tunnelling Coy. R.E.
5.	1st Cameronians.		
6.	1st Middlesex R.	12.	Bde. Transport Officer
7.	2nd A.& S.Hrs.	13.	2nd Division.
8.	5th Scottish Rif.	14.	5th Infantry Brigade.
		15.	6th Infantry Brigade
		16.	"Z" Group, R.F.A.

To be attached to 19th Infantry Brigade Relief and March Table.
Operation Order No. 59.

Unit.	Relieved by.	Time of Commencement of relief.	Rendezvous for guides.	Billets.	Remarks.
2nd A. & S. Highrs. (Sub-Section Z.2)	1st Queens. (R.West Surrey R.)	11 am.	Brigade Headquarters.	GONNEHEM (V.18) E of LA CLARENCE R	
1st Middlesex R. (Sub-section Z.1.)	2nd Highland Light Infantry.	1 pm.	CAMBRIN CHURCH.	GONNEHEM (V.18) W of LA CLARENCE R	2nd Highland L.I. will have dinners at CAMBRIN from 12 to 1 pm. Route to GONNEHEM via CHOQUES.
2nd R.Welsh Fus.	2nd Oxford & Bucks. L.I.	-	-	BUSNETTES.	2nd R.Welsh Fus. to be clear of present billets at 10 am.
5th Scottish Rifles.	7th L'Pool R.	-	-	VENDIN - LEZ - BETHUNE.	5th Scottish Rifles to be clear of present billets at 1-30 pm.
Brigade Sapping Platoons.	Details.	-	-	SESSE LA VALLEE.	Sapping Platoon to be clear of present billets at 9 am.
1st Cameronians.	-	-	-	RUE D'AIRE BETHUNE.	Remain in present billets.

26/10/15.

Major,
Brigade Major, 19th Infantry Brigade.

DAILY REPORTS.

War diary

Daily Report up to 12 noon 17th October, 191[illegible].
[illegible] Infantry Brigade.

OPERATIONS.

Yesterday morning the [illegible] Infantry Brigade relieved the [illegible] Infantry Brigade (7th Division) in the line from [illegible] - [illegible] - [illegible] road exclusive. The [illegible] Middlesex Regiment relieved the 2nd Gordon Hdrs. and half the 8th Devons and the [illegible] Hdrs. relieved the 2nd Border Regiment and half the 8th Devons.
The attitude of the enemy has been quiet though at times very jumpy. He appears to be nervous and was continually firing in short bursts of both rifle and machine gun fire during the night.

[illegible] Right Battalion.
The enemy have been very quiet opposite this battalion. He opened bursts of rifle fire on collecting parties for the dead, which hampered them. Four bodies were brought in with difficulty.
At [illegible] four trench mortar bombs fell [illegible] behind our lines at [illegible]. No damage was done. Enemy's working parties at point [illegible] and opposite "[illegible]" [illegible] were dispersed by rifle and maxim gun fire. Sniping was persistent throughout the night, but ceased at daylight. There is a fixed rifle which fires down the [illegible] - LA [illegible] road at intervals during the night. No enemy maxim guns opened fire and there was no retaliation of hostile artillery fire on the trenches held by this battalion.
Left Battalion.
Vigorous sniping was kept up by our men during the night in order to prevent the enemy working on his front line. About [illegible] yesterday afternoon the enemy were active with trench mortars and rifle grenades. Most of these exploded between [illegible]. Our artillery promptly retaliated, whereupon the enemy ceased firing.

WORK.

Owing to the Brigade relieving the [illegible] Infantry Brigade not much work other than clearing up could be done. Fire trenches, communication trenches and fire steps cleaned up and repaired. Wiring was carried out all along the line. Much time was spent packing up grenades, bombs and rifle ammunition. [illegible] are entirely strange to trench life, and so instruction had to be given to them as to how to carry out various work etc.
It is intended to strengthen both front and rear lines, to thicken the parapet in places and to establish a system of firing steps almost continuous along the front line. Wiring parties will be at work nightly and communications and dug-outs will be improved. New dug-outs will be continued.

INTELLIGENCE.

Lights.
About [illegible] p.m. and [illegible] a.m. during the bombardment [illegible] great [illegible] and red flares were sent up by the enemy.
Wire.
The enemy seems to have strengthened his wire considerably since the Brigade last held this line. [illegible] the wire opposite [illegible] and the [illegible].
He was seen working on his wire last night but was stopped at once by machine gun fire.
Patrols.
The Right Battalion sent out patrols but owing to the intense darkness and thick mist, nothing could be done. Patrols will go out every night to ascertain the amount of work the enemy is doing, and further information about the wire will be forwarded as information is gained. No machine gun emplacements have been located.

MISCELLANEOUS.

[illegible] Trench Mortar Battery had no opportunity of firing his guns. No hostile movement [illegible] observed.

Sheet 2.

DISPOSITION OF THE BRIGADE BY 9-0 A.M. TOMORROW WILL BE AS FOLLOWS :-

In the Trenches
        Right   1st Bn: Middlesex Regiment.
        Left   2nd Bn: Argyll & Sutherland Highlanders.
Forward supporting Battalion, 1st Bn: The Cameronians.
Rear supporting Battalion,   5th Scottish Rifles.
Reserve,   2nd Bn: Royal Welch Fusiliers.

                                          Brigadier General,
17th October, 1915. Commanding 19th Infantry Brigade......

War Diary

Daily Report up to [...] 29th October 191[...]
1 th Infantry Brigade.

Right Batn:- The enemy have become very quiet opposite this front, and have quieted down a great deal since yesterday. Sniping was persistent at times, but inflicted unusual and uncommon.

[Centre] Battalion:- The enemy has been quiet opposite this battalion. [...] working party was located working near point 87 and was dispersed by our machine gun fire at [...] p.m. Patrols have been working, and [...] our night [...] patrols were sent out throughout the night and reported two hostile sentries to be posted at intervals of [...] along.
Their wire is strong and in fair condition.
The enemy sent over two small [...] on the left of the battalion, but prompt retaliation from our trench mortars stopped any further attempts.

Left Battalion:- The enemy opposite the right company were very active during the night, but were silenced by retaliation from our trench mortars. Rifle grenades were [...] for two hours to which the enemy failed to reply. The enemy on the left of the battalion were however exceptionally quiet. [...] of the enemy's wire were believed to have been accounted for yesterday.

The work of rebuilding of parapets and fire steps was carried out along the front line. Collection of [...] and refuse was done, which occupied considerable time. [...] latrines have been dug.
Wire has been strengthened and improved along the whole front. Chevaux de frises and wire rolls have been put out. [...] trench has been cleared of [...] and made passable. [...] dugouts have been commenced. [...] which was very badly knocked about on the [...] has been rivetted and improved. [...] loop holes have been put in. It is intended to carry out the programme of work sent in to the Division in yesterday's daily report.

Artillery:- No hostile our artillery units have been located, and no hostile patrols have been seen.
The 9[...] guns (1 th Battery) between [...] Street [...] Avenue, 3 only of which suffer in pattern, and no bombs appeared to cause a good deal of damage to the enemy's [...]
dugouts etc., are also to be dug out [...]

Disposition of Battalions 1th Infantry Brigade:-
In the trenches :- on the right [...] 1st Batn [...]
on the left [...] [...] Batn [...]
In support :- [...] 1st [...]
[...] [...] [...] Battalion [...]
Reserve:- [...] [...] [...]

[...] Bishop, Lt.
1th [...] Brigade, B.M. [...] [...] 1st Infantry Brigade.

Daily Report up to 12 noon 19th October, 1915.
19th Infantry Brigade.

OPERATIONS.. The enemy have been much quieter during the past 24 hours. Hardly any sniping by day, though it is fairly persistent at night, probably owing to our burying parties and patrols which are out most of the night.
The enemy has shelled our trenches but has done no damage. He shelled a working party working on the line of trenches East of BRADNELL Trench. He also shelled the artillery observation post at the junction of WILSONS WAY and the LANE.

Z.8.
Right battalion. At 9-30 pm, 11-45 pm and 3 am a hostile working party working on the parapet and wire was located by point 97, which was dispersed by machine gun fire. The enemy work at this point nightly and snipers will be posted opposite this point in future to disperse the enemy directly he starts working. An enemy's patrol was located and fire on but without effect. The enemy fired on our collecting parties for dead from MINE POINT with a machine gun. This gun could not be exactly located. The artillery retaliated effectively stopping the enemy's fire.
At 7 am this morning the enemy fired rifle grenades and trench mortars at the trenches West of Point D. The artillery again silenced the enemy.
A hostile machine gun fired at our working parties at 3am this morning. The gun, as far as possible, was located in the German trench between the crater D and T sap.
It was very misty this morning and it was very difficult to locate the gun.
Five dead bodies were buried last night.

Left Battalion. The enemy were very active with trench mortar bombs and rifle grenades during the night, but the bombers and trench mortars retaliated each time. The damage done could not be ascertained but it sufficed to silence the enemy.
Vigorous sniping was kept up by us throughout the night in order to stop the enemy's working parties from working on their parapets and wire.
This morning, the enemy between 11 and 1 pm put over about 40 light shells mostly time shrapnel. Most of these burst by the LANE, KINGSWAY, SUNKEN ALLEY and all along the MAISON ROUGE line of dug outs. A few casualties were caused.
The enemy is reported to be mining underneath the left company of this battalion. This fact has been reported to the R.E. and
~~the enemy~~

WORK.. Right Battalion. Parapets have been repaired and strengthened all along the front line. The work of straightening out the communication from ARTHURS KEEP commenced.
Five bodies were buried out in front.
25 rifles were brought in. The wire was repaired all along the front. General clearing up.

Left Battalion. No. 18 Soyau and 19 was widened to allow stretchers to pass down. Parapets in JILL STREET and JACK STREET thickened. Fire steps improved. Some wiring was done and "Chevaux de Frise" put out.

INTELLIGENCE. Lights.
Many red and green flares were sent up during the night. Whenever a red flare went up, the enemy opened short bursts of rifle fire. A searchlight, mounted evidently on a car played on the Right battalion at intervals during the night.
Uniforms.

Uniforms.
This morning four Germans (JAEGERS) were seen including an officer. They were engaged in sniping which they did by firing over the parapet. As the sniper fired another with glasses directed fire for him. They appeared to think themsleves under cover of a traverse but could be clearly seen Their uniforms were very new and were of lightish grey green. they wore small round hats (Peltzmutzer) with a dark green or black band. The disc in front of their caps was black or dark green with white outside. The officer could be distinguished from the others as he had a shiney peak to his cap. These men were fired on. Further observation this morning shew that at intervals along the German parapet groups of loopholes in pairs, close together. They appear to be in a traverse, well protected, well masked, with overhead cover. These observations were seen through a Ross magnifying telescope. Nothing could, however, be seen with the naked eye, telescopic rifle, or periscope.

Miscellaneous.
During the night, opposite the left battalion, the enemy appeared to fire from loopholes by groups of twos and threes, as though sentries were posted close together.
A German was seen crawling about last night in front of the left battalion's wire. He was fired upon, result was unknown.

Disposition of the Brigade by 9 am tomorrow.

In trenches right.	1st Middlesex Regt.
In trenches left.	2nd A. & S. Highrs.
In forward support.	1st Cameronians.
In rear support.	5th Scottish Rifles.
In reserve.	2nd R.Welsh Fusiliers.

19/10/15.

Brig-General,

Commanding 19th Infantry Brigade..

Daily Report up to 12 noon 20th October, 1915.
19th Infantry Brigade.

OPERATIONS.

Enemy have been very quiet. There has been little sniping except at dawn and dusk, when it is fairly persistent daily.

Z.2. Right Battalion. The enemy have been abnormally quiet opposite this battalion, while he made frequent use of flares at dawn. In reply to our trench mortars, rifle grenades and bombs were fired at these trenches at point D. but very effective retaliation on MINE POINT by our artillery suffered to silence him. The enemy has not fired his heavy trench mortar bombs since the Brigade have been in line the 16th October, which looks as if he has removed them. At 7-50 p.m. and 8-36 p.m. hostile working parties near the railway line opposite the right front of this battalion were dispersed by machine gun fire. A hostile machine gun was located a few yards to the West of point 97.
Battalion scouts were out all night. No hostile patrols were met, and they reported that the enemy were quiet in their trenches. During the heavy gun fire last night the enemy sent up many flares of all colours, his sniping was also very heavy.

Left Battalion. Enemy quiet but showed moderate activity during the night. Our bombers were active. A few light shrapnel were fired at MAISON ROUGE dug-outs.

WORK.

Right Battalion. Continuation of repairs of parapets in all the Companies front and of the wire entanglements. Straightening out the communications to ARTHURS KEEP. Collection of tins and refuse from parapets. Nine dead bodies were buried in front, and a quantity of rifles and equipment was brought in. Sap to Crater D. improved and overhead cover provided. Latrines completed in this section. Sniping loopholes were put in the front parapet.
Left Battalion. Wiring in fron continued. Parapet and firing points improved in HIGH STREET and BACK STREET. Widening the LANE and TOWER RESERVE Trench.

Re work. Conversion of KINGSWAY into a fire trench commenced. Deepening new trench joining TOWER RESERVE TRENCH and KINGSWAY. Dug-outs in left battalion near left company H.Q., commenced. Notice boards begun.

INTELLIGENCE.   Nil.

Disposition of Brigade.
In trenches Right   2nd Royal Welch Fus:
In trenches Left   1st Cameronians.
ANNEQUIN   2nd A. & S. Hdrs:
BEUVRY   6th Scottish Rifles.
BETHUNE   1st Middlesex Regt:

Brigadier General,
20th October, 1915.   Commanding 19th Infantry Brigade.....

Daily Report up to 12 noon 21st October, 1915.
19th Infantry Brigade.

OPERATIONS. There is little to report. The enemy has been fairly quiet; but was very jovial last night opposite our left. He seems to submit to our trench mortars and grenades, and hardly ever retaliate.
The 1st Middlesex Regt: were relieved by the 2nd Royal Welch Fusiliers from R.1. - BOYAU 15 and the 1st Bn: Cameronians relieved the 2nd Argyll & Sutherland Highlanders on the left, to the BETHUNE - LA BASSEE road. This morning we were relieved by the 6th Infantry Brigade of the trenches between GUN STREET and the main road.
Z.2. Right Battalion. There has been no shelling on this front nor have the enemy sent over any trench mortar bombs. It has been very quiet. The enemy's snipers were not active. On the other hand our snipers were very active and succeeded in killing a German.
Left Battalion. The enemy have been very quiet opposite the left battalion. The enemy fired a few rifle grenades and at midnight a few trench mortars which did no harm. His snipers were very active opposite this battalion and kept up a "perfect battle" throughout the night.
The Germans have become rather bold, and showed themselves up to their hips over the parapet last night at dusk. Our snipers engaged them and shot one of them. Since then they have not reappeared.

WORK. Right Battalion.
The parapet along this front has been thickened. Loopholes were put in. Wiring was done all along the front. Fire steps have been repaired and are now almost ready for the wooden platforms. Some rivitting was done and traverses were stregthened. A new system of latrines is being organised. Some new ones were dug.
Left Battalion.
Some wiring was done. Traverses were rivetted. Most of the labour was taken in filling 1,800 sandbags for use.

Re work. (a). Work on the new second line continued with two parties totaling 320 men.
(b). Continued work at ESSARS with 2 sections.
(c). 24 notice boards were made and painted.
(d). Inspected R.A. observation posts with G.O.C., R.A., 1st Corps. There is a good deal of work required.

INTELLIGENCE. Lights.
Several red and green lights were sent up on the right opposite HOHENZOLLERN.
Uniforms.
A German was seen on the extreem right of the 2nd Royal Welch Fus: wearing a grey green uniform and a peakless gray cap with a dirty white band. He was shot when showing head and shoulders over the parapet.
Working Parties.
A hostile working party was seen at point A.28.a.5.8.. The supporting Battery was informed and dispersed them.
Another party was heard North of point 88 at 9-45 p.m. last night. They were dispersed by machine gun fire.

MISCALENEOUS. Two or three times during the night the enemy shouted and called across to the Cameronians. No answer was given.

Sheet 2.

PATROLS. An Officer's patrol from the right Battalion went out at 9-0 p.m last night. The object of the patrol was (a) to reconnoitre the ground towards the enemy's trench,(b) to find a sap head or shelter from which the enemy had been sending flares,(c) to encounter an enemy's patrol,and(d) to bring in identity discs and equipment from the dead out in front.
The patrol went out as shown in the attached sketch. 50 yards out a faint trail was struck leading towards the enemy's trenches. A hundred yards from the starting point the trail forked as shown in sketch. On the North side where a shell hole and a pit. Both of these had been used by the enemy and were dry. The Northern branch of the trail went out in a N.N.W. direction and apparently had been well used, this was not followed up. On going forward on the main trail the patrol came under fire from point A. The trail up to this point was in a slight fold of the ground, this deepened and was more worn towards point B. At this point there was a pit similar to the former one, and in it was found the body of a man of the Middlesex Rigiment and the legs of another man. The pit was dry and had been used. The trail then turned slightly North and 25 yards on (point C in sketch) was the parapet of the enemy's sap. There was no wire in front. The patrol could also see a line of parapet to the right. (Point D.) This was further back. The total distance from the our parapet to point C. was about 175 yards. No enemy patrols were met with.
The patrol were successful in bringing in 2 rifles and bayonets, 2 identity discs, 180 rounds of ammunition, 2 sets of web equipment, 1 pair of wire cutters and 1 vigilent periscope. There is further equipment to bring in.
The Patrol reported in at 10-45 p.m. There were no casualties.

Brigadier General,
21st October, 1915.   Commanding 12th Infantry Brigade....

Daily Report up to 12 noon 22nd October, 1915.
19th Infantry Brigade.

OPERATIONS.   The enemy have been very quiet. Usual heavy sniping at
dawn and dusk and between 8-0 p.m. and 9-0 p.m.

Right Battalion.   The Royal Welch Fus: Grenadiers have
located two targets in the Crater D. which will be bombed
tonight. The Trench Mortar battery attached to this section
fired 25 rounds between 9-30 a.m. and 10-30 a.m. in retaliation for enemy's rifle grenades. Hostile sniping was very
moderate except between 4-0 a.m. and 6-0 a.m. when it
increased somewhat. A hostile machine gun opened fire on
our wire parties at 7-15 p.m. It could not be located.
Six German field howitzer shells fell behind the German
trenches last night near point A.27.b.9.7. Fire ceased after
two red flares were fired from the German front line trenches
at that point. At 12-45 a.m. a German working party was
working at point A.27.b.9.3.
At 10-30 a.m. this morning an enemy's working party was seen
at A.23.c.4.2. This was reported to F.O.O. An hostile
machine gun has been located at A.21.d.4.2.

Left Battalion.   From 10-0 p.m. to 11-0 p.m. last night
there was an interchange of hand grenades. Little damage
was done. The enemy apparently saw the place from which our
grenadiers had been throwing bombs, and fired small trench
mortars at them.
The Ball Grenades gave the locality away. Owing to the accu-
racy of our snipers shooting the enemy was forced to withdraw
his periscopes several times.
Usually from 2-0 a.m. to 4-0 a.m. the enemy ceases sniping
and the snipers are relieved by machine guns which open
sudden bursts of fire along our parapet. During the morning the enemy has been sniping at our periscopes.
The centre Company claim to have hit 3 Germans in the Trench.

WORK.   Right Battalion.   Wiring parties were out. Loopholes and one
snipers post were put in. New latrines were dug and new
grenade posts and stores were made. Firing steps were improved
It is intended to continue rivetting and construction of
fire-steps as soon as wood is available.

Left Battalion.   Traverses built. Firing steps and parados
rivetted. Some wire was put out.

INTELLIGENCE. Miscellaneous.
At 3-45 a.m. this morning a searchlight played on our left
battalion. Its ray of light appeared to come from LES
BRIQUES FARM or in the neighbourhood of AUCHY.
An enemy's aeroplane engaged one of ours at 4-10 p.m. yesterday with machine gun fire. Our aeroplane made off as if hit,
and landed East of the FORET (A?EMIE) Cottages.

Patrols.
Two patrols from the right battalion went out last night
with the object of reconnoitring the ground between our
own and the German trenches and also the enemy's wire.
The night was a bad one for patroling as it was raining hard
and little could be seen or heard. One or two old disused
trenches near the Crater opposite point D. were found. The
patrol worked along these and finally stopped 50 yards from
the German line. Parties of the enemy were heard working
on their wire, and at intervals talking could be heard. The
patrol could not get near enough to the enemy's wire, owing
to the enemy working, to ascertain its strength etc., The
patrol brought in some equipment.

22nd October, 1915.   Brig-General.
                                Commanding 19th Infantry Brigade.

19th Infantry Brigade.

Daily report up to 12 noon 23rd October, 1915.

OPERATIONS. The enemy have been fairly quiet on the whole except for a few shells last night and the usual sniping and grenade throwing.

Right battalion.

In consequence of the enemy having been seen working on their wire and parapet along RAILWAY trench, between 11 pm and midnight on the night of 21/22nd October, a fire attack was arranged last night. In co-operation with the Artillery was opened at 11 pm for two minutes with previously laid rifles, 3 machine guns, rifle grenades and the West bomb throwers. The Trench Mortar Battery also co-operated, firing about 30 rounds. Fog hindered accurate observation but groans were heard for some time afterwards in front of the enemy's line.

At 3-55 pm a German hoisting the white flag near Point A.27.b.9.5. was shot by one of our observers. Later two more Germans working on their parapet at PETES POST were shot.

Enemy's sniper's loophole at HIGH POINT was destroyed by our Trench Mortars.

Left battalion.

The enemy fired a few shells at BACK STREET and HIGH STREET and again at 10 pm and again at 12 midnight.

From 12 midnight the enemy's sniping grew less and after dawn enemy was quiet on right and left, but in the centre reciprocal sniping and grenading continued.

Work.

Right battalion. Wiring parties were sent along the whole front. Communication trenches cleaned. Support trenches were repaired and improved.

Left Battalion. Some wire put out. Two traverses constructed. The latrines dug and two sniping posts built. Revetting and construction of fire steps continued.

INTELLIGENCE. Miscellaneous. Enemy fired heavily at our aeroplanes yesterday. They appeared to be firing section volleys and three or four machine guns opposite our left battalion also fired before the combined firing mentioned took place.

German work parties were reported along RAILWAY trench at 7-30 pm., 8-15 pm., 9-50 pm., and 10-15 pm last night, driving in stakes and working on parapet.

About 10 pm last night the enemy were shouting across the crater. One remark was "Don't forget your tea and sugar next time you come over".

Patrol. An officer's patrol went out from the right battalion with the object of reconnoitring a trench about 50 yards in front of the line, and just South of the VENDELLES Road, and also to find out if the enemy working parties were out. The trench in question appears to be that shewn faintly on photograph 1239. Opposite our front (along PP in sketch) it was shallow and evidently used but little, if at all, but after turning the corner by the road it was found to be well used. The patrol was fired on by a

listening post at about point C. It returned by the
route indicated on sketch, finding a very shallow
trench at F and a well used foot path at G. Working
parties were located driving in pickets and wiring.
There were no casualties.

Please return the attached sketch.

23/10/15.   Lieut-Colonel,
                                        Commanding 10th Infantry Brigade.

19th Infantry Brigade.

Daily report up to 12 noon, 24th October, 1915.

OPERATIONS.

1. Enemy very quiet, but his snipers are alert. His trench mortars were active several times, but were silenced by our artillery.

Right Battalion. In co-operation with the artillery, heavy fire was opened on RAILWAY TRENCH for two minutes at 9 pm last night in the hopes of catching enemy working parties. Owing to fog it was difficult to judge the effect. The enemy retaliated with 12 trench mortar bombs near Boyau 15, six shells fired into the rear of point B, 20 shells in rear of support trench between Boyaux 14 & 15 and 10 shells between saps 5 and 51. There were no casualties.
Enemy sniping very active by night but weaker by day.

Left Battalion. At 9-5 pm last night the hostile trench battery were immediately silenced by our howitzers who replied in 50 seconds.
During the evening the enemy put a few shells along the line RUSSELLS REDOUBT - BACK STREET.
This morning the enemy opened fire with trench mortars but was again silenced by our howitzers.

WORK.

2. Right Battalion. Four wire parties worked last night. Improvement of front line continued. Filling up excavations, and undercutting with sandbags and levelling fire steps. Three loopholes put in. TALBOT ROW ALLEY cleaned.

Left Battalion. Improvement of fire trench continued; six bays being completed. 50 yards of "Chevaux de Frise" and other wire put out. One latrine and one observation post made.

INTELLIGENCE.

3. A machine gun was located at A.27.b.9.8.
At 7-10 pm hostile wire parties were observed along RAILWAY trench. At 2-10 pm yesterday a German was seen for a very short time just South of HERVILLE. His face, cap, and shoulders were distinctly visible. He had a red band round his cap which looks as if the 14th Jaegers had been relieved.
Further signs that the enemy in front of the left battalion is not the same as those who were there on 25th September, are that those there at present have tried to shout across and show themselves more than was usual. Our snipers claim to have shot some.
The enemy put up a dummy head and shoulders last night, opposite EWA.

24/10/15.

( ) Lieut-Colonel,
Commanding 19th Infantry Brigade.

19th Infantry Brigade.
Daily Report up to 12 noon 25th October, 1915.

OPERATIONS. Yesterday afternoon and evening the enemy shelled more than usual, probably in retaliation for our bursts of fire the previous two nights, and the registration of the 7th Siege Brigade R.F.A.

Right Battalion. Twice during the afternoon the enemy put light shells on the support trench near A.27.b.1.3. and A.27.b.1.2. 12 High Explosive, probably 5.9", fell on support trenches near the VERSAILLES road. These were fired from some position a little North of ARCHY. Our howitzers replied. At 10-30 p.m. six more light shells fell near BOYAU 15 and six trench mortar bombs near point D. Considerable damage was done to the trenches by the shelling; but no casualties.

Left Battalion. At 9-0 p.m. enemy shelled support trenches and fired also fired some trench mortars and rifle grenades. Our artillery and trench mortars replied effectively.

WORK. Right Battalion. Wiring was continued last night. The damage done by the shelling was repaired. Improvements of the fire trench were continued. One grenade station built, and 3 loopholes constructed.

Left Battalion. Wiring was continued. Improvement of fire trench continued including 4 traverses built.

INTELLIGENCE. Miscellaneous. After one of our shells had exploded a finger was blown over into our trenches.
A working party was digging in trench A.27.b.7.9. during the day.

Patrol. An Officer's patrol went out last night with the object of reconnoitring the disused trench at A.27.b.6.7. which was studied before on the night of the 22nd/23rd. Nearer the road where the trench had before been found to be used, the enemy had scooped out a prolongation of the trench for about 3 yards and had also thrown out a T of about the same distance. The patrol was fired on in the course of its tour. A German loophole was brought in. There were no casualties.

Lieut-Colonel,
25th October, 1915.   Commanding 19th Infantry Brigade.....

19th Infantry Brigade.
Daily Report up to 12 noon, 24th October, 1915.

OPERATIONS.
Right Battalion. The 2nd Royal Welsh Fus: were relieved yesterday afternoon by the 1st Middlesex Regt: without incident. In the evening about 12 light shells fell in rear of our line along the VERMELLES - AUCHY road. The enemy is very active in his attempts to interfere with our working parties at night by machine gun and rifle fire.

Left Battalion. The 1st Cameronians were relieved by the 2nd Argyll & Sutherland Highdrs: yesterday morning without incident. The enemy has been exceptionaly quiet sending over no shells and very few trench mortar bombs and rifle grenades. There is even very little sniping.

WORK.
Right Battalion. Owing to the bad weather the work done has been chiefly clearing trenches of mud and strengthening trench walls which now need revetting.

Left Battalion. The bricking of MAISON ROUGE Trench was continued. Clearing and strengthening the trenches after the heavy rain required all the remaining labour.

INTELLIGENCE. The enemy is busily engaged on strengthening his own defences. This morning some heavy shells, believed by R.A., to be of 9" calibre, fell at and near the CASSE ROAD at AUCHYHILL.

Lieut-Colonel,
24th October, 1915. Commanding 19th Infantry Brigade.

10th Infantry Brigade.

Daily report up to 12 noon, 27th October, 1915.

OPERATIONS.   Right battalion.

The enemy was very quiet throughout the last 24 hours. The enemy was heard working by whistle direction frequently during the night.

Left battalion.

Last night the enemy snipin was heavier than usual. He was very active with trench mortars yesterday afternoon and again this morning. Our guns and trench mortars replied and silenced the enemy. Yesterday afternoon a German was seen working with his head and shoulders showing above the parapet. He was shot by our snipers, who distinctly saw him fall. The uniform could not be observed as he was working in shirt sleeves.

WORK.   Right battalion.

Revetting of trenches continued. Sap 5, in part, converted into fire trench for flank defence. Two dugouts and two observation posts constructed.

Left battalion.

Wiring continued. Continued revetting parapet in PATRICK STREET, HIGH STREET, MAIN STREET and front line. Two new latrines built. Rebricking of L.E.S. and H.S. road continued.

INTELLIGENCE.   Enemy light guns, probably three in number, were located just North of trees at LES BRIQUES. A machine gun was observed from 12 yards South of SAP 5, the direction being 40 degrees (true bearing).

27/10/15.   Lieut-Colonel,
                                          Commanding 10th Infantry Brigade.

19th Infantry Brigade.
Daily Report up to 12 noon, 28th October, 1915.

OPERATIONS. Right Battalion. The enemy has been very quiet for the past 24 hours. His working parties were less active last night, but traffic was again heard near AUCHY. Today he was active in firing at our aeroplanes.

Left Battalion. There has been practically no sniping from the enemy during the last 24 hours. The enemy fired a few trench mortars and light shells yesterday afternoon and again this morning but no damage was done. Several times during the night the enemy shouted across to us, sometimes saying that they were coming over here on the 30th and sometimes that they were going away altogether on that date.

WORK. Right Battalion. Wire strengthened. Trenches cleared and strengthened. Continued conversion of Sap S. into fire trench for flank defence. Further work none

Left Battalion. Parapet of front trench from GUY STREET to North end of HOLLOWAY is being repaired and work on parapets in PATRICK STREET and GAOL STREET continued. Further work done on improving front line and BOYAUX 15 and 16.

INTELLIGENCE. Wire. The enemy's wire is intact wherever it can be seen; but opposite our trench from North end of HOLLOWAY to GUY STREET none can be seen for about 50 yards owing to the broken ground. Opposite our trench between BOYAUX 15 andd 17 it appeared to be very strong consisting of apron fence, chevaux de frise and concertina wire.

Machine guns. Machine guns located by observation of flashes at, or just North of, point 95. Reference Map No 36 c N.W.Sheet 1., square A.27.b.9.5.

                                                        Lieut-Colonel,
28th October, 1915.   Commanding 19th Infantry Brigade....

Daily Report up to 12 noon, 29th October, 1915.

19th Infantry Brigade.

OPERATIONS. Right Battalion.   The enemy has been very quiet during the past 24 hours. At 10-15 am six small shells were fired at the front trenches near BOYAU 14. but no damage was done. Our artillery retaliated on MINE POINT.

Left Battalion.   Three light shells fell near BOYAU 16. last night, about 8-0 p.m. and about 3-0 p.m. 4 trench mortar bombs fell near BOYAU 15. These had been fired in reply to ours. A few light shells at intervals during the past 24 hours fell at Western end of WILSON'S WAY.

WORK. Right Battalion.   The wire was strengthened at various points along the front, otherwise the work was confined to the clearing of trenches and the revetment of places where they had fallen in.

Left Battalion.   The wire was strengthened at various points along the front. Repairing of parapet of front trench completed for 25 yards. Bricking of MAISON ROUGE trench continued. Work on RUSSELLS KEEP, BOYAUX 15, 16, and 19 and HIGH STREET continued. Way cut from MAISON ROUGE trench through road to the brickstack near Western end of WILSON'S WAY.

INTELLIGENCE. Wire.   There is no change in the enemy's wire.
Lights.   Red and green lights have been observed to our right usually between 6 and 8 p.m.
This morning, between 10 and 11 a.m. the enemy shelled the main LA BASSEE road 50 yards West of HARLEY STREET with light percussion shrapnel. There were at least two casualties but owing to the relief it is not certain whether all reports are in.

Lieut-Colonel,

29th October, 1915.   Commanding 19th Infantry Brigade.

(Brigade transferred
to 33rd Division
25.11.15)

Headquarters,

19th INFANTRY BRIGADE.

(2nd Division)

N O V E M B E R

1 9 1 5

Brigade Operation
Orders Nos. 60 to 69
inc.
Daily Reports.

Headquarters, 19th Infantry Brigade.

November 1915

(Copied from previous diary)

30th) October
31st)

1st) November
2nd)
3rd)   In billets training.   Operation Order
4th) GONNEHEM.   No. 60 attached.
5th)

//

WAR DIARY
or
INTELLIGENCE SUMMARY.

Army Form C. 2118.

(Erase heading not required.)

Hour, Date, Place	Summary of Events and Information	Remarks and references to Appendices
6th Nov. Cambrin	The relief of the 6th Inf Bde was carried out yesterday without incident. A new operation order (O attached) was issued. The trenches require a great deal of work	Casualties off
7 Nov Cambrin	The enemy were active today with minenwerfers. Some of [our?] did considerable damage	Killed — 4. Wounded — 1
8th Nov. Cambrin	Our trenches were heard shelled in front. This was an enemy retaliation.	Wounded — 1.
9th Nov.	An officers patrol went out from the 5th S.R. between Save Centre & our front. The patrol were fired on but there were no casualties.	
10th Nov.	Today in the afternoon the enemy exploded a mine. No damage was done to our trenches and no attack followed. On the whole a [quiet?] [day?] Operation order No 61 attached (subsequently cancelled)	Wounded — 1.

Army Form C. 2118.

WAR DIARY
or
INTELLIGENCE SUMMARY.
(Erase heading not required.)

Instructions regarding War Diaries and Intelligence Summaries are contained in F. S. Regs., Part II. and the Staff Manual respectively. Title pages will be prepared in manuscript.

Hour, Date, Place	Summary of Events and Information	Remarks and references to Appendices
11th Nov. Cambrin	The 5th S.R. were today relieved by the South Staffords and the 1st Bn. The Cameronians were relieved by the Warwicks & 22nd Bde. 7th Division. The relief took place without incident. Operation order 62 attached.	Casualties O/R Wounded — 1.
12th Nov. Cambrin	The Bde. today took over the old front 6 October and relieved the 5th Infantry Bde. The 2nd Royal Welch Fusiliers and the 1st Middlesex went into the front line with the 2nd Arg. Suff'd. Highlanders in support. Operation order 64 attached.	Wounded — 3.
13th Nov. Cambrin	The enemy were very quiet today. Nothing of interest took place.	
14th Nov. Cambrin	The enemy were quiet again today but there have been exchanges of artillery fire.	Wounded — 2.
15th Nov.	The trenches are in a better condition now and a great deal of work is being done on them.	Killed — 2 Wounded — 6.

WAR DIARY or INTELLIGENCE SUMMARY.

(Erase heading not required.)

Army Form C. 2118.

Hour, Date, Place	Summary of Events and Information	Remarks and references to Appendices
November 16th CAMBRIN	Work continues on trenches. Great improvement in communicating trenches.	Capt Turio 10th gets took over Baalflagg from Major R.M. Fro appd H.E. Brown G.S.O. 2 "13" Corps. Wounded 3 O.R.
November 17th CAMBRIN	Quiet on the whole. Still plenty of work to be continued on	Wounded 2 O.R.
" 18th	2 A & A relieved Middlesex in ZZ subsectors 5 O.R " Z1 " 2 R.W. 4 " Enemy snipers were active otherwise all quiet	O.O. No 63 attached
" 19th	Gloomy repairing of trenches continued. Progress with floors of trenches continued.	
" 20th	Fairly quiet on whole. Enemy's artillery slightly active	Killed 1 O.R. Wounded 2 O.R.
" 21st	2 R.W. Fus were relieved by 2 Ox. Bucks 2 A & A " " " 2 H.L.I. 1 Middx " " " 2 Worcesters 1 Camn " " " 1 O.R.	O.O. No 64 attached
" 22nd 23rd 24th 25th 26th 27th	Training in Rest Billets.	O.O. No 65 attached O.O. No 66 attached Killed 1 O.R. wounded 17 O.R. (1 wounded 10A wounded 10R O.O. No 67 attached

Army Form C. 2118.

WAR DIARY
or
INTELLIGENCE SUMMARY.
(Erase heading not required.)

Instructions regarding War Diaries and Intelligence Summaries are contained in F. S. Regs., Part II. and the Staff Manual respectively. Title pages will be prepared in manuscript.

Hour, Date, Place	Summary of Events and Information	Remarks and references to Appendices
November 28th: GONNEHEM. O.O. No 68 attached	In billets resting	
29th "	Trenches via Keel Camp " " @BEUVRY. @BUNCHETT.	O.O No 69 attached
30th "	Relief cancelled. Battns. & HQrs move to BETHUNE.	

E.B. Rowe Capt
for Brigadier General
Commanding 19th Brigade

BRIGADE OPERATION ORDERS NOS.

    60
    61
    62
    63
    64
    65
    66
    67
    68
    69

SECRET

Copy No. 2

19th Infantry Brigade Operation Order No. 60.

Reference map BETHUNE Combined sheet, 1/40,000.

3rd November, 1915.

1. 19th Infantry Brigade will relieve 6th Infantry Brigade in Section "A" (CUINCHY) on November 5th, 6th and 7th.

2. Reliefs of battalions will take place as shewn in the attached Relief and March Table.

3. The relief of Machine Guns will be carried out under arrangements between Brigade Machine Gun Officers.

4. No. 62 Trench Mortar Battery will remain in the trenches and will be attached to 19th Infantry Brigade.

5. 115th Field Company, R.E. (Less 3 sections) will remain in "A" Section and will be affiliated for work to 19th Infantry Brigade.

6. Transport will move under battalion arrangements.
    Instructions will be issued later by the Staff Captain regarding Transport billets.

7. Commanding Officers, Company Officers, Grenade officers of 1st Cameronians and 5th Scottish Rifles, Brigade Machine Gun Officer, O.C.19th Brigade Trench Mortar Battery will visit the trenches at 11 am on 4th November.
    Guides will be furnished by 6th Brigade Headquarters.

8. The usual trench stores will be taken over, and a list forwarded to Brigade Headquarters as soon as possible after relief.

9. Brigade Headquarters, on completion of relief on 6th November, will be established at F.19.d.6.3.

Major,
a/Brigade Major, 19th Infantry Brigade.

Issued at 5-30 pm.
Copy. No.1 Office.   Copy No.9. 19th Bde. T.M.Battery.
       2 War Diary.   10 62nd T.M.Battery.
       3 Staff Captain.   11. Bde. Transport Officer.
       4 2/R.Welsh Fus.   12. 2nd Division.
       5 1/Cameronians.   13. 5th Infantry Brigade.
       6 1/Middlesex R.   14. 6th Infantry Brigade.
       7 2/A.& S. Hrs.   15. "A" Group, R.F.A.
       8 5/Scottish Rifles.

RELIEF AND MARCH TABLE issued with 10th Brigade Operation Order No. 80.

Date.	Unit.	From.	To.	Relieving.	Time.	Remarks.
Nov. 5th.	1st Cameronians.	BETHUNE. (Rue d'Aire)	ANNEQUIN.	2nd South Staffords.	3 pm.	On arrival come under orders of G.O.C. "A" Section.
--do--	5th Scottish Rifles.	VENDIN.	BEUVRY.	5th Liverpool Regt.	1 pm	--do--
--do--	2nd R.Welsh Fusiliers.	BUSNETTES.	BETHUNE (Rue d'Aire)	1st Cameronians.	3 pm.	Remain under orders of G.O.C. Reserve Brigade.
Nov.7th.	1st Middlesex Regt.	GONNEHEM	ANNEQUIN.	1st King's Regt.	1 pm.	
Nov.7th.	2/A.& S.Hrs.	GONNEHEM.	BEUVRY.	1st Hertfordshire Regt.	1 pm.	

SECTION "A" (CUINCHY).

Date.	Unit.	Sub-Section (including keeps and support points.)	Rendezvous for guides for platoons and posts.	Relieving.	Time leading platoon to reach rendezvous.
Nov. 6th.	1st Cameronians	A.2 (including BRICKSTACKS KEEP, LOVERS REDOUBT, CABBAGE PATCH REDOUBT)	HEDGEROW LANE.	1st King's Regt.	10 am.
--do--	5th Scottish Rifles.	A.1 (including LANE REDOUBT, STAFFORD REDOUBT, CUINCHY SUPPORT POINT.	--do--	1st Hertfordshire Regt.	12 noon.
--do--	2nd R.Welsh Fusiliers.	HARLEY STREET (including BRADDELL POINT, PONT FIXE South, CAMBRIN SUPPORT POINT.)	--do--	1st R.Berkshire Regt.	1-30 pm.

[signature]
a/Brigade Major, 10th Infantry Brigade.

War Diary *Cancelled*

Copy No.

19th Infantry Brigade Relief Order No. 61

Referebce Trench Map.

1. Reliefs will be carried out on 11th November, 1915. as per attached table.

2. Machine gun reliefs will be carried out tomorrow under instructions issued through Brigade Machine Gun Officer. The Machine Gun Officers of 2nd Royal Welch Fusiliers and 1st Middlesex Regiment will take over guns in A.1. and A.2. respectively on completion of relief on 11th November.

3. Lists showing S.A.A., Grenades, and trench stores in sub-section and supporting points will be handed over, copies being sent to Brigade Headquarters except those of stores etc in Support Points.

4. A programme of work carried out by the relieved Battalion during their tour in the trenches will be given to the relieving battalion.

5. Relieved battalions will send in the daily report up to the time of relief.

Major,

Brigade Major, 19th Infantry Brigade...

Issued at 6 p.m.

Copy No. 1. 2nd R. Welch Fus:
" 2. 1st Cameronians.
4. 2nd A. & S. Hdrs:
6. 1st Middlesex R.
5. 5th Sco: Rifles.
3. 2nd Division.
7. 5th Infantry Brigade.
8. "A" Group, R.F.A.,

Relief not carried on 11th

10th Infantry Parade

ORDER OF MARCH

Unit followed.	Direction of march.	Location for halts.		
				during the export point as kept.
	(1) Coy. (2) Coy. (3) Coy. Export Points	(A.M.) (A.M.)	10 am	Export Point (Coy) 1 platoon Export Point (Prep) 1 platoon Exp. First Export Point(Coy) 2 platoon
	A.M. AAA	A.M. (A.M.MAJ.)	11 am	Platoon Parade 3 platoon Grand Assembly 1 platoon Grand Assembly 2 platoon
	AAA.	H.Q.NCO'S.		Except H.Q. 1 platoon Gate 1 platoon Except pistol 1 platoon
	HHY-H.Q.(INF).		1 pm	MICS (Coy) 1 platoon (Pr) 1 platoon

signature

10th Infantry Parade.

Copy No......

19th Infantry Brigade Relief Order No. 62.

Reference Trench Map and
BETHUNE 1/40,000 Map.

11th November, 1915.

1. Relief Order No. 61 is cancelled.
   The Brigade will be relieved tomorrow in "A" Section by 22nd Infantry Brigade of 7th Division and on 13th November will take over "Z" Section from 5th Infantry Brigade.
   Reliefs will be carried out as per Relief Table attached.

2. The new Brigade area will be as follows:-
Northern boundary.

   THE LANE (exclusive) - CAMBRIN SUPPORT POINT - TOURBIERES and CARTERS REDOUBTS (all inclusive) thence to canal at F.1. d.O.O. (exclusive of LE PREOL and LE QUESNOY).

Southern Boundary.

   Boyau 6 - SIMS KEEP - LEWIS ALLEY - LEWIS KEEP (all inclusive).

3. The following "keeps" will be taken over by the Brigade
                          on 12th November.

The Keep.			
CAMBRIN S.P.	By 2/A.& S.Hrs.	From 2/R.Welsh Fus.	½ platoon at 2-15 pm
TOURBIERES REDOUBT.	--do--	1st Middlesex R.	1 Section at 2-15 pm
CARTERS REDOUBT.	--do--	1st Middlesex R.	1 Section at 2-15 pm

                    on 13th November.

Z.1. Subsection.

SIMS KEEP.	By 2/R.Welsh Fus.	1 Platoon.
ARTHURS KEEP.	--do--	1 Platoon.

 Subsection.

RUSSELLS KEEP.	By 1st Middlesex R.	1 Platoon.
LEWIS KEEP	--do--	1 Section.

4. Relief of machine guns will be carried out on 12th and 13th November under instructions issued through Brigade Machine Gun Officer.
   9 guns will be relieved tomorrow in "A" Section and will go into billets in HARLEY STREET: the remaining 6 guns will be relieved on 13th November.
   The whole 15 guns will relieve guns of 5th Infantry Brigade in "Z" Section on 13th of November.

5. 62nd Trench Mortar Battery will move out of "A" Section tomorrow and be billetted with 34th Brigade Ammunition Column under instructions already issued.
   19th Brigade Trench Mortar Battery (4 guns) will be relieved by 22nd Brigade Trench Mortar Battery tomorrow. Guides to be at No. 1 HARLEY STREET at 10-30 am. It will be billetted in HARLEY STREET and relieve 5th Brigade Trench Mortar Battery in "Z" Section on 13th November.

6. Transport will remain in present billets.

7. 11th Field Company, R.E. will move under separate instructions and be attached to 6th Infantry Brigade. 5th Field Company, R.E. will be affiliated to 19th Infantry Brigade in "Z" Section.

(2).

8. On completion of relief of "A" Section tomorrow and until relief of "Z" Section commences on 13th November 2nd R.Welsh Fusiliers will be under the command of G.O.C. 22nd Infantry Brigade.

On reaching billets tomorrow and until relief on 13th November is completed 2nd A. & S. Highrs., 5th Scottish Rifles will be under the command of G.O.C., 5th Infantry Brigade.

9. List of trench stores handed over will be sent into Brigade Headquarters as soon as possible.

10. On completion of relief tomorrow Brigade Headquarters will be RUE DE LILLE, BETHUNE till 12 noon 13th November when it will be established at the CHemist's Shop, CAMBRIN.

H.E.Braine
Major,
Brigade Major, 19th Infantry Brigade.

Issued at 11-30 pm.

Copy. No. 1 2nd R.Welsh Fus.
2. 1st Cameronians.
3. 1st Middlesex Regt.
4. 2nd A. & S. Highrs.
5. 5th Scottish Rifles.
6. 62nd Trench Mortar Battery.
7. 19th Bde. Trench Mortar Battery.
8. 11th Company, R.E.
9. "A" Group, R.F.A.
10. 2nd Division.
11. 5th Infantry Brigade.
12. 22nd Inf. Bde. (7th Division).
13. File.
14. War Diary.
15 Staff Captain.
16. "Z" Group. R.F.A.

To be attached to
Relief Order No. 62.

RELIEF TABLE.
12th November, 1915.

19th Infantry Brigade.

Unit.	Relieving.	Rendezvous for guides.	Time.	Subsection or billets after relief.	Relieving.	Remarks.
2/R.War.R. (22nd Bde)	1st Cameronians	HEDGEROW LANE.	10-30 am.	BEUVRY (South)	Glasgow Highrs	
1/S.Staffs R. (22nd Bde)	5th Scottish Rifles.	HEDGEROW LANE.	11-30 am.	BEUVRY (North).	2/A.& S.Hrs.	
19th Bde. Sapping Platoons.	—	—	—	CAMBRIN CHURCH.	1 Coy. Oxs & Bucks L.I.	Sapping Platoons to leave present billets at 10-30am
2/A.& S.Hrs.	—	—	—	CAMBRIN AND ANNEQUIN (South).	Oxs & Bucks L.I.	March from BEUVRY at 10-30 am.

13th November.

Unit.	Relieving.	Rendezvous for guides.	Time.	Subsection or billets after relief.	Relieving.	Remarks.
2nd R.Welsh Fus.	2/R.Welsh R.	HEDGEROW LANE.	10-30 am.	Z.1.	—	No troops to wait on LA BASSEE ROAD near CAMBRIN SUPPORT POINT.
2/R.Welsh Fus.	1st Queens R. (5th Bde).	Junction of HARLEY STREET & LA BASSEE RD.	11 am.	—	—	
1st Middlesex Regt.	2/Worcester R. (5th Bde)	5th Bde. H.Q. (Chemist's shop)	9 am.	Z.2.	—	
1st Cameronians.	—	—	—	—	BETHUNE.	To be clear of BEUVRY at 10 am

11/11/15.

Brigade Major, 19th Infantry Brigade.

War Diary

Copy No. 11

19th Infantry Brigade Relief Order No. 63.

Reference Trench Map and
Bethune Map, 1/40,000.

17th November, 1915.

Reliefs will be carried out on 18th and 19th November as follows :-

(1) 2nd Bn. Argyll & Sutherland Highlanders will relieve 1st Bn. Middlesex Regiment in "Z.2." Sub-section on 18th November, commencing at 10 am from CAMBRIN SUPPORT POINT, where guides will be provided.

(2) (a) 5th Scottish Rifles will relieve 3 Companies 2nd R.Welsh Fusiliers in "Z.1" Sub-section from Boyau 6 to VERMELLES ROAD (exclusive) on 19th November, commencing at 10 am from CAMBRIN CHURCH, where guides will be provided.

(b) One Company, 2nd A. & S. Highrs. from MAISON ROUGE will relieve one Company 2nd R. Welsh Fusiliers in "Z.1" Sub-section from VERMELLES ROAD (inclusive) to Boyau 15, on 19th November, commencing at 9 am from MAISON ROUGE, where guides will be provided.

BILLETS.   On the 18th instant, 1st Middlesex Regt. will occupy billets vacated by 2nd A. & S. Highrs. at ANNEQUIN.

On the 19th instant 3 companies 2nd R.Welsh Fusiliers will occupy billets vacated by 5th Scottish Rifles at BEUVRY. One Company will remain at MAISON ROUGE.

All reliefs and moves to be reported as completed.

                                                                Captain,

                        Brigade Major, 19th Infantry Brigade.

Issued at 6 pm.

Copy No. 1 2nd R.Welsh Fusiliers.
        2. 1st Cameronians.
        3 1st Middlesex Regt.
        4 2nd A. & S. Highrs.
        5. 5th Scottish Rifles.
        6 2nd Division.
        7 6th Infantry Brigade.
        8 22nd Infantry Brigade.
        9 "Z" Group, R.F.A.
        10. File.
        11. War Diary.
        12 Staff Captain.

Secret

War Diary

Copy No. 14

19th Infantry Brigade Relief Order No. 64.

Reference BETHUNE 1/40,000 and
Tronch Map.

19th November, 1915.

RELIEF.
1. On the 21st November three battalions of the 5th Infantry Brigade will relieve 3 battalions of the 19th Infantry Brigade in support and reserve billets.
   Moves will be carried out in accordance with attached Relief Table.

MOVES.
2. On 21st November, the following moves will take place:-

  (a) 1st Middlesex Regiment on relief by 2nd Highland Light Infantry at 12 noon to march to GONNEHEM and BETHUNE.
    Billetting party to meet the Staff Captain 19th Infantry Brigade at Brigade Headquarters GONNEHEM at 11 am.

  (b) 2nd R.Welsh Fusiliers on relief by 2nd Oxs. & Bucks. L.I. at 12 noon to march to GONNEHEM.
    Billetting party to meet Staff Captain, 19th Infantry Brigade at Brigade Headquarters, GONNEHEM at 11 am.

  (c) 1st Bn. The Cameronians on relief by 2nd Worcester Regiment at 1 pm. to march to BUSNETTES.
    The billeting Officer to be sent on 20th instant to see the billets occupied by 2nd Worcester Regiment.

3. On 21st November the 20th Royal Fusiliers of the 98th Infantry Brigade will be attached to 19th Infantry Brigade.
   Moves in connection with this are shown in the attached Relief Table.

4. Completion of reliefs and moves to be reported to Brigade Headquarters.

                                              Captain,
                                Brigade Headquarters, 19th Inf. Bde.

Issued at 6 pm.

    Copy No 1 2nd R.Welsh Fus.
           2   1st Cameronians.
           3   1st Middlesex R.
           4   2nd A. & S. Highrs.
           5   5th Scottish Rifles.
           6   2nd Division.
           7   5th Infantry Brigade.
           8   Staff Captain.
           9   19th Bde. Sig. Section.
          10   20th R.Fus.
          11   98th Inf. Brigade.
          12   6th Inf. Brigade.
          13   File.
          14. War Diary.
          15   "Z" Group R.F.A.

To be attached to Relief Order No. 54.

RELIEF TABLE.

19th Infantry Brigade.

Unit.	Relieving.	From	Billets or Sub-section after relief.	Remarks.
		21st November, 1915.		
1st Middlesex Regt.	2nd H.L.I. 20th Royal Fusiliers.	ANNEQUIN (S).	GONNEHEM BETHUNE.	½ Battalion to billet one night in MONTMORENCY BARRACKS, BETHUNE with ½ Battalion 20th Royal Fusiliers.
1st Cameronians.	2nd Worcester Regt.	(RUE D'AIRE) BETHUNE.	BUSNETTES.	
2nd R.Welsh Fus.	2nd Oxs. & Bucks. L.I.	BEUVRY (N)	GONNEHEM.	One Company at MAISON ROUGE to join Battalion at BEUVRY (N) on relief by 2nd A.& S.Highrs.
4 Platoons, 2/A.& S.H.	1 Coy., 2/R.Welsh F.	Trenches.	MAISON ROUGE.	
½ Bn. 20th R.Fus.		BETHUNE.	Trenches Z.1 & Z.2.	For instruction.
		22nd November, 1915.		
½ Bn./Middlesex R.	-	BETHUNE.	GONNEHEM.	Leaving at 10 am.
½ Bn. 20th R.Fus.	-	BETHUNE.	Trenches Z.1 & Z.2.	For instruction.
½ Bn. 20th R.Fus.	-	Trenches.	ANNEQUIN (S).	1 Battalion 5th Inf.Bde. at ANNEQUIN (N) and 1 battalion of 7th Division at LE PREOL come under orders of 19th Inf.Bde. until 23rd.

19/11/15.

E.W.Rowers
Captain,
Brigade Major, 19th Infantry Brigade.

SECRET. *War Diary* Copy No......... 16

19th Infantry Brigade Relief Order No. 65.

Reference Combined Bethune Sheet 1/40,000

21st November, 1915.

1. On 23rd November, the 19th Infantry Brigade will hand over the front from Boyau 6 to GUN STREET (exclusive) to the 6th Infantry Brigade, as per relief and march table attached.

2. The relief of machine guns will commence at 3 pm under arrangements made between Brigade Machine Gun Officers.   On relief sections will rejoin their units in their new billets.

3. 19th Brigade Trench Mortar Battery will be relieved by 6th Brigade Trench Mortar Battery.

   6th Trench Mortar Battery will remain in the trenches, and be attached to 6th Infantry Brigade.

4. Transport will move under battalion arrangements.

5. Lists of stores handed over will be given to relieving units, copies being sent to Brigade Headquarters.

6. The 3 Corporals and 8 Privates attached to No.6 Trench Mortar Battery will report at Brigade Headquarters at 10 am on 23rd November.

7. On 24th November 2nd Argyll & Sutherland Highrs. and 5th Scottish Rifles will move to BELLERIVE, and L'ECLEME, and the 19th Infantry Brigade will join 33rd Division.

8. Brigade Headquarters, on completion of relief on 23rd will be established in GONNEHEM (V.18.a.)

E.K. Purss Captain,
Brigade Major, 19th Inf. Brigade.

Issued at 9 pm.

Copy No. 1   2nd R.Welsh Fus.
        2   1st Cameronians.
        3   1st Middlesex Regt.
        4   2nd A. & S. Highrs.
        5   5th Scottish Rifles.
        6   20th Bn. R.Fus.
        7   2nd Division.
        8   6th Inf. Bde.
        9   5th Inf Bde.
      10   41st Bde. R.F.A.
      11. 98th Inf. Bde.
      12. Bde. Sig. Officer.
      13. 19th Bde. Trench Mortar Battery.
      14. 6th Trench Mortar Battery.
      15. Staff Captain.
      16. War Diary.
      17. File.

To be attached to Relief Order No. 65.　　　RELIEF AND MARCH TABLE.　　　19th Infantry Brigade.

Unit.	Relieved by.	Rendezvous for guides.	Time.	Billets after relief.	Remarks.
		23rd November, 1915.			
2nd A. & S. Highrs.	2nd South Staffords.	CAMBRIN SUPPORT POINT.	9 am.	BETHUNE.	Billeting party to report to Town Major, BETHUNE at 10 am.
5th Scottish Rifles.	1st R.Berks. R.	CAMBRIN CHURCH.	10 am.	VENDIN.	
½ Bn.20th R.Fus.				ANNEQUIN.-(N)	From trenches after relief of 2/A.& S.Hrs. by 2nd S.Staffords.
Headquarters & ½ Bn.20th R.Fus.	18th R.Fus.			ANNEQUIN (N).	20th R.Fus. come under orders of 5th Inf.Bde. after relief.
19th Bde. T.M.Battery	6th Bde. T.M.Battery			LA VALLEE.	Relief to be arranged with O.C.6th Bde. T.M.Battery.
		24th November, 1915.			
2nd A.& S.Highrs.				BELLERIVE.	Times to be notified later.
5th Scottish Rifles.				L'ECLEME.	Times to be notified later.

signature

Brigade Major, 19th Infantry Brigade.　　　Captain, Captain.

21/11/15.

Copy No....7...

19th Infantry Brigade Relief Order No. 66

Reference BETHUNE Combined sheet 1/40,000

22nd November, 1915.

The following moves are substituted for those under November 24th in 19th Infantry Brigade Relief Order No. 65.

(a) The 2nd Bn. Argyll & Sutherland Highrs. will move from BETHUNE to MONT BERNENCHON at 1-30 pm.

Billetting parties to meet Staff Captain at Road Junction, Q.31.c.9.6. at 12 noon.

(b) The 5th Scottish Rifles will move from VENDIN to BELLERIVE at 1-30 pm.

Billetting party to meet Staff Captain at Road Junction V.12.b.8.7. at 11 am.

Captain,

Brigade Major, 19th Inf. Brigade.

Issued at 7-30 pm.

Copy No. 1 2nd R. Welsh Fusiliers.
         2 1st Cameronians.
         3 1st Middlesex Regt.
         4 2nd A. & S. Highrs.
         5 5th Scottish Rifles.
         6 2nd Division.
         7 Bde. Sig. Officer.
         8)
         9) Office.
        10)

War Diary

SECRET.

Copy No.... 9 ......

19th Infantry Brigade Operation Order No. 67.

Reference Map BETHUNE
Combined Sheet 1/40,000.

1. The following moves and transfers will take place tomorrow.

   (a). The 1st Bn: Middlesex Regiment will march from GONNEHEM to LES CHOQUAUX at 10 a.m. and will come under the orders of the 98th Infantry Brigade at 12 noon. Billeting party to meet Staff Captain at Road Junction, W.18.a.0.8. at 10 am

   (b). The 2nd Bn: Argyll & Sutherland Highlanders at MONT BERNENCHON will be transferred to 98th Infantry Brigade at 12 noon.

   (c). 18th and 20th Royal Fusiliers at BETHUNE will be transferred from 98th Infantry Brigade to 19th Infantry Brigade at 12 noon.

2. The completion of these moves and transfers will be reported to Brigade Headquarters.

                                              Captain,
28th November, 1915.   Brigade Major, 19th Infantry Brigade.

Copy No. 1. 2nd R.Welch Fus:
         2. 1st Cameronians.
         3. 1st Middlesex Regt:
         4. 2nd A. & S.Hdrs:
         5. 5th Scottish Rifles.
         6. 33rd Division.
         7. 98th Infantry Brigade.
         8. Staff Captain.
         9. War Diary.
        10. File.

Copy No. 8

19th Infantry Brigade Operation Order No. 68.

Reference BETHUNE Combined sheet 1/40,000.

28th November, 1915.

1. The following moves will take place tomorrow.

    (a) 1st Cameronians BUSNETTES to BETHUNE at 10 am.

    Billetting party to report to Town Major at 9-30 am.

    (b) 5th Scottish Rifles FELLERIVE to BETHUNE at 10 am.

    Billetting party to report to Town Major at 9-30 am.

    (c) 2nd R.Welsh Fusiliers GONNEHEM to OBLINGHEM at 11am.

    Billetting party to meet Staff Captain at Level Crossing, W.26 central at 10 am.

2. The Completion of these moves will be reported to Brigade Headquarters at GONNEHEM.

Captain,

Brigade Major, 19th Infantry Brigade.

Copy. No. 1. 2nd R.Welsh Fusiliers.
2. 1st Cameronians.
3. 1/5th Scottish Rifles.
4. 18th Royal Fusiliers.
5. 20th Royal Fusiliers.
6. 33rd Division.
7)
8) Office & File.
9)

Secret

Preliminary Instructions for Relief.

1. On November 30th, 1915 the 19th Infantry Brigade will relieve the 21st Infantry Brigade.

2. They will hold the line as follows :-

   5th Bn: Scottish Rifles from WILLOW ROAD to LORGIES ROAD (inclusive) with MAIRIE REDOUBT, and will find its own relief.
   1st Bn: Cameronians from LORGIES ROAD (exclusive) to the junction of SCOTTISH TRENCH and NEW TRENCH (exclusive) and POPPY REDOUBT. Relief (2nd Royal Welch Fusiliers) will be billeted in LE QUESNOY
   18th Bn: Royal Fusiliers from NEW TRENCH (exclusive) to FIFE ROAD (inclusive) and LEES REDOUBT, and LE PLANTIN, East, North and South. Relief Battalion (20th Bn: Royal Fusiliers) will be billeted in FERME DU ROI.
   20th Bn: Royal Fusiliers will find the garrisons of GIVENCHY KEEP, HILDER REDOUBT, MOAT HOUSE, HERTS REDOUBT and WINDY CORNER from one Company.

3. At 9 a.m. November 29th, the Brigade Grenade Officer, Company Commanders, Machine Gun Officer, and Bombing Officer of 5th Scottish Rifles, 1st Cameronians and 18th Royal Fusiliers, will visit the trenches, also one officer from the Company of the 20th Bn: Royal Fusiliers, detailed to hold the Keeps.

4. Two motor busses will be at 19th Infantry Brigade Headquarters at 7-30 a.m., where the officers of the 1st Cameronians and 5th Scottish Rifles should be at that hour. They will call at the Headquarters of the 18th Royal Fusiliers, 54, RUE DE LILLE, BETHUNE about 8-15 a.m., to pick up the officer of the 18th and 20th Royal Fusiliers, and will then proceed to the 21st Infantry Brigade Headquarters alongside the LA BASSEE Canal (Square F.10. b.9.0.).

5. On 29th November at 2-30 p.m. the following officers and N.C.Os. will report at 21st Infantry Brigade Headquarters and will be attached to units of the 21st Infantry Brigade for the night:-

   5th Scottish Rifles.
   One Officer per Company) Of the Company in the front line.
   One N.C.O. per platoon   )

   1st Cameronians.
   One Officer per Company) of the two Companies in the front
   One N.C.O. per Platoon) line.

   18th Royal Fusiliers.
   One Officer per Company) Of the two Companies in front and
   One N.C.O. per Platoon) support line..

6. A Motor Bus will be at Headquarters, 18th Royal Fus: at 2 p.m. where these parties should collect.

7. Please acknowledge.

28th November, 1915.

Captain,
Brigade Major, 19th Infantry Brigade....

SECRET.   Copy No. 11

19th Infantry Brigade Operation Order No. 69.

Reference Bethune Combined sheet, 1/40,000
& 1/10,000 Trench Map.

                                                29th November, 1915.

1. 19th Brigade will relieve the 21st Brigade in the GIVENCHY Section on 30th November. Reliefs will be carried out as per table attached.

2. The new Brigade area will be as follows :-

   The Southern boundary of the area runs from WILLOW ROAD (A.9.d.4.4.) to the Canal at F.18.a.5.8. (ORCHARD REDOUBT and PONT FIXE being included in 2nd Divisional area), thence along the Canal to its junction with the BEUVRY canal, and thence past the South of LE QUESNOY and rejoins the canal above PONT TOURNANT.
   The Northern boundary is the junction of FIFE Road with the front line, inclusive to the Brigade, thence along FIFE Road, as far as its junction with the old British line, thence Westward including LE PLANTIN North, & TUNING FORK West, and GORRE WOOD.

3. The line will be held as follows:-

Right Battalion 5th Scottish Rifles.
1 Company in front line.   )
1 Company in GUNNER SIDING &   ) WILLOW ROAD to LORGIES ROAD
MAIRIE REDOUBT.   ) (inclusive).
2 Companies at WINDY CORNER.   )

Centre battalion 1st Cameronians.
2 Companies in front line &   )
POPPY REDOUBT.   ) LORGIES ROAD (exclusive) to
1 Company in SCOTTISH TRENCH.   ) junction of SCOTTISH TRENCH
1 Company in NEW CUT.   ) & NEW TRENCH (Exclusive).

Left Battalion 18th Royal Fusiliers.
1 Company in front line.   )
1 Company in GEORGE STREET.   ) Junction of SCOTTISH TRENCH &
5 Platoons in LE PLANTIN.   ) NEW TRENCH (inclusive) to
3 Platoons in Redoubts.   ) FIFE ROAD (inclusive).

Support.
1 Battalion, 2nd R.Welsh Fus. At LE QUESNOY.

Reserve.

20th Royal Fusiliers.   at FME.DU ROI.
1 Battalion (less 1 Company).
in redoubts).

4. The following redoubts and keeps will be taken over by the Brigade :-

MAIRIE REDOUBT.	1 Platoon,	5th Scottish Rifles.
POPPY REDOUBT.	½ Platoon,	1st Cameronians.
LEES KEEP	½ Platoon)	
LE PLANTIN E.	½ Platoon)	18th Royal Fusiliers.
LE PLANTIN N.	1 Platoon)	
LE PLANTIN S.	1 Platoon)	

(2)

GIVENCHY KEEP.	1½ Platoons	)
	(less 2 N.C.Os. & 6 men)	)
HILDER REDOUBT.	½ Platoon.	)
MOAT HOUSE REDOUBT.	½ Platoon.	) 20th Royal
HERTS REDOUBT.	1 Platoon.	) Fusiliers,.
WINDY CORNER KEEP.	½ Platoon.	)
MARAIS E.	1 N.C.O. & 3 men.	)
MARIAS S.	1 N.C.O,& 3 men.	)

5. Relief of Machine Guns and 19th Trench Mortar Battery will be carried out under instructions issued by the Brigade Machine Gun Officer.

6 Sapping Platoons will be detached from their units on the morning of the 30th. They will march independently to LE QUESNOY, and report to Staff Captain at Road Junction, F.8.b.8.8., at 9-45 am.

7. Secret Trench Maps, Brigade Defence and Trench maintenance schemes will be taken over and a receipt given.

8. List of trench stores taken over will be forwarded to Brigade Headquarters.

9. No. 9 Trench Mortar Battery will, on completion of relief, be transferred to 19th Brigade.

10. 19th Brigade Headquarters will close at GONNEHEM at 2 pm and will be established near the Canal, F.10.b.9.0. at 4 pm.

            E.H. Rhodes   Captain,

         Brigade Major, 19th Inf. Brigade.

Issued at 9 am.
Copy No. 1 2nd R.Welsh Fus.
    2 1st Cameronians.
    3 5th Scottish Rifles.
    4 18th Royal Fusiliers.
    5 20th Royal Fusiliers.
    6 33rd Division.
    7 21st Infantry Brigade.
    8 19th Trench Mortar Battery
    9 Bde. Signal Officer.
   10)
   11)Office & File.
   12)

To be attached to Operation Order No. 59.   19th Infantry Brigade.

19th RELIEF TABLE.
30th November, 1915.

Relieving Unit.	Unit relieved.	Sub-section or Billet.	Rendezvous for Guides.	Time.	Remarks.
Scottish Rifles.	2nd Wiltshire R.	Trenches (Right)	VAUXHALL BRIDGE. (A.13.b.5.5.)	10-30 am	
1st Cameronians.	2nd Yorkshire R.	Trenches (Centre).	WINDY CORNER. (A.8.c.3.9.)	11.30 am.	
18th Royal Fusiliers. (less 1 Company)	4th Camerons.	Trenches (left)	ESTAMINET CORNER.	4-30 pm.	An Officer of the Camerons will meet the battalion at F.4.b.5.2. at 4 pm & direct them to ESTAMINET CORNER.
1 Company, 18th R.Fus.	2nd Yorkshire R.	Trenches (left)	WINDY CORNER.	11.30am.	
1 Company, 20th R.Fus.	—	Keeps and Redoubts.	WINDY CORNER.	12 noon.	2 N.C.Os. & 6 men of this Company for MARIAS E & S to be at 21st Bde. H.Q. at 10am.
2/R.Welsh Fus.	R.Scots. Fus.	LE QUESNOY.	—	—	March at 10 am, billetting party to meet Staff Captain at LE QUESNOY (road Junction at F.8.b.8.8) at 9 am.
3 Companies, 20th Royal Fus.	Bedford Regt.	FERME DU ROI.	—	—	March at 9-30 am. Billetting party at FERME DU ROI at 8-30am.

29/11/15.

E.K. Moore

Captain,
Brigade Major, 19th Infantry Brigade.

20th Infantry Brigade.
======================

Correction to Relief Table attached to Operation Order
No. 49.

In line 4 for
"19th Royal Fusiliers less 1 Company" read
"19th Royal Fusiliers less 1 Company".

In line 5 for
"1 Company Royal Fusiliers" read
"2 Company Royal Fusiliers".

E. Rice Captain,
20th November, 1914. Brigade Major, 20th Infantry Brigade.

DAILY REPORTS.

File.

Daily Report up to 12 noon, 7th November, 1915.
18th Infantry Brigade.

OPERATIONS. The relief of the 8th Infantry Brigade was carried out without incident yesterday.

Right Battalion. At 6-0 p.m. last night about 20 light shells and some rifle grenades were fired into our trenches between the LA BASSEE road and HILL 60 ALL, and there was considerable sniping from the crater just South of the LA BASSEE road. At 11-0 a.m. this morning a minenwerfer fired about 20 times against the same place from a position just South of the LA BASSEE road and about 40 yards from our trenches.

Left Battalion. A sniper reports having hit some Germans whom he saw carrying planes by the wheel embankment, in the early [illegible]. The enemy has been quiet and nothing [illegible] until nearly noon when a large number of trench mortar or minenwerfer fires from our left [illegible] and [illegible]. Our artillery retaliated but as the enemy continued the Stoke Battery was called in [illegible] two canisters.

Right Battalion. The support and fire trenches were cleaned and also [illegible] in the fire trench, and the crater part of [illegible] was also been cleaned. Cleaning and clearing [illegible] was also done in the [illegible].

Left Battalion. The fire trench, [illegible] HAZE [illegible] and the [illegible] were cleaned. 1 coil of [illegible] was [illegible] sandbags were filled.

[illegible]. The enemy's wire appears intact. A yellow sign was followed by one red light and two coloured signals are observed 15 minutes before the enemy started their usual fire against the right [illegible].

There was an unusual amount of [illegible] in the enemy's lines last night. Working parties were also heard. Light transport was heard behind the enemy's lines [illegible] 8-0 p.m. and 7-0 p.m. last night and sounds as if they were being unloaded.

7th November, 1915.

Daily Report up to 12 noom, 8th November, 1915.
19th Infatry Brigade.
****

OPERATIONS. Right Battalion. About a dozen "rum-jar" minenwerfer were fired at about 10-30 a.m. on our trenches South of the LA BASSEE road. No damage was done. We retaliated with "West" Bomb throwers. Enemy sniping is very accurate; three periscopes were broken.

Left Battalion. The minenwerfer fired by the enemy yesterday about noon did considerable damage. Four men were blown to pieces by one which fell at the junction of Saps 7 and 10 and the parapet on JERUSALEM HILL was completly obliterated by two others. About 8-30 p.m. the enemy landed two minenwerfer between ARLINGTON STREET and DAVIS STREET but no damage was done. About a dozen small shells were fired at the BULGE and WORCESTER LANE. Our guns retaliated. The enemy's sniping was heavy in the night but unusually quiet by day.

WORK. Right Battalion. The "housemaiding" of GRAFTON STREET, EDGWARE ROAD and CONDUIT STREET was continued. A lot of work was also done in repairing latrines. All keeps were cleaned and firing steps improved and the support and fire trenches were cleaned and in places rivetted. Bricking of the LANE and GLASGOW STREET continued.

Left Battalion. Cleaning and improvement of the trenches was continued. The BULGE was cleaned and revittment began. Repairs were began where the trench was damaged yesterday by minenwerfer and the construction of new fire steps was continued.

INTELLIGENCE. Wire. The enemy's wire seems intact.
Lights. About 7-30 p.m. a green star shell followed by a white one and then a red light were shown by the enemy and a burst of machine gun and rifle fire followed.
Germans were heard working in the small trench close to our front line just South of the LA BASSEE road. Voices were also heard during the night in the large crater opposite TOWER TRENCH and an enemy party appeared to be working in the crater just South of the LA BASSEE road. The Germans shouted across once or twice during the night but unintelligibly.
The large minenwerfer which fired yesterday was located as having fired from the neighbourhood of FRANKS KEEP.

Lieut-Colonel,
8th November, 1915. Commanding 19th Infantry Brigade......

19th Infantry Brigade.
Daily Report up to 12 noon, 9th November, 1915.

OPERATIONS. 1. Yesterday afternoon in consequence of our artillery shelling canal banks the Germans retaliated on our trenches firing 30 heavy shells and some "rum jars" into A.1. subsection damaging the front parapet and blocking the trenches. This shelling came from a N.E. direction. He also shelled and mortared trenches of A.2. at same time but not so heavily and damage here was slight. One of his heavy shells burst in his own front trench. 6 shells were blind. Our guns retaliated.
The night was unusually quiet especially opposite subsection A.2.
Today enemy shelled HUNTERS STREET and WORCESTER LANE about 10 a.m. for an hour, with field guns, doing little damage.
Between 12-10 p.m. and 12-30 p.m. he shelled KINGSCLERE (A.2. Battalion H.Q.,) and North end of CUINCHY Village. No damage.

WORK. 2. **A.1 Subsection.** Damage done by shell fire repaired. Continued work on cleaning and boarding trenches. Firing steps revetted and strengthened, especially GRAFTON STREET, MARYLEBONE ROAD, PRAED STREET and front trench.
PARK LANE, REDOUBT, CUINCHY SUPPORT POINT and STAFFORD REDOUBT trenches floored with boards.
Work on cleaning and bricking communication trenches continued.

A.2. Subsection. General repairs and revetting to trenches and cleaning, especially WORCESTER LANE, HUNTER STREET, WHITECHAPEL STREET and BRICKFIELD Terrace. Front trenches partly boarded. Work on boarding, clearing and revetting communication trenches and 2nd line fire trench continued.

R.E. 350 men worked on 2nd and 3rd lines under R.E. supervision 200 men of Sapping Platoon assisted Infantry in front line trench

INTELLIGENCE. 3. A searchlight was working during the night in neighbourhood of LES BRIQUES. Several star shells of various groupings, mostly red and green, were sent up, but nothing happened to indicate their meaning. Voices were again heard in large crater just South of the LA BASSEE road.
An Officer's patrol along LA BASSEE Road encountered no hostile patrols. Saps 3 and 4 were found to be filled in.
Enemy heard working in his trenches opposite Subsection A.2.
A red, white and blue flag has been put up on the LA BASSEE road. Enemy's wire reported intact and to be very strong and in good order opposite centre of subsection of A.2.

9th November, 1915.   Lieut-Colonel,
                                              Commanding 19th Infantry Brigade......

19th Infantry Brigade.
Daily report up to 12 noon, 10th November, 1915.
==

OPERATIONS.   Right Battalion.   The enemy put several "rum jars" into
               our trenches on the South of the LA BASSEE road between
               9 a.m. and 12 noon. In the afternoon the enemy sent over
               more "rum jars" into our trench near the Brickstacks, but
               they were located and silenced by our guns.

               Left Battalion.   Yesterday the enemy shelled the embankment
               and the "Cameronians" headquarters in retaliation to our
               artillery. Some slight damage was done to parapets, which
               have since been repaired. Our trench mortars fired last
               night at 5 p.m. There have since been occasional interchange
               of mortars.
               One of our snipers last evening hit a German and the body was
               visible for some time.

WORK.   Right Battalion.   About 40 yards of BACK STREET have been
               floored and the Sap at South end of QUARRY TRENCH has been
               partially cleared. The night was spent in clearing in
               fallen in trenches. Some of the water has been cleared by
               pumps. Parts of SHORT CUT and TOWER BRIDGE have been
               revetted.

               Left Battalion.   The parados have been built up in the front
               line and three bays of BURIAL STREET have been revetted
               with sandbags.
               WORCESTER LANE has been repaired. The CATS PATH has
               been cleared of water and footboards have been laid down.
               JERUSALEM HILL, WHITECHAPEL ROAD and BRICKFIELD TERRACE have
               been cleared.

               R.E.   125 men worked under R.E. supervision in second
               line Some dug-outs and emplacements were made in front line
               and an artillery observation post was made.
               The Bomb Store in HARLEY STREET has been roofed.

INTELLIGENCE. The enemy's wire seems intact.
               An Officer's patrol of the 5th Scottish Rifles went out last
               night to the four craters on our front from near SUE BRIDGE
               to the South end of QUARRY TRENCH.
               Three of the craters have not been used but in the most
               Northerly one an emplacement of sandbags probably for a
               trench mortar was found. A gallery ran back from this crater
               to the German line.
               The patrol was fired on when getting through our wire but there
               were no casualties.

                                                      F. Rowley Lieut-Colonel,
               10th November, 1915.   Commanding 19th Infantry Brigade....

13th Infantry Brigade.
Daily report up to 12 noon, 11th November, 1915.
-:-:-:-:-:-:-:-:-:-:-:-:-:-

OPERATIONS.   Right Battalion. The enemy exploded a mine about 5-45 p.m.
to the right of OUR MINE. No damage was done to our
trenches and no attack followed.
A German sniper just south of the LA BASSEE road, was silenced by one of our sentries at dawn this morning.

Left Battalion. The enemy opposite this section were quiet
and there was less sniping than usual. The enemy's artillery
however has been active, but with no results. Yesterday
between 2-00 p.m. and 3 p.m. the enemy put a few shells near
CASSAVA PATCH, THE SUICIDE ACRE and DIE HARD REDT. At 10 a.m.
a few shells burst in CUINCHY VILLAGE.
One of our snipers yesterday hit a German as he passed a
gap in his trench. The sniper states that the German was
a big man, but he could not describe his uniform.
At 1 p.m. about 6 large shells fell at HDQTS. Three burst
in the Officers' Mess.

WORK.   Right Battalion. The last 24 hours have been spent by the
Battalion in clearing the trenches where they have been
blocked by the falling in of walls and parapets. The water
and mud has been cleared as much as possible by pumps and
mud scoops. The fire steps have been scraped and strengthened.
The trench at CULLUM STREET, CUINCHY has been paved for some
yards?X. Bn. TRENCH has been cleared where it had fallen
in. The telephone dug-outs have also been repaired.

Left Battalion. The parados in the front line have been
revetted with hurdles for some yards. The front line has been
cleared and pumped and footboards have been laid down.
WOLFE ST. has been repaired in several places where the
sides had fallen in. POTTICOAT LANE and COLUMN LANE have
been cleared, and JUBILEE AVE., WILLOW WALK AVE. and
SHIRECOCK AVENUE have been repaired and revetted.
The firing positions in BOMBA REDOUBT, PUP REDOUBT
and HAPPY GOLF have been rebuilt. MAUDE LANE has been
cleared.

The Sapper platoons have rebuilt the PUMP and have cleared
WOLFE ST. and the new drain near the DUDLEY. Bres-
therb obstacles and posts have been put up in front of
the trenches where required. Parts of the parados of the
firing trench up to all spots have been boarded.
The old trench from the OLD KEEP RUIN to the firing line
have been cleared and the wire across the gap at the gap
has been repaired as far as possible.

R.E. staff have worked under the supervision of Major ?? R.E.
The making of dug-outs and emplacements in the front line has
continued.
Artillery observation posts were cleared up by R.E. staff.

INTELLIGENCE. The enemy's wire seems intact.
Some working parts were working on the ridges concerned in
rear of their front line. They have also been working
at the following places :- RAILWAY T.T., MINE A.B.C.
with timber and sandbags.
The ??" Battery opened fire on the working party.
56"

F. ?? Lieut-Colonel,
11th November, 1915.   Comd. 13th Infantry Brigade.

19th Infantry Brigade.

Daily report up to 12 noon, 12th November, 1915.

OPERATIONS.
The 5th Scottish Rifles were today relieved by the South Staffords and 1st Bn. The Cameronians were relieved by the Warwicks of 22nd Brigade, 7th Division.

RIGHT BATTALION. A.1.

The enemy were quiet opposite this section. During the night a few shells burst in the right company's front without doing any damage.

LEFT BATTALION A.2.

During the night the enemy were quiet except for shelling the DUMP near the canal and destroying a fair amount of the work which had been done there.

His Artillery was active near RAILWAY HOLLOW and the BRICKSTACKS during the afternoon. Our trench mortars fired with success on the German working parties.

PONT FIXE was shelled by heavy howitzers all the afternoon. The garrison telephone dug-out was destroyed and some damage done on the far side of the canal.

WORK.
The last 24 hours have been spent in clearing the trenches where the sides have fallen in and a certain amount of flooring and revetting has also been done.

The SAPPING Platoons have been revetting and reconstructing front trenches and have cleared trenches that have fallen in.

The North end of TRAFALGAR and some of JAMES ST. have been revetted.

Yesterday afternoon's shelling and last night's rain has destroyed a great deal of the work that has been done. Parapets have slipped badly and several of the communication trenches have collapsed.

Only plank revetment or corrugated iron sheets with pit props will prevent this state of affairs continually occurring.

A.1. Work. Work was continued on the dug-outs in front line and the Artillery observation posts in   .

INTELLIGENCE.
The enemy's wire seems intact. Germans were heard talking in the craters opposite right of A.1. Sub-section.

12/11/15.

F. Rowley   Lieut-Colonel,
Commanding 19th Infantry Brigade.

19th Infantry Brigade.

Daily report up to 12 noon, 15th November, 1915.

OPERATIONS.   The Brigade relieved the 5th Infantry Brigade this morning.
The enemy's artillery was less active last night and confined
chiefly to the area round Battalion Headquarters of Z.2.
Shells burst in Battalion Headquarters and Officers' latrine.
Very little damage otherwise.

WORK.   The last 24 hours have been spent in clearing landslides and
preparing trenches for floorboards. Two earthworks are
ready for shelters, work delayed owing to reliefs this
morning.
Trenches very wet and landslides frequent. Work is being
organized and special parties are at work this afternoon.

INTELLIGENCE.   Nil.

DISTRIBUTION.
Z.1.. 2nd Royal Welch Fus:
Z.2.. 1st Middlesex Reft:
CAMBRIN and ANNEQUIN (South)........ 2nd A. & S. Hdrs:
BEUVRY..................................... 5th Scottish Rifles.
BETHUNE (Rue d'Aire)................ 1st Cameronians.

                                                  Lieut-Colonel,

15th November, 1915.   Commanding 19th Infantry Brigade.....

19th Infantry Brigade.

Daily report up to 12 noon, 14th November, 1915.

OPERATIONS.
Right Battalion. The enemy's machine guns traversed the parapet at intervals during the night. The snipers also were very active. The enemy shelled with small shells during the afternoon and evening.

Left Battalion. The enemy were very quiet last night, and no patrols were met. At 9 p.m. a working party at point 41 was dispersed. Twelve small shells burst at the head of BURBURE ALLEY at 2-45 p.m. yesterday.

WORK.
Right Battalion. The last 24 hours have been spent in clearing the trenches and boyaux where they have fallen in. The parapet is being repaired and made bullet proof. Footboards were put in and soak-pits were made. Two dug-outs were roofed in.

Left Battalion. The last 24 hours have been spent in clearing the front line, the second line and boyaux of water and landslips. Some of the parapets and pardos have been built up. Four collapsed dug-outs and two latrines have been cleared. Three landslides in WILSON STREET have been removed and the whole trench has been improved. Eighty yards of parapet has been improved for better firing positions. 150 yards of WILSON'S WAY have been cleared. In RUSSELL'S KEEP five landslides have been removed and ten yards of trench has been revetted.

INTELLIGENCE.
Right Battalion. Last night the flashes of machine guns were located as follows :- point 85, point 70, and point 41. The enemy's searchlight played on our lines during the night from apparently well behind their lines. Six green flare lights were fired over our lines at 5-45 p.m. then two more were put over followed by three shells.

A/

Sheet 2.

INTELLIGENCE.
(continued)

A small party were heard working on the enemy's ~~trench~~ wire about midnight.

About 12-30 a.m. the enemy's shells appeared to be coming from the direction of AUCHY.

This morning earth was observed being thrown up at point 87, on the railway.

Two hostile aeroplanes circled over enemy's lines about 8-20 a.m.

Left Battalion. Smoke from an engine was observed near railway junction in square 28c. The enemy are believed to be behind the far lip of the new crater and bombs were thrown during the night.

L. Rowley Lieut-Colonel,
14th November, 1915. Commanding 19th Infantry Brigade...

19th Infantry Brigade.
Daily report up to 12 noon, 15th November, 1915.

1. OPERATIONS. Subsection Z.1. The enemy's field guns were active at intervals during the last 24 hours and various parts of this subsection were shelled. Two men were slightly wounded and a little damage was done to parapets. Between 4 p.m. and 4-30 p.m. five large shells burst just short of the right of the subsection. The enemy's snipers were inactive during yesterday. At night sniping was very active on both sides, especially between 5 p.m. and 7 p.m. An enemy wiring party was fired on in front of POPES NOSE. At 2 p.m. men were observed working in the enemy's front line just North of POPES NOSE and were stopped working by fire.

Subsection Z.2. Enemy last night were working on the left front of this subsection. They were also working in the new crater. Between 2 p.m. and 4-30 p.m. the enemy put over a number of trench mortar bombs and hand grenades into the left and centre companies. The enemy's snipers were very active throughout the night.

2. WORK. Subsection Z.1. The last 24 hours have been spent in repairing parapets and pardos and in clearing trenches and boyaux of mud and water. Footboards were fixed in the front line and wire was put out.
Two positions for dug-outs were completed and five fire steps were repaired and made serviceable.

Subsection Z.2. The front line was cleared and rivetted with sandbags. Some landslides were built up and Boyaux 20 and 16 were cleared and repaired. Two traverses in front line were rebuilt and two dug-outs were started. Some of the parapet was rebuilt and 20 yards of the trench were boarded in the front line. The third line was cleared and the fire positions improved.
Work continued on new headquarters in Z.1. and Z.2.

3. INTELLIGENCE.

The enemy's wire seems intact.
Machine Guns opened fire from points 95, 97, and A.27.b.9.5.
A small searchlight was observed at 7-50 p.m. and at 12-5 a.m. near the point at A.27.b.9.7.
A stationary light was observed near the same spot at 1-10 a.m. This appeared to be on the parapet and remained there for five minutes.
What appeared to be a light cart, was heard moving from left to right between enemy's front and second lines, near the Railway line at 7-5 p.m.
The enemy are doing a considerable amount of work in strengthening the trench in rear of LONG FARM; thick wire has been put up on stakes at A.21.b.3.2. Fresh earthwork was noticed at FRANKS KEEP.
An Officers patrol of the 2nd R. Welch Fus: went out last night to trace old trenches and to locate machine guns near the POPES NOSE. find if they were used by hostile patrols and to fix locality of machine guns near the POPES NOSE. Reference sketch attached. The patrol went out from the left of the subsection to trench "AA" which was found to be full of "French" wire. The wire it is believed was placed there by one of our brigades and ends at "B."
"C C " was unoccupied by the enemy. A.A. was followed in a southerly direction and was in parts 5 feet deep. At one point a dug-out had been commenced, and there are numbers of our entrenching tools lying about this trench. Enemy were working at "L" and "T"
The machine gun in POPES NOSE was to the North of it about one foot below the parapet in an open emplacement. The flash showed very plainly. There were no casualties and the patrol returned at midnight.
15/11/15.   Commanding 19th I.B.   Lieut-Colonel

19th Infantry Brigade.

Daily report up to 12 noon, 16th November, 1915.

1. OPERATIONS.   Right Battalion.
   Our own and the enemy's snipers were active during the night.
   The enemy's artillery was active throughout the last 24 hours,
   shells from light field guns and howitzers burst between the
   front and third lines. Some slight damage was done to parapets
   The shells appeared to be coming from AUCHY LES LA BASSEE.
   A hostile working party was located at 9-45 p.m. in front of
   RAILWAY TRENCH. They were at once fired on; but they retalia-
   ted with machine guns.

   Left Battalion.
   The enemy sniped steadily throughout the night and also sent
   over a few rifle grenades in answer to our trench mortars.
   A hostile working party was dispersed by Machine Gun fire.
   Near the new crater the enemy were much quieter than usual.

2. WORK.   Right Battalion.
   The last 24 hours have been spent in reconstructing and revetting parapets pardos and traverses. Firesteps have been improved and footboards have been laid on piles. Wire was put out in
   front of the first line.
   The above work was done on all three lines and also on ARTHURS
   and SIMS KEEPS

   Left Battalion.
   The trench round the new crater has been improved. Yesterdays
   work was continued. The revetting and clearing of trenches
   was carried on, and HIGH STREET and BACK STREET are now passable
   for stretchers. Some brick flooring was laid in WIMPOLE STREET
   The communication trenches from WIMPLOE STREET to the third
   line were revetted.

3. INTELLIGENCE.
   Machine Guns were observed at POPES NOSE, Point 79, A.27.b.9.5.
   A.27.b.9.4.,
   At 11-40 p.m. about 12 small fires sprang up 50 yards in front
   of the right of Z.1. subsection. These fires burned for 5
   minutes. Enemy then sent up a flare in this direction and
   opened fire with a machine gun. No report was heard previous
   to the springing up of the fires.
   The ground was examined and a few small circular patches of burnt
   grass were found.
   A hostile aeroplane was observed over the enemy's lines at12-30
   p.m.   Oposite Z.2. subsection a German Officer was observed.
   He wore a spiked helmet with a red band round it.
   A patrol went out last night at 10 p.m. from where the front
   line cuts the VERMELLES ROAD. They were fired on by a machine
   gun. No hostile patrols were encountered. As it was too light
   to be out in front the patrol returned.

                                                Brigadier General,

16th November, 1915.   Commanding 19th Infantry Brigade......

19th Infantry Brigade.

Daily report up to 12 noon, 17th November, 1915.

1. OPERATIONS.   Right Battalion.
The enemy's artillery was active during the night, about 70 "whizz-bangs" burst in the centre of the Z.1. area. Some little damage was done to parapets. The guns appeared to be firing from the direction of AUCHY LES LA BASSEE. A hostile machine gun fired at intervals from PORTE NORD. We replied with our machine guns. The enemy fired 6 rifle grenades into the front line near POINT 15 at 11-15 p.m. The enemy's snipers were much less active than usual. During the night we fired on and dispersed a German wiring party just north of SUB-SECTOR.

Left Battalion.
Our sniping and machine gun fire kept down the enemy's fire last night. An enemy's working party was heard in rear of the new crater. Yesterday a few trench mortar bombs fell between POINT 15 and 17.

2. WORK.   Right Battalion.
The last 24 hours have been spent in rebuilding parapets, paydos and traverses. The work of repairing firesteps was carried on; but unfortunately, much of this work was undone by the gas experts who, while inspecting the cylinders, pulled down the fire steps in places.
Some footboards were put down and two dug-outs were made. Fresh wire was put out and gaps in the old wire were repaired. Some iron loopholes were set in the parapet.

Left Battalion.
The work of cleaning the trenches and revetting was continued. ... and ... were almost wholly revetted. Loopholes were made and some wire was put out in front. The traverses in ... ... were repaired and some fire steps in LEVIS ... were rebuilt. The bricking of ... ... was continued.

3. INTELLIGENCE. Yesterday opposite the left of Z.2. subsection the enemy were seen carrying planking along their trench. This looks as if it were for use in mines.
Heavy transport was heard ... a.m. and 7 a.m. moving on the road from ... HAIGHT to AUCHY.
Two green flares were sent up in enemy's lines back of POINT 7.
At various parts of the enemy's front trench fresh earth has been thrown up.
The enemy have driven in a number of stakes in front of their front line opposite the centre of Z.1. subsection. Owing to the dull weather it is so far impossible to tell if fresh wire has so far been fixed to the stakes.

Brigadier General,
17th November, 1915.   Commanding 19th Infantry Brigade.

10th Infantry Brigade.

Daily report up to 12 noon, 18th November, 1915.

1. OPERATIONS. This morning the 1st Bn: Middlesex Regt relieved was the 2nd by
Bn: A. & S. Highlanders.

The enemy's snipers were active between 8 p.m. and 9 p.m.
but on the whole they were less active than usual.

A hostile machine gun opened fire from POPES NOSE at 5-30
p.m. During the afternoon, however, our rifles had been
fixed to cover this point, so when the machine gun flashes
were observed we opened fire with the laid rifles. The
machine gun did not again fire from POPES NOSE.

During the night the enemy shelled the area round the right
of HIGH STREET and ARMENTIERES KEEP with "whizz-bangs"

2. WORK. During the last 24 hours repairs to parapets were carried
out. Two dug-outs were built and some floorboards were
laid. The parapets in some places have collapsed owing
to the gas experts examining their cylinders. These men
pull down the fire steps and make no attempt to rebuild
them.

3. INTELLIGENCE. The enemy's wire seems intact.

Hostile transport was heard at 5-45 p.m. moving from North
to South for 15 minutes. At 6-15 p.m. it was again heard
moving in the opposite direction. This transport appeared
to consist of from 4 to 6 heavy vehicles and seemed to be
moving along the road near point A.22.b.3.0.

The enemy opposite D.2. subsection last night shouted over
some remarks in English.

A patrol sent out last night and reports that the new crater
is unoccupied but that the enemy side of the crater is
held by a small party.

Brigadier General,
18th November, 1915.   Commanding 10th Infantry Brigade.....

19th Infantry Brigade.
Daily report up to 12 noon, 19th November, 1915.

1. OPERATIONS.
Today the 5th Scottish Rifles relieved the 2nd Royal Welch Fusiliers in Z.1. Relief was carried out without incident. One Company of 2nd Royal Welch Fusiliers occupied MAISON ROUGE LUG-OUTS vice 1 Company 2nd A. & S. Hdrs. who took over the line occupied by left Company 2nd Royal Welch Fus:.

Right Battalion.
Enemy's sharpshooters were far less active than usual during last 24 hours. Hostile working party located at 11-15 p.m. working at A.27.b.?.6. They were dispersed by machine gun and rifle fire and were not heard again during the night.
Hostile artillery were active between 4-41 p.m. and 6-15 p.m. Ten light H.V. Shells burst on and about HIGH STREET and between 6-30 a.m. and 8a.m. nine burst near ASKEW Rd.

Left Battalion.
Enemy working party working on their front line opposite Right Company were dispersed by our fire.

2. WORK.
Right Battalion.
The last 24 hours have been spent in strengthening and repairing the parapet and pardos. Traverses were rebuilt and footboards put down. Wiring was continued and two dug-outs were put up.
Two positions for dugouts prepared and communication trench cleaned up.

Left Battalion.
Clearing and repairing of communication trenches was continued. Footboards were laid in ROWS 19 and BACK Row 2. The parapet was revetted and strengthened. One dug-out was completed and three more dug-outs prepared.

3. INTELLIGENCE.
Transport rather heavier than usual was heard between 7-8 p.m. and ???. This transport appears to come and go along the road through ???, north to the L.B. of ???. Enemy sent up a great many flares during the night, some of these on bursting threw out two separate lights, one lighting the ground forward and one the ground near the enemy. At 6-40 a.m. enemy sent up 3 green lights opposite J. Subsection. A great deal of coughing was heard in the enemy's lines during the night.
At 3-10 a.m. two red lights were put up opposite A.2. Subsection.
Patrol Report.
Two patrols went out last night from the Battalion in L.2. to reconnoitre the new crater. They discovered that the Germans are in the new crater and heard them talking and hammering with a wooden mallet. Very lights were fired which appeared to come out of the new crater.
Mining.
At 6-30 p.m. the left company of Battalion in L.2. subsection reported that the Germans could be heard mining under the trench, near the fork of GULL STREET. The 180th Company R.E. were communicated with and decided to counter mine at once. This was about 11 p.m. At 2 a.m. the O.C., 180th Company R.E. sent a message to say that it was not mining but some other noise, and the counter mine was not blown up. The other noise appears to have come from the leaking of some petrol tins full of water making a noise like mining.

Brigadier General,
19th November, 1915. Commanding 19th Infantry Brigade.

19th Infantry Brigade.
Daily report up to 12 noon, 20th November, 1915.

1. OPERATIONS. Right Battalion.

On this front the enemy have been fairly quiet. Hostile working parties were heard working on their wire and were dispersed by our rifle fire.

Left Battalion.

Hostile artillery were busy at 10-30 p.m. and onwards firing on BACK STREET and HIGH STREET. Hostile trench mortars were active but were silenced by our artillery.

The enemy's sharpshooters on the whole were more active than usual last night.

2. WORK. Right Battalion.

Trench boards were laid in fire trenches. Parapets rebuilt and revetted in second line.

Two dug-out positions completed.

Left Battalion.

BRAINES WAY, BOYAU 19, BOYAU 18, HIGH STREET and BACK STREET repaired and footboards placed.

Firing steps repaired in nearly whole of front line.

RUSSELLS KEEP repaired and cleared up.

3. INTELLIGENCE. Heavy transport was heard lasting for two hours crossing our front along main road running through AUCHY LES LA BASSEE from S. to N.

At 6-30 p.m. last night two red lights were put up opposite right Company of 2.2. about Point A. These two lights were followed by heavy hostile trench mortar fire.

At 7 p.m. the enemy was heard dumping stuff between points 79 and 97. Reference 36cN.W. Sheet 1.

Patrol report.

An Officers patrol examined ground around new crater. Sound of working was heard although very slight. The new crater was bombed and the enemy dispersed because all sounds of working stopped. The report was confirmed by another patrol at 5-15 a.m.

Brigadier General,
20th November, 1915. Commanding 19th Infantry Brigade..

19th Infantry Brigade.

Daily report up to 12 noon, 21st November, 1915.

1. OPERATIONS.

Right Battalion.

On this front the enemy sharpshooters have been quiet. Hostile working parties were again observed working on their wire and were dispersed by machine gun and rifle fire.

Left Battalion.

At about midnight last night SOME Germans made a bomb attack against our bomb post at the near lip of the crater near MINE POINT. They were repulsed by our bombers and forced to retire. They again attempted another bomb attack at 4 a.m. and were repulsed. Our bombers claiming to have hit some Germans as groans and obscene language were heard. Hostile snipers and machine guns were quiet.

2. WORK.

Right Battalion.

Firing platforms in first two lines improved. Parapets rebuilt and trenches generally cleaned up. Footboards laid. One more dug-out prepared. Wire improved in front of first line.

Left Battalion.

Trenches cleaned up generally. Footboards relaid. Revetting of parapets continued and wire was put out.

3. INTELLIGENCE.

A house opposite Z.2. subsection was seen to be on fire at 5-30 p.m.

Light transport again heard on AUCHY - HAISNES road about 6-30 p.m.

Patrol Report.

A patrol went out from the Battalion in Z.1. subsection between points 97 and 79 to reconnoitre the disused trenches on our front to see if any evidence of an attempt to occupy them had been made by the enemy. They found no evidence whatsoever and the patrol returned without casualties.

Brigadier General,

21st November, 1915.   Commanding 19th Infantry Brigade.

19th Infantry Brigade.
Daily report up to 12 noon, 22nd November, 1915.

Right Battalion.

1. OPERATIONS.
The enemy on this front were fairly quiet during the night. Their machine guns and snipers were more active but were silenced by our bursts of fire.

Left Battalion.
Last night the enemy having been discovered mining towards our parapet directly South of Etna salient at 6-15 this morning the 180th Company R.E. exploded a counter mine, and directly after the crater formed, under cover of heavy fire from our front line trenches, was rushed by a party of 10 bombers and 15 men (casualties 1 killed 4 wounded). The crater is now being consolodated by this party and connected by a sap to the front line trench. This new crater has been named GIBSON'S Crater.

2. WORK.

Right Battalion.
Revetting and flooring constructed in 1st and 2nd lines.
3 new sites for dug-outs cut, one dug-out completed.
Fresh wire was put out in front of fire trenches.

Left Battalion.
Twenty five yards of parapet and parados completed, also firing steps remade. HIGH STREET, BACK STREET, BOUAUX 16, 18, and 19 repaired.
Sap to GIBSON'S Crater dug for 22 yards.
Sap to old New Crater continued.

3. INTELLIGENCE.
Light transport was heard on the AUCHY road intermittingly during the night.
Many lights were sent up from the enemy's trenches during the night. A green light was sent up at 9 p.m. but nothing further happened.

Patrol Report.
A patrol again went out from the Right Battalion in Z.1. subsection to examine disused trenches in front of our line. They saw no signs of recent occupation and returned without incident.

Brigadier General,
22nd November, 1915.   Commanding 19th Infantry Brigade.

2 DIVISION

~~#1~~

19 INFANTRY BRIGADE

H.Q.

1914 AUG — 1915 NOV

TO 33 DIVISION

Unallotted.

Assembled in France 22.8.14.

The Brigade was not allotted permanently to any Division during August 1914.

B. H. Q.

19th INFANTRY BRIGADE

AUGUST 1914

Attached is narrative of events 22nd August to 1st September 1914.

19th Inf: Bde.

August 1914. Page 1.
2nd to 31st inclusive. Army Form C. 2118.

WAR DIARY
or
INTELLIGENCE SUMMARY.
(Erase heading not required.)

N.B. The Brigade has not had all its officers constantly having this during August

Hour, Date, Place	Summary of Events and Information	Remarks and references to Appendices
22–23/8. VALENCIENNES	Bde. beginning to assemble.	
23/8. VALENCIENNES	Assembly complete except two regts of Arty – Regmt. lightly holding equipment-ridge for H.Q – Coys. to aid in mng in – Bde. Brig: rep: departed & left H.Q. VIVRE CHAIN / 7h when about 10a.m. — During the afternoon the Brigade was ordered to hold its ground. The position was on the left of the line. Fresh orders as per message on page 2 — Bde moved night 23/pm to 1st Bde. all ran to relieve towards ELOUGES. Exch.	Got Maj gen Drummond Lichnowky Johnson Staff-Capt Capt. Fitz Gerald Bde Major Maj Turner D.S.O. of 2/5th 1st A Churchill ad of Major LME Lewes of 1st Capt Clayton Welsh R.C. 2/R.W.F. 2/A.S. H. Commanding Chamberlayne 1/app R. Hunt staff officers
24/8. QUIVRE CHAIN	The relief went on uneventfully. Orders to with to ELOUGES... Bde. was placed under the orders of Cav. Div.... Capt. Wise From ELOUGES the division has been through LE FENELAIN ... to Pont 13 Rules.	

19th Inf Bde August 1914 –

Instructions regarding War Diaries and Intelligence Summaries are contained in F. S. Regs., Part II. and the Staff Manual respectively. Title pages will be prepared in manuscript.

WAR DIARY
or
INTELLIGENCE SUMMARY.
(Erase heading not required.)

Army Form C. 2118.

N.B. The Brigade was not allotted permanently to any div. – during August

Hour, Date, Place	Summary of Events and Information
4 am – 23/8 FENLAIN	Brigade ordered to leave hurriedly as part of the general movement – Slightly engaged near ROMERIES & VUISSY –
	Casualties as per margin –
	Reach LE CATEAU 10 pm. day: march 19 miles
	From 23rd to 25th Aug inclusive the 19th Bde was on the extreme left of the line – Brigade placed under the orders of G.O.C. 5th Div
26th/8 LE CATEAU	4/30 am found the town was blocked with a miscellaneous collection of vehicles of other formations, notably an ambulance hastily loading up the wounded of previous day's fighting. But this was cleared away just in time. About 6/30 am the Germans advanced and some of them actually got into the outskirts of the town. There was a little street fighting. The Brigade had originally been ordered to be clear of the town by 5/30 am but this was afterwards altered to, I think 6/30 or 7.
	The Brigade having got clear of the town with hardly a casualty took up a position

Remarks and references to Appendices

Casualties 23rd

Unit	Officers K	Officers W	Officers M	OR K	OR W	OR M
~~HQ~~	–	–	–	–	–	–
~~2 RWF~~	–	–	–	–	–	–
1/Midd x	–	1		4	12	
		1		4	12	
24th						
1/Cams	–	–	–	–	–	4
2/A.S.H.	–	–	–	2	9	4
25th	–	1	–	6	21	8
RWF.	–	–	–	–	–	12
2/A.S.H.	–	–	–	2	–	–
	–	1	–	8	21	20
26th						53
2/RWF	–	–	–	–	–	
1/Mid	–	2	–	2	24	–
2/A.S.H.	–	–	11	–	–	300
HQ 26th		3 / 1 x	11	10	45 / 1	373
27th						
2/RWF.	–	–	–	–	–	68
1/Cams	–	–	–	–	–	40
	–	4	11	10	46	481

x Maj. Johnson [illegible] many of the "missing" were killed or wd.

(9 29 6) W 3332—1107 100,000 10/13 H W V Forms/C. 2118/10.

19th Suffolk Regt August 1914

Army Form C. 2118.
page 3

WAR DIARY
INTELLIGENCE SUMMARY.
(Erase heading not required.)

Hour, Date, Place	Summary of Events and Information	Remarks and references to Appendices
26/8 contd.	for statmt. see Rev. room front of 19th Bn & note my RUEMONT Road about 1½ m. N. of from the forces fd were about 10 am higher echelons 12/14th H.B. were deployed & sent forward to occupy trenches the & repos N. of 152 Road hitherto held out the same trench 150 M. N. two T/(Army ammunn were sent forward to get out & Sup Rd as we were RUEMONT to trust to retirn this ended so critical but these 2Bns were severely engaged — ! The L/I & H and I/had orders in this chfr. hand to use in posts to be kept thd & the free ready all day that ensued ably — Abt 2 p.m. the Bn was ordered to fall back to pass RUEMONT tanks we undertvd they there rested though, ad which how it believd in been there with orders along the road to St QUENTIN. The enemy infantry which had not advanced	

19th Infy Bde - Aug 1914 -

WAR DIARY
or
INTELLIGENCE SUMMARY.
(Erase heading not required.)

Army Form C. 2118.
page 4 -

Hour, Date, Place	Summary of Events and Information	Remarks and references to Appendices
26/8 One horse	Advance of our head of the Bd during the day and began to take on. The retirement was conducted in good order at first, but no 15th Bde to front of ours. The place I halted this Bde also is so densely packed in 15th Bde with troops, gunners, infantry by different units following & onward unity to luggage carts, wagons etc. The position during the day is one family heavy. The retirement was continued with humidity to trenches. Throughout the day the Brigade was kept bivoyid - Divd artillery firing from places heard in front heavy French troops seen that was having the honest to man.	Our Major 17th Bde Col Ward returns Command of the Brigade Mag- you formerly Wounded having been placed sick list. Col Ward will find it nice— during taking Bdr hosp. Mag- Ross takes Battalion.
27/8	In the evening HAM was reached & the Bde bivouaced by the rly stn at hopes which when the - they had	8th bivouaced at GREZ num Ham LE CATEAU — OISEY 40 miles
The troops the	End of page - about 50 miles since leaving LE CATEAU	

INTELLIGENCE SUMMARY.

(Erase heading not required.)

Instructions regarding War Diaries and Intelligence Summaries are contained in F. S. Regs., Part II. and the Staff Manual respectively. Title pages will be prepared in manuscript.

Hour, Date, Place	Summary of Events and Information	Remarks and references to Appendices
28/8 at E.25.	The Bttn. were ready to move at 4/30 am. but received orders at [illegible] that PONTOISE was [illegible] — was to be the [illegible] — was [illegible] to carry [illegible] buddy in head up. [illegible] were [illegible] and it not been for the help of — and [illegible] bugger in carrying [illegible] who were [illegible] [illegible] would [illegible] being home their [illegible] — Buys [illegible] [illegible] Capt Fletcher [illegible] without medical aid.	**Casualties Officers** 23rd Aug R. Lobing offcr [illegible] 26th " Maj Johnson [illegible] R.L.P.I above wounded — 24th Aug [illegible] W. C.E. Miller W " S.T. MacLean W " Capt Fletcher W " Fenton R. Brice W " C.E. Miller W " H.E. Kennedy W " L.E.A. Slater W " A.R. Woodgreen W " F.W. Gretton X " G.R. Conrad Noon W " R.M.G. Ayton
29/8 PONTOISE	Being to do been turned out POINTOISE. but not noted out.	
30/8 PONTOISE	March to CUCOISI. 15 miles about. Arrived out.	
31/8 CUCOISI	Meaut to have SENTINES — but was told not — by Bttn Cdr Starting 15th hearnt the trenches had been [illegible] by the enemy. Arrived.	Above belong to 2/M.H. have [illegible] Arrived [illegible] [illegible] Capt Fairbairn, Bng Gnd offr [illegible] the W-on [illegible] to be wounded —

27/8/14. Cmdg 19th Bgde

STORY OF 19th BRIGADE.

Supplied by Gen. Smith Dorrien AFB

Narrative of Events of 19th Infantry Brigade, from its formation (22nd August), up to and including 1st Sept. 1914.

(a)

22nd Aug.   Battalion entrained at Havre for Valenciennes.

23rd Aug.   Was informed on arrival at Valenciennes that the Battalion now formed part of the 19th Infantry Brigade formed the day previous, under the command of Major-General L. Drummond, C.B.

On detraining, the Brigade marched to Conde-Mons Canal, taking up an outpost line along it.

The same evening enemy attacked 1st Middlesex Regiment, but failed to effect a crossing. Casualties, 4 other ranks killed, Major Blakeney and 10 other ranks wounded.

24th Aug.   Brigade retired by independent movement of battalion via Elouges on Jenlain, where a defensive position was prepared, but no attack was made.

25th Aug.   Started from Jenlain at 4 a.m. for Haussy. Supported Cavalry there at midday and were shelled, retired to Solesmes and thence to Le Cateau, through the outposts of 4th Division.

26th Aug.   The Brigade left Le Cateau about 6 a.m., being the last troops to leave the town. Middlesex Regt. found the rearguard. Enemy attacked the town causing some street fighting, but were repulsed by the rearguard, who got clear with few casualties. The Brigade was then ordered to take up a position in Reserve west of the Le Cateau - Reumont Road. About 10 a.m. the 1st Middlesex Regt. and 2nd Argyll & Sutherland Highlanders were ordered to the right flank where two companies of the former battalion entrenched, holding the extreme right flank of the British position. Two battalions, viz. 2nd R. Welch Fus. and 1st Cameronians were about same time detached to the 14th Infantry Brigade near Reumont.

About 11 a.m. the Argyll & Sutherland Highlanders deployed and advanced to a forward position in the firing line supported by two companies of the Middlesex Regt. The remaining two companies held the right flank, assisted by two companies of the Royal Scots Fus., who had been placed under the orders of the O.C. 1st Middlesex Regt.

The preparation of the trenches was much assisted by a Section Field Coy. R.E., whose particular number and the name of C.O. I regret I cannot recall. Both battalions on the right flank were exposed to heavy shell fire and considerable infantry fire all day, but owing to good entrenching, the casualties were comparatively small. Between 2 and 3 p.m. approximately heavy masses of the enemy (infantry) could be seen moving opposite our right flank, and this being brought to my notice I proceeded to that flank and remained there till the conclusion of the action. I am therefore unable to speak of what happened to the remainder of the Brigade.

At about 3 p.m. there appeared to be a general retirement on our left, and receiving no orders, also being without information as to locality of Brigade Hq., I assumed local command. (It was subsequently ascertained that General Drummond had met with an accident, and the Brigade Major killed or wounded).

At 4 p.m. the Cavalry Brigade, which was in position about three miles on our right and who had throughout the day prevented the enemy from attacking us by means of their shell fire, began to retire. Finding the troops near me practically the only troops left in the Field, I judged it expedient to retire also, as it appeared that we were likely to be outflanked by the enemy in great strength. The retirement was carried out in perfect order, by successive units, under shell fire, the men being very steady. On arrival at Reumont we saw large bodies of our own troops retiring ahead of us. As far as could be judged the companies of the Royal Scots Fus. were the last to leave the field. The retirement was continued in darkness to Estrees, where this portion of the Brigade bivouacked.

27th Aug.	Retirement continued to West of St. Quentin via Ham to Ollezi, where the brigade concentrated and came under orders of G.O.C. 5th Division, Colonel Ward, 1st Middlesex Regt. being appointed to command vice Major-General Drummond, and Major R.J. Ross, 1st Middlesex Regt. being appointed Brigade Major vice Captain Johnson (wounded and missing).
28th August	The Brigade acted as rearguard to 5th Division, marching via Noyon to Pontoise.
29th Aug.	The Brigade took up defensive position on River Oise.
30th Aug.	After blowing up bridges at Pontoise at dawn, brigade marched to Attichy over River Aisne to Couloisy.
31st Aug.	Marched from Couloisy through Foret de Compiegne to St. Sauveur, where Brigade took up outposts in conjunction with 12th Brigade. Hqs. being sent to Sentines. Brigade brought under orders of 4th Division.

(b).

1st Sept.	During the morning news was brought that a battery had been severely handled in the morning fog. The Cameronians and Middlesex were ordered onto high ground south of Sentines to clear up situation. Shortly after arrival a message came from General Briggs, Commanding 1st Cavalry Brigade, that he was in difficulties, and asking for assistance at the village of Nery. The 1st Middlesex Regt. with Cameronians in support, were directed on the village, where it was found that a battery of enemy's guns were firing on the cavalry bivouac at short range. On coming under effective infantry fire the enemy abandoned their guns, eight of which fell into the hands of the Middlesex Regt. together with about 30 prisoners. One Coy. Middlesex Regt. pursued in the direction of the enemy with their limbers, capturing an ambulance wagon with two medical officers and wounded Germans.

The Brigade then found the rearguard and covered the retirement of the 4th Division, taking up that night a defensive position at Fresnoy.

In connection with above operations, I would, as officiating Brigade Commander, bring to notice the name of

Major R.J. Ross, 1st Middlesex Regiment

my acting Brigade Major, who under circumstances of great difficulty, owing to the hurried organization of the Brigade, rendered me valuable assistance under very trying circumstances

(Signed) B.H. Ward, Lieut-Colonel,
1st Middlesex Regiment.
(late Commanding 19th Infantry Bde.)

No permanent allotment

B. H. Q.

19th INFANTRY BRIGADE

SEPTEMBER 1914

Hg 1st Inf Bde

Army Form C. 2118.
Page 1-

WAR DIARY
or
INTELLIGENCE SUMMARY.

Sept 1914.

(Erase heading not required.)

Hour, Date, Place	Summary of Events and Information	Remarks and references to Appendices
SENTINES. 1st Sept.	About 4 am a few Uhlans galloping along the village street created some sensation but calm soon prevailed — 2 hours later the Brigade having just arrived to the hills to the southern of the village was met by a messenger who asked for help urgently for the 1st Cav Bde (under Gen Briggs) which had got into difficulties at NÉRY and had suffered very heavily. Col Bird at once marched the 1st Brigade to their relief about 1 mile. The enemy appeared to have got right round the Cavalry and had succeeded in placing two guns to within 800 yards of their camp. The Cavalry had a great many casualties & kept their horses were lying dead in rows. Although very tired before an incident in which the enemy were driven off the 12 field Guns captured, the 10 guns took about 60 prisoners — Soon afterwards the march to FRESNOY was resumed. Enemies reached about 8 pm. Distance 14 miles.	Casualties Very slight due end of month

(9 29 6) W 3332—1107 100,000 10/13 H WV Forms/C. 2118/10.

Army Form C. 2118.

19th Inf. Bde. Sept 1914. page 2

WAR DIARY
or
INTELLIGENCE SUMMARY.

(Erase heading not required.)

Instructions regarding War Diaries and Intelligence Summaries are contained in F.S. Regs., Part II. and the Staff Manual respectively. Title pages will be prepared in manuscript.

Hour, Date, Place	Summary of Events and Information	Remarks and references to Appendices

FRESNOY. 2nd Sept. March to LONGPERRIER near DAMARTIN about 13 miles —

LONGPERRIER. 3rd. March about midnight 2/3rd Sept. LAGNY across the MARNE about 9am — in the afternoon to CHANTELOUP 2 miles — fine — Very hot day —

CHANTELOUP. 4th. Resting all day —

CHANTELOUP. 5th. March to GRISY about 14 miles —

Army Form C. 2118.

WAR DIARY
or
INTELLIGENCE SUMMARY.
(Erase heading not required.)

Instructions regarding War Diaries and Intelligence Summaries are contained in F.S. Regs., Part II. and the Staff Manual respectively. Title pages will be prepared in manuscript.

Hour, Date, Place	Summary of Events and Information	Remarks and references to Appendices
Sept 5th CHANTELOUP	Bde move to GRISY. By General Hon F Gordon taken over command of Bde. and Captn C P Hayward Coldstream Guards takes up duties of Bde Major.	
Sept. 6th GRISY	Bde marches in rear of 4th Div and goes into bivouac at VILLNEUVE ST DENIS.	
Sept 7th VILLNEUVE ST DENIS	Bde forms part of left column of 4th Div and marches to LA HAUTE MAISON – Kept touch in general with enemy – Bde bivouac.	
Sept 8th LA HAUTE MAISON	Orders issued to attack in direction of PIERRE LEVEE at 5 a.m. Enemy found to have withdrawn during night – Bde moves forward to SIGNY – SIGNET bit beneath Bde of left Column of 4th Div. On ridges just S of MARNE this advanced guard 1st MIDDLESEX Connaughts shell fire from N branch of river – MIDDLESEX remain in possession of ridges N of SIGNY-SIGNET – Connaughts in reserve – A and S Highlanders and 1st RWF Bde move 3 p.m. to LES CARRIERS under orders of G.O.C. 11th Inf. Bde – Welsh Fusiliers move down with LA FERE and kept Sherwoods under cover and in hours in N bank of MARNE. Connaughts relieve Middlesex on ridge. At S Highlanders & WELSH FUSILIERS rejoin Bde 3 p.m. Bde marches 9.30 p.m. to JOUARRE where Connaughts left in bivouac at SIGNY-SIGNET.	Casualties Welsh Fus. 4 NCOs and men wounded. Connaughts 3 " " wounded. A&S Hrs 1 man killed Middlesex 3 NCOs and men killed – 30 wounded WELSH FUSILIERS 1 Officer 1 man Killed 10 NCOs & men wounded Connaughts 1 Officer 11 men wounded Middlesex
Sept 9th SIGNY-SIGNY		
Sept 10th JOUARRE	Bde (less Connaughts) move at 3.30 a.m. Crossing MARNE by pontoon bridge at LA FERE and arrive on left flank General of 4th Div. Bivouac to night at CERTIGNY – when Connaughts rejoin.	

Army Form C. 2118.

WAR DIARY
or
INTELLIGENCE SUMMARY.
(Erase heading not required.)

Instructions regarding War Diaries and Intelligence Summaries are contained in F. S. Regs., Part II. and the Staff Manual respectively. Title pages will be prepared in manuscript.

Hour, Date, Place	Summary of Events and Information	Remarks and references to Appendices
Sept 11th CERTIGNY	Btte marched 7a.m. in rear of 4th Div. and billeted for night at Bte MARTZY St GENEVIEVE. Very wet 12 men wounded for night.	
Sept 12th MARTZY ST GENEVIEVE	Btte marched in rear of 4th Div to BUZANCY when it billeted for night. Very wet afternoon.	
Sept 13th BUSANCY.	March 3 p.m. through SEPTMONTS to near CARRIÈRE L'ÉVÊQUE. Where bivouac for the night.	

Army Form C. 2118.

WAR DIARY
or
INTELLIGENCE SUMMARY.
(Erase heading not required.)

Instructions regarding War Diaries and Intelligence Summaries are contained in F. S. Regs., Part II. and the Staff Manual respectively. Title pages will be prepared in manuscript.

Hour, Date, Place	Summary of Events and Information	Remarks and references to Appendices
Sept 14 ~~BUSANCY~~ CARRIERE LEVEQUE	Bttn marched at 12.30. a.m. k bivod SEPT VENIZEL, as reserve to 4th Div on heights N of River AISNE near BUSY LE LONG	
Sept 15 VENIZEL	Middlesex and Cameronians movie at 2.30 a.m. N of R. AISNE to covr pontoon bridge – very wet day and night – all much bivouac in woods – very boggy and unhealthy –	
Sept 16 VENIZEL	A and S Highlanders men bivouac at 8 p.m. to BUSY LE LONG in support of 10th Inf Bde – No other change of position.	
Sept 17th VENIZEL	Very wet all day – A & S Highlanders sheltered in bivouac at BUSY LE LONG. 1 man killed.	
Sept 18th VENIZEL	Very wet night 17/18 and all day 18th – Received orders to join 2nd Corps, but orders cancelled –	
Sept 19th VENIZEL	Welsh Fusiliers movi back 9 a.m. N of BUZZY to entrench position on Plateau –	
Sept 20th VENIZEL	19th Bde movd 9 p.m. to SEPTMONTS (4 miles) and goes into billets –	
Sept 21st SEPTMONTS	Welsh Fusiliers and Middlesex entrained on Plateau SW of ACY –	
Sept 22 " " "	A & S Highlanders and Cameronians entrench on Plateau SW of ACY –	

WAR DIARY
or
INTELLIGENCE SUMMARY
(Erase heading not required.)

Army Form C. 2118.

19th Infantry Bde.

Hour, Date, Place	Summary of Events and Information	Remarks and References to Appendices
Sept 23d SEPTMONTS	2 Battalions entrenched on ACY plateau.	
" 24th "	2 Battalions entrenched ACY plateau	
" 25th "		
" 26th "		
" 27th "	Bde ordered 5.30 a.m. to march to SERCHES, as enemy reported to be crossing AISNE at CONDÉ. Order cancelled before Bde marched off. 2 Companies sent out to collect wire and mend roads.	
" 28th "		
" 29th "	3 Companies employed improving gun epaulements.	
" 30th "	1 Company employed entrenching Staff ACY.	
	(9th Inf Bde relieved at SEPT MONTS)	J. Gordon Brig Genl. Comdg 19th Inf. Bde

No permanent allottment

B. H. Q.

19th INFANTRY BRIGADE

OCTOBER 1914

19th Infantry Bde.

Army Form C. 2118.

WAR DIARY
or
INTELLIGENCE SUMMARY.
(Erase heading not required.)

Instructions regarding War Diaries and Intelligence Summaries are contained in F.S. Regs., Part II. and the Staff Manual respectively. Title pages will be prepared in manuscript.

Hour, Date, Place	Summary of Events and Information	Remarks and references to Appendices
October 1st to 4th Septmonts	In reserve to 3rd Corps.	
5th Septmonts	March 7.30 p.m. to St REMY	
6th St REMY	March 7.30 p.m. to VEZ	
7th VEZ	March 5.30 p.m. to BETHISY St PIERRE	
8th BETHISY	March 2 p.m. PONT St MAXENCE	
9th Pont St MAXENCE	March 7 a.m. to ESTREES St DENIS. Commenced entraining 6 p.m.	
10th HAZEBROUCK St OMER	First train of Bde arrivd St OMER 11 a.m. Commenced Sent on and put towards RENESCURE. Whole Bde clear arrived by midnight 10/11.	There might possibly be a point to content ? movement from ambush ?
11th St OMER	March to RENESCURE to cover detrainment of 4th Division at St OMER.	
12th RENESCURE	March 6.30 a.m. through HAZEBROUCK and MERVIN to BARRE - St SYLVESTRE STRAZEELE. On extended patrol in line in touch with enemy about STRAZEELE.	
13th BORRE	19th Brigade concentrated at ROUGE CROIX forming Corps reserve while 4th and 6th Division attack enemy in line VIEUX BERQUIN - METEREN - BERTEN.	
14th ROUGE CROIX	Attack continues and enemy retires 9 a.m. 12 noon 19th Inf Bde with 1 Bat. R.A. from out of St SYLVESTRE. Advance guard to MONT DE LILLE coming in touch with Enemy.	Casualties 3 men wounded

WAR DIARY
INTELLIGENCE SUMMARY.
(Erase heading not required.)

Army Form C. 2118.

Hour, Date, Place	Summary of Events and Information	Remarks and references to Appendices
15th Oct. MONT DE LILLE	R. Welsh Fusiliers & other [troops?] of North Country. Trench small body of troops of North Country. The 19th Brigade moved to STEENWERCK arriving there at 12 midnight 15/16 morning march to 4th Divn which took over from us via R. LYS.	
16th STEENWERCK	March 4.10 p.m. via NEUVE EGLISE to VLAMERTINGHE as a reserve to 4th Corps.	
17th to a 18th Oct. VLAMERTINGHE	In billets VLAMERTINGHE	
19th " " "	March 2 pm to LAVENTIE (23 miles) as reserve to 3rd Corps. [20?] by motor buses) (Commanders go by motor) Fusiliers [committed?] to entrench on the line FAUQUISART — CROIX BLANCHE. At 12 noon the White brigade ordered to march on FROMELLES which place was reached at 3 p.m.	
20th LAVENTIE	7. a.m. Cameronians and Welsh Fusiliers. The situation at this time was as follows. The right of the 3rd Corps was at RADINGHEM; the left of the 2nd Corps about AUBERS. The space between them two Points being held by French Cavalry. Two Battalions, the Welsh Fusiliers and Middlesex were pushed forward to the line Post FROMELLES — PONT DE PIERRE to hold a line slightly in rear of the French Cavalry. The enemy were in touch with our Divn at RADINGHEM during the & were engaged with 6th Divn at RADINGHEM during the afternoon. The two Bns in reserve bivouacked about a mile N.W. of FROMELLES for the night.	

WAR DIARY
or
INTELLIGENCE SUMMARY.
(Erase heading not required.)

Army Form C. 2118.

Instructions regarding War Diaries and Intelligence Summaries are contained in F. S. Regs., Part II. and the Staff Manual respectively. Title pages will be prepared in manuscript.

Hour, Date, Place	Summary of Events and Information	Remarks and references to Appendices
21st Oct FROMELLES	During the night 20/21 orders were received from 3rd Corps that 19th Bde. should occupy FROMELLES and LE MAISNIL and then fill the gap between 2nd and 3rd Corps. To carry out this object the 2nd H. and S. Fus. moved at 4 a.m. to LE MAISNIL (which they found held by French Cavalry and Cyclists) while the Welsh Fusiliers extended their front so as to hold from the SW corner of FROMELLES to PONT DE PIERRE to a Central position about BAS MAISNIL. The Cameronians and Middlesex moved at 7 a.m. Towards 11 a.m. the enemy opened a very heavy shell fire on LE MAISNIL which continued throughout the day. At 12 noon Middlesex (less 2 Coys) were sent forward to support the H. and S. Fus.— The enemy developed a strong infantry attack against LE MAISNIL during the afternoon. Some French Cyclists holding ground on the left flank of this defeat gave way at 5 p.m. whereupon the position became untenable and the H. and S. Fus. and Middlesex retired on BAS MAISNIL before a largely superior force of the enemy. A line was taken up for the night astride the FLEURBAIX — LE MAISNIL Road about LA BOUTILLERIE	Casualties. Officers Other Ranks Killed — 6 Wounded — 5 — 44 Missing — 3 250 * * Many of these men were killed and wounded which had to be abandoned owing to retirement.

Army Form C. 2118.

WAR DIARY
or
INTELLIGENCE SUMMARY.
(Erase heading not required.)

Instructions regarding War Diaries and Intelligence Summaries are contained in F. S. Regs., Part II. and the Staff Manual respectively. Title pages will be prepared in manuscript.

Hour, Date, Place	Summary of Events and Information	Remarks and references to Appendices
Oct 22. LA BOUTILLERIE	19th Inf Bde taking up a defensive position on the line Fauquet - LA BOUTILLERIE - ROUGES BANCS. in touch with 16th Inf Bde on the left and with French Cavalry on the right - Enemy attacked overnight parties but went on their effort.	Casualties. Officers. Other Ranks. Killed - 1 15 Wounded - 2 38 Missing - 1 19
Oct 23 " "	"	Killed 2 Wounded 7
Oct 24 " "	Enemy heavy by their trench constructed trenches within 500 to 700 yds of our lines. During the night 24/25 the enemy showed heavy fire from his own call along the line but made no real attempt to push forward.	Killed 5 Wounded 24
Oct 25 " "	1st Bn Royal Fus. relieved French troops on our right and joined up their with the 8th Indian Bde (Ret. later relieved French Cavalry on our left Oct 24.) Enemy made no serious attempt to attack - a good deal of shelling and sniping.	Killed 1 Wounded 25
Oct 26 " "	"	26 Killed 1 Wounded 29 / 50
Oct 27 " "	"	27 Killed 1 Wounded 8 / 34
Oct 28 " "	"	28 Killed 5 Wounded 41
Oct 29 " "	"	29 Killed 1 Wounded 5 / 22

Army Form C. 2118.

WAR DIARY
or
INTELLIGENCE SUMMARY.
(Erase heading not required.)

19th Infantry Bde.

Hour, Date, Place	Summary of Events and Information	Remarks and references to Appendices
Oct. 30th LABOUTILLERIE 12.30 a.m.	A heavy attack made by the enemy on the whole of front held by 19th Inf Bde. attack started 12.30, a.m. and continued till dawn. Some of enemy succeeded in entering right of our trenches. Dead Germans found 4 to number of 300 were counted in front of trenches on morning. A party of 50 enemy penetrated between two of our trenches but were all of their supporters in (Capture). The regiments opposed to us were 223 and 224.	Casualties Officers / Other ranks killed 23 wounded 4 / 47
Oct 31st " "	Enemy remained in trenches, opposite to us making no further effort to attack. A good deal of sniping and shelling	killed — 5 wounded — 10

No permanent allottment

B. H. Q.

19th INFANTRY BRIGADE

NOVEMBER 1 9 1 4

Army Form C. 21

WAR DIARY
or
INTELLIGENCE SUMMARY. November. 19th Inf. Bde.

(Erase heading not required.)

Instructions regarding War Diaries and Intelligence Summaries are contained in F.S. Regs., Part II. and the Staff Manual respectively. Title pages will be prepared in manuscript.

Hour, Date, Place	Summary of Events and Information	Remarks and references to Appendices
		Casualties
		Officer / Other ranks
		Killed / Wounded
LA BOUTILLERIE 1. November.	A good deal of shelling by hostile artillery — About 5 Hrs out withdrawn to ERQUINGHEM when they come under 4th Div —	K. 1 / 3 W. — / 11 ✗
2nd Nov. " "	The enemy are active sniping and shelling our line of trenches. Their artillery appears on line of trenches a battery of heavy howitzers, a battery in Action, a battery of 4.5 howitzers, and at least one Horse Artillery Battery, the guns of which are pushed up to short range — Our artillery in the	K. — / 2 W. — / 11
3rd Nov " "	section attached to the Brigade consists of two Field Batteries 24th Bde. R.F.A. 1 Howitzer Battery and 2 Six inch Howitzers —	K. — / 4 W. 2 / 26
4th Nov " "	The hostile infantry display much activity sapping up towards our trenches and throwing their hostile parallels — In most places the hostile	K. — / 6 W. 2 / 15
5th Nov " "	trenches are from 200 to 400 yds from our own —	K. — / 2 W. — / 7
6th Nov. " "	On the 7th and 8th Nov. the lines held by the Middlesex Regt were very heavily shelled causing heavy casualties. Hostile guns could not be located, and the only reply that could be made was for our guns to shell enemy's trenches —	K. — / 2 W. A.W. 14 / 16½ ✗ 11½
7th Nov " "		K. — / 13 W. 1 / 42

(9 29 6) W 3332—1107 100,000 10/13 H W V Forms/C. 2118/10.

Army Form C. 21

WAR DIARY
or
INTELLIGENCE SUMMARY.
(Erase heading not required.)

November
19 Inf. Bde.

Hour, Date, Place	Summary of Events and Information	Remarks and references to Appendices
8th Nov. LA BOUTILLERIE		Casualties Officers Other ranks K. — 5 W. 2 27
9th Nov. "		K. — 3 W. — 5
10th Nov. "	A and S Coys made a night attack near PLDEGSTEERT acting under orders of 11th Inf Bde. night 9/10	K. 2 W. 5 #132
11th Nov. "		K. — W. — Nil
12th Nov. "		K. — W. — Nil
13th Nov. "	During last 4 days both artillery Bombardment much reduced.	K. 2 W. — 4

Army Form C. 2118.

19th Inf. Bde.

WAR DIARY
or
INTELLIGENCE SUMMARY.
(Erase heading not required.)

Instructions regarding War Diaries and Intelligence Summaries are contained in F. S. Regs., Part II. and the Staff Manual respectively. Title pages will be prepared in manuscript.

Hour, Date, Place	Summary of Events and Information	Remarks and references to Appendices
		Casualties — Other Ranks
		Officer
Nov 14th LA BOUTILLERIE	6pm. The 19th Inf Bde relieved by 20th Inf Bde – Bde withdraws to billets at BAC ST MAUR. A and S Hrs return from being attached to 11th Inf Bde –	K. 1 W. 4
Nov 15th BAC ST MAUR	In billets BAC ST MAUR	K. Nil W.
Nov 16th BAC ST MAUR	" "	K. Nil W.
Nov 17th BAC ST MAUR	Bde relieves 10th Inf Bde taking over line of trenches from L'EPINETTE to LA RUAGE just East of HOUPLINES – line held by Cameronians on left, with Fus in centre, A and S Hrs on right. Middlx in Bde Reserve –	K. Nil W.
Nov 18th HOUPLINES	Enemy not nearly so active as at LA BOUTILLERIE. A certain amount of sniping but little hostile artillery fire agst our line – Enemy's trenches within 100 yds on left of line, but their centre and left, between 500 and 800 yds distant –	Nil –

Army Form C. 2118

WAR DIARY
or
INTELLIGENCE SUMMARY. 19th Inf. Bde
(Erase heading not required.)

Instructions regarding War Diaries and Intelligence Summaries are contained in F. S. Regs., Part II. and the Staff Manual respectively. Title pages will be prepared in manuscript.

Hour, Date, Place	Summary of Events and Information	Remarks and references to Appendices
Nov. 19th HOUPLINES.	5th (Territorial) Bn Scottish Rifles join the 19th Inf Bde and billet at ARMENTIERS.	Casualties Officers Men K. W. 4
Nov. 20th "	This section of the line supported by 2, 4.5" Howitzers and 1 Batty R.F.A. Enemy having shown little activity with their artillery, and confined themselves to Sniping.	k. w. 1
Nov. 21st "		K. Nil. W
Nov. 22nd " Nov. 23rd " Nov. 24th "		Nil Nil k w 1 latter
Nov. 25th "	Middlesex Regt relieve Welsh Fusiliers, and become Bde reserve.	k w 1
Nov. 26th "		Nil
Nov. 27th "	5th Bn S.R. send up one Company to Cameronians Trenches, one Company to A and S Hrs trenches. These two Companies remain the 2 days & nights and are then relieved by the other Companies.	K 1 W
Nov. 28th "		K W 1
Nov. 29th "		K W 1
Nov. 30th "		Nil - K 1 + 42 W 13 + 208

CM Fitzwere (aft
BM

Forms/C. 2118/10.

(2 DIV)
(Box 1364)

No permanent allottment

B. H. Q.

19th INFANTRY BRIGADE

DECEMBER 1914

Army Form C. 2118.

19th Infantry Bde

WAR DIARY
or
INTELLIGENCE SUMMARY.
(Erase heading not required.)

Instructions regarding War Diaries and Intelligence Summaries are contained in F. S. Regs., Part II. and the Staff Manual respectively. Title pages will be prepared in manuscript.

Hour, Date, Place	Summary of Events and Information	Remarks and References to Appendices
		Casualties
		Officers / Other ranks
Dec 1st HOUPLINES		Nil
„ 2nd „	Welsh Fusiliers relieve Camerons in the trenches. The latter coming into Brigade Reserve	Nil
„ 3rd „		Nil
„ 4th „	A good deal of rain fell during this period, and much work resumed in trenches to keep them in order.	Nil
„ 5th „		Killed — 1 / Wounded — 5
„ 6th „	Enemy's infantry and artillery in trenches and artillery inactive — Hostile snipers active —	Nil
„ 7th „		K — 2 / W — 1
„ 8th „	Night attack made by enemy. This first intimation of activity was the enemy opening at 7.30 p.m. wales of musketry fire from opposite night of A and S Coys — The Seen Learshah trenches A and S Coys handled artillery and forward the enemy to within 150 yds of centre of A and S Coys — 50 men to within 150 yds	K — 2 / W — 5
„ 9th „	This parts of enemy opened fire but soon after wards withdrew to their trenches — A few of the enemy also advanced towards the centre and right of the Middlesex. Fire from the trenches of A and S Coys and Middlesex then before I suered and our artillery opened in support —	K — 6 / W — 13

19 M Inf

Army Form C. 2118.

WAR DIARY
or
INTELLIGENCE SUMMARY.
(Erase heading not required.)

Instructions regarding War Diaries and Intelligence Summaries are contained in F. S. Regs., Part II. and the Staff Manual respectively. Title pages will be prepared in manuscript.

Hour, Date, Place	Summary of Events and Information	Remarks and references to Appendices. Casualties Officer / Other ranks
Dec. 10th HOUPLINES	Hostile artillery was opened on our trenches and on HOUPLINES — All firing ceased about 8.30 p.m. — The General in charge opined was that enemy intended to make an attack, but failed to push it home —	K. — / W. 2
Dec. 11th " "	Cameronians relieved A and S Hrs in the trenches, the latter go into 6 Div reserve at Lunatic Asylum ARMENTIERES — Brigade ordered to show activity = so as to prevent enemy withdrawing troops to Neuve Ypres to that northern wards, where an attack by allies was in progress. Sub. Command. Sri pms more active and artillery covered hostile trenches daily	K. — / W. 2 — / 2 19 M.H.
Dec. 12th		K. — / W. 1 / 6

Army Form C. 2118.

WAR DIARY
or
INTELLIGENCE SUMMARY.
(Erase heading not required.)

19th Infantry Bde.

Hour, Date, Place	Summary of Events and Information	Remarks and references to Appendices
		Casualties Other ranks
		Officers
Dec 13th HOUPLINES		K —
14th "	During this period the Enemy showed little activity with his artillery, and made no attempt to push his trenches closer to ours.	W — 1
15th "		K — 1
16th "		W — 3
17th "		K 1, W 1 — 2
18th "		K —, W — 2
19th "		K Nil
20th "	Hants & The relieve Middlesex in the trenches the latter going into 6 Div reserve at Asylum ARMENTIERES.	W — 6, K — 2, W 1

Army Form C. 2118.

WAR DIARY
or
INTELLIGENCE SUMMARY.
(Erase heading not required.)

19th Infantry Bde.

Hour, Date, Place	Summary of Events and Information	Remarks and references to Appendices
		Casualties
		Officers / Other Ranks
Dec 21st HOUPLINES	In spite of wet state of trenches, Men have had little sickness during this time - Average daily admittance to hospital about this period 15 per day from the Brigade.	Nil
22nd "		K 2
23rd "		W 2
24th "		K 4
25th "		W 2 / 1st 5 Nil 3+51
26th "	The Brigade relieved by 18th Infantry Bde and went into billets in SW outskirts of ARMENTIERES as III Corps reserve.	Nil
27th ARMENTIERES	In Billets as reserve to III Corps. Brigade exercised in route marching daily.	Nil
28th "		Nil
29th "		Nil
30th "		Nil
31st "		Nil

F. Gordon
B. General
Commanding 19 Inf Bde.

ATTACHED 6 DIVISION

19 INFANTRY BRIGADE

1915 JAN — 1915 MAY

To 27 DIVISION

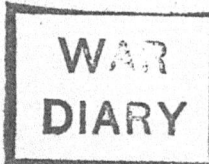

Headquarters,

19th INFANTRY BRIGADE.

(6th Division)

J A N U A R Y

1 9 1 5

D.A.A.G
The Base.

War Diary for January 1915 herewith.

Feb 2ⁿᵈ
1915

J Gordon
Bʳ General
Commanding
19ᵗʰ Infantry Bde

Army Form C. 2118.

WAR DIARY or INTELLIGENCE SUMMARY.

(Erase heading not required.)

January 1915

19th Infantry Bde.

Instructions regarding War Diaries and Intelligence Summaries are contained in F. S. Regs., Part II. and the Staff Manual respectively. Title pages will be prepared in manuscript.

Hour, Date, Place	Summary of Events and Information	Remarks and references to Appendices — Casualties —		
			Officers	Other ranks
		Killed / Wounded		
Jan 1st ARMENTIERES	In Corps reserve (3rd Corps).	K.	nil	
		W.		
Jan 2d ARMENTIERES	Relieve 16th Inf Bde. in line of trenches running between TOUQUET and RUE DUBOIS, 3 miles South of ARMENTIERES.	K.		1
		W.		1
Jan 3d BOIS GRENIER	Very heavy rain during the last week, trenches in a very bad state owing to the wet.	K.		
		W.		3
Jan 4th " "	This Section supported by 12th Bde RFA. 1 Battalion in the trenches, Cameronians, 1 Middlesex and 2 Hand 5th and 5th RW.	K.		nil
		W.		
Jan 5th " "	in Bde reserve 2 Welsh Fus and 5th RW. Scottish Rifles.	K.		1
		W.		1
Jan 6th " "	Wet weather continues and all communication trenches knee deep in parts. The erection of breastworks becomes necessary	K.		1
		W.		1
Jan 7th " "	and is commenced, material being supplied by the 1st London Fd. Co R.E.	K.		1
		W.		1
Jan 8th " "	Welsh Fusiliers relieve Cameronians in the trenches.	K.		1
		W.		1

Army Form C. 2118.

WAR DIARY
or
INTELLIGENCE SUMMARY.
(Erase heading not required.)

19th Infantry Bde.

Instructions regarding War Diaries and Intelligence Summaries are contained in F. S. Regs., Part II. and the Staff Manual respectively. Title pages will be prepared in manuscript.

Hour, Date, Place	Summary of Events and Information	Remarks and references to Appendices Casualties		
		Officer	Other ranks	
		Killed	Wounded	
Jan 9th BOIS GRENIER	Wet weather continued and period of transition between trenches and breastworks leads to much intermittent in troops holding the front line.			4
Jan 10th " "		K		
		W		2
Jan 11th " "	Enemy being in an bad a state as ourselves, and forced to work their own trenches, and in fact at their relief show little activity. Sniping or shelling	K		4
		W		1
Jan 12th " "		K		2
		W		
Jan 13th " "		K		1
		W		6
	Camerinians relieve A and S Hrs. in the trenches.			
Jan 14th " "	Little in movement in the weather, but Breastwork accommodation daily increased, and more dry dug outs than provided	K		3
		W	1	7
Jan 15th " "		K		1
		W		2
Jan 16th " "		K		
		W		
Jan 17th " "		K		1
		W		2

Army Form C. 2118.

WAR DIARY
or
INTELLIGENCE SUMMARY.
(Erase heading not required.)

19-Inf Bde.

Hour, Date, Place	Summary of Events and Information	Remarks and references to Appendices
		Casualties Officers OR Killed Wounded
Jan 18th BOIS GRENIER	Cameronians relieve Hamps S Hrs relieve Middlesex	K 1 / 1
Jan 19th	Cameronians take over line held by Welsh Fusiliers – 2 Companies 5th S.R. take over a portion of the centre of the line.	W 2
Jan 20th	Trenches thus held by 2 Bns (which are relieved every 5th day by the 2 Battalions in reserve) and by 2 Companies S.R. (which are relieved every 3rd day by the other 2 Companies of their Battalion).	K 1 / W 3
Jan 21st		K 1 / W 2
Jan 22nd		K nil / W nil
Jan 23rd	Little in front went in the weather but good progress made with breastworks —	K 2 / W M'5 2
Jan 24th		K M'5 / W M'5
Jan 25th		K nil / W nil
Jan 26th	Bombardment carried out by supporting batteries against hostile trenches in our front to test concentration of fire on enemy's works and breastworks	K 1 / W

Army Form C. 2118.

WAR DIARY
or
INTELLIGENCE SUMMARY.
(Erase heading not required.)

19th Infantry Bde.

Hour, Date, Place	Summary of Events and Information	Remarks and references to Appendices
		Casualties
		Officers / Other ranks
Jan 27th Bois GRENIER	Dry weather sets in – Trenches much improved –	Killed / 2
		Wounded / 2
Jan 28th	Breast works now within measurable distance of completion along all the front which will be required –	K. / nil
		W / nil
Jan 29th	All men in front line now well accommodated in dry dug outs	K / 2
		W /
Jan 30th		K / 1
		W /
Jan 31st		K / 1
		W /
		Total Casualties for this month K 14 / 1
		W 60 / 1
		— / 2
		75

F. Gordon Br. General
Commanding 19th Inf Bde.

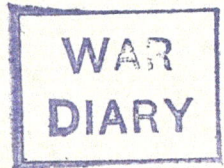

Headquarters,

19th INFANTRY BRIGADE.

(6th Division)

F E B R U A R Y

1 9 1 5

February 1915.

Army Form C. 2118.

WAR DIARY
or
INTELLIGENCE SUMMARY.
(Erase heading not required.)

19th / 1st Bde

Instructions regarding War Diaries and Intelligence Summaries are contained in F.S. Regs., Part II. and the Staff Manual respectively. Title pages will be prepared in manuscript.

Hour, Date, Place	Summary of Events and Information	Remarks and references to Appendices	Officers	O.R.
BOIS GRENIER Feb 1st	19th Infantry Bde continues to hold the same line, with 2 Battalions and 2 Co 5th Scottish Rifles in the trenches — The two regular Bns do 5 days in the trenches and then 5 in reserve in billets, the 2 Co 5th SR, 3 days in the trenches and 3 in reserve in billets —	Killed Wounded	—	1 1
" " Feb 2nd		Missing Killed Wounded Missing	— 1 — —	1 3 1
" " Feb 3rd	Artillery bombardment by 12th Bde RFA Carried out against a portion of the Enemy's trenches opposite our left Battalion	Killed Wounded	— 1	1 2
" " Feb 4th	Hostile artillery, with cooperation of two of their Search lights, bombarded our front line of trenches, and also the roads by which our ration wagons move up. Bombardment started 7pm and lasted 45 minutes — Our guns opened a hot fire in return on the Enemy's trenches — No transport damaged —	Killed Wounded	1 1	6 13

Army Form C. 2118.

WAR DIARY
or
INTELLIGENCE SUMMARY.
(Erase heading not required.)

19th Bn. February

Hour, Date, Place	Summary of Events and Information	Remarks and references to Appendices
BOIS GRENIER Feb. 5th	A great deal of work necessary in the trenches to maintain parapets and treadwork. —	Officers O.R. Wounded — 1
" Feb. 6th	New work carried out on supporting points close in rear of fire trenches. —	Killed ※ 1
" Feb 7th		— 1
" Feb 8th	The enemy shows no particular activity, but is active sniping. —	Wounded 1 —
" Feb 9th		Killed — 1 Wounded — 8
" Feb 10th	The artillery appeared to be firing spasmodically at the trenches, and at BOIS GRENIER, but did little damage. —	Killed — 2 Wounded — 4
" Feb 11th		Wounded 1 —
" Feb 12th		Wounded — 4
" Feb 13th		Wounded — 2
" Feb 14th		Wounded 1 — 2

Army Form C. 2118.

WAR DIARY
or
INTELLIGENCE SUMMARY.
(Erase heading not required.)

February

Instructions regarding War Diaries and Intelligence Summaries are contained in F. S. Regs., Part II. and the Staff Manual respectively. Title pages will be prepared in manuscript.

Hour, Date, Place	Summary of Events and Information	Remarks and references to Appendices
BOIS GRENIER		O/R
Feb 15		wounded — 5
" 16		wounded — 2
" 17	4th Canadian Battalion attached for a week to be instructed in trench duties.	wounded — 1
" 18		killed — 3
		wounded — 3
" 19		killed — 1
		wounded — 1
" 20	There is little improvement in the weather. This whole country is water-logged, and it is only possible to maintain trenches by constant bailing and pumping.	— — 1
" 21		killed — 2
" 22		drowned — 2
		wounded — 3
" 23		— — 1

Army Form C. 2118.

February

19th Inf Bde

WAR DIARY
or
INTELLIGENCE SUMMARY.
(Erase heading not required.)

Instructions regarding War Diaries and Intelligence Summaries are contained in F.S. Regs. Part II. and the Staff Manual respectively. Title pages will be prepared in manuscript.

Hour, Date, Place	Summary of Events and Information	Remarks and references to Appendices
BOIS GRENIER Feb 24	Canadian Section Bn attached for a week trip in shelter in trench duties –	off o.R. killed — 1.
Feb 25		wounded — 2.
Feb 26		wounded — 1 missing — 1
Feb 27		— —
Feb 28		killed — 1

F. Gordon
Brigadier General
1/3/15 — Comdg 19th Inf Bde

Headquarters.

19th INFANTRY BRIGADE.

(6th Division)

M A R C H

1 9 1 5

Army Form C. 2118.

19th Infantry Bde WAR DIARY March 1915

or INTELLIGENCE SUMMARY.

(Erase heading not required.)

19 1/8

Hour, Date, Place		Summary of Events and Information	Remarks and references to Appendices
			O. O.R.
1 March	Bois Grenier	⎫ The situation remains the same in our front; daily registration by our own and hostile artillery, but no organized bombardment on either side. Sniping by day active; by night little sniping except in front of our left. A great improvement in the weather. Master the trenches drier, and there is much to show for work and material put into them. In addition to general strengthening of the front line, work in connection with supporting points and defence of the main second line is carried out by Battalions in reserve. ⎬	Killed — 1
2nd " "	"		
3rd " "	"		Killed — 1
4th " "	"		19 " K. 2. W 3 Wounded — 3
5th " "	"		Wounded — 1
6th " "	"		Wounded — 3
7th " "	"		Wounded — 2
8th " "	"		5"8" W. 7 Wounded — 1
9th " "	"		Killed — 4 Wounded —

L by Brigadier

Army Form C. 2118.

WAR DIARY
or
INTELLIGENCE SUMMARY.

19 Inf Bde   March 1915

(Erase heading not required.)

Instructions regarding War Diaries and Intelligence Summaries are contained in F. S. Regs., Part II. and the Staff Manual respectively. Title pages will be prepared in manuscript.

19/M

Hour, Date, Place	Summary of Events and Information	Remarks and references to Appendices
March 10th BOIS GRENIER	Bombardment of hostile trenches in our front carried out on 10th and 11th. This activity	O. OR Wounded — 4
March 11th " "	displayed to prevent enemy throwing his line to support the neighbourhood of NEUVE CHAPELLE.	Killed — 1 Wounded — 2 9.1.15 K.S.W.10
March 12th " "	1 Platoon Welsh Fusiliers, under Lt Mostyn, made a raid by night on enemy's trenches with hand grenades. They succeeded in throwing grenades into the enemy front trench and retire covered by fire of 72nd Batty R.F.A. Casualties 1 man killed and 2 wounded.	Killed — 1 — 3 Wounded — 5
March 13th " "	1st Bn Middlesex Regt takes over trenches at RUE DU BOIS from 16th Inf Bde on our left.	Killed — 2 Wounded — 2
March 14th " "	Hostile artillery shew very little activity between March 10th and 17th.	Killed — 2 Wounded 1 — 10
March 15th " "		Killed — 3 Wounded — 5

T Brig Genl
19 Bde

Army Form C. 2118.

WAR DIARY
or
13th Inf Bde INTELLIGENCE SUMMARY. March 1915

(Erase heading not required.)

Instructions regarding War Diaries and Intelligence Summaries are contained in F. S. Regs., Part II. and the Staff Manual respectively. Title pages will be prepared in manuscript.

Hour, Date, Place	Summary of Events and Information	Remarks and references to Appendices
March 16th BOIS GRENIER		Casualties O.OR 19
		13th 16th K.7. W.1.=20 Wounded – 6
" 17th " "	Middlesex are relieved at Rue Du Bois by 16th Infantry Bde.	Wounded – 1
" 18th " "		Wounded – 1
" 19th " "	6th & 13th North Staffords are attached to 19th Inf Bde for 5 days to be instructed in trench duties.	Killed – 1 Wounded – 1
" 20th " "		Killed 1 – Wounded 1 – 4
" 21st " "	Between the 16th and 21st hostile artillery more active; shelling, but very little damage done.	17th–20th K.1+1.W.1+6 Wounded – 4

F.J. Bridgwood
Brig General

Army Form C. 2118.

WAR DIARY
or
INTELLIGENCE SUMMARY.

(Erase heading not required.)

19 hy Bat   March 1915

1906 A

Hour, Date, Place	Summary of Events and Information	Remarks and references to Appendices
March 22. BOIS GRENIER		killed O.OR — 2
		wounded — 2
March 23 " "		killed — 1
		wounded — 1
" 24 " "	Work on two main communication trenches, to provide access to our line by day, started.	wounded — 4
		2Lt W. K 3 W.H.
" 25 " "		— 1
" 26 " "	Active patrolling carried out between 25th and 28th to locate a German position and then determine the regimental (?)write up—	wounded — 1
" 27 " "		wounded 1.5
" 28 " "		wounded — 5
		25-28 W 1 + 4

J. by Brigfield

Army Form C. 2118.

WAR DIARY
or
INTELLIGENCE SUMMARY.

(Erase heading not required.)

19th Inf Bde   March 1915

Hour, Date, Place	Summary of Events and Information	Remarks and references to Appendices
March 29th BOIS GRENIER	Hostile artillery shelled an advanced parallel that we had opened up 50 yards from Centre of our line —	Wounded — 2 O.R.
March 30th		Wounded — 1
March 31st		Killed — 2 Wounded — 6 29-31 & 2.w.9
		TOTAL. O.R. Killed 0 2 Wounded 2 23 3 95

F Gordon Brig Genl
Cmd'g 19th Inf Bde

Headquarters,

    19th INFANTRY BRIGADE.

        (6th Division)

      A P R I L

       1 9 1 5

Army Form C. 2118.

WAR DIARY
or
INTELLIGENCE SUMMARY. 19th/1st Bde
April 1915

(Erase heading not required.)

Instructions regarding War Diaries and Intelligence Summaries are contained in F. S. Regs., Part II. and the Staff Manual respectively. Title pages will be prepared in manuscript.

Hour, Date, Place	Summary of Events and Information	Remarks and references to Appendices — Casualties Officers & Other ranks
BOIS GRENIER April 1st	Cameronians take over trenches at RUE DU BOIS from 16th Inf Bde, which Bde is withdrawn into reserve.	April 1 Killed — 2 Wounded — 6
" " 2nd	The situation remains the same in our front; daily registration by our own and hostile artillery. Sniping by day active on both sides, by night little sniping.	2 Killed — 1
" " 3rd		3 Wounded — 2
" " 4th		4 Wounded — 1
" " 5th		5 Wounded — 7
" " 6th	16th Inf Bde relieves Cameronians at RUE DU BOIS.	6 Killed — 1 Wounded 1 2
" " 7th	The fine weather has to some extent dried up the trenches — work commenced on two main communication trenches (1700 yds and 900 yards in length respectively) by which the front line can be reached by day. A supporting line also commenced running from 100 to 200 yards in rear of fire trenches.	7 Wounded — 1
" " 8th		8 Wounded — 1
" " 9th		9 — —
" " 10th		10 Wounded — 1
" " 11th		11 Killed — 1 Wounded 1 3
" " 12th		12 Killed — 2 Wounded — 1
" " 13th		13 Wounded — 1

Army Form C. 2118.

WAR DIARY
or
INTELLIGENCE SUMMARY.   19th Inf. Bde.
(Erase heading not required.)   April 1915

Instructions regarding War Diaries and Intelligence Summaries are contained in F. S. Regs., Part II. and the Staff Manual respectively. Title pages will be prepared in manuscript.

Hour, Date, Place	Summary of Events and Information	Remarks and references to Appendices
BOIS GRENIER April 14th	Active patrolling in front of our lines is carried out by night as frequently but few hostile patrols are found in front of their wire.	14 — Casualties (Officers & other ranks)
" 15		15 Killed — 1
" 16	The enemy presumably seeing new work on Communication trenches and different trenches being carried out has started shelling at night, mostly between 9 and 11 p.m., big fire being directed into the proved in rear of our fire trenches, and at our Communication trenches —	16 wounded — 4
" 17		17 wounded — 1
" 18		18 wounded — 2
" 19		19 Killed — 1
" 20		20 wounded — 2, killed — 1
" 21	The Enemy's infantry maintain a passivist attitude and are making no attempt to push forward their trenches —	21 wounded — 2
" 22		22 wounded — 2
" 23		23 wounded — 1, 5
" 24	Our guns bombard hostile trenches and communication trenches in combination with rifle fire from machine gun fire. This activity oversers'sed in order to attract enemy's attention and prevent his detaching troops to the North. Hostile artillery replies with 150 shells fired mostly at our fire trenches (wounding 11 men) —	2 wounded — 1

Army Form C. 2118.

WAR DIARY
or
INTELLIGENCE SUMMARY.

(Erase heading not required.)

19th Inf Brigade
April 1915.

Hour, Date, Place	Summary of Events and Information	Remarks and references to Appendices
		Casualties
		Officers Other ranks
BOIS GRENIER April 25.	The two main Communication trenches are now completed and work on the Subsidiary line well advanced.	25 wounded — 11
26		26 wounded — 1
27	The hostile artillery opposite us is showing most activity, shelling BOIS GRENIER in Communication trenches, and fire trenches, and also firing salvos at night at our working parties.	27 killed — 2
28		28 wounded — 1
29	Our artillery retaliate to this night firing by shooting at enemy's wire	29 wounded — 5
30	entries and at their Communication trenches.	30 killed — 3
		wounded — 5
		Total killed — 15
		wounded 3 · 67
1/5/15	F. Gordon, Brig Genl	
	Comdg 19th Infy Bde	

<u>Attached to 27th
Division 31.5.15.</u>

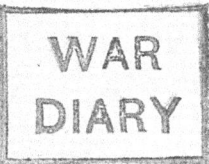

Headquarters,

<u>19th INFANTRY BRIGADE.</u>

(6th Division)

<u>M   A   Y</u>

1 9 1 5

Army Form C. 2118.

WAR DIARY
or
INTELLIGENCE SUMMARY 19th Infantry Bde

May 1915.

(Erase heading not required.)

Hour, Date, Place	Summary of Events and Information	Remarks and References to Appendices	Casualties	
			Offrs.	O Ranks
MAY 1st BOIS GRENIER	The ground having dried up, steady progress is made in providing a supporting line from 100ˣ to 200ˣ in rear of fire trenches. Subsidiary communication trenches lead in from the two main communication trenches to the fire trenches are taken in hand — The enemy appears to our line slow little activity except with their artillery — The hostile artillery registers our trenches daily, and every 3 or 4 days carries out a small organised bombardment of some area in rear of our lines — As however hostile guns employed are mostly field guns little damage is done.	1 Killed	—	1
2" " "		2 Killed	—	2
3" " "		3	—	1
4" " "		4 Wounded	—	1
5" " "		5 Killed	—	1
6" " "		6 Wounded	—	1
7" " "		7	—	1
8" " "		8	—	1
9" " "		9 Killed	—	1
		Wounded	—	2
10" " "		10 Wounded	—	1
11" " "		11	—	1
12" " "		12 Wounded	—	1

Army Form C. 2118.

WAR DIARY
or
INTELLIGENCE SUMMARY.

(Erase heading not required.)

Instructions regarding War Diaries and Intelligence Summaries are contained in F. S. Regs., Part II. and the Staff Manual respectively. Title pages will be prepared in manuscript.

Hour, Date, Place	Summary of Events and Information	Remarks and references to Appendices

Casualties

Hour, Date, Place	Summary of Events and Information		Offr.	O.Ranks
May 13th – BOIS GRENIER		13	–	1
May 14th "		14 Wounded	–	3
May 15th "		15 Wounded	–	3
May 16th "	In order to attract the enemy's reserves and prevent them moving South to assist in repelling the attack of the 1st Army 19th Inf. Bde. and Supporting artillery show activity by bombarding enemy's trenches, cutting his wire with artillery fire and opening bursts of rifle and machine gun fire. Hostile wire where cut is kept under fire throughout the night, and hostile working parties attempting repairs driven in.	Killed 16 Wounded	– –	2 1
" "		17 Killed Wounded	– –	2 2
May 18th " " "	Normal activity on front of hostile artillery. A number of rifle grenades are fired at own right and centre sections by the enemy. The distance between the lines, however, being from 250x to 300x, Their aim is inaccurate and a few casualties only are caused.	18 Killed	–	1
May 19th " " "		19 "	–	1
May 20th " " "		20 "	–	1
		21 Killed Wounded	– –	3 5
		22 Wounded	–	1

WAR DIARY or INTELLIGENCE SUMMARY

Army Form C. 2118.

MAY 1915 — 19th Infantry Brigade

(Erase heading not required.)

Instructions regarding War Diaries and Intelligence Summaries are contained in F.S. Regs., Part II. and the Staff Manual respectively. Title pages will be prepared in manuscript.

Hour, Date, Place	Summary of Events and Information	Remarks and references to Appendices

MAY24 BOIS GRENIER /25	The 4th Gds. on the right cannot get a firm footing in the BRIDOUX road: 2 further attacks by 4 (West Riding T.F.) Brigade & remnants of our Regiment in making small advances & even inclined to fall back.
	70 yds in front of their line. The Commanders are much hampered in the right direction of their fire from intensely heavy & ... all of these appointed them with mg fire from ... & all thought the night 24th. 24Pers & 2xPbs known shelled destroyed all the high ground between spot repairs close into the Trench Bay's trenches & Dead Cow farmers.
		Casualties
		Offrs ORanks
		23 Killed — 5
		    Wounded
		24 Wounded — 1
		    Killed — 1
		    Wounded
		25 Wounded — 2
		27
		28 Wounded — 2
		    Killed — 1
		    Wounded — 1
		29 Killed — 1
		30 Wounded — 2
		— Killed — 14
		Total Wounded — 35
		
		New
		Wire
		7/2.

	Quiet	
Mon 26 27 " "	Quiet. On 31st May 27th Div. in late inn-ground relieved from 11th Div. & the 27th Brigade was attached to	
Mer 28 & 31 " "	the 27th Division. 27th Division to be described as 19th Infantry Brigade and to be known as ... to the to the an the ... to the ...	
	30/31 May Reliefs passed and rearrangement from 19th Brigade to the old lines — defences	
		F. Gosselin Capt Brigade Major 19th Inf. Bde.

1 June 1915

Forms/C. 2118/11.

ATTACHED 27TH DIVISION
19TH INFY BDE

2 DIVISION

BDE HEADQUARTERS
JUN-JLY 1915

From 6th Division on
31.5.15.

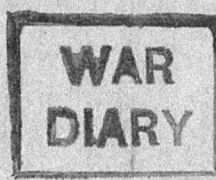

Headquarters,

19th Infantry Brigade.

(27th Division)

J U N E

1 9 1 5

Attached:

Operation Order.
Intelligence Reports.

WAR DIARY
INTELLIGENCE SUMMARY

Army Form C. 2118.

JUNE 1915
19th Infantry Brigade

Hour, Date, Place	Summary of Events and Information	Remarks and references to Appendices	Casualties	
			Killed	Wounded
BOIS GRENIER				
1st - 10th June.	General 10 days, no incidents except enemy	O.R.	-	-
2	quiet	O.R.	-	1
3		O.R.	1	-
4	(Bois de Biez)	O.R.	1	2
5	The Brigade took over trenches on left (half 81" by Rue these)	Offr		
6	of the 28th June. Militia provides the Brigade line 3½	O.R.	2	9
	Bn. L. Fus., Gor. + 1/5 Bn. Bde. was Reserve	O.R.	3	3
7		O.R.	2	1
8		O.R.	1	6
9		O.R.	1	-
10		O.R.	2	2
11		O.R.	1	-
12		O.R.	-	1
13		O.R.	1	-
14	Brigadier General [...] No. F. Gordon C.B. [...] in command	O.R.	2	9
15 (Tues. June)	of the 19th Inf. Bde. Septr. 1914, landed over command to	O.R.	-	3
16.	Lt Col. Robertson (Cameronians), Several Post [...]	O.R. Offr O.R.	2 1 1	2 1 1

WAR DIARY or INTELLIGENCE SUMMARY.

(Erase heading not required.)

Army Form C. 2118.

JUNE 1915
19th Infantry Brigade

Hour, Date, Place	Summary of Events and Information	Remarks and references to Appendices
BOIS GRENIER		Casualties killed wounded
17 June	See Daily Summaries attached	OR — 4
18 "		OR 1 5
19 "		OR 1 1
20 "		Offr 1 —
		OR 4 9
		Offr 1 —
		OR 1 3
21 "		OR 1 5
22 "		OR 1 2
23 "		OR 1 8
		Offr — 1
24 "		OR 1 1
25 "		Offr 1 3
		OR — 2
26 "	(Counter attack delivered on Bois du Biez finished by 8.20 A.M.) Brigade on 27th June ordered to move & 1 armed front line — have 2/ Bn. to front line & 1 1/2 Bn. in 2nd Reserve & 1 Bn. Divisional Reserve. On same night Right Bn 1/N Lancashires relieved & 1 Bn from 25th Inf. Bde (3rd Div) relieved them & attached for duty & front.	OR — 1
		OR 1 1
		2.O. No. 4 of 3/2/15 attached
	Reinforcements attached here & there during the period	2 6

Tebut 1st 1915

J.E. Mayne Captain & Adc
4th 15 Infantry Bde

Forms/C. 2118/11.

OPERATION ORDER NO. 41.

SECRET.

19th Infantry Brigade Operation Order No: 41.

Copy No: 1

26th June, 1915.

1. The following reorganization of the line will be carried out on the night of the 27th/28th June:-
   (a) 2nd Battn. Argyll & Sutherland Highlanders in subsections 60 - 62 will be relieved by a battalion of the 81st Infantry Brigade and march to billets at GRIS POT.
   Details of the relief to be arranged between Commanding Officers concerned at a time and place to be notified later.

   (b) The Cameronians will take over subsection 49, (i.e. from their present right flank to the BOIS GRENIER - BRIDOUX Road inclusive) from a battalion of the 25th Infantry Brigade.
   Details of relief will be arranged between Officers Commanding units direct.

2. This reorganization will necessitate the readjustment of the brigade front as follows:-

   (i) Right Battalion will hold subsections 49, 50, 51, and 52 with support trenches in rear up to and including FLAMENGRIE FARM.
   2 platoons will be kept in support - one in support of subsection 49, the other in support dug-outs in rear of subsection 53 for the defence of FLAMENGRIE and WATER FARMS.

   (ii) Centre ½ battalion (5th Scottish Rifles) will hold subsections 53, 54 and half-55, with support trenches in rear from FLAMENGRIE FARM, exclusive, to support trench 55, inclusive.

   (iii) Left battalion will hold subsections half-55, 56, 57, 58 and 59, with support trenches 56 to 59 both inclusive.
   1 platoon and 2 sections will be kept in support in rear of DEAD COW FARM for the defence of BURNT FARM, DEAD COW FARM and RAILWAY FARM, 2 sections to each.

The above readjustments will be carried out at 9.pm on the evening of the 27th/28th June; details being arranged between Officers Commanding units concerned.

3. All ammunition and grenades, and other trench stores on charge will be handed over to the relieving units.

4. Artillery support will be reallotted as follows:-

   Subsections 49 - 52:   364th Battery, R.F.A.,
   Subsections 53 - 55:   96th Battery, R.F.A.,
   Subsections 56 - 59:   11th Battery, R.F.A.

Page 2.

4. On and after the evening of the 27th June, of the 2½ battalions in billets, one Regular Battalion will be in Divisional Reserve, and the other Regular Battalion and the ½ battalion 5th Scottish Rifles in Brigade Reserve.

The units in Brigade Reserve will find 2 Companies every night for Inlying Picquet on the Subsidiary Line - one Company in vicinity of NEW FARM, and one Company in the vicinity of BILLET FARM.

The Regular Battalion in Brigade Reserve will also find the 4 machine guns on the subsidiary line - 2 at MOAT FARM, and 2 at BILLET FARM.

The Battalion Machine Gun Officer, with 2 cyclist orderlies, will be billeted at BILLET FARM.

When moving into positions on the subsidiary line and on returning to billets, the company at NEW FARM will use the GRIS POT - BOIS GRENIER Road and track off it and the company at BILLET FARM will use the route via LA VESEE.

6. A new Table of Reliefs which cancels Table issued on 22nd June last, will be issued today.

H E Roanne

Captain,

Issued at   2   p.m.   Brigade Major 19th Infantry Brigade.

Copy No: 1 retained,
        2 H.Q.27th Div.,
        3 25th Inf.Bde.,
        4 81st Inf.Bde.,
        5 2nd R.W.Fusiliers,
        6 The Cameronians,
        7 1st Middlesex Regt.,
        8 2nd A. & S.Hrs.,
        9 5th Scottish Rifles (trenches),
      10 5th Scottish Rifles (H.Q.),
      11 "A" Group, R.F.A.,
      12 19th Field Ambulance,
      13 19th Inf.Bde.Amm.Column,
      14 Brigade Signal Officer,
      15 Brigade Transport Officer.

S E C R E T.
This table cancels
that issued on
23rd June, 1915.

B.M. 252.   26th June, 1915.

19th INFANTRY BRIGADE - RELIEF TABLE:

26th JUNE - 8th JULY:

Showing positions of Battalions every evening AFTER reliefs are completed

UNITS:	JUNE:						JULY:							
	26th	27th	28th	29th	30th	1st	2nd	3rd	4th	5th	6th	7th	8th
The Cameronians:	R.	R.	R.	Bde. Res. I.P.	Bde. Res. I.P.	Div. Res.	Div. Res.	Div. Res.	R.	R.	R.	R.	R.
2nd Royal Welsh Fusiliers:	Bde. Res. I.P.	Div. Res.	Div. Res.	R.	R.	R.	R.	R.	Bde. Res. I.P.	Bde. Res. I.P.	Div. Res.	Div. Res.	Bde. Res.
5th Scottish Rifles.	C.	C.	C. Rel. I.P.	C.	C.	C.	C.	C. Rel. I.P.	C.	C.	C.	C.	C. Rel. I.P.
1st Middlesex Regiment:	L.	L.	L.	L.	L.	Bde. Res. I.P.	Bde. Res. I.P.	Bde. Res.	Div. Res.	Div. Res.	L.	L.	L.
2nd Argyll & S. Highlanders:	BOIS	Bde. Res. I.P.	Bde. Res.	Div. Res.	Div. Res.	L.	L.	L.	L.	L.	Bde. Res. I.P.	Bde. Res. I.P.	Div. Res.

NOTES:
1. The tours of duty in Brigade and Divisional Reserve will be from 9.pm to 9.pm
2. The Companies on Inlying Picquet will be in position at 9.30.pm each night and will return to billets next morning, starting three quarters of an hour before sun rise, marching by separate platoons (Sun rise 27th June 3.50.am
3. Machine guns will remain on the subsidiary line during their whole tour of duty.

DEFINITIONS:
R   = Right Battalion in trenches 49 - 52, ½ 55,
C   = Centre ½ battalion in trenches 55 - ½ 55,
L   = Left Battalion in trenches ½ 55 - 59.
Bde.Res. = Battalion in Brigade Reserve,
Div.Res. = Battalion in Divisional Reserve.
I.P. = Two Companies on Inlying Picquet on Subsidiary line
Rel. = Relief of ½ Battalion, 5th Scottish Rifles

Captain,
Brigade Major 19th Infantry Brigade

INTELLIGENCE REPORTS.

19th INFANTRY BRIGADE

INTELLIGENCE SUMMARY, 5.am 10th - 5.am 11th June:

1. During the day there was very little sniping except on the right opposite sub-sections 50 - 51 where it was above the normal. Fairly quiet after 11.pm till dawn when sniping became more active, but slackened when we replied to it.

2. Look out posts could see no movement in enemy's lines, except opposite 60 - 61 where a hostile working party was seen behind the trenches. The snipers of The Cameronians took steps to look out for them and eventually shot two of them.

3. The enemy's artillery was particularly aggressive all day especially during the early part of the night. Field guns, 5.9 howitzers and heavier howitzers being used, the suspected an 8" from a single howitzer in the direction of ENCLOS.

9.50. - 10.10.am, a few shells at LA VESEE.

10.30. - 11.am, 3 shells fell between Subsection 61 and Battalion Headquarters.

10.50. - 11.10.am, area between rear of subsections 53, 54, 56, 57, and BURNT FARM shelled with 5.9 howitzers from direction of WEZ MACQUART - damage 1 dug out broken, no casualties.

3.30 - 3.45.pm., Trenches 53, 54, 55 shelled.

3.30 - 4.25.pm., about 38 5.9" howitzer shells were put on to level crossing I 21 a from direction of ENCLOS. No damage except to houses.

3.30 - 4.35.pm, 38 5.9" howitzer shells fell about level crossing I 21 a and 4 struck DEAD COW Farm and support line in vicinity. Fired from single howitzer at about one minute's interval from direction of FORT D'ENCLOS

4.15 - 4.25.pm, Field guns from LA VALLEE fired 7 rounds shrapnel into FLAMENGRIE FARM. Our guns were shelling enemy's trenches at the same time, so enemy retaliated on FLAMENGRIE observation post.

6.0 - 7.0.pm., A heavy howitzer of large calibre shelled area I.25 60% of these shells were blind. Direction FORT D'ENCLOS.

9.15.pm Enemy used trench mortars and rifle grenades against subsections 60 - 61, 96th and 87th Batteries replied in retaliation and The Cameronians replied with machine guns, mortars and rifle grenades.
The Cameronians' casualties 1 killed, 7 wounded - 4 dangerously.

10.15 - 10.25.pm About 24 shells in salvos of four fell in area DEAD COW Farm and support trenches in vicinity. Shrapnel from light howitzers from direction of LA FLEUR D'ECOSSE.

4. Small hostile working parties heard cutting grass and driving in stakes. Normal amount of ordinary transport heard but small quantity of heavy transport heard at 2.20.am moving East to West near enemy's trenches.

At end of communication trench opposite right of sub section 55 enemy has erected a small earth covered hut.
Working party opposite sub section 60 were noticed to be of fine stature and of mature age wearing dark uniform and rounds caps
No hostile patrols met.
Wind light from N.N.W.
Night very dark.

12/6/15.
Brigadier General,
Commanding 19th Infantry Brigade.

12 June

Daily Intelligence Report, 19th Infantry Brigade.

Enemy fairly quiet from midnight till dawn when sniping increased, but it did not last long

Engine whistle heard at 10.pm and 1.am.

Men seen in trenches yesterday opposite subsections 50 — 53 were wearing short blue coats and dark blue caps fitting tightly on the head, like a skull cap and with a small rim. At 4.am heavy transport was heard moving East to West. Mounted groups of 20 at intervals of 200 yards with 2 men every 20 yards between the mounted men were observed at bend in road in I.34.a.: after going down road to LA VALLEE they were lost to view; the noise of transport ceased at 6.15.am.

During the day enemy in trenches very inactive, no movement and no signs of work seen; not much sniping except on extreme right where it was annoying - sniper suspected in No: 3 Farm or in trees near.

Hostile working party of 50 men was seen in morning at farm North of road in I.34.a. 4.3. - a careful watch was kept on them and the artillery managed to catch them at 2.pm causing casualties.

Between 2.20 and 2.50.pm enemy shelled level crossing in I.21.a. Several shells were blind and the shooting was not so accurate as yesterday.

Hostile aeroplane flew over trenches about 3.30. to 4.pm but retired on our aeroplanes approaching.

87th Battery shelled No: 3 Farm at 4.pm as enemy suspected of sniping from there

During the afternoon men were seen in LE QUESNE Farm dressed in dark blue uniforms and some in shirtsleeves, carrying planks. A screen is erected in front of the farm to cover working party. It is being watched and artillery are warned.

Captive balloon observed far away to the South about 1.pm.

13/6/15

Brigadier General,
Commanding 19th Infantry Brigade.

5.pm. 13th June, 1915.   19th Infantry Brigade

INTELLIGENCE REPORT

NIGHT:

1. A fairly quiet night with increase in sniping at daybreak. No hostile patrols seen and only a single man seen working outside the parapet except opposite Subsection 50 where there was a small party. Rifle grenades were fired at 10.pm at our party working on wire opposite Subsection 51. There was more than the usual amount of transport on the move. Engine whistles were fairly frequent and a train was heard moving at about 11.30 in I.33.b. Two traction engines also heard. A single white light was sent up from German trench opposite 52, the reason for which was not apparent.

DAY:

2. Quiet. Little sniping, and very little signs of work or movement in the enemy's trenches.
The only human beings seen behind the line were 2 cyclists riding from the DISTILLERY towards DEQUESNE Farm on WEZ MACQUART - BOIS BLANCS Road and a man in a helmet and a so called dark green uniform, working in a trench as if laying a wire. On examination the uniform was thought to be dark blue instead of green which somewhat reduced the value of the information.
A hostile aeroplane reconnoitred trenches at 11.30.am
The only shells fired were 3 shrapnel at junction of trenches S.W. of FLAMENGRIE Farm.

3. A patrol consisting of Lieut. Mostyn and Corporal Evans went out from subsection 50 at 10.pm and reached a well known hostile listening post 10 yards from enemy's wire, which was found unoccupied. Party of enemy heard working on parapet and mending wire. Much talking heard in main trench and from the amount of noise made the trench seems strongly held. There were no tracks in long oats which covered most of the ground except quite close to enemy's wire. This would be a good spot to take anyone who could distinguish a Bavarian's from a Saxon's accent.

4. A careful reconnaissance from an observation post showed a wire entanglement in front of the German second line opposite Subsection 57. The communication trench leading back to Hotel on road (see 1/10,000 map) seemed also wired. The Hotel itself and houses round seemed strongly fortified and wired and appeared very little damaged by artillery. The Distillery seemed strongly fortified and 150 yards East of it, North of the road, a strong fortified work was noticed on high ground with a good field of fire. In the front line trench opposite Subsection 57 their appeared to be a tube of some sort. It looked anything from a machine gun to a gas tube or a hose pipe: it was impossible to tell clearly what it really was

14/6/15.

Brigadier General,
Commanding 19th Infantry Brigade.

5.pm 14th June, 1915.   19th INFANTRY BRIGADE

INTELLIGENCE REPORT

NIGHT:

1. At 5.25.pm a motor lorry was observed moving towards RADINGHEM on road I.33.b 2.4. About 5.30.pm our 2 Vickers trench mortars in RHE DU BOIS trenches bombarded German trenches opposite. Enemy retaliated with 52 shells from field guns near WEZ MACQUART, and with numerous rifle grenades and trench mortar bombs. He rather got the best of it at first, but we got the upper hand eventually and silenced his large trench mortar. 9 put of 20 of our 35 bombs did not burst. 2nd A. & S.Highlanders had one casualty - not severe.
Between 6 and 7.pm about 18 howitzer shells were fired in direction of BOIS GRENIER Road.
Fairly quiet night. Little more activity on the right where at 12.15.am rifle grenades were fired at grass cutting parties in front of sections 51 and 53 as well as heavy sniping; one man killed. Counter sniping quietened enemy down. Flares were sent up but no trace of any enemy could be seen. Normal transport heard. Searchlight was on at intervals from 11.pm to midnight. Small hostile working parties heard for short periods.

DAY:

2. Quiet morning - but sniping active in front of Section 50. Party of enemy seen going from HOUSSIE Farm into Farm at I.27.a 7.3. About
About 1.pm few shells from field guns put into Railway Farm from direction of LA FLEUR D'ECOSSE.
Enemy gave a liberal allowance of shelling to BOIS GRENIER and farm buildings in that neighbourhood.
He also seemed to be registering PARK ROW (left main communication trench)
Total 43 howitzer shells and 48 from field guns, former from South of LA VALLEE, latter from about LA FLEUR D'ECOSSE (line DISTILLERIE I.27.b - I.28.d central.)
Men in shirt sleeves and dark blue trousers seen working in LE QUESNE Farm.
Later about a dozen men in dark uniform and an officer in shining helmet seen entering the Farm.
7 pigeons seen to circle up from the farm and fly towards ARMENTIERES -- whether carriers is not known.
At 4.30.pm a covered van and horse cam from LA HOUSSIE and stopped at road junction in I.33.a for 20 minutes.

3. During the night the following patrols went out:-
   (i) L/Corpls.MARCIOTTA and BARTON and Pte.Myers and Jones under 2nd Lieut.Nare, 1st Middlesex Regiment to bomb a saphead in front of Section 57. After crossing the COURANT DE LA CHAPELLE they reached within 20 yards of the saphead. Enemy opened fire from sap as soon as patrol crossed the stream; patrol advanced and threw 3 bombs which missed; 3 further boms landed in sap and firing ceased and further 3 more bombs were thrown to catch anyone retiring. It was too dark to see what casualties were caused. There was no firing from hostile main trench and no casualties.
   (ii) Corpl.Jones, Ptes.Oliver and Williams, under Capt.Childe-Freeman 2nd R.W.Fusiliers - object to waylay a German patrol which had been seen the night before. 2 attempts were made, one at 8.45 and again at 10.45.pm but nothing could be seen or heard.

15/6/15.   Brigadier General,

                                              Commanding 19th Infantry Brigade.

5.pm. 15th June, 1915.   19th Infantry Brigade.

INTELLIGENCE REPORT:

NIGHT:

1. At 9.pm 2 H.E. shells fell behind 53 and at 11.20.pm 6 shrapnel from direction of Les Bas Champs Farm O.9.b and some rifle grenades were fired at our working party opposite 51 and 52. Otherwise a quiet night. Only small hostile working party seen outside trenches and some hammering heard inside the trenches. Very little movement observed in front line trenches after 5.pm except between 6 and 8 pm. Second line trenches seemed to be held as smoke was seen coming out of them at 7.am in the morning. Sausage balloon seen at dawn far behind enemy's lines; direction East by South. Carts loaded with hay accompanied by 10 men seen in square I.32 a. A revolving light with exposure every other second seen on a direct line with LILLE Citadel, from 10.pm to 1.am Heavy transport heard moving S.W. at 9.45.pm and train heard at 10.10.pm

DAY:

2. Quiet and less sniping on extreme right than usual. 2 heavy howitzer shells fell near NEW FARM H.19.d. No other shelling reported. No movement seen behind enemy's line except working party supposed to be at I.36.a 8.4.
New machine gun cupola noticed slightly behind front line trenches at I.26.d 4.2, and covered with grass.

3. A patrol of 2 N.C.Os and 5 men under 2nd Lieut.Higgins, 2nd Royal Welsh Fusiliers went out from 51 in the hope of waylaying a hostile patrol; but too many flares and the fact of being observed and being fired on prejudiced any chance of success.

16/6/15.   P R Robertson   Brigadier General,

                                              Commanding 19th Infantry Brigade

5.pm 16th June, 1915.   19th Infantry Brigade

INTELLIGENCE REPORT

NIGHT

1. At 6.45.pm a hostile aeroplane reconnoitred our trenches but retired when rifle fire opened on it: during firing enemy resorted to rifle grenades. An iron loophole was pierced by german bullet - latter sent to C.E., 3rd Corps. During afternoon 3 carts seen near ENNETIERES.

   Quiet night, sniping less than usual especially on the right where during the last few nights it has been particularly aggressive.

   Revolving light at LILLE again observed. An abnormal amount of heavy transport heard opposite 57 from 9.40 to 11.10.pm moving South on RADINGHEM - LA VALLEE Road.

2. Patrols during night reconnoitred ground and found enemy busy on his wire and front trenches in various places and cutting grass - These patrols were fired on.

   Special patrol from 50 heard Germans talking in trenches. Difficult to distinguish whether Saxon or Bavarian, probably former, certainly not Prussian.

DAY:

3. Particularly quiet day. Very little sniping. At 10.am hostile aeroplane, pursued by one of our aeroplanes, was seen to drop several hundred feet but recovering disappeared over the German lines. At 12.26 pm one of our aeroplanes was brought down by shell fire and fell very steeply to the ground some 400 yards behind German lines. Party of enemy seen working on LA VALLEE - RADINGHEM Ridge. Very little movement otherwise.

ARTILLERY:

4. During early afternoon a few shells fired into WATER FARM BURNT FARM and in direction of GRIS POT. 27 shells fired from field gun (probably at I.29.b) at I.14.b 8.2 set haystacks on fire. Probably caused by detachment of infantry located in subsidiary line exposing themselves too freely.

17/6/15.   Brigadier General,
                                          Commanding 19th Infantry Brigade.

5.pm 17th June, 1915.   19th Infantry Brigade

INTELLIGENCE REPORT

EVENING AND NIGHT:

1. 6.30 - 7.pm enemy put 28 shells from field guns near LA VALLEE into sections 52, 53, 54, and 55: 3 men wounded. 4 18 pdr. shells fired in retaliation.
These shells came from single gun believed to be in the hedge at S.E. corner of O.3.d. on in hedge in O.3.a. Range is short and difficult to time but cross bearings will be taken.
Raton Farm and Billet Farm (I.19.c) and LA VESEE (I.19.a) shelled with 4.2 howitzers from ENGLOS.
Men and women seen on cross roads I.33.a5.9 - No other movement observed.

Quiet night; patrols report hostile working parties out repairing parapet and cutting grass. Numerous coloured lights, red and green were sent up by the enemy. In early hours of morning rifle grenades fired into 56, 57 and 60 and 61 and trench mortars in addition into the latter; no casualties reported. Section 60 replied with mortars and rifle grenades. LILLE revolving light again seen.

DAY:

2. Between 5 and 5.45.am and 8 and 8.30.am about 80 shells from field guns were put into Sections 51 and 52 - damage slight - one casualty slight.
Quiet during rest of day - no movement seen except few men carrying timber to LA MOTTE HOUSSAIN Farm (I.32.c. 0.6) and a working party on redoubt in I.36.b. 8.8 which looks a very strong work.

ARTILLERY:

3. 14 18 pdrs shells fired into pagoda shaped earth work close to parapet in front of 55 which our infantry believed to be a Head Quarters dug out; enemy retaliated as above with 20 shells into 54 and 55.

4.   ### PATROLS:

Reports of 4 patrols are attached. The one marked A was the special patrol sent out by request of 3rd Corps which resulted in the officer being convinced that the enemy in front were Saxons. Enemy seem to be patrolling more than usual and to be occupying more than his usual number of listening posts, probably owing to extra precaution on account of large working parties on his front.

18/6/15.   Brigadier General,

                                        Commanding 19th Infantry Brigade.

Report on patrol 16th June.

Patrol consisting of two officers went out last night in front of section 50 with the object of listening to the enemy talking, They proceeded as shown by arrows on attached sketch towards A where an enemy working party could be heard cutting grass in front of their main trench. Patrol approached cautiously to within about 50 yards when they heard slight movement about 15 - 20 yards in front of them which came apparently from covering party lying in long grass. Patrol lay still for about an hour listening to enemy working party who were talking quite a lot and could be heard fairly distinctly The enmy did not appear to have observed patrol but continually sent up flares and also parachute fares which they very rarely use at all in vicinity of F on sketch.where our patrol of 15th - 16th went out and probably left very clear tracks in high oats which are in front of this part of our line. They also made use of a trench searchlight S which they have not used for a long time and fired fairly frequently down shallow ditch which runs from F to our lines. There appeared to be six or seven of the enemy cutting grass; the strength of the covering party was doubtful but distinct movement and an occasional cough was heard at four different points B,C, D, E in front of patrol. About 11.30.pm working party withdrew and patrol returned to our trenches at 12 midnight.

(Sd) P.Mostyn, Lieut.

Headquarters

19th Infantry Brigade.

Patrol Report

No: 1 Patrol: Sergt. Taylorl) The Cameronians.
               L/Corpl.Kirkwood)
Object: Sniping and observation.
Went out at 1.55.am on 16th
Returned at 9.pm   on 16th.

      This patrol was out all day in the grass.
    At 3.20.am. they saw a party working on their parapet under cover of slight mist, one Herman was wearing a Khaki forage cap.
    At 4.15.am They heard Germans working with metal plate.
    At 11.15.am a small party of Germans seen in the "Hotel".
    They report a machine gun emplacement as shown in sketch.
    They claim to have shot a German working on the parapet in the morning and another doing the same in the evening.

No: 2 patrol: Captain J.D.Hill and Sergt.McGowan. (Grenade Section) went out at 9.15.pm and returned at 11.45.pm Report hearing a lot of talking in German trenches.

No: 3 Patrol: Lieut.Minchin and Sergt.Coyne, went out to within 100 yards of enemy's trenches.
    They saw a patrol of about 12 of the enemy. Sergt.Coyne opened fire and they distinctly heard a groan. The enemy's patrol then retired.

An observation post in a tree last morning report seeing five Germans in or near their parapets. They were wearing dark uniform one man was seen to have a dark cap with a red band.

17/6/15.   (Sd) J.Chaplin, Major,
                                    Commanding The Cameronians.

5.pm 18th June   19th Infantry Brigade

INTELLIGENCE REPORT

1. EVENING and NIGHT:

At 7.pm 2 German aeroplanes closely reconnoitred the trenches.
Engine whistle again heard.
No movement seen behind enemy's line.

2. DAY:

From 5.40.am to 6.20.am enemy bombarded sections 60, 61 and
62 with field guns, howitzers, trench mortars, heavy and
light, and rifle grenades. Some shells also fired into
DEAD COW FARM, RAILWAY FARM and DESPLANQUES FARM - Casualties -
5 - one died of wounds. 2 hostile batteries located - one at
I.29.a. 5.0, the other near I.35. Total hostile projectiles
fired about 80 shells, 50 trench mortar bombs from 4 mortars,
and innumerable rifle grenades. We could only retaliate with
7 trench mortar bombs, 20 rifle grenades and at 6.10.am with
17 rounds from 2 18 pdr. batteries.
Quiet throughout the day - no movement seen except a few men
carrying timber from LA MOTTE HOUSSAIN FARM.
2 Anti-aircraft guns located firing from I.36.a 2.8

3. PATROLS:
        two
A patrol of/men under Lieut. Wyatt, The Cameronians, from
subsection 56 went out to locate and bomb a German working
parties. Enemy were found cutting grass with a small
covering party. A grenade was thrown at this party. Other
patrol reports small parties of the enemy working on wire and
that a trip wire now exists in parts with small alarm bells
attached.

19/6/15.   Brigadier General,

                                          Commanding 19th Infantry Brigade.

5.pm 19th June: 19th Infantry Brigade

INTELLIGENCE REPORT

1. **Evening and Night:**

About 5.30.pm hostile aeroplane reconnoitred trenches and area in rear - reported as fired on both by our and German anti-aircraft guns. It finally alighted over the ridge East of Beaucamps where there is apparently an aeroplane park. Led horses seen in front of houses at I.36.d 1.6, which is suspected of being an aeroplane park Lauduster
Quiet night - increased sniping at dawn. 3 rifle grenades fired at 54. Enemy had parties cutting grass.
A patrol from 54 heard a great deal number of wheezy coughs as of oldish men. About midnight coloured lights seen bursting in the air and were very numerous - might be anti-aircraft gun shells bursting.

2. **Day:**

5.am an aeroplane marked with rings reported as being brought down opposite FLEURBAIX.
About 9 - 11.30.am LA VESEE was intermittently shelled; altogether 53 howitzer and field gun shells falling.
The section of heavy battery near L'ARMEE was heavily shelled between 8.15 and 9.15.am by heavy howitzers, and 42 shrapnel and light howitzer shells being fired. Battery untouched though ground ploughed up all round and close to it
At 3.40.pm 9 shells fired from single gun at H.12.c 8.8
Quiet day in the trenches - a few shells fired into area of trenches during day - about 10 howitzer shells being put into communication trench behind 63.
A kite of coloured paper representing german flag was flying in front of subsection 62. Hostile observing station seems to be in some tall trees about I.26.a 7.4
Men seen using MOTTE HOUSSAIN Farm communication trench.
Large working party seen by artillery F.O.O. working on CAPINGEN Ridge J.31.a and work being done in Farm HOUSSAIN O.2.a

3. **Patrols:**

(a) A special patrol consisting of 2nd Lieut Peterkin and 1 man 1st Middlesex Regiment went out at 3.pm - report attached.

(b) Lieut.Hudleston took a patrol out at 9.30.pm to ascertain what working parties enemy had out and their whereabouts. No working parties found opposite 50 - 53 - later large noisy working party heard opposite 54, hammering in stakes. Lieut.Hudlestone was out for 3 hours and heard much talking and whistling in the trenches and reports the line strongly held.

(c) 2 patrols went out from 57 and 58 under Lieuts. Wyatt and Gray, The Cameronians, to endeavour to waylay German patrols and listening posts. A German grass cutting party was seen by first patrol, but patrol unable to get round them. A third patrol went out later - this and the second patrol saw no German moving anywhere.

20/6/15.   Brigadier General,
                                        Commanding 19th Infantry Brigade.

5.pm 24th June.   19th Infantry Brigade.

INTELLIGENCE REPORT:

1. **Evening and Night:**

Sniping active between 8 and 9.pm opposite 50 - 53 and heavy sniping between 1.30 and 2.am opposite 60 - 62, and at daybreak. Heavy firing at patrols and many flares sent up. Small working parties reported on hostile parapet just before dawn. Few rifle grenades fired. Lille light seen from 10.15.pm and 1.40.am. Enemy not patrolling and such working parties seen were behind their wire and listening posts were close to wire and wired in. About 8.pm enemy shelled area H.17.c with 5.9" howitzers. During night between 11.pm and 2.am odd shells were fired into area H.18.a and b.

2. **Day:**

3 Captive balloons seen at 9.am - a long way off S. by W. Quiet day and enemy not showing himself much. 2nd Royal Welsh Fusiliers in RUE DU BOIS lines fired trench mortar about 11.am, enemy replied with trench mortar and rifle grenades at subsection 61, 62; casualties 2 killed, 4 wounded. 53A battery retaliated with a few rounds. Rifle grenades urgently needed in this section Small hostile working parties seen, some dressed in grey, light green coat, others in blue, and one man wearing grey flat cap with dark coloured band.
One of the parties at head of communication trench opposite 50 was fired on and scattered by 11th battery - another opposite 55 was also fired shelled and appeared to have been obliterated. During afternoon DESPLANQUES Farm, BOIS GRENIER and GRIS POT were shelled.

3. **Patrols:**

Special patrols were sent out to endeavour to waylay hostile patrols, listening posts or covering parties.

(a) Lieut.Hudlestone and 6 picked N.C.Os. and men of 1st Middlesex Regt. went out from 50 and 51 but could find no one - 3 scouts wounded, 2 severely.

(b) Lieut.Rooke and 6 men of The Cameronians went out from 57 and threw bombs at listening post,- screams and groans heard and much confusion followed. They opened fire and Lieut.Rooke was killed and one man is missing.

(c) Lieut.Mostyn and Corpl.Bennett of 2nd Royal Welsh Fusiliers went out from 60 along the railway. Only enemy seen was a party behind his wire on his parapet. Bombs were thrown but result not known. Hostile wire reconnoitred; there was a lot of wire in front of 60 but did not appear to be very strong opposite 61. A great deal of loose wire laying about between the 2 trenches.

4. Order of battalions from the left of line:-
        2nd Royal Welsh Fusiliers,
        2nd A. & S.Highlanders,
        ½ Battalion, 5th Scottish Rifles, (T.F.)
21/6/15. 1st Middlesex Regt.   Brigadier General,

                            Commanding 19th Infantry Brigade.

5.pm 21st June   19th Infantry Bde.

INTELLIGENCE REPORT:

1. **Evening and night:**

15 pdr.
At 5.30.pm a few H.E./shells from Battery about O.3.d fell near FLAMENGRIE FARM and subsection 54.
About 5.30.pm till shortly after 6.pm parapet in front of 50-55 and 59-62 was shelled with lyddite and percussion shrapnel, and succicient damage was done to necessitate repairs to parapet - wire in front of 50,51, 54 and 55 was also attacked, but long grass made results difficult to observe. LILLE light again seen during night from 10.pm to 2.am
Coloured lights and star shells of various kinds and colours sent up by enemy in all directions. Engine whistles heard on railway
Great deal of sniping during night probably caused by activity of patrols.

2. **Day:**

Quiet - a few enemy observed working in various parts of his line in grey uniform - one man seen in round grey felt hat with red band, another opposite 55 in helmet with "179" in figures marked on front of its cover.
An observation balloon seen to the South. Some movement seen at cross roads in I.36.c 2.5 and at house in I.36.c 1.6
10 shells fell about farm RUE FLEURIE I.7 during afternoon.
Distillerie I.27.b suspected of harbouring snipers was shelled during afternoon. Black smoke seen issuing from factory chimney in WEZ MACQUART I.23.a

3. **Patrols:**

Special patrols were sent out during the night: nothing was seen opposite 50 - 53; small working parties came out for a short time opposite 54, 55 - 2 strong hostile patrols met opposite 58,59 who advanced on flanks of Argyll and Sutherland Highlanders, after a listening post of 8 men had opened fire - No hostile patrols seen opposite 61 - 62.
Details of 2 of above patrols are attached.

4. **Distribution of units from Right to Left:**

        1st Middlesex Regiment,
        ½ Battn. 5th Scottish Rifles.,
        2nd A. & S.Highlanders,
        2nd Royal Welsh Fusiliers.

22/6/15.   Brigadier General,

                                                   Commanding 19th Infantry Brigade.

5.pm 22nd June.   19th Infantry Brigade

INTELLIGENCE REPORT:

1. Evening and Night:

Quiet evening: LILLE light agin seen at 12.7 am. 7 lights about size of a star seen within area about 800 yards behind German lines opposite 61. Lights were at one minute's interval and remained in the air for 30 seconds. Sniping heavy between 2 and 3.am Some rifle grenades fired into 55. Hostile searchlight used from extreme left and East of Railway.
Information gained by patrols last night showed that the 179 Saxon Regiment is opposite the Brigade, that their trenches are strongly held, and that they fight well.

2. Day:

Quiet day - little sniping and no signs of enemy except some work with shovels in front trenches in front of 60. No hostile shelling since last report. A small mound noticed 3 days ago in front of farm I.33.b 4.6 now appears to be covered with sods.
Some wagons and carts and small parties of men were seen between 5 and 6.pm passing cross roads I.36.c

3. Patrols:

Strong fighting patrols were sent out by 1st Middlesex Regiment, 2nd Argyll & Sutherland Highlanders and 2nd Royal Welsh Fusiliers to capture hostile patrols and gain information as to the identity of the enemy opposite my front.
Patrols of 1st Middlesex Regiment saw nothing opposite 50 - 53, enemy quiet and not patrolling. Patrol of 2nd Royal Welsh Fusiliers opposite 62 were fired on by hostile patrol who retreated at once. - After 3 hours search nothing more could be seen and patrol returned. This patrol reconnoitred trenches opposite 62, found them boarded but unoccupied and probably disused for some time.
Opposite 56 - 59 the 2 patrols sent out by 2nd A. & S.Hrs. obtained valuable information. The Right patrol from 56 found a new flanking trench strongly held but no hostile patrols in front. The left patrol from 58 - 59 under Lieut.Aitken divided into 2 parties and found strong parties of the enemy in front who attempted to surround each of the parties. The left party under Sergeant Macpherson fought its way through and being reinforced by 2 more sections drove off the enemy who were attacking the right party. Several of the enemy were bayonetted and 7 are reported as being shot.
2nd A. & S.Hrs casualties - 1 killed, 1 wounded, 1 missing. An overcoat and helmet were brought in showing that the 179th Saxon Regiment were still in occupation of the German trenches along my front.

Copy of report by O.C. 2nd A. & S.Hrs. is attached.

23/6/15.   Brigadier General,

                                        Commanding 19th Infantry Brigade.

19th Brigade.

Report on Reconnaissances carried out
on the night of June 21st – 22nd.

Reconnaissance by right Company (Section
of line 5b). To find out whether traversed
sap shown in aeroplane photograph of
June 12th was being continued to form
a salient to the enemy's trenches –
whether any work was being done on it –
whether it was strongly held.

Reconnaissance by left Company (Section 58·
59) to endeavour to gain the information
required by G.H.Q. as to what
troops were in front of the right of
the 3rd Corps.

My orders were that both reconnaissances
were to be carried out by parties of not
less than fifty men.

The O.C. 11th Battery R.F.A. was asked
to lay 2 guns on enemy's parapet
in front of Sections 5b and 59.

The captains of right and left Companies
were connected up direct with the C.C.

46

battery. The O.Cs. Welsh Fusiliers and detachment 5th Scottish Rifles were asked to lay a machine gun on parts of the enemy's parapet.

These precautions and the strength of the parties detailed were on account of the late activities in front of the line in the endeavour to gain the information required by G.H.Q. and serious opposition was anticipated.

The Right Company Reconnaissance was carried out by B Company. Captain Clarke who detailed 50 men under 2nd Lieut Bankier to proceed in 3 parties to the Sap mentioned.

They met with no opposition until the left party arrived close to the Sap when they were challenged and heavily fired on by a party outside the Sap.

The centre and right parties approached the Sap and got round it.

It was found that the Sap does not continue any further than what is shown in the photograph and there is no attempt being made to join it up to the parapet to its left (enemy side). It appeared to be

47

Strongly held — An attempt was to have been made to enter the sap but as the three parties lost touch it had to be abandoned.

2nd Lieut Bankier displayed great coolness and intelligence in conducting this reconnaissance —

Left Company Reconnaissance —
was carried out by D company Captain Purves who detailed 50 men under Lieut Aitken to proceed to the enemy listening post where they had bolted a post of 8 men the previous night —

They were to divide in two parties on each side of the Sap leading to the listening post and in the event of the post again running away to remain concealed until the enemy patrol came out to investigate —.

The left of the party lost touch with the right. The right got to its position near the Sap and concealed itself — The left meanwhile got away to its left and came upon a large body of Germans which attacked it and surrounded a party under Sergeant

Macpherson who however gallantly fought his way through and brought it eventually back to the breastwork with only two casualties — As the right party under Lt. Aitken was still out and apparently surrounded Sergt. Macpherson with two fresh sections himself armed with two revolvers went out again and fought his way back to Lieut Aitken driving the Germans before him — Lieut Aitken meanwhile realising that the left party had lost touch with him sent Scouts to the left & found Germans retiring. He wheeled his party to the left and fired on the Germans who made off for their trenches with Lieut Aitken's party in pursuit. When he got the helmet & coat which was thrown away by a hurrying German — Strong German reinforcements now were reported moving on both flanks striving to surround Lieut Aitken's party & Sergeant Macpherson's party which had now joined him — Lieut Buchanan was sent out with two sections & did good work in covering the retirement of the patrol — The enemy eventually

was driven off & opened a
heavy fire from a position in
front of their wire —
The patrol was by then behind
the breastworks —
Casualties were one man killed - one
man dangerously wounded - one
man missing —
The enemy's Casualties were heavy.
Sergt. Macpherson is known to
have accounted for seven —

The list of men asked for by G.O.C. 19th Brigade
will be forwarded later

22/6/15.   B.C. Gore   Lt Col
            Comdg 1/Argyll & Suth Highrs

5.pm 23rd June: ENTELLIGENCE REPORT: 19th Infantry Brigade.

1. **Evening and Night:**

    At 8.pm a great deal of cheering was heard in the German lines opposite 60 - 61. Quiet night but more sniping than usual; numerous flares used and a searchlight, probably on a motor, was very active along the front.

    LILLE revloving light seen from 9.pm till dawn.

2. **Day:**

    Transport reported heard by all units from dawn till after 10.45.am - direction uncertain, but suspected to be on RADINGHEM - LA VALLEE Road.
    Road shelled by our artillery with 5 rounds from 18 pdr.

    Quiet day - sniping was annoying in morning opposite 50 - 53: some snipers located in trees and these were stopped by a few rounds of shrapnel

    Very little shelling - a few 4.2" shells fell at LA VESEE during afternoon.

    German breastworks seem to have had a great deal of work done on them recently.

3. **Patrols:**

    Nothing to report.

4. **Distribution:**
    From Right to Left:

    The Cameronians, 2 Companies 5th Scottish Rifles,
    2nd A. & S.Highlanders, 2nd R.W.Fusiliers.

24/6/15.   Brigadier General,
                                       Commanding 19th Infantry Brigade.

5.pm 24th June: 19th Infantry Brigade.

INTELLIGENCE REPORT.

1. **Evening and night:**

At 6.30pm 4 H.E. shells burst near battery at L'ARMEE; between 6 and 7.pm 10 15 pdr. shells fell in subsection 55. Quiet night - steady sniping all night at 60 - 61, while sniping increased at dawn opposite rest of front. Rifle grenades fired into 55. Odd coloured lights seen during the night. Enemy working parties out opposite 54,55 putting up wire between their present wire and ditch which runs in front of it.

2. **Day:**

Quiet - rather more sniping in centre. Our howitzers obtained 2 direct hits on machine gun emplacements opposite 60; enemy retaliated with trench mortars; 3 rifle grenades fired at 50 51. Artillery replied with 6 rounds.

3. **Patrols:**

Nothing to report. Enemy working on wire in front of 54-55.

4. **Distribution:**

Right to Left:

The Cameronians - 2 Companies 5th Scottish Rifles - 2nd Argyll & Sutherland Highlanders - 2nd Royal Welsh Fusiliers.

25/6/15.   Brigadier General,

                                 Commanding 19th Infantry Brigade.

5.pm 25th June.   19th Infantry Brigade

INTELLIGENCE REPORT:

1. Evening and Night:

Large fire reported at 7.pm near farm in vicinity of LE PARADIS; our artillery had been shelling this farm during the afternoon. Section 61 reported that the 4.5" howitzers had knocked out a trench mortar that had been shelling them. Between 6 and 6.30.pm subsection 61 shelled with field guns - several rifle grenades also fired into subsection 60; one man killed and 2 officers and one man slightly wounded.

Quiet night. Sniping more active opposite 60 - 62 than elsewhere. About midnight about 3 rifle grenades were fired into 55.

2. Day:

Quiet day - no shelling - misty day and difficult to observe any movement. 3 layers of sandbags with loopholes, added during the night to German 2nd line trenches opposite 55; a pump seems to be used in farm I.32.a 9.0

Working parties in fair numbers seen by Artillery F.O.O. on CAPINGHEM ridge.

About 5.pm 4 H.E. shells burst in I.13.c and H.18.b, breaking telephone wires.

3. Patrols:

Small patrols of enemy seen. These hostile patrols seemed to be in close communication with their trench as whenever met star shells were immediately sent up from trench.

The following patrol signals were noticed:

    Long low blast on whistle: = "Retire"
    Noise as of stick rubbing)
    on sheet of corrugated iron:) = "Advance"

    Very's lights sent up by patrol: = "Reinforce"

4. Distribution: Right to Left
    The Cameronians - 2 Companies 5th Scottish Rifles -
    1st Middlesex Regiment - 2nd A. & S. Highlanders.

26/6/15.   Brigadier General,
                                              Commanding 19th Infantry Brigade.

5.pm. 26th June.   19th Infantry Brigade:

Intelligence Report.

1. **Evening and night**:

Quiet night. Sniping more brisk up to midnight opposite 60, 61
than elsewhere. Usual increase in sniping between 2 and 3.am
At 2.15.am machine guns at 50 were turned on to snipers in trees
opposite with apparently good effect. Between 10.30 and 11.pm
Germans put 9 shells into trench S.52 and communication trench -
probably on account of noise of my working parties hammering in
stakes for wiring there. 364th Battery replied with 12 rounds
At 10.pm transport heard opposite 55, probably carrying trench
material as sounds of planks being thrown down heard.
2 Grenades fired into 55.

2. **Day**:

Quiet day - one rifle grenade fired into 51. Between 8 and 8.30 am
enemy fired 6 4.2" howitzer shells into BOIS GRENIER and 3
15 pdr shells into 53. Probably a reprisal to our 4 rounds
from 18 pdr. into trenches opposite 52, 53 at 7.am
Between 3 and 4.pm, 8 rounds 4.2" howitzer shells fired into
55 - 57 and between 4.30 and 5.30 GRIS POT houses shelled with
4.2" howitzers - one direct hit on a house. Working party still
active on CAPINGHEM ridge and usual traffic at LA GRANDE COUR
Cross Roads I.36 b and d. Captive balloon seen to the South.
Hostile working party seen again at LE QUESNE; party twice
visited by officers, one with red cap band and one with blue
cap band. German seen in front trenches opposite 55 with dark
coloured cap with black strip.

3. **Patrols**:

Patrols from 54 and 55 report enemy cutting grass, and light
transport heard which stopped opposite 56, 57. Enemy were
wiring a new trench parallel to their main trench opposite left
of 55, probably the trench shown in latest photograph enfilading
Courant de la Chapelle. Sniper post discovered 150 yards from
German trench.
A patrol of 2nd Lieut. Dewes and Corporal Wilshan, 1st Middlesex
Regiment reconnoitred during daylight the new German trench
opposite left of 55 shown on new photograph. The trench is
2 feet deep and leads up to a listening post near a foot bridge
over the Courant; post is heavily wired and wire ran back
and connected with wire opposite main breastworks. The patrol
brought in a hostile British Rifle lost in the skirmish a few
days ago and also a German bomb - this bomb was set in a ditch
the patrol worked up with a trip wire attached to the friction
tube.

27/6/15.

Brigadier General,

Commanding 19th Infantry Brigade.

5.pm 27th June, 1915.   19th Infantry Brigade.

INTELLIGENCE REPORT

1. 5.pm - 5.am.

About 6.30., 25 men, a motor car, and a cart seen at O.5.a:5.3; 5 of the men were dressed in canvas clothing.
Quiet night. Sniping up to midnight more active opposite 58,59 - and usual activity at dawn. 2 rifle grenades fired into 55. The place where they came from was fired at, which seemed to cause the enemy some annoyance. Hostile working parties out on parapet which were fired at. Some coloured lights and a red star shell were seen. Enemy believed to have carried out a relief on night 26th/27th June opposite 50-52.

2. 5.am - 5.pm.

Quiet day in trenches. No movements of enemy seen.
At 10.15.am 4 military wagons were seen on RADINGHEM - LA VALLEE Road and were fired at, first shell burst between 3rd and 4th wagon and all broke into a gallop, when 2nd shell burst over them. This is very probably the road along which the transport reported reported at night travels.
Between 4.15.pm and 4.30.pm a few 4.2" howitzer shells were sent into L'ARMEE between H.18.b and H.12.c: a party of R.G.A. at the time were preparing the ground in the neighbourhood.
Between 4 and 5.pm, 5 4.2" howitzer shells burst above GRIS POT and between 3.30 and 5.pm, 17 4.2" howitzer shells fell about LA VESEE and farm in neighbourhood.
1st Middlesex Regiment Tree look-out post report the hostile battery thought to be in I.29.a 5.2: bearing from I.20.b.7.3 was 117 degrees magnetic. The puffs of smoke were clearly seen.
Company of infantry were seen on Road I.36.d 11 to O.6.b O.6

3. Patrols:

Nothing special reported by night patrols
A patrol of 2 N.C.Os. 5th Scottish Rifles (Lance Corporals J.M. Stewart and J.C.Stewart) went out from centre of 55 at 1.am and returned at 9.am They reached a point about 30 yards from German trench. They report that 10 to 15 yards in front of main wire entanglement their wire was stretched taut between the trees. The wire of the main wire entanglement was abnormally thick with very close barbs and were nailed on the top of posts. The breast and knee wires were not taut but hung loose. Grass was not trampled on and trees full of birds' nests which would show that no snipers use these trees and not much patrolling is done at this spot. Except for an occasional sniper the hostile trenches were perfectly quiet after 3.am. There was no difficulty in getting out and back by daylight to the German wire at this particular point.

28/6/15.   Brigadier General,
                                              Commanding 19th Infantry Brigade.

5.pm 28th June.   q 19th Infantry Brigade.

19th INFANTRY BRIGADE INTELLIGENCE REPORT.

1. 5.pm - 5.am

Quiet night - usual sniping up to midnight, and heavy between 2.30 and 3.am. 2 rifle grenades fired at 53 during night.

2. 5.am - 5.pm

Very quiet day in trenches. Slight shelling in Brigade area during afternoon. Between 3 and 4.pm, 2 15 pdr. shells fell in vicinity of DESPLANQUES Farm, 4 4.2" howitzer shells burst on BOIS GRENIER Road near SHAFTESBURY AVENUE and 12 rounds between LA VESEE and GRIS POT and a few rounds on the RUE DELETTREE, H 18 causing casualties.

Hostile working parties seen hard at work on CAPINGHEM Ridge and in ENGLOS Village.

Wagons and parties of the enemy seen on the RADINGHEM - LA VALLEE Road. They were shelled by 11th Battery - one wagon hit and the road made very unhealthy. Enemy added new wire opposite 59.

One rifle grenade was fired at 51.

3. Patrols.

Patrols neither saw nor heard any movement of the enemy.

Brigadier General,
Commanding 19th Infantry Brigade.

5.pm 29th June, 1915.   19th Infantry Brigade.

INTELLIGENCE REPORT:

1. 5.pm - 5.am

At about 5.30.pm 33 18 pdr. and 4.2" howitzer shells fell North
of Desplanques Farm I.14.a
About 10.pm 2 shells burst in front of farms at I.13.b, one
farm being hit. Quiet night with heavy sniping at daybreak a
opposite 53 - 55. Usual number of star shells. After a heavy
burst of fire on one of our working parties, when 2 red lights
were sent up, a searchlight was turned on to our trenches which
had been fired at. Signs of mining were reported by subsection
49, but the R.E. expert sent down could not fin
suspicious   as sound had ceased. During night the Germans opposite 49
shouted out that they would sing to us and asked the Cameronians
to sing to them; opportunity taken to put out wire while
Germans were singing.

2. 5.am - 5.pm

Quiet day though hostile snipers more active during afternoon.
Very little movement seen in enemy's lines. About 30 men seen
working at 6.40.am on ridge opposite 53. Opposite 54 2 men
seen wearing usual cap and tunic while 2 others had on
slightly blue caps with no red band. Opposite 49 a German was seen
with grey uniform broad red band in cap, and with grenade badge
in cap. Several direct hits by our artillery observed on
buildings behind German lines. No shells fired at the trenches
since last report, but enemy's artillery more active this last
few days on area in rear of trenches, shelling the whole area
intermittently throughout the day. At 11.30.am 4 heavy
howitzer shells burst about L'ARMEE, 2 hitting the houses where
anti aircraft guns usually go. About a dozen shells fell in I.7
and half a dozen in I.8; a few round GRIS POT and LA VESEE, one
hitting the Estaminet at LA VESEE Corner. About 30 shells
fell along the road from Streaky Bacon Farm (H.18.c 5.8) as
far as H.23.a. a good many fell at road junction H.17.d 4.3
at 6.pm

3.   Patrols:

Nothing unusual to report.

                                          Brigadier General
                                 Commanding 19th Infantry Brigade

5.pm 30th June   19th Infantry Brigade

INTELLIGENCE REPORT.

1. 5.pm - 5.am

About 6.pm about two dozen shells were put into road at I.19.c and d and between 30 and 40 15 pdr H.E. burst near cross roads in H.17.d
At 11.pm, 11 15 pdr. shells were fired into I.14.a and I.1.c.
At 11.40.pm, 8 shells fell in L'ARMEE from direction of LA VALLEE.
Quiet in the trenches during the night; usual heavy sniping at daybreak; LILLE revloving light seen from 9.pm till 1.am.

2. 5.am - 5.pm

Quiet day - enemy noticed baling his trenches, otherwise no otherwork observed near trenches. Enemy have dug a new sap opposite the right half of section 53 and wired it heavily. Enemy opposite 57,58 have been using a dummy head and shoulders, showing it in various places, but no notice was taken of ut. Hostile working parties along the whole CAPINGHEM - ENGLOS ridge. GRAND MARAIS Farm still being used by the enemy as smoke observed coming from Farm.
At 9.30.am a single 4.2" shell fell in the favourite spot 300 yards East of HOSPICE FARM.
Between 11.30 am and 12.30.pm and at 1.15.pm, 15 to 20 shells burst in ARMENTIERES and CHAPELLE D'ARMENTIERES.

3. Reconnaissance

A reconnaissance made from a tree, of that portion of the enemy's front West of the Railway, gives the following information:-
Hostile wire consists of "Chevaux de Frise" and low wire entanglement, with iron railings in many places attached to the wire. Owing to long grass it is invisible in many parts. The depth of the wire averages from 20 to 30 yards. 300 yards West of Railway, a sap to hold 12 men was distinctly seen. For 200 yards from Railway enemy's parapet is 2 feet 6 inches high and beyond, for 300 yards, 4 feet.6 inches high. The loopholes here are almost entirely iron plate blinded with sandbags. A deep borrow pit is in front of the breastworks. The main communication trench is of high command and revetted with earth thrown up from borrow pits on both sides.
Second line of defence runs from DISTILLERIE to farm I.27.a 9.4, with breastwork 20 yards in front of the DISTILLERIE, revetted with sandbags and bricks. The farm is loopholed. Strong "Chevaux de Frise" and low wire entanglement is in front of DISTILLERIE and a low wire entanglement is in front of Farm.
About 30 to 40 yards in rear of front trench is a support trench, which was probably the original old front fire trench. It is strongly wired in front.

30/6/15.   P.R. Robertson   Brigadier General,
                                                Commanding 19th Infantry Brigade.

To 2nd Division 19.8.15.

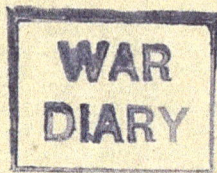

Headquarters,

19th Infantry Brigade.

(27th Division)

J U L Y

1 9 1 5

(19th-31st)

(Note: Diary for
period 1st to
18th July not
received by this
Section).

Attached:

Operation Orders.
Intelligence Reports.

WAR DIARY / INTELLIGENCE SUMMARY

Army Form C. 2118.

JULY, 1915.
19th Inf. Bde.

Instructions regarding War Diaries and Intelligence Summaries are contained in F.S. Regs., Part II. and the Staff Manual respectively. Title pages will be prepared in manuscript.

(Erase heading not required.)

Hour, Date, Place	Summary of Events and Information	Remarks and references to Appendices
BOIS GRENIER and LAVENTIE		Casualties
		Ranks Officers
19. July.	Overnight of 19/20 July the Brigade was relieved in the BOIS GRENIER sector by the 82nd Inf Bde & the	1. OR — 1
	27th Division. The Brigade marched to Rest Billets	2. OR — 1
	in the neighbourhood of STEENWERCK. Itinerary & time	3. OR — 3
	of arrival of 23rd July. Op. Order No. 42 attached	4. OR — 5
Daily Rank attached		5. OR 5/1 — 1
22nd July	The Brigade was inspected by Lt. Genl (in Ch) Sir H.S. RAWLINSON	6. OR — 1
	Comdg IVth Corps. Exf. Officers' Mess was inspected in	7. Off 5/5
	turn & complimented each of them on their work in the	8. Off 5/3 OR 2
	trenches during the long stay into the IIIrd Corps.	9. OR — 1
23rd July	The Brigade moved from billets in STEENWERCK &	10. OR — 3
	taking trenches South of LAVENTIE from Lat 154th Inf Bde	11. OR — 1
	of XIth (Highland) Division. Trenches were in a very bad	12. OR — 1
	state & reinforced plateau very important. Much work	13. OR — 1
	had to be done to bring them to a proper state of defence. Operation	14. OR
	Order No. 43 attached.	15. OR — 1
30/31 July	The line held by the Brigade was reorganised. 5th R.W. was into the	16. OR — 1
	outer defences & the Right-comp-Bn-first three taken as a left from ₁/₂ strongly	17.
	Report (Bln.) of 30 + 31 July attached	18.
	LAVENTIE. appendix W. 1915. — No E. Maude Major	19.
		20. — 1
		21. OR — 1
		22. OR — 3
		23. OR — 1
		24. OR — 1
		25. OR — 3
		26. OR — 1
		27. OR — 4
		28. OR — 1
		29. OR/y — 1
		30. OR — 1
		31. — 1

OPERATION ORDERS.

Copy No: 1

19th Infantry Brigade Operation Order No: 42

18th July, 1915.

1. The Brigade will be relieved on the night 19th - 20th July, by the 82nd Infantry Brigade; and will move to billets in district West and South West of STEENWERCK (A.17).

2. Details of reliefs will be arranged between battalions concerned, at 19th Infantry Brigade Headquarters at 2.pm today.

3. Battalions will assemble and march to new billetting areas, as per March Table which will be issued later. Billets will be handed over to representatives of relieving units at a time also to be notified later.

4. Regimental transport, except that actually required for baggage from the trenches will move independently under battalion arrangements so as to reach their new lines during daylight.

5. The following trench stores, in addition to ammunition will be handed over to relieving battalions and receipt taken:-

> Picks,
> Shovels,
> Pumps,
> Loopholed plates,
> Braziers,
> Trench boxes,
> Ladders,
> Buckets,
> Sniperscopes,
> Grenades,
> Very's lights,
> Vermorel sprayers.

6. The Sapping Platoons will move with Brigade Headquarters. The parties at present at the Brigade Grenade School will rejoin their units on morning of 20th July.

H.E. Paine
Captain,
Brigade Major 19th Infantry Brigade.

Issued at 10.15.am

Copy No: 1 Filed,
2 2nd R.W.Fusiliers,
3 The Cameronians,
4 1st Middlesex Regt.,
5 2nd A. & S.Hrs.,
6 5th Sco.Rifles (Billets)
7 5th Sco.Rifles (Trenches)
8 27th Division,
9 82nd Infantry Brigade,
10 19th Field Ambulance,
11 19th Bde.Ammunition Column.
12 19th Brigade Train,
13 19th Brigade Supply Column,
14 Brigade Transport Officer.

B.M./B.3

1. Herewith March Table to be attached to Operation Order No: 42 of to day.

The times of starting are arranged to fit in with the crossings of other units and will be strictly adhered to.

2. During daylight no large body of troops will be moved on the roads towards the positions of assembly

3. 5 motor ambulances, one for each unit, will be stationed at CROIX DU BAC from 4.pm till 7.pm in case they may be required.

One horse ambulance will be at the position of assembly of each of the trench battalions at 10.30.pm to accompany them on the march. A guide will meet each ambulance on its arrival at battalion billets and conduct it to the 19th Field Ambulance billets.

4. Brigade Headquarters, after reliefs are completed, will be at A.22.a 1.7

5. Please acknowledge receipt by wire.

18/7/15.

Captain,
Brigade Major 19th Infantry Brigade.

Issued with Operation Order No: 42.   MARCH TABLE: 19th Infantry Brigade.

UNIT	Place of assembly and starting point	Time of starting	ROUTE.	Billeting area.
2nd Royal Welsh Frs.	Road junction, H.14.a via road junction H.15.c and CROIX DE ROME.	3.15.pm	FORT ROMPU - BAC ST MAUR Bridge - CROIX DU BAC - Pt.VANUXEEM (A.29.8) - le Pt.MORTIER - road junction A.21.d - road junction A.20.a 5.2	All farms on road between Fme du BC and LA ROSE Fme. A19 A/4
2nd A. & S. Highlanders	Road junction H.4.d 6.7	3.30.pm	ERQUINGHEM Bridge - cross roads B.27.d - CROIX DU BAC (G.6.c) - Pt.de la BOUDRETTE - road junction G.10.a - road junction G.3.d	Farms in A.26.c.d and G.2.b
Hd.Qrs. and 5th Battn. Sco.Rifles.	Road junction H.5.b 7.6 (not shown on map) reached by road past Brigade H.Q. and track in H.6.d 7.7	3.30.pm	ERQUINGHEM Bridge - cross roads B.27.d - CROIX DU BAC - Pt.VANUXEEM (A.29.c) - le Pt.MORTIER (G.4.a)	Farms on road from A.27.d to A.21.d
The Arghrohians	Farm at H.17.d 2.0	On completion of relief.	Road junctions in H.22.b 9.1 and H.16.c CROIX DE ROME - FORT ROMPU - BAC ST MAUR bridge - CROIX DU BAC - road junction G.5.b - le SEQUEMEAU A.30.c - STEENWERCK - lo Gd.BEAUMART A.22.a	Farms on road from A.20.b to A.19.d
1st Middlesex Regiment.	La ROLANDERIE Fme. H.11.c	On completion of relief.	ERQUINGHEM Bridge - cross roads B.27.d - road junction l'HALLOBEAU B.25.c 7.6 - road junction A.18.c 4.2 - STEENWERCK	Farms on road in A.15.a.b.
1 Battn. 5th Sco.Rifles.	Farm at road junction H.11.d 6.6	On completion of relief.	Road junction H.5.d - ERQUINGHEM Bridge - thence by route as for other half Battalion.	Along road from A.27.d to A.21.d

Issued at 7.15.pm
18/7/15.

W.R.Knowle Captain,

Brigade Major 19th Infantry Brigade.

SECRET   o/c

BATTLE ORDER

Officer Commanding
5 Battns, 197th *Train Amm Col, Supply Col.*

The Brigade will relieve the 184th Infantry Brigade (61st Division) on the night 23rd – 24th July.

Detailed orders will be issued later.

21st July, 1916.

[signature]

Captain,
Brigade Major 30th Infantry Bde.

19th Infantry Brigade Operation Order No:43

Copy No: 1

Ref 1/40,000
map, sheet 36.
Sketch map
attached.

22nd July, 1915

1. The Brigade will relieve the 154th Infantry Brigade (51st Division) and take over the trench line between M.24.b 7.9 and N.8.c 4.7 with the various supporting posts in rear, on evening of 23rd July. The above includes the portion of the trench line 50 yards East and West of the FAUQUISSART - TRIVELET road with supporting post E.4 which will be taken over the same night from the SIRHIND Brigade of the Lahore (Indian) Division.

2. (a) The 2nd Royal Welsh Fusiliers will take over part of E lines and part of F lines as far as (X) with supporting posts E.4: F.1: F.2.
   (b) The 2nd Argyll and Sutherland Highlanders will take over the remainder of F. lines with supporting posts F.3: F.4: and F.5.
   (c) The 1st Bn. Middlesex Regiment will be in billets along the RUE DU BACQUEROT (M.17.d to M.6.d) and will find garrisons for second line posts 11, 12, 13, 14, 17 and 18. Post 11 will be taken over from the SIRHIND Brigade.
   (d) The 5th Bn. Scottish Rifles will be in Brigade Reserve in LAVENTIE.
   (e) The 1st Bn. The Cameronians will be in Divisional Reserve in the RUE DE LA LYS   G.27, G.54.

3. Details of reliefs of E and F lines and 2nd line posts will be arranged between Officers Commanding 2nd Royal Welsh Fusiliers, 2nd A. & S. Highlanders and 1st Bn. Middlesex Regiment   and Commanding Officers of outgoing battalions, at the 154th Infantry Brigade Headquarters (G.35.c 6.3) at 2.pm to day.
The Brigade Machine Gun Officer will meet the 154th Infantry Brigade Machine Gun Officer at the same place and time.

4. Further orders with March Table will be issued later.

Captain,

Issued at 8.am

Brigade Major 19th Infantry Brigade.

Copy No: 1 Filed,
2 Staff Captain,
3 2nd R.W. Fusiliers,
4 The Cameronians,
5 1st Bn. Middlesex Regt.,
6 2nd A. & S. Highlanders,
7 5th Scottish Rifles,
8 19th Field Ambulance,
9 19th Brigade Amm. Column,
10 19th Brigade Train,
11 19th Brigade Supply Column,
12 Brigade Transport Officer,
13 H.Q., 8th Division,
14 H.Q. 154th Inf.Bde.
15 H.Q. Sirhind Brigade.

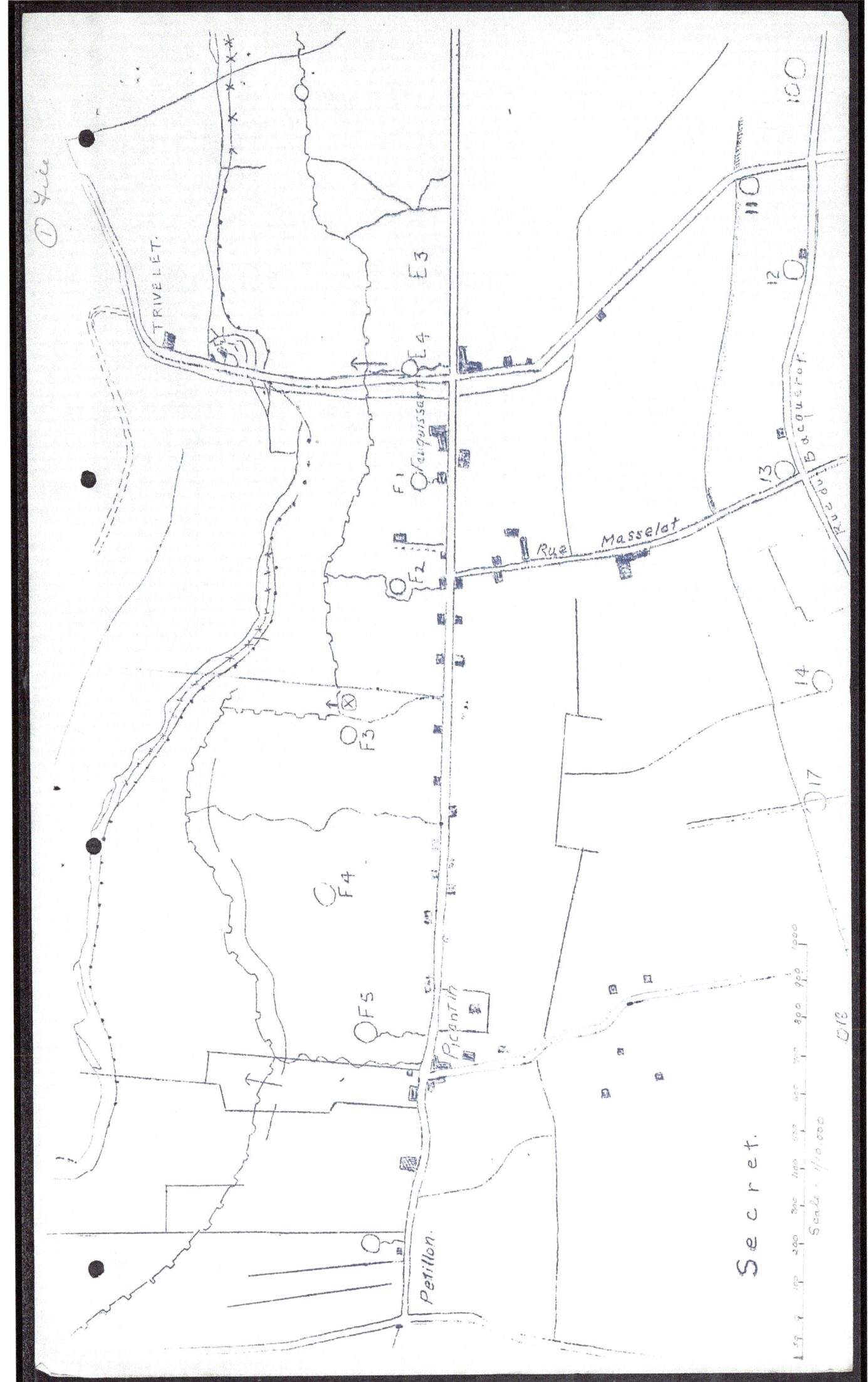

Copy No: 1

19th Infantry Brigade After Order

    to be attached to Operation Order No: 43.

Reference 1/40,000 map.   22nd July, 1915.

1. The Battalions of the Brigade will move to-morrow as per March Table attached.

2. The usual trench stores will be taken over. Periscopes, hyposcopes, telescopic rifles, hedging gloves, wire cutters, and catapults are not being handed over by the relieved battalions.

3. Regimental transport will move independently under battalion arrangements.

4. The sapping platoons will move with their regimental transport. The sapping platoon officers will meet the Staff Captain at LAVENTIE Station (M.4.b 0.10) at 3.pm

5. Present Brigade Headquarters will be closed at 6.pm and open at M.4.b 3.5 at the same hour.

Issued at 9.45.pm

                                                      Captain,

                                  Brigade Major 19th Infantry Brigade.

Copy No: 1 Filed,
        2 Staff Captain,
        3 2nd R.W.Fusiliers,
        4 The Cameronians,
        5 1st Middlesex Regt.,
        6 2nd A. & S.Highlanders,
        7 5th Scottish Rifles,
        8 19th Field Ambulance,
        9 19th Brigade Amm.Column,
      10 19th Brigade Train,
      11 19th Brigade Supply Column,
      12 Brigade Transport Officer,
      13 H.Q. 8th Division,
      14 H.Q. 154th Infantry Bde.,
      15 H.Q. Sirhind Brigade.

To be attached to
Operation Order,
No: 43.

MARCH TABLE. BATTALIONS 19th INFANTRY BRIGADE

23rd JULY, 1915.

Unit	Starting point.	Time of passing starting point.	ROUTE.	BILLETS.
2nd A. & S. Highlanders:	Road junction, G.9.c 3.9	5.pm.	SAILLY Bridge.	Halt near road junction G.27.d till the evening when battalion will move forward to trenches via M.5.b
2nd Royal Welsh Frs:	Road junction, A.20.a 6.1	3 30.am P.M.	Road junction G.9.c – SAILLY Bridge.	Halt near road junction G.27.d till the evening when battalion will move forward to trenches via G.27.b and LAVENTIE.
1st Middlesex Regiment:	Cross roads, A.22.a	7.45.pm	LE Pt.MORTIER – Pt.de la BOUDRETTE – A.10.d – SAILLY Bridge – road junction G.27.d – to M.5.b	The battalion will be met by guides at 10.pm at road junction M.5.b whence companies will be guided to their billets in Rue du BACQUEROT.
5th Scottish Rifles.	Cross roads at le Pt.MORTIER G.4.a	7.15.pm	Pt. de la BOUDRETTE – SAILLY Bridge – road junctions at G.27.d and G.34.d	North end of LAVENTIE.
The Cameronians	Road junction A.25.d 2.5	7.30.pm	; SAILLY Bridge.	Area G.27.b.c and d.

22/7/15.

[signature]
Captain,
Brigade Major 19th Infantry Bde.

SECRET

RELIEF ORDERS.   Copy No. I

                              30
                              ~~31st~~ July, 1915.

Reference attached map (issued to five Inf. Bns. only)

1. From to-morrow night, the front held by the Brigade will be from FAUQUISSART - TRIVELET road (inclusive) to the SAILLY - FROMELLES Road (exclusive).

2. The 1st Bn. The Cameronians will, tomorrow evening, take over from the 2nd Bn. East Lancashire Regt. (24th Infantry Brigade), sub-sections 1.P., 1.Q., 1.R., on the present left of the Brigade front, with the supporting posts 1.A., 1.X., and 1.B. in rear.
   Details of relief have been arranged between Officers Commanding Battalions concerned.

3. The 3rd Battery, R.F.A. will cover the line held by the 1st Bn. The Cameronians.

4. Besides S.A.A., Sniperscopes, megaphones, rifle grenade stands, catapults, water tanks, gongs, grenades, green signal rockets and Very pistol ammunition, are trench stores, and will be handed over by the Officer Commanding 2nd East Lancashire Regiment.
Periscopes, Very pistols, and Vermorel Sprayers will not be handed over.
Officers Commanding 1st Bn. Middlesex Regiment, and 5th Scottish Rifles will hand over to 1st Bn. The Cameronians by 4 pm tomorrow, 3 and 2 Vermorel Sprayers, respectively.

5. The 2nd Bn. Royal Welch Fusiliers will relieve the garrisons in posts 11, 12, 13, 14, 17, and 18 in the RUE DU BACQUEROT by 6 pm tomorrow.
The remainder of the battalions (less 1 Company), with machine guns will relieve the 1st Bn. The Cameronians in billet line, by 8 pm.
Detailed arrangements to be made between Commanding Officers concerned.
Headquarters and 1 Company, 2nd Bn. R.Welch Fusiliers will remain in LAVENTIE.

6. Headquarters of Battalions in trenches will be as follows:-
   5th Scottish Rifles.   M.12.c.5.6.
   1st Middlesex Regt.   M.6.d.2.1.
   1st Cameronians.   M.6.d.6.4.

7. Rocket signals by night for the Brigade will be Green from evening of 31st July, inclusive.

8. At 6 am, 1st August, the 2nd Argyll & Sutherland Highrs. will be in Brigade reserve, the Brigade finding no Divisional reserve battalion.

9. On completion of relief, O.C., 19th Infantry Brigade will assume command of the line mentioned in para. 1 above.

                                              Major,
                              Brigade Major, 19th Infantry Brigade.

            P.M.
Issued at 7 ~~am~~.
Copy. No. 1 Filed.   Copy. No. 8. 19th Fd. Amb.
  "   2 Staff Captain.   "   10. 19th Bde. Ammn.Col.
  "   3 2nd R.Welch Fus.   "   10. 19th Bde. Train.
  "   4 1st Cameronians.   "   11. Bde. Transport Off.
  "   5 1st Middlesex R.   "   12. 24th Inf. Bde.
  "   6 2nd A. & S. Highrs.   "   13. 8th Division.
  "   7 5th Scottish Rifles.   "   14. G.O.C., R.A., 8th Div.
                                       "   15. 9th Bde. R.F.A.

Copy No. 1

SECRET.

RELIEF ORDERS
of
19th Infantry Brigade.

31st July, 1915.

Reference: 1/40,000 map, sheet, 36.

1. After completion of relief tomorrow evening (1st August) the front line held by the Brigade will extend from Communication trench No. 10 (exclusive) (N.13.c.5.9.) to the SAILLY - FROMELLES Road, exclusive (N.9.c.6.8.)
   The southern boundary of the Brigade area will be RUE MASSELOT - Road Junction M.10.d. - LAVENTIE - LAVENTIE STATION - NOUVEAU MONDE - (all inclusive).
   2½ battalions will be in front line and 2½ battalions in Brigade reserve.

2. Tomorrow evening (1st August) the 5th Scottish Rifles will hand over the trench line from FAUQUISSART - TRIVELET road (inclusive) to No. 10 Communication trench (inclusive) and Posts E.4, F.1, to units of the BAREILLY Brigade (MEERUT Division).
   On completion of relief, 2 Companies, 5th Scottish Rifles will move to billets in LAVENTIE.
   Details of relief have been arranged by the Officers Commanding units concerned.

3. The 2nd Bn. R.Welch Fusiliers will, tomorrow evening, 1st August, hand over posts 11, 12, and 13 on the RUE DU BACQUEROT to units of the BAREILLY Brigade.
   Details to be arranged between Officers Commanding units concerned.
   On completion of relief, 2nd R.Welch Fusiliers will have 2 companies and 4 machine guns on the RUE DU BACQUEROT and 2 companies with Headquarters in LAVENTIE.

4. The 2 Companies, 2nd R.Welch Fus. on the RUE DU BACQUEROT will find the garrisons for posts as follows:-
   Post No. 14 (CELLAR)   - 1 Section.
   Post No. 17.(DEAD END) - 2 Sections.
   Post No. 18.(PICANTIN) - 2 Sections.
   The remainder of the two companies will be billetted as laid down in para 4 of Secret memorandum O.8 of 24th July, 1915.
   The Machine guns will not be placed in the posts.

5. Picks, shovels, periscopes, Very pistols, Vermorel sprayers, and latrine buckets will not be handed over to relieving units.

6. Artillery support on the Brigade front will be given by the 9th Brigade, R.F.A. until 10 pm, from which hour it will be given by the 90th Brigade, R.F.A.

2nd August

Major,
Brigade Major, 19th Infantry Brigade.

Issued at 5 pm.
Copy No. 1 Filed.
"   2 Staff Captain.
"   3 2nd R.Welch Fus.
"   4 1st Cameronians.
"   5 1st Middlesex Regiment.
"   6 2nd A. & S. Highrs.
"   7 5th Scottish Rifles.
"   8 19th Fd. Amb.
"   9 19th Bde. Amm. Col.
"   10 19th Bde. Train.
"   11 Bde Transport Officer.
"   12 Bareilly Brigade.
"   13 8th Division.
"   14 9th Bde. R.F.A.

INTELLIGENCE REPORTS.

5.pm. 1st July: 19th Infantry Brigade

19th INFANTRY BRIGADE

5.pm - 5.am

Between 6.30 and 7.pm wagons ans carts, some loaded with timber were seen on road I.36.d 0.1, going to ENNETIERES and to PARADIS. Paarties of men seen carrying bundles from 7 to 8.pm about I.34.a 7.5.

At 7.30.pm, 8 rounds from 4.5" howitzers were put into hostile trench opposite 51 in retaliation for rifle grenading of our trenches.

Night quiet - but sniping became heavy between 1.30 and 2.15.am opposite 49 - 52 but less at dawn as usual opposite 54 - 55. Revolving light seen at LILLE as usual. Various star shells, floating red light and a rocket white light 1,000 yards behind German trenches were seen. No unusual transport sounds were heard. Battalion in 49 reported that troops on their right were heard shouting across to the enemy.

At 4.am hostile trenches and communication trenches in rear, opposite 49,50 51 were bombarded with lyddite and shrapnel; 80 rounds fired the larger portion at the front trenches.

At 4.10.am 2 small parties of enemy in I.34.a. 7.5 were fired on by 11th Battery and seen to cause casualties.

A large hostile working party at 0.4.b 5.7 were scattered by a salvo of 5 rounds and probably caused loss as shells burst amongst them.

At 4.20 am. enemy replied to out bombardment with 97 shells from a mixed battery of field guns and 4.2" howitzers and a heavy howitzer into subsection 49, 53 and 54 and on support trenches in rear - some damage done and 1 man killed and 2 wounded. Firing ceased at 5.25.am Hostile battery seemed to be in direction of Fort ENGLOS. BOIS GRENIER and road to East was also shelled.

5. am - 5.pm

Quiet day - no sign of hostile working parties except a few men working on support line where much work has been done lately.

                                                                    Brigadier General,

                                       Commanding 19th Infantry Brigade.

5.pm 2nd July: 19th Infantry Brigade.

INTELLIGENCE REPORT

1. 5.pm - 5.am

About 6.10.pm a few howitzer shells fell near L'ARMEE.
At 7.45.pm, 4 15 pdr. shrapnel and 4 rifle grenades were fired on and behind subsection 52 near WATER FARM, and some against parapet of 54. Steps were taken to reply to these at once by howitzer fire on trenches opposite. Between 7 and 8.pm parties of enemy seen at I.34.a 7.5
LILLE revolving light again seen. Heavy sniping opposite 50 - 53 from 1.30 to 2.30.am, otherwise fairly quiet. Very quiet opposite 54 - 55 to midnight, enemy opposite singing from 9.30 to 10.30.pm and no flares were sent up.

2. 5.am - 5.pm

Quiet morning - very little seen of enemy and little signs of work except boards being carried along trench.
At 10.am 11th Battery dispersed working party on LA VALLEE - RADINGHEM Road.
About 4.15.pm, 20 15 pdr. shells were fired at 51, 52, 53 - 364th Battery retaliated.
At 4.40.pm enemy threw 2 bouquets of 4 shells each into 54 and later 6 single shells into 55 and 5 shells into rear of FLAMENGRIE Farm.
Enemy seen in trench wearing small grey soft cap similar to French Kepi, no coloured bands noticed.

3. Patrols:

Subsection 55 noticed a patrol of 8 Germans, following scouts of 1st Middlesex Regiment. Patrol sent out but Germans immediately returned. No other enemy patrols seen or heard. He is not patrolling much lately.
The night before last enemy fired rifle grenades into 54 and our listening post opened rapid fire in direction of supposed rifle grenade party. Enemy shouted out "All right we've got some more for you Jock's" and fired again. Fire was again opened and rifle grenades ceased. Officer of 1st Middlesex Regiment who was out on patrol on left reported that he saw 3 Germans of this party being carried back.
Patrol of 3 men under Lieut.Mostyn, 2nd R.W.Fusiliers went out last night from opposite right of subsection 50. At 10.30.pm when about 60 yards from enemy's trench sounds of a number of men marching along boards in the trench could be heard. These sounds continued at short intervals along their line and in different places until 11.45.pm The furthest East movement was heard was opposite centre of subsection 50 and it extended a long way to the Westward past German trenches opposite the BRIDOUX Road Salient,- which looks very much like a relief taking place. Patrol examined enemy's wire which was intact and returned at 12.40.am. No hostile patrol or working parties were observed.

                                            Brigadier General,
                                        Commanding 19th Infantry Brigade.

5.pm 3rd July   19th Infantry Brigade

INTELLIGENCE REPORT

1. 5.pm - 5.am

From 7 to 8.pm parties of Germans were seen in I.54.a & b carrying sacks - probably ration parties.
Between 6.30 and 7.pm hostile aeroplane passed over trenches twice - rifle and machine gun fire being opened on it. Enemy retaliated by shelling and firing rifle grenades at 52 and 53, and a few shells fell into RAILWAY and DEAD COW Farms. At 9.pm last night white flare sent up behind enemy's lines in rear of BOIS BLANCS, but nothing occurred. 3 rifle grenades fired at 51 at 2.am Heavy sniping during night opposite 50 - 53. Sniping opposite 54,55 commenced at 1.40.am and became very active after 2.am. Various star shells and coloured lights seen during night. LILLE light was not seen during night. Enemy heard working with timber and metal sheets during night. Music heard in enemy's trenches.
At 4.30.am usual working party seen at 0.4.b - 11th Battery fired at them and work ceased.

2. 5.am - 5.pm

Quiet in trenches - sniping increased in afternoon. Certain amount of shelling done by enemy during the day - on road and subsidiary breastwork between NEW and RATION Farms, LA VESEE and on subsections 50 and S.52,S.53 and S.58 - about 90 shells in all; both shrapnel and H.E.
GRIS POT shelled billets shelled at 4.pm - casualties 1 killed and 2 wounded.
Enemy seen working at intervals on broken parapet opposite 54, and fired at. No other hostile movement observed.

3. Patrols.

Nothing to report.

                                                Brigadier General
                                           Commanding 19th Infantry Brigade

5.pm 4th July   19th Infantry Brigade.

INTELLIGENCE REPORT

1. 5.pm - 5 am.

At 5.30.pm 4, 77mm and 10, 4.2" howitzer shells burst in H.16 and along road in H.17.d - the 4.7" guns were firing, and enemy was probably searching for them.
About 10 soldiers were seen cutting hay and loading up a transport wagon in I.34.b 8.1
Hostile aeroplane flew over lines at 6.45.pm but did not come within range.
Normal night on the left. Opposite centre and right enemy began sniping at 9.pm last night and continued until 2.30.am and at times sniping was very heavy. One shell landed near S.54 at 11.pm
After coloured rockets were sent up by Brigade on right, enemy sent a large number of flares up.
Between 7.15 and 7.30.pm - the 11th and 364th 18 pdr. batteries, and A/53 4.5" howitzer battery in combination with one another opened a rapid salvo fire on large parties of Germans that had been carefully located the 5 previous evenings between 7 and 8 pm These parties have been watched, they come up the road from LA VALLEE to the angle at HALTE I.34.a 3.5, some then proceed North to the road angle I.28.c 5.3, by a newly constructed road (this road is fit for wheeled traffic, motor ambulances and carts have been seen on it) others go up the railway line and separate at a communication trench junction to LE QUESNE (I.33.a) and to the houses at I.27 central. Roughly 100 Germans have been counted nightly in parties in the area shelled. The howitzers shelled GRAND MARAIS and road from there to road angle at HALTE, the 11th Battery road angle at HALTE to road junction I.34.c, and 364th Battery on to LA VALLEE road junction. All guns waited till Germans were fairly distributed all along the roads and opened together. It is almost certain that quite fair losses must have been caused to the enemy. All parts fired on had been carefully registered beforehand.

2. 5.am - 5.pm

Hostile aeroplane flew over line at 8.40.am - out of range.
Quiet day - normal sniping.
At 4.pm 6 5.9" howitzershells burst over GRIS POT.
At 4.15.pm heavy howitzer shell fell just behind parados of 57, killing four and wounding 5 men.
Soldiers again seen with horse and cart collecting hay near LA VALLEE.
Some Germans seen on LA VALLEE - RADINGHEM Road carrying planks.
No working parties seen on CAPINGHEM ridge today.

3. Patrols

Patrols from 54, 55 report enemy working on their wire and cutting grass till about midnight.
Patrols from 58 - 59 report continuous talking along German trenches as if they were strongly held. Transport heard moving North to South from 10.45.pm till 1.am.
Patrols from right nothing to report.

Brigadier General,

Commanding 19th Infantry Brigade.

5.pm 5th July   19th Infantry Brigade.

INTELLIGENCE REPORT

1. 5.pm - 5.am

Fairly quiet night but increased sniping. At about 10.pm enemy were shouting about WARSAW, and became very noisy about 11.pm and were playing the Marseillaise on mouth organs and shouted across opposite 54 "Who's over there". New light seen - it went up Green and came down Red. Rifle grenades fired at 54 about 10.pm. Large number of star shells put up by enemy during the night but ceased on heavy reply being given at dawn.

2. 5.am - 5.pm

Quiet day - enemy sniping from trees about 1.pm opposite the Right. Fire was opened by one Company and a man was seen to fall from a tree. Sniping ceased after this. About 8 shells fell during the morning near trenches 53, 54, and 57, most of them H.E, from howitzer near FORT ENGLOS 2 were blind. Heavy haze all day, very difficult to see any movement.

3. Patrols:

The Cameronians on the right sent out a bombing party to bomb the enemy, but no enemy patrols were met. This and other patrols and listening posts report noise heard like iron sheeting or hollow metal being unloaded and noise like sawing metal also heard.

Officers patrol from 2/A. & S.Hrs. on the left saw large working parties cutting grass and improving wire in front of 58 and 59, with covering parties out.

Our patrols fired on both - results not known.

Brigadier General,
Commanding 19th Infantry Brigade.

5.pm 6th July   19th Infantry Brigade

INTELLIGENCE REPORT
5.pm - 5.am

Between 4.30 and 7.pm enemy's artillery was unusually active, shells being put into area between LA VESEE and L'ARMEE - 4 men being wounded in billet near latter place. Our shelling seems to have annoyed the enemy as his shelling of our trenches and of area in rear came after and was all in retaliation.

About 7.pm 5 shells were fired at 50, 53 and 55. Fairly quiet night except opposite 54,55 where enemy kept up intermittent fire all night and fired 5 rifle grenades at various times. It is impossible to reply to their rifle grenades, except by patrols lying in wait for them in case they come out to their forward saps, as our rifle grenades can not be fired at that range - a handicap which the enemy takes every advantage of. Green parachute light sent up opposite 54 also 2 rockets.

No: 2 Mountain Battery fired 50 rounds during evening at roads and tracks in area FLEUR d'ECOSSE - LA VALLEE - GRAND MARAIS (I.29 and I.34) These roads have been used nightly for reliefs and rations, etc.

5.am - 5.pm

Quiet day in trenches. During morning at odd times about 24 shells, all H.E., were fired at various points in front trenches with a few into "Shaftesbury Avenue". About 11.am one of our aeroplanes appeared to be hit and came back over our lines, the engines stopping when over FLAMENGRIE FARM.

Farms at H.12.b 0.2 were shelled by a battery from near WEZ MACQUART from 2.30 to 3.pm - about 20 shells mostly percussion howitzer being fired - Farms used as billets hit 5 times. In addition to the shells fired into the trench area, enemy's artillery during the day fired 4.2" shells along the RUE FLEURIE and L'ARMEE in early morning. - Our 11-th Battery retaliating on Farms, etc. opposite, enemy put 20 shells to West of BOIS GRENIER. During afternoon 20, 77m.m and 5.9" shells burst about road North of L'ARMEE and some 43 shells between LA VESEE, GRIS POT and L'ARMEE. On 96th and A.53 batteries retaliating, enemy's fire ceased.

Patrols

Patrols nothing to report except following:

Two officer's patrols from A. & S.Highlanders sent out from 57 & 59. First patrol got close to enemy's party working on wire and was challenged by a strong covering party and forced to retire. Second patrol from 57 got within a few yards of enemy flag put up in cleared space 50 yards in front of their wire. A party of 15 Germans were observed 20 yards on their right rear. Patrol retired pursued by the enemy to a ditch where enemy were bombed and driven off.

A patrol consisting of L/Corpl.McNeil and Pte.Stewart, 5th Scottish Rifles sent out from 55 spent from 2 am to 11 am in the morning examining German wire and listening posts. Near a ditch 80 yards from German trenches a hollowed tree was found which had obviously been used as a sniper's post. Some listening posts located - some were fitted with wooden seats - each for 2 or 3 men. The wire entanglement seems varied somewhat; in some parts it was not very strong, but generally it was very strong and thick - too thick to crawl through. Samples of wire were brought in, an empty cigarette packet and a cartridge case, also a card board box with stamp dated 2nd June,1915, addressed to a soldier of the 3rd Company, 1st Battalion, 179th Regiment, 47th Brigade, 24th Division, 19th Army Corps.

Brigadier General,
Commanding 19th Infantry Brigade.

5.pm 7th July   19th Infantry Brigade.

INTELLIGENCE REPORT.

1. 5.pm - 5.am

Quiet night with steady sniping up to midnight particularly on the left where it continued up to 2.am

Between 3.20 and 3.45.am 10 men fully armed left hostile second line I.27.b 3.8, and 12 men seen to come in, both moving to and from RUE DU BOIS and 2 cyclists seen riding from Distillerie to RUE DU BOIS.

2. 5.am - 5.pm

Quiet day - enemy not sniping much till about 4.pm.

A black and yellow flag has been placed by enemy in front of their trenches opposite 54. Men seen wearing Khaki helmet with black spike.

At 9.45.am 11th and A/55 Batteries dispersed a working party near LA VALLEE - RADINGHEM ROAD.

During morning enemy put 6, 5.9" shells into BOIS GRENIER - FLEURBAIX Road, 20, 77m.m shells into barrier on BRIDOUX Road I.31.a and in S.51. 96th battery retaliated on German trenches opposite 54.

During afternoon LA VESEE and GRIS POT were shelled with 4.2" howitzers, about 24 rounds fired, and 2 shrapnel shells burst over entrance of SHAFTESBURY AVENUE.

3. Patrols

Patrols had nothing to report. Germans heard talking in their trenches - but do not seem to be patrolling.

Brigadier General,
Commanding 19th Infantry Brigade.

5.pm 8th July   19th Infantry Brigade

INTELLIGENCE REPORT

5.pm - 5.am

During afternoon about 5.30.pm a few shells were fired at 54 and 55 and towards GRIS POT.
Quiet night, enemy sniping less than usual and made very little reply to our firing. Very few Very's lights sent up by them. One shell fired at 9.pm into entrance of Shaftesbury Avenue.
Subsections 54 and 55 have not been bothered by rifle grenades lately since patrols lay out for them recently and opened rapid fire where grenades came from.

5.am - 5.pm

Quiet day with occasional sniping shots. Between 12.25 and 1.15.pm 15 5.9" shells fell in GRIS POT, LA VESSEE and RUE DELPIERRE. At 3.pm 3 more 5.9" shells fell in huts near GRIS POT and 2 in BOIS GRENIER. At 4.40.pm 3 more 5.9" shells fell in BOIS GRENIER. 7 rifle grenades were fired from subsection 50 at enemy's trenches - 2 just reached and burst on his parapet, the remainder were short, one being blind. A new machine gun emplacement discovered opposite 50. Opposite 57 small hut has been located within a few yards in rear of enemy's front line which is occupied, perhaps a company headquarters.
Between 7 and 8 am small parties of the enemy observed working on their communication trench which runs from trench opposite 58 towards railway - about 10 men were seen using this trench at 3.am this morning. Enemy busy at work on CAPINGHEM Ridge.

Patrols

A patrol from the Cameronians under Lieut.Gordon went out at 9.15.pm ; 3 working parties were seen on their wire, but no patrols met. On return of patrol fire was opened on these working parties - result not known.
Other patrols had nothing to report except that enemy working parties heard hammering in stakes between 9.30 and 10.30.pm - no hostile patrols met.
On cross examination further information was obtained from patrol of 5th Scottish Rifles mentioned in report of 6th July. At night the sentry posts in hostile trenches seem to consist of groups of 2 men to every 5 to 10 yards. The enemy " stands to" between 2 and 3 am and the sniping which is heavy during that time seems to be a regular parade as words of command were distinctly heard which when given immediately stopped the heavy sniping, while the ordinary deliberate sniping continued. The llok out by day seems poor, as although there were several periscopes visible and many pointing at the patrol, which at times was exposed, no notice was taken of them. A special kind of thick wire is freely used, too tough for our wire cutters, with barbs one inch long. It is very thick in places, so thick that as described " a mouse could not get through it". An embrasure was noticed in the parapet, either for field gun, trench mortar or rifle grenade stand, probably the latter; it was not a machine gun emplacement.

Brigadier General,

Commanding 19th Infantry Brigade.

5.pm 9th July   19th Infantry Brigade.

INTELLIGENCE REPORT

1. 5.pm - 5.am

At 7.30.pm. Germans were seen lying in wait behind a flag which they had put up opposite 56, and special steps are being taken to deal with the ambuscade tonight.
Quiet night, hostile sniping not at all aggressive, except the usual heavy sniping at dawn. This heavy sniping by words of command may probably be a means of practising fire control and fire discipline on the part of the Germans.
At 9.30.pm a burst of fire was opened on our working parties in front of 57 - no casualties.
At 10.pm enemy's working party located opposite 51 - a party went out to get to our rifle grenade range and dispersed them with rifle grenades.
At 5.am enemy threw a few shells from field guns at LA VALLEE into trenches near Flamengrie and Water Farms.

2. 5.am - 5.pm

Quiet day - small enemy working parties were observed in front trenches and on second line; one party wore white duck jackets
Small party seen using communication trenches, wearing usual round cap with red band and coat or blanket rolled over shoulder.
Portions of the hostile second line have been freshly loopholed and wire has been put up behind their first line. Some of the higher trees have been artificially thickened opposite Water Farm.
Small parties of the enemy seen at odd times on LA VALLEE - RADINGHEM Road.
At 6.am 2 5.9" H.E. shells burst near LA VESEE, and at 9.30 am, 3.77mm shells were fired into BOIS GRENIER.
Between 11 and 12 noon the enemy fired 32 4.2" H.E. and Shrapnel from direction of FLEUR D'ECOSSE into area round New Farm - *hitting* artillery observation station there.

3. Patrols

No hostile patrols seen or heard , 2 or 3 small parties seen working on wire and cutting grass.

9/7/15.   Brigadier General,

                                                Commanding 19th Infantry Brigade.

5.pm 10th July   19th Infantry Brigade.

INTELLIGENCE REPORT

1. 5.pm - 5.am.

At 6.10.pm, 8 4.2" shells fell between BURNT FARM, PARK ROW AVENUE, and LA VESEE: 2 guns were firing; direction LA PARADIS.
Quiet night from midnight till dawn - certain amount of snipin opposite the Right. Normal transport sounds heard opposite centre. Man seen with flat grey cap, dark blue band; another in dark blue cap with yellow braid and white badge.

2. 5.am - 5.pm

At 7.5 am 2 shells fired at Flamengrie Farm.
Enemy shelled support and front trenches on left from 7.40 to 8.5 am with a single field gun from beyond the Distillerie, and again from 8.20 to 8.30.am 27 shells altogether fired, distributed between Dead Cow Farm and front and support trenches 58, 59; some direct hits on the farm and some slight damage; 11th battery retaliated.
Quiet day, few small working parties seen: two men seen at No: 3 Farm were sniped at with telescopic rifle and disappeared; one man observed with khaki-grey spiked helmet and black waterproof jacket - also a small party carrying boards. Working party seen on CAPINGHEM Ridge were shelled by our artillery, and men seen to drop.
Besides above, no other movement observed.
2 Sausage ballonns were up to the South opposite 8th Division front.

3. Patrols

Patrols out all night. On the Right no patrols or working parties on wire were seen, except opposite BRIDOUX Salient where enemy were seen working on wire. Small wire party heard opposite 56 at 10.30.pm - opposite here also enemy were heard working in their trench joking and laughing.

10/7/15.

                                        Brigadier General,
                                   Commanding 19th Infantry Brigade.

5.pm 11th July   19th Infantry Brigade.

INTELLIGENCE REPORT

5.pm - 5.am

At 7.pm. a working party was seen behind farm West of BRIDOUX Road.
Red, Green and white flares were sent up at 9.pm from direction of
LA FLEUR D'ECOSSE.
Quiet night though sniping heavier than usual between 2 and 3.am
Opposite 54 at dawn 2 men firing from parapet were hit by our
snipers; periscopes also were smashed, some of which were of large
size.
About 10.pm a few shrapnel were fired at 54, just before which 2 red
and one green lights had been sent up from German trench opposite.

5.am - 5.pm

Quiet day on left and centre; on right enemy's snipers were more
active than usual. Opposite 53 enemy has put up fresh wire close
to his front trench and some wire in rear of it. Opposite 55 a pole,
similar to a wireless pole has been erected. Men seen observing
and sniping over parapet all with usual greyish flat cap.
At 12.30.pm enemy bombarded 50 with 30, 77mm shrapnel. 364th
battery retaliated with 12 shrapnel into trenches opposite and
A/53 battery with 4 shrapnel.
A working party seen at 0.15

Patrols

Patrols last night report all very quiet in hostile line; a few
parties seen on wire and cutting grass with covering parties in
front.
The flag referred to in Intelligence Report of 9th July - behind
which Germans had been seen lying in wait - was brought in today.
3 Scouts (L/Corpl.Margiotta and Barton and Pte.Jones) of 1st
Middlesex Regiment went out at noon today and found two flags.
They were not observed until flag was planted on our parapet when
very vicious sniping at once commenced.
In addition to the above a third flag was brought in by Lieuts.
Bucknall and Hare who were out on patrol for 4½ hours this
afternoon. The flag was hung on a tree 70 yards in front of German
lines and on enemy's side of the Courant de la Chapelle. Soon after
taking the flag a bomb exploded at the tree where the flag had been.
Sapheads and listening posts which had been used by the enemy the
night before were reconnoitred. In one of the listening posts a
signal wire was found leading back to the German lines. The wire
entanglement in front of the German trenches was examined and found
to be very strong and there were no signs of it being removed or
thinned. A working party was heard by the patrol in front of
German 2nd line. Both patrols were out in front of No: 56.
Two of the flags were large, 3 feet square. The third was 6 inches
square with "GOD KILT THE KAISER, WE WILL MAKE YOU WANT US" written
on it. All were German colours.
Yesterday afternoon Lieut.Hare 1st Middlesex Regiment, with L/Corpl.
Barton and Pte.Jones reconnoitred what is presumably the
flanking sap shown in photograph opposite 55 - 56. The Courant de
la Chapelle was bridged: from near it a natural ditch improved into
a trench ran back to the sap head, the sap itself faced our trenches
obliquely and had flank protection of steel plates with bombproofs.
The sap was 3 feet deep and 5 feet wide. Patrol think enemy use
this part of the Courant de la Chapelle for drawing water. The wire
round the saphead was old and rusty.

11/7/15.   Brigadier General,
                                            Commanding 19th Infantry Brigade.

5.pm 12th July, 1915.   19th Infantry Brigade

INTELLIGENCE REPORT

1. 5.pm - 5.am

At about 7.pm 3 H.E. shells fell at junction of Haymarket and
Shaftesbury Avenue and 4 on the subsidiary line. Between 8 & 9.pm
single 4.2" shells were burst over the La Vesee road.
An unusual number of coloured lights, mostly red and green, were
sent up by the enemy during early part of night. More than normal
amount of "Very's" lights were also sent up. A quiet night. The
usual vigorous sniping at dawn was abruptly stopped on the Right
by A/53 howitzer battery throwing 4 rounds into hostile trenches
opposite.
The guns firing between 8 and 9.pm were located by flashes about
Les BAS CHAMPS Farm (O.9.b) Coloured lights mentioned above always
preceded the firing, so that it is possible the enemy may have
various combinations of lights as signals for targets - lights
seemed to be sent up from farm close in rear of front line.

2. 5.am - 5.pm

Quiet day - Hostile shelling consisted of a H.E. shrapnel on to
La Vesee Road junction and at about 4.pm 25 4.2" howitzer shells
fell near NEW Farm - the artillery observing station had a fairly
hot time of it. At the same time 6 77mm shells fell in S.56, S.57.
Two pigeons seen flying from German lines westward.
Enemy opposite 55 has raised his parapet and strengthened it with
extra sandbags - here men were seen wearing caps of light bluish grey
with narrow band either white or very light blue. Few odd small
working parties seen on front line. Usual work going on on
CAPINGHEM Ridge and along LA VALLEE - RADINGHEM Road.

3. Patrols

Patrols were sent out throughout the night as far as enemy's wire.
All except one patrol on extreme right reported that no enemy working
parties were out on their wire or even in front of their parapet. The
wire was intact which was corroborated by daylight observation in
early morning. A new listening post was discovered opposite 57 which
held 6 men.
A patrol under Lieut. Mostyn, 2nd R.W.Fusiliers went out from 50.
They moved across about 250 yards of enemy's front and tried to get
near wire but were fired at very heavily both from 2 listening posts
and from enemy's main trench by maxims. Enemy were driving in stakes
in his wire line and doing it very silently, and his listening posts
were particularly alert.

12/7/15.

                                            Brigadier General,
                                      Commanding 19th Infantry Brigade.

13th July, 1915.   19th Infantry Brigade

INTELLIGENCE REPORT

1. 5.pm - 5.am

In I.34.d a gun position or an ammunition store shows up very distinctly when the sun shines on it.

About 8.20.pm party of enemy seen carrying timber near LA MOTTE HOUSSAIN Farm. Hostile aeroplane flew over the line at 6.10.pm at a great height.

LILLE revolving light seen from 9.30.pm. Small parties of enemy seen at various points in rear of their lines in early morning.

A quiet night. Sniping at dawn considerably decreased. The latest consignment of German flares are not good - several failing to ignite properly and others giving poor light.

At 6.30.pm enemy shelled PARK AVENUE with 77 mm gun - 11th battery replied on LA HOUSSOIE and GRAND MARAIS.

2. 5.am - 5.pm

Quiet day - little sniping; a small working party dispersed by our snipers opposite 55. Hostile aeroplanes flew along line at 3.10.pm - out of rifle/range.

At 4.pm Farm in I.34.c was burned to the ground by 53.A Howitzer Battery. The Farm was probably a bomb store as it blew up. Odd parties of the enemy seen near LA VALLEE and on the ridge were fired at by our artillery and dispersed.

About 5.pm about 30 5.9" howitzer shells were fired into GRIS POT billets damaging the houses - and about 30 rounds of 4.2" howitzers fired along the BOIS GRENIER Road.

A/53 howitzer battery burst 2 lyddite and 2 shrapnel over hostile gun firing at I.29.d 3.3.

3. Patrols:

Patrols report enemy working on wire and cutting grass opposite the left and centre. No parties seen on the right.

Hostile wire intact all along the front.

13th July, 1915.

Brigadier General,
Commanding 19th Infantry Brigade.

5.pm 14th July.   19th Infantry Brigade.

INTELLIGENCE REPORT

1. 5.pm - 5.am

Between 5.30 and 6.pm enemy continued their artillery activity of 5.pm and put 12 4.2" shells into ERQUINGHEM and 20 77mm shells round Moat Farm, 3 hitting the Farm.

About 7.pm a German working party was seen working on parapet opposite 60 and evidently hidden by grass from this trench: it was enfiladed by 2nd A. & S.Highlanders machine gun in 58. Two men working in front line opposite 51 were fired at and dropped; a periscope was hit.

Enemy put up several star shells during night. Parties were cutting grass opposite 55 between 10.pm and midnight. LILLE light seen between 10.pm and 1.55 am. Sniping intermittent opposite centre and left and very active between 1.30 and 2.30.am opposite the right.

Two hostile aeroplanes flew over trenches at 7.30.am

2. 5.am - 5.pm
little sniping

Quiet day in the trenches:- nothing seen except one man in the factory at LA HOUSSOIE. At 7.30.am 24 5.9" H.E. and shrapnel burst in BOIS GRENIER.

Between 11.30 am and 12.30.pm enemy shelled RUE FLEURIE with 12 4.2" howitzer shells hitting the farms there.

Our batteries shelled small parties of enemy and registered farm at O.11.d 4.0, hit a cart and wounded a man.

3. Patrols

Patrols report enemy's wire intact and that enemy were working on it opposite the left trenches. Opposite the centre working parties were heard in and behind hostile trenches, the latter seemed to be working with bricks. A patrol of 12 men was seen opposite 56 and fired on by machine gun. All was quiet on the right, no hostile working parties were seen, though hostile listening posts were out.

14/7/15   Brigadier General,
                                        Commanding 19th Infantry Brigade.

5pm. 15th July   19th Infantry Brigade.

INTELLIGENCE REPORT

1. 5.pm - 5.am

Quiet night very little sniping, except on the right where it was heavy up to midnight. LILLE light seen during night. Several flares of enemy failed to ignite. Normal sounds of transport heard.

2. 5.am - 5.pm

Quiet day in the trenches, little sniping except again on the right where it was more than usual. Opposite right enemy have what looks like a large periscope in the trees - a man seen wearing khaki uniform similar to our infantry.

At 5.15 and 8.15am this morning enemy put 6 and 4 77mm H.E. into BOIS GRENIER and again at 10.15.am fired 20 4.2" H.E. and 77mm shells at BOIS GRENIER observation station getting 3 direct hits. Enemy very busy with large working parties on CAPINGHEM ridge all day. The earthwork seems completed and barbed wire entanglements seems now being erected. A/53 howitzer battery dispersed parties throughout the day. Working party in saphead opposite 55 was dispersed by 6 rounds from 96th Battery.

3. Patrols

Patrols report enemy's wire intact. In places opposite the left battalion it is being strengthened with a trip wire in front. A daylight patrol from 57 reports that a short parallel has been dug close behind wire.

15/7/15

Brigadier General,
Commanding #9th Infantry Brigade

5.pm -16th July   19th Infantry Brigade.

INTELLIGENCE REPORT

1. 5.pm - 5.am

The 2nd A. & S.Highlanders reported that at 8.20.pm a column of infantry which took 7 minutes to pass a point was seen probably on the VERT BALLOT - RADINGHEM Road at O.10.d; two batteries were also seen trotting on the same road, the guns could be distinctly seen through a powerful telescope with men sitting on the limbers. Wagons were also seen, some covered; these were not closed up but were somewhat straggly. Another battery was seen walking on the ENNETIERES - ESCOBECQUES Road.
14 4.7" french shells were fired into 53,54, between 7.30 and 8.pm, 5 at 11.pm and 8 77 mm shells at 4.am near FLAMENGRIE Farm - and shells near Battalion Headquarters of Right Battalion at 8.40.pm. A german baling water was shot on the parapet opposite 53. Man seen wearing service cap with broad red band. A German seen descending from a tree and fired at, result not known. Fairly quiet night, with sniping heavier on the right.

2. 5.am - 5.pm

Enemy very quiet except on right where there was a good deal of sniping all day. Our aeroplanes very active. Two aeroplanes seemed to have a duel in the air, result not known. Enemy has erected a barrier of branches on road in I.34.d behind which about 40 Germans were seen. 364th battery shelled large 15feet periscope reported yesterday but failed to dislodge it.
Two or three explosions heard in morning in or immediately behind German front line opposite 56 which sounded like blasting: this also occurred yesterday.
2 77 mm shells burst near Rue Fleurie about 4.30.pm and about a dozen shells were fired into various parts of the left battalion.

3. Patrols:

A patrol of the Cameronians under Lieut.Bucher went out from 53 and saw enemy working on their wire and driving in iron stakes. 2 grenades were thrown at the working party with good effect. Transport was heard in close proximity to the enemy's trenches. Other patrols also report enemy were working on their wire and were hammering in metal stakes. Strong covering parties were out which appears to be the normal procedure lately. German trenches in some places appear to have had overhead cover added to them. Enemy's wire everywhere intact.

16/7/15.   Brigadier General,

                                             Commanding 19th Infantry Brigade.

5.pm 17th July   19th Infantry Brigade.

INTELLIGENCE REPORT

1. 5.pm - 5.am

A quiet night, though a good deal of sniping on the right up to 10.pm. Enemy's fireworks still of rather a poor quality. A large searchlight played on our trenches about midnight. Normal transport sounds heard at 10.pm moving South.

2. 5.am - 5.pm

Very quiet day probably owing to gusty weather. Enemy seems to be roofing in his front line. German seen wearing greenish cap with white buttons and two thin stripes of darker green. Usual working parties on RADINGHEM ridge, many carrying planks and transport also seen on ridge. An enemy sniper was shot opposite 53 after a steady sniping duel lasting 3 hours.

At 7.am 12 rounds H.E. shrapnel from 77mm guns were burst near and over Brigade Headquarters at H.6.d and at H.12.b Between 4.30 and 6.pm level crossing by DESPLANQUES Farm was shelled intermittently. A new work being built at O.11.b 2.9

Our guns shelled working parties on Capinghem ridge and wagon on LA VALLEE - RADINGHEM Road.

3. Patrols.

Patrols report no signs of working parties and no hostile patrols met. Our patrol went out from 51 and fired 3 rifle grenades but result not known. Enemy's wire now has large number of wire posts added to it.

17/7/15.   Brigadier General,
                                       Commanding 19th Infantry Brigade.

5.pm.18th July   19th Infantry Brigade.

INTELLIGENCE REPORT

1. 5.pm - 5.am

Exceptionally quiet night and more noticeable on the right where enemy are usually more noisy. This sudden peace on the right might probably mean a relief was taking place. Sniping commenced at 1.am. Opposite centre sounds were heard as if enemy were working with wood in their trenches.

2. 5.am - 5.pm

Enemy very quiet - nothing much to be seen either,. One or two men seen moving in their second line. Movement again noticed in LE QUESNE Farm which is either a Headquarters of sorts or a store depot. About 6 shells fell in left battalion area during the day.

3. Patrols.

As a relief on the right was suspected, Lieut.Tayet of the Cameronians went out and burst 10 rifle grenades on enemy's trenches - results not known. Patrols report enemy's wire intact and that no work was being done either in or in front of their trenches.

                                        Brigadier General,
                                Commanding 19th Infantry Brigade.

	"A" Form.		Army Form C. 2121.
	MESSAGES AND SIGNALS.		No. of Message

Prefix....Code....m.	Words	Charge	This message is on a/c of:	Recd. at....m.
Office of Origin and Service Instructions.	Sent			Date
	At....m.		Service.	From
	To			By
	By		(Signature of "Franking Officer.")	

TO: 8th Division

Sender's Number.	Day of Month	In reply to Number	A A A
*NM 83	24		

Daily Report aaa operations nothing fresh to Not already reported in Situation reports aaa WORK aaa Right battalion made incinerators and Latrines aaa cleaned up and disinfected dugouts aaa cleared up refuse aaa made fire steps and put in 3 new dug outs aaa. Left battalion Busy cleaning up trenches and putting them in Sanitary condition and Strengthening parapet which was very weak aaa No R.E. material was available today aaa Intelligence Right Battalion enemy working on wire last night. Enemy Sniping slight aaa M.G. Worked opposite F.1. Sausage balloon up over AUBERS between 4.45 and 11.30 am

From

Place

Time

The above may be forwarded as now corrected. (Z)

Censor. | Signature of Addressee or person authorised to telegraph in his name.
* This line should be erased if not required.

(T1809) Wt. 14142—C.1. 45000 pads. 4/15. Sir J. C. & S.

"A" Form.
MESSAGES AND SIGNALS.
Army Form C. 2121.

Prefix	Code	m.	Words	Charge	This message is on a/c of:	Recd. at	m.
Office of Origin and Service Instructions.							
			Sent			Date	
			At	m.	Service.	From	
			To				
			By		(Signature of "Franking Officer.")	By	

TO

| Sender's Number. | Day of Month | In reply to Number | |
| | | | AAA |

enemy's wire very strong and intact.
Hostile aeroplane passed over line
at 5 hrs. Flying very high.
Left Battalion - Sniping very heavy
at Salient. 19 Heavy shells fired
into trenches about 3.15 p.m. enemy's
wire very strong and intact.
Two working parties seen during night.
This afternoon a very heavy bullet
or small shell came at frequent
intervals over the parapets in F.3. They
were fired singly and not in
rapid succession. During night a sound
was heard as if a machine
were working with a very creaking
wheel opposite the Salient

From 19
Place
Time

The above may be forwarded as now corrected.
Censor. Signature of Addressor or person authorised to telegraph in his name.
* This line should be erased if not required.

(T1809) Wt. 14142—641. 4500 pads. 4/15. Sir J. C. & S.

DAILY REPORT, 25th July, 1915.   19th Infantry Brigade.

OPERATIONS: 1   Enemy quiet. Very quiet night except for some sniping between 2 and 2.30.am on the right.
At 10.am this morning 16 shells were fired at trenches on right of salient and communication trench in rear. Most of them went over - no damage done.

WORK: 2.   (i) Battalions in front trenches strengthened parapet and put out wire. Wire was found very weak and paretically useless and in many places non-existent. Some existing dug-outs cleaned and disinfected, others filled in and new ones built. Iron loopholes placed in position. Incinerators constructed and latrines, wash houses and refuse pits built.
Working parties out till dawn on front parapet and on wire.
(ii) Sapping platoons worked on 3 communication trenches in rear of left battalion. A great deal of work being done on communication trench on extreme right of salient. Ground in rear of front line reconnoitred for further work.

INTELLIGENCE: 3.   3 enemy working parties seen working in front of parapet. One was heavily fired at by rifle and machine guns and casualties caused. Party did not re-appear the rest of the night.
At 5.45.am hostile aeroplane was circling round behind enemy's lines, probably directing as fire as hostile heavy gun was firing at the time. Gun seemed to be some distance beyond AUBERS. Between 5 and 7.pm last evening enemy fired from his trenches at our aeroplanes volume of fire was not heavy.
Sound of creaking wheel again heard - could it be the wheel of mining shaft ?

PATROLS: Patrols of Right Battalion found enemy working on front with covering parties out. One patrol reconnoitred house on TRIVELET Road and found it empty with a few lying down fire trenches in rear. Enemy made no attempt at concealment. A patrol on left found no obstacles between our trenches and enemy - a large excavation half way between trenches was discovered, large enough to hold 6 men - and a certain amount of trip wire was found. A working party discovered here was heavily sniped by us all night after patrols returned.
Patrols of left battalion saw 2 hostile patrols of 8 men each. Enemy's wire was intact and strong.

Brigadier General,

Commanding 19th Infantry Brigade.

Daily Report, 26th July: 19th Infantry Brigade

OPERATIONS: 1. Enemy quiet. Right Battalion got the 19th battery to fire on a hostile working party at 317 - result not known.
Enemy shelled:-

     4.30.pm 7 shells Rue Tilleloy,
     6.20.pm 15 shells South of LAVENTIE.
     7.15 - 7.30.pm 19 shells South of LAVENTIE.

WORK: 2. <u>Right Battalion</u> put in dug-outs - strengthened parados and added firing steps - cut grass and put out wire entanglements - 2 trenches for listening posts dug and prepared.

<u>Left Battalion</u> strengthend and rebuilt parapets, and thickened and raised parados - revetting being carried out as far as material available allowed - firing steps were added - wire strengthened and in places where non-existent new wire has been put up.

INTELLIGENCE 3. Enemy seem to have large working parties out nightly from 9.pm till 2.am working on their wire and cutting grass and men could be seen standing on their parapets. Near the TRIVELET Road and in front of F.3 they have a covering party, in other places they appear to work without one. As soon as our patrols and working parties are in these hostile parties are fired on. As our wire is in such a deplorable condition and the grass in front is so long large working parties have to be employed nightly in front on this work as well as on work in front of the parapets. It is difficult therefore to put a stop to his activity at night until my line has been put into a fitter state of defence. Arrangements have been made however to open rapid rifle fire and machine gun and artillery fire all along the front at 11.30.pm tonight in the hope of catching these working parties.
The enemy snipes very little by day or night and does not appear to patrol at all. In the trenches and at work he laughs, talks and sings all night.
Last night on the right he was shouting from his parapet to find out who we were.
A trolley was heard several times by all patrols running in rear of the enemy's trenches from the TRIVELET Road up to the mine crater. Whenever it stopped there was great activity amongst the enemy and planks were heard being thrown out. The creaking wheel mentioned yesterday may belong to this trolley.
Enemy's wire seems strong and intact; opposite F.3 it was Chevaux de Frise and stakes supporting very rusty barbed wire.
Enemy's flare lights were of very poor quality.
<u>Transport heard</u>
     At 9.pm light transport on Rue Deleval for 15 minutes.
     At 10.pm 1 cart on road in N.20.c 2.10 moving S.W.
     At 11.50.pm a hand cart came up to trenches on the TRIVELET Road.
     At 1.am light transport moving from Rue Deleval towards AUBERS.

2 machine guns were located opposite Right Battalion.
<u>Hostile aeroplanes</u> seen behind German lines between 6.15 - 6.40.pm
<u>Observation Balloon</u> over AUBERS yesterday till 7.25.pm and went up again at day break today.
<u>Patrols</u> found that ground opposite E and F lines had no obstacle between our and German wire. Opposite F.3 was a series of shallow pits giving head and shoulder cover, 2 yards apart well concealed and unoccupied. 2 saps found running out from mine crater, unoccupied and looked like listening posts. Owing to bright moon and wind towards enemy effective patrolling is difficult.

26/7/15.   Lieut.Colonel,
                                                     Commanding 19th Infantry Brigade

DAILY REPORT to 12 noon 27th July.   19th Infantry Brigade.

OPERATIONS: 1. Enemy quiet. His artillery fired as follows:-
During afternoon - Rue Tilleloy - Rue Masselot with 77 mm guns (twice), communication trenches Nos. 13 and 14 with 10.5 cm howitzers. Our guns registered german trenches, shelled 2 working parties and considerably damaged 2 sally ports and fire trenches early this morning. Enterprise proposed last night was cancelled owing to relief of SIRHIND Brigade not being completed - Will be carried out tonight.
Opposite F.1 a large grass cutting party East of TRIVELET road was marked down and 5 rounds rapid fire of 100 rifles previously laid and a machine gun was turned on them. Shouts and groans and a considerable disturbance heard. Enemy retaliated with 4 trench mortars and a rifle grenade (2 bombs blind) and again at 2.am with 3 trench mortars and 2 rifle grenades.
Working party opposite F.3 also fired on by our *heavily*

WORK: 2. Parapets and parados strengthened. Trenches narrowed and filled in - fire steps made - wire strengthened. All sapping platoons and extra working parties improving communications and digging new trenches. Latrines put in, traverses erected and washhouses made. Ground has been reconnoitred and organized working parties have been working on shelter trench line.

INTELLIGENCE: 3. <u>Transport</u> One or two heavy wheeled carts heard between 12.20 and 12.25. moving S.E. from Farm Deleval. Again heard moving N.E. along Rue Deleval from 12.50 to 12.55.am
<u>Working parties</u> heard working from 11.pm till 1.am along whole front of right battalion. They were fired at as in 1 above as soon as our parties were in.
AUBERS Balloon came down at 7.30.pm. Went up for an hour at 6.45.am and up again at 9.20 and still up.
<u>Trench mortars</u> Spot fired from was 205 degrees magnetic from end of No: 12 communication trench.
<u>Uniform</u>. Few of the enemy seen showing themselves above the parapet wearing green tunics.
<u>Miscellaneous</u>. Sniping was much heavier than usual during night and at dawn, probably owing to their working parties having been forced to cease work.
<u>Patrols</u>: Met no hostile patrols. A noise which sounded like heavy chains working on a winch was heard opposite F.2. This was also reported by patrols of Right battalion as if enemy were working with heavy chains or employing a winch. Trolley again heard.
~~Miscellaneous~~ At 9.40.pm opposite F.2 a piano and violin was heard playing and also considerable cheering.
A patrol visited the crater and found a single row of "chevaux de frise", 4 feet long and 18 inches high in front of it, with wooden frames to strengthen it. On the flanks were two rows of iron stakes, 4 paces apart. A stake was brought in which shows the ingenuity of the enemy, no noise is made putting it in. The wiring of the stakes is very poor and sags a good deal. Saps reported last night proved to be great blocks of earth only. 5 germans came out of crater and sent up flare.

27/7/15.   Lieut Colonel,
                                    Commanding 19th Infantry Brigade.

Report to 12 noon, 28th July.   19th Infantry Brigade

OPERATIONS: 1. Enemy quiet except for some heavy rifle fire and trench mortaring after 11.30.pm in retaliation for our activity. Patrols went out from Right battalion last night and located positions of hostile working parties. By previous arrangement 19th and 20th batteries opened fire at 11.30.pm also rifle fire from 400 fixed rifles and machine guns. The enemy had large working parties out and probably suffered casualties.
He sent up many flares and fired rapidly into the air evidently expecting an attack. He retaliated with 4 trench mortars, some rifle grenades and 7 shells between 11.50.pm and 12.10.am
Enemy's artillery put 4 rounds 10.5 cm howitzer shells into No: 13 communication trench and at 11.30 am this morning shelled our trenches opposite 334.

WORK: 2. Parapets and parados strengthened. Traverses constructed, dug outs made, wire put out. Listening posts on right made-- fire trenches narrowed.

INTELLIGENCE   3. **Lights** A Red light went up at 11.40.pm after our second burst of rifle and artillery fire opposite F.1.
   Balloon Came down last night and has not been up today.
   Artillery Battery firing last night was on a bearing of 142 degrees from trench on left edge of TRIVELET Road; Trench mortar on a bearing of 100 degrees from same place.
   Strength Judging from rifle fire in reply to our burst at 11.30.pm the trenches in front are strongly held by Night.
   Wire New wire entanglements have appeared in front of F.2 on a front of 70 yards. The parapet has also been strengthened. A large working party was working on this until interrupted last night.
   Transport heard between 12.30 and 1.45.am in direction of point 300 moving S.W.
   Miscellaneous One German was shot by our shiping post in rear of F.1. A man was seen to leave the house with white gable end on Rue D'enfer about 6.30.pm. House is about 1,500 yards behind enemy's lines.
Trolley again heard at point 324.
   Patrols Patrols from left battalion went up to hostile wire but saw no hostile working parties last night. Hostile patrol met opposite F.3 and were fired upon and disappeared.

28/7/15.

Lieut.Colonel,
Commanding 19th Infantry Brigade.

Daily report to 12 noon, 29th July, 1915.

19th Infantry Brigade.

Operation 1. Enemy quiet. His Artillery put 10 4.2 Howitzer shells into rear of E.4, and RUE TILLELOY yesterday afternoon. Sniping heavy on the salient, quiet elsewhere. Four rifle grenades fired at F.3, only one burst.
Enemy snipes very little and very inaccurately, and he does not appear to have good loopholes.
Our batteries shelled odd enemy working parties reported by Infantry.

Work. 2. Work on rear parapets and rear trenches continued – both strengthened and refaced – dugouts fitted in – trenches narrowed and traverses added, firing steps constructed and old dugouts filled in – latrines and wash houses completed – steel loopholes erected, none existed before. Communication trenches to shelter trench line dug.
560 men working in shelter trench line and main communication trench 13 and new communication trench 16.

Intelligence. 3. Working parties.
No hostile working parties were seen or heard in front of enemy's parapet opposite right battalion last night. Opposite left battalion, parties were seen cutting grass and wiring. A bombing party was sent out, but found party had returned to their trenches.
Yesterday afternoon men were observed putting up low wire in front of their second line opposite F.1. The men were not visible from the trenches, but seen from Battalion observation tree, so fire could not be opened. Persistent work going on all day at 310.
Lights.
A large number of lights seen last night. Green rocket at 10-30 pm from AUBERS RIDGE.
9-50 pm – two red lights opposite E.4.
9-45 pm.- One white light in rear of trench opposite F.2. No meaning can be discovered for these lights.
2 Red and 1 green light fired backwards opposite F.3. at 9 pm, shortly after enemy shelled our back roads.
Flare from AUBERS RIDGE went up white, turned green, then red, then green again. Nothing happened afterwards.
Patrols.
Aeroplanes and balloons.
At 6-40 am hostile aeroplane dropped two white lights over our trenches. Usual balloon up today. Two hostile aeroplanes seen over our trenches at 6 am, flying very high.
Strength of enemy.
About 20 rifles fired on one of our aeroplanes from between 320-322. The rifle fire from between 323-333, opposite salient, was much heavier. The line opposite the salient evidently more strongly held by day than the East of the line.
Transport.
Light transport was heard on road between 287-306 at 9-30 pm moving East. Single wagon heard at midnight in same spot moving fast to East.
Patrols.
A patrol visited house on TRIVELET road, and the orchard next it. Both unoccupied. Further on, close to wire, a listening post was discovered, and voices heard coming from it. Enemy discovered working on wire West of road opposite SIRHIND BRIGADE.

29/7/15.

Lieut-Colonel,
Commanding 19th Infantry Brigade...

19th Infantry Brigade.

Weekly report on Exploits.

The only enterprises undertaken during the past week have been those of patrols, unless the affair reported in the Daily Report of 28th July is called an enterprise.

Patrols have gone out nightly, at least one patrol from each Battalion being under an officer. These patrols have so far been small and have gone out merely with the intention of gathering information and of finding the lie of the ground, as the lines are strange. Some patrols have penetrated within the enemy's advanced wire.

Reports of these patrols, and the information gained, have already been sent in to you.

30th July, 1915.   Lieut-Colonel,
                               Commanding 19th Infantry Brigade.

Daily report to 12 noon, 30th July, 1915.

19th Infantry Brigade.

Operations.
1. Quiet. Some sniping at night and some bursts of Machine Gun fire. Trench Mortar fired at TRIVELET road barricade:- mortar located at 316. Enemy seems to have fixed rifles on roads and houses in rear of trenches, and sniping has been very persistent during night.
Enemy's guns shelled with 77 m.m. guns:- No. 13 Communication trench during morning - WANGERIE (4 rds), Laventie (2 rds) and trenches during afternoon - No. 13 Communication trench, heavily, and RUE TILLELOY in rear, in evening.

Work.
2. Work continued in thickening parapets, parados, and traverses. Dug outs put in: wire strengthened: machine gun emplacements built: trenches cleaned up: fire steps added: fire trenches narrowed: 3 listening posts, 50 yards long, dug and wired from F.4: work on communication trenches continued, 200 men employed. Owing to whole Brigade being on move, no other working parties could be found.

Intelligence,
3. Working parties.
During night, enemy had small parties on his line opposite right battalion, and was working in his trench at 319 during morning.

Aeroplanes.
7 am and 9 am.

Miscellaneous.
Trolley heard again last night~~: working opposite~~ near crater: ~~Signal lamp observed working opposite salient:~~
Signal lamp seen working near 356.

30th July, 1915.

Lieut-Colonel,

Commanding 19th Infantry Brigade.

19th Infantry Brigade.

Daily Report up to 12 noon, 31st July, 1915.

Operations.
1. Enemy quiet. Less sniping than usual on the left during the last 24 hours. His Artillery was active this morning between 10 am and 12 noon. Field guns fired at Breastwork of F.4. and on RUE TILLELOY in rear of F.2. Seemed to be a single gun close up to trenches somewhere about 370. Later a 15 pr. battery near 329 shelled shelter trench line and RUE TILLELOY in rear of F.4. - about 40 shells fired. Left Battalion observation tree was knocked over. Enemy sniped vigorously between 1-15am and 2 am.

Work.
2. Work continued on thickening parapet and parados, narrowing trenches and putting out wire.- a few new dugouts put in - old dugouts in front parapet filled in - refuse pits and latrines dug - 2 new Machine Gun emplacements put in, trench mortar emplacements made in F.3. - firing steps added.
Work on shelter trench line and communication trenches continued - 520 men working.
Forts 11, 12, 13, 17, and 18 required parapets thickened and revetted - 80 men worked on these.

Intelligence.
3. Less sniping than usual, probably because more cover now exists for the troops and Communication trenches are getting better Enemy appears very jovial and loud laughter heard opposite F2 last night. He is inclined to conversation on the right, and asked who we are.

Transport.
The trolley heard most of the night near the mine crater, and the unloading of bricks and stones heard there several times in the night.
Transport heard to stop at 295 at 10-45 pm. Noise near enemy's front line like sound of lawn mower, possibly the same as the creaking chain reported recently.
A handcart was moving just in rear of enemy's trenches, putting some sort of metalling down. Patrols think transport comes up pretty close to hostile trenches. enemy probably laying in stones and boarding for winter trenches. Train whistles heard in AUBERS.
Working parties.
Patrols located party cutting grass and mowing opposite F.4 - our machine gun fire stopped this work. Other working parties in front of right battalion driving in stakes.
Lights.
White light like small electric light seen on enemy's parapet from 8-30 pm to 9-30 pm - light seen at 316 at same time and raised on a pole for a few seconds.

31/7/15.

Lieut-Colonel,

Commanding 19th Infantry Brigade..

mouse/stray/BBB

www.ingramcontent.com/pod-product-compliance
Lightning Source LLC
Chambersburg PA
CBHW081434300426
44108CB00016BA/2366